your view

northwest
development agency

cumbria·cumbria·cumbria·cumbria·cumbria·cumbria·cumbria·cumbria·cumbria·cumbria·cumbria·**cumbria**·cumbria·cumbria·cumbria·cumbria·cumbria·cumbria·cumbria·cumbria·cumbria·cumbria·cumbria

ncashire·lancashire·lancashire·lancashire·lancashire·lancashire·lancashire·lancashire·lancashire·lancashire·**lancashire**·lancashire·lancashire·lancashire·lancashire·lancashire·lancashire·lancashire·lancas

anchester·manchester·greater manchester·greater manchester·greater manchester·greater manchester·greater manchester·**greater manchester**·greater manchester·greater manchester·greater manchester·greater manchester

cheshire·cheshire·cheshire·cheshire·cheshire·cheshire·cheshire·cheshire·cheshire·cheshire·**cheshire**·cheshire·cheshire·cheshire·cheshire·cheshire·cheshi

merseyside·merseyside·merseyside·merseyside·merseyside·merseyside·merseyside·merseyside·merseyside·**merseyside**·merseyside·merseyside·merseyside·merseyside·mersey

Show your true colours

The Siemens C45. With so many ringtones, CLIPit™ covers and screen graphics to choose from, matching your mobile to your personality couldn't be easier. Visit our website and download what suits you best. What does your phone say about you?

Be inspired

SIEMENS

C45

![Manchester 2002 – THE XVII COMMONWEALTH GAMES]

Publishing Director
Elisabeth Bolshaw

Senior Editor
Keith Ryan

Editor
Nick Cheek

Subeditor
John Cooper

Consultant Editorial Board
Jason Harborow
Jo Flaherty
Alison Leese

Art Director
Elroy Toney

Designers
Keri Murphy
Saydul Karim
Joanna Lory

Picture Editor
Beverley Ballard

Illustrator
Toby Leigh

Head of Production
Pippa Williams

Production Controllers
Lucy Grove
Lisa-Marie Lewis

Production Co-ordinator
Amy Sollitt

Group Advertisement Director
(Agency Sales)
Mark Winthrop

Sales Manager
John Lord

Managing Directors
Dean Citroen
Oren Wolf

Published by
Citroen Wolf Communications
4 Holford Yard
Cruikshank Street
London WC1X 9HD
Tel: +44 (0)20 7713 5555
Fax: +44 (0)20 7713 5588
E-mail: general@cwcomms.com
ISDN: +44 (0)20 7278 5253

Printed in the UK by
Southernprint (Web Offset) Ltd
Tel: 01202 628365
Fax: 01202 621262

Colour origination by
Colour Systems Ltd
Tel: 020 7520 8630
Fax: 020 7520 8639

contents

43
David Moffatt tells Nick Keith the story behind the 2002 Games in Manchester

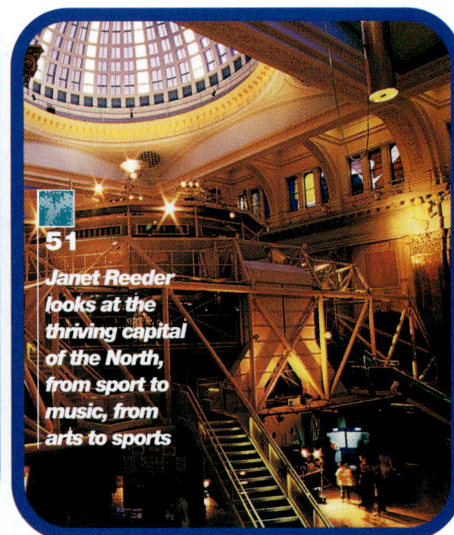

51
Janet Reeder looks at the thriving capital of the North, from sport to music, from arts to sports

62
Next stop: Melbourne. We introduce the next Commonwealth Games – are you ready for 2006?

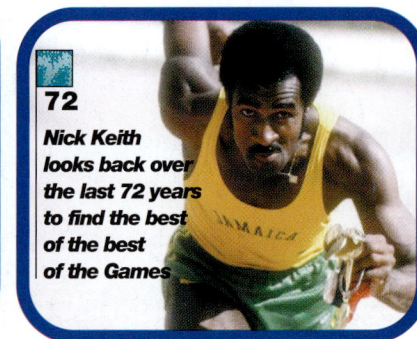

72
Nick Keith looks back over the last 72 years to find the best of the best of the Games

28
Nigel May on the latest from Manchester 2002, including a chance to win one of five Commonwealth Games goodie bags

Hulton Getty

Greg Caray

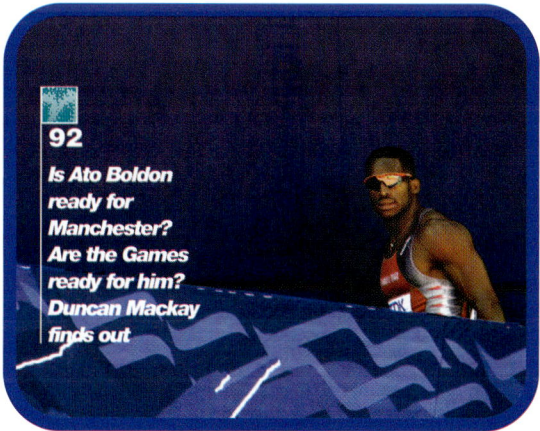

Stu Forster (Allsport); Stewart Darby

ROCK SOLID

Even before the Battle of Marathon the Rock was used by Hercules as a test of strength and endurance when he separated Europe and Africa.

The Pillars of Hercules are still ROCK SOLID and an integral part of The Commonwealth. The Rock of Gibraltar has excellent sporting facilities catering for training camps in most major sports, such as Athletics, Basketball, Football, Hockey, Martial Arts, Netball, Shooting (Clay, Pistol, Smallbore), Squash, Volleyball and Watersports, along with many other sporting activities.

Contact our
Sports Development Unit or the
Gibraltar Tourist Board and find out more:

GIBRALTAR
Ms Michelle Smallwood
Sports Development Unit
Victoria Stadium · Bayside Road
Gibraltar
Tel: (350) 76522 · Fax: (350) 42749
Email: vicstad@gibnynex.gi

LONDON
Gibraltar Tourist Board
178/179 Strand
London WC2R 1EL
www.gibraltar.gov.uk
Tel: (44) 20 7836 0777
Email: info@gibraltar.gov.uk

Gibraltar
TOURIST BOARD

98

It's important to create the right impression – Graham McColl checks out the opening and closing for the Games 2002

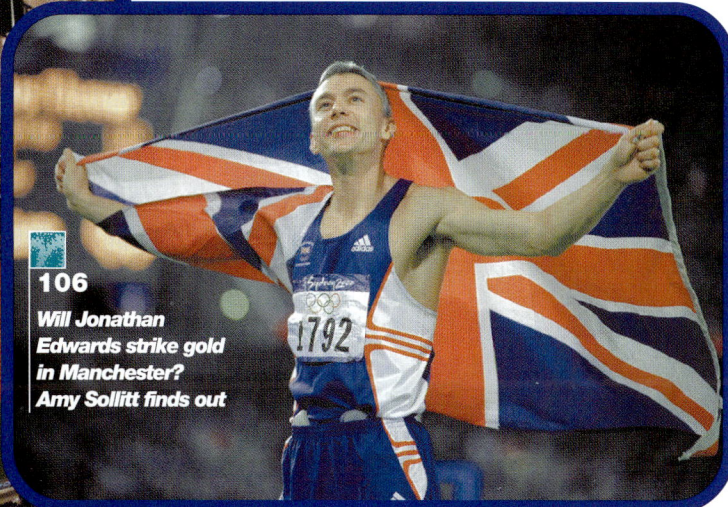

106

Will Jonathan Edwards strike gold in Manchester? Amy Sollitt finds out

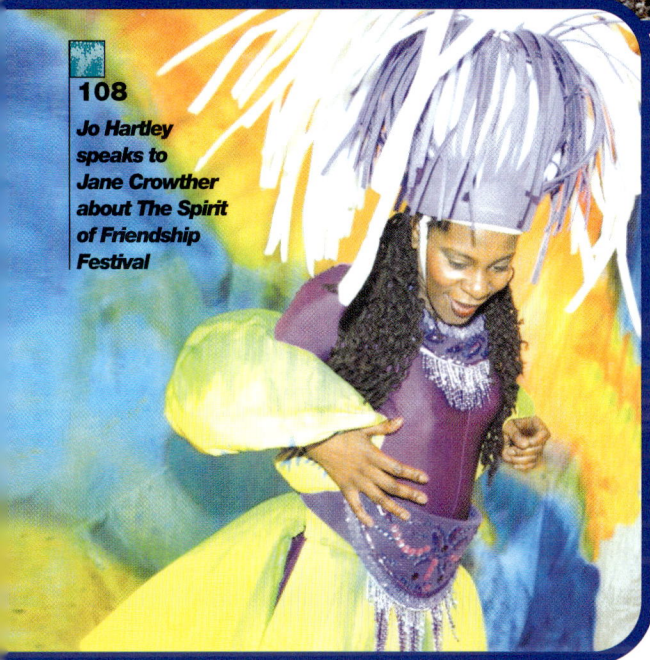

108

Jo Hartley speaks to Jane Crowther about The Spirit of Friendship Festival

96 THE COUCH POTATO'S GUIDE TO THE GAMES

If you can't make it to the 2002 Commonwealth Games, then kick back, grab a four pack of Boddies and a bar of Cadbury's Dairy Milk and watch the Games from the comfort of your living room

105 DEAN MEAN FIGHTING MACHINE

Dean Macey is England's brightest decathlon star – he finished fourth in Sydney and took bronze at the World Championships. Now he's got the Commonwealth gold in his sights, as Nikki Racklin discovers – will anyone stand in his way?

302 OFFICIAL MERCHANDISE FOR THE GAMES

Tony Marshall (Empics); Clive Brunskill (Allsport)

Welcome to the XVII Commonwealth Games in Manchester

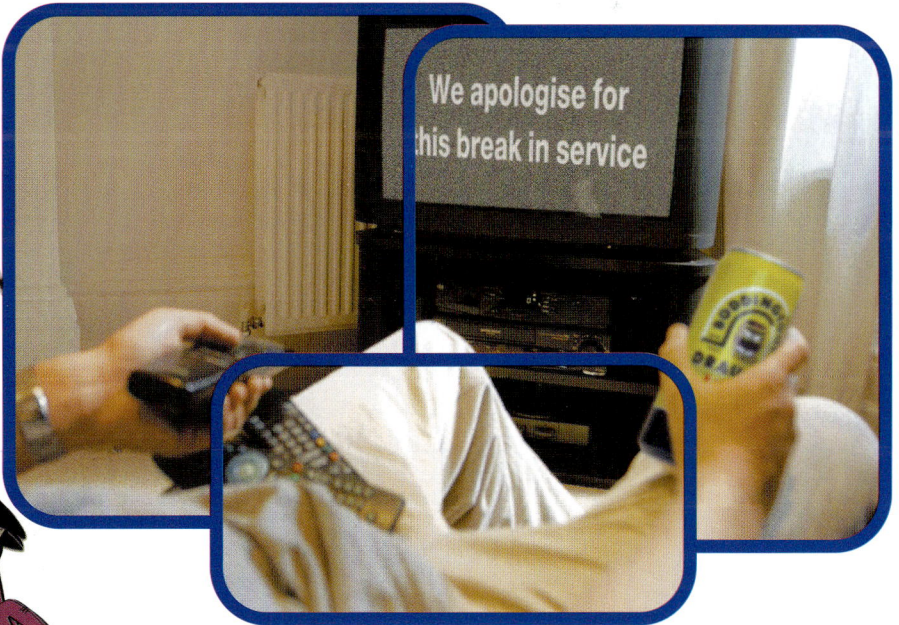

We apologise for this break in service

Foreword

HRH The Earl of Wessex

On behalf of the Commonwealth Games Federation, may I welcome you to England, Manchester and the XVII Commonwealth Games. I have the honour of having been President of the Commonwealth Games for the past 12 years, and I am delighted to be involved in the first Games to be held in this country during that time.

Manchester is our proud host city and through the organisers, Manchester 2002 Limited, and in partnership with Manchester City Council, Sport England and the government, they have worked long and hard to deliver these Games.

Sport is an uplifting and unifying activity. It brings together nations, and it unites people across international and cultural boundaries. The XVII Commonwealth Games will be the largest multi-sport event ever to have been organised in the United Kingdom and I am sure it will further cement the friendship that exists between all the Commonwealth countries.

The stage is set for 11 days of world-class sport in top quality facilities. Over 5,000 competitors from 72 nations will be participating in 17 sports. We all wish them every success, personal achievements and happy memories to last them a lifetime.

On behalf of the people of Manchester, the volunteers and the organisers, I want to thank you for taking the time to come and support these Games. Your presence and interest is much appreciated by everyone involved.

Edward

HRH The Earl of Wessex

Foreword
The Rt Hon Tony Blair MP

The Commonwealth Games is a truly special occasion. It's a remarkable event which represents all that is best about the Commonwealth.

Over the 11 days of the Games, we will see in Manchester an astonishing diversity of nations and cultures. But we will also see a friendship, based on links between our countries and citizens, which are rooted in history but remain strong in the modern world. We will witness fierce competition, but also a genuine warmth between sportsmen and women and competing countries.

I am sure, too, these Games will leave a lasting impression on all who come here, of Manchester as a vibrant and modern city with a warm welcome for athletes, officials and spectators alike. They will also leave behind a legacy of superb sporting facilities which will serve the city, surrounding area and region for decades to come.

I was privileged to lay the foundation stone for the City of Manchester Stadium in 1999 and returned this spring to see the finished stadium. This wonderful venue and the huge enthusiasm I found here for this festival of sport further increased my confidence that the XVII Commonwealth Games will be a huge success.

I am looking forward to coming back to enjoy the unique atmosphere which surrounds these remarkable Games. I hope you all enjoy your time in Manchester. I am sure Manchester will enjoy you being here.

The Rt Hon Tony Blair MP
Prime Minister

Foreword

Charles Allen
Chairman, Manchester 2002 Ltd

If I may re-work a phrase from a well-known playwright from Stratford-upon-Avon, just down the road from Manchester, "if sport be the food of regeneration, play on."

Manchester, this great city at the heart of England, is on the move. It is changing from an industrial giant to a vibrant city of commerce, media, retail and service industries, with a cloak of inspiring architecture and an attitude of friendly expertise to suit the 21st Century. At its centre in this Golden Jubilee year are the Commonwealth Games.

This wonderful event could not have happened without the vision and generosity of our funders: Manchester City Council, the government and the lottery funds of Sport England. Nor could we have succeeded without the active support of our Sponsors and Partners who have shared our ambition and passion for the Games, not only with financial assistance, but also with products, services, experience and staff.

So, I offer you, members of the media, a particular welcome. You will see great competition during the ten days of the Games, many records will be broken and there will be many stories to tell of the way in which Manchester came alive to host the Games and you – the visitor.

You are assured a warm welcome and facilities for the important job you will do recording and reporting the Games to the Commonwealth.

Our Media Services team is dedicated to your needs, our Crew 2002 – the volunteer workforce – is everywhere in the city to help and guide you to the best that the Games and the city have to offer.

Enjoy the Games, enjoy England's North West and, above all, enjoy yourself.

Charles Allen
Chairman, Manchester 2002 Limited

Foreword
Tanni Grey-Thompson, OBE

As one of the athletes taking part, I'm really looking forward to this year's Commonwealth Games. The Games have a special place in the hearts of many sportspeople. It's an incredibly friendly event with a superb atmosphere – you really get to know the other athletes around the village and, for me, around the track.

For many athletes, this is their favourite competition because of the spirit surrounding the Games. Athletes from all over the Commonwealth are very proud of the Game's unique heritage. For sportspeople from smaller nations, it's a fantastic opportunity to compete against the more recognised countries and to show what they can do.

As a Welsh athlete, it's amazing to me that the Games are taking place in Britain. The crowds will obviously be incredibly excited and there will be really strong emotions for those sportspeople who are competing on home soil. Manchester is an excellent venue for the Games – the stadium and sporting facilities are absolutely stunning and the track is extremely fast.

There has been so much commitment put into the Games. For example, a while ago, I went to a volunteers presentation and met some of those people who'll be helping out – they were so excited. That's good for the athletes – the enthusiasm is really going to rub off on them.

For those attending, I'd say have fun and get ready for a week of great sport. Also, bring loads of flags and cheer as loud as you can. It's great for athletes from all nations to see as much wholehearted support as possible.

Finally, to those who made it all happen – all those taking part would like to offer a big thank you. Manchester has done a great job. It's often easy to underestimate the amount of work that goes into a competition like this. It has taken years and years of dedication and the people behind the scenes – who don't always get the recognition they deserve – have all put in a tremendous amount of work and they deserve a lot of credit for making these the biggest and most successful Games ever.

Tanni Grey-Thompson

Tanni Grey-Thompson, OBE
Paralympic gold medallist

The greatest show on earth

After years of careful planning and exceptional effort, Manchester welcomes you to the greatest show on earth – the XVII Commonwealth Games, the most significant multi-sport event to be held in this country since the Olympics of 1948. These largest-ever Games will include a total of 5,250 athletes and team officials from all 72 Commonwealth nations, and territories will participate in 14 individual sports and three team sports at the Games.

The likes of Colin Jackson, Maria Mutola and Ato Boldon will all grace the magnificent new City of Manchester Stadium, the 38,000-seat centre piece of the Games. The stadium also plays host to an awe-inspiring opening ceremony that will be a blaze of colour and pageantry, as competitors from the around the Commonwealth represent their nations with pride in the arena. On 4 August, after 10 days of intense and spectacular competition, the stadium will be the scene of an equally impressive closing ceremony. Victors and vanquished will join in celebration of a very special friendship that gives the Commonwealth Games their unique appeal.

Proving that Manchester is fully committed to promoting and staging an "inclusive Games", elite athletes with a disability will be included in the main sports programme and their results will count toward the final medal tally. There will be 200 athletes with disabilities competing in eight separate events and the competition will be fierce.

So welcome, everyone, to the XVII Commonwealth Games – visitors from around the world, spectators watching eagerly from home and champions hungry for gold. This will indeed be the greatest Games the Commonwealth has ever seen.

Keith Ryan, Senior Editor
Citroen Wolf Communications (Publishers)

Getting around the Games

1 City of Manchester Stadium

This is the big one – the centrepiece of the Commonwealth Games. The stadium plays host to the Opening and Closing ceremonies and has a 38,000 seat capacity.

2 National Squash Centre

This is the new home of the Squash Rackets Association. With six new permanent fixed courts and one moveable show court, it is undoubtedly one of the premier squash facilities in the world.

3 Table Tennis Centre, Sportcity

This new facility includes six indoor tennis courts in two large halls, each housing three courts. The facility represents a world class venue for the sport.

4 National Cycling Centre

This venue hosted the World Track Cycling Championships in 1996, as well as the 2000 Championships. It is an internationally renowned Velodrome with seating for 3,500 spectators.

5 Belle Vue Regional Hockey Centre

This is the nominated venue for the hockey events and has undergone a recent £3 million redevelopment. It includes two water-based hockey pitches among many other new sports features.

6 Manchester Aquatics Centre

This is the new £32 million swimming pool complex located close to the city centre. It houses two 50-metre pools as well as separate diving and leisure pools.

7 Forum Centre, Wythenshawe

The Forum complex (close to Manchester Airport and the regional motorway network) is the stage for the preliminary rounds of the boxing, as well as all boxing training facilities.

8 Salford Quays

The Quays provide an outstanding backdrop as the venue for the walks as well as the triathlon event. The walks take in the centre of the Quays, while the triathlon takes full advantage of the setting.

9 Heaton Park

The park is the venue for the lawn bowls There are four greens for the Commonwealth Games competition and it will provide a regional centre of excellence for lawn bowls as a legacy after the Games.

10 Manchester Evening News Arena

The Manchester Evening News Arena is the largest multi-purpose indoor entertainment and sports arena in Europe and will play host to the netball and boxing competitions for the Games.

Rivington, Bolton

The mountain bike events take place on the slopes of Rivington Pike (see map below), near Horwich.

Bolton Arena

The venue for badminton at the Games is the magnificent new Bolton Arena (see map below).

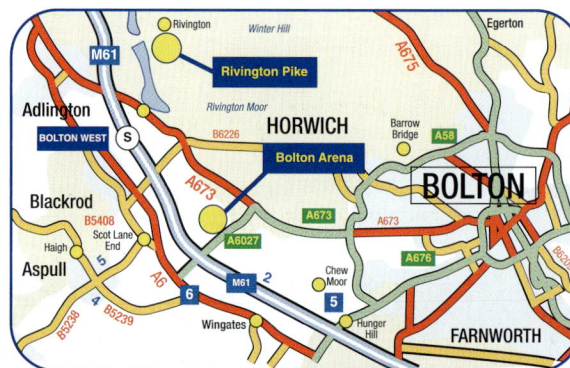

11 The G-MEX and MICC

Capable of hosting anything from rock concerts to the World Table Tennis Championships to major art exhibitions, the G-MEX is the venue for gymnastics, judo and wrestling, with seating capacity for up to 6,000 spectators while the Commonwealth Games are in progress.

National Shooting Centre, Bisley

Bisley's NSC (see map above) provides the only facility in the world capable of holding all Olympic and fullbore disciplines on one site.

BOLTON

M66 M62

18

19

17

M60

16

15

14

A667

A666

A666

A6

A572

A580

A56

A6044

A6044

A56

A576

A576

A665

A576

A664

A6104

A664

9

M60

21

22

A62

M60

SPORTCITY

3

2

MANCHESTER

A5185

A5185

A576

A576

A5185

A5066

CLOWE STREET

CHEETHAM HILL ROAD

CHEETHAM HILL ROAD

ROCHDALE ROAD

OLDHAM ROAD

TRINITY WAY

ADELPHI ST.

SILK ST.

A6041

CHAPEL STREET

DEANSGATE

CROSS ST.

GREAT ALLCOATS ST.

10

11

PORTLAND STREET

OLDFIELD ROAD

REGENT ROAD

CHESTER ROAD

MANCUNIAN WAY

A57(M)

UPPER BROOK STREET

A662

A662

23

M602

A57

A570

A57

SALFORD QUAYS

A5081

A5603

3

2

1

4

1

A635

A57

24

6

A34

5

A5184

10

9

8

A6144(M)

A181

A56

A6010

A6010

A5079

A6

M60

25

7

A5145

A5103

A626

27

26

6

5

A6

M60

4

A34

A5145

M60

WYTHENSHAWE

7

MANCHESTER INTERNATIONAL AIRPORT

60

Going for gold
is all about realising dreams.

PILKINGTON

We've already realised ours- self-cleaning glass.

Gold Award for innovation.
Batimat Show, Paris 2001.

Introducing the first glass to clean itself continuously.

Every athlete dreams of winning a medal - while every homeowner might well dream of windows that clean themselves. Now, thanks to Pilkington **Activ**™ – winner of a leading industry award for innovation – at least one of those dreams is a reality.

New Pilkington **Activ**™ is the world's first self-cleaning glass, using a unique dual action process. Firstly, an invisible layer reacts with natural UV energy to break down organic dirt; then it causes rainwater to 'sheet' down the glass, washing the dirt away without leaving streaks.

Visit **www.activglass.com** to find out more about this latest innovation from Pilkington – a company that, as one of the world's foremost glass manufacturers, always leads the field.

Pilkington **Activ**™ The world's first self-cleaning glass.

Pilkington Activ™
self-cleaning glass

Caught in the Web

Anybody who has logged on to the official Commonwealth Games website can see what a slick, info-packed resource it is and how vital it is to the Games. Since its launch, the site has gone from strength to strength –

Visit the official Commonwealth Games website at www.commonwealthgames.com

the professionalism and talent involved is obvious. It was set up in a basic form about two years ago. It needed to have an e-retail element for tickets and merchandise, and there were loads of initial requests from universities for info about the Games. That was phase one in setting it up – providing information and tickets. Originally, the site was receiving about 200 hits per week and those numbers have grown. The website was designed in-house and was originally a holding site. Then the company began working with sponsorship partners to make sure that the site

delivered its key objectives. It needed to be dynamic and accessible, and provide e-commerce services prior to the Games. There are about ten people who work on the site, updating things on a daily basis, but that number will increase. The site recently had 570,000 hits in a week, with an average user-time of 16 minutes (during the Games, this number could reach up to 200,000 hits a day). Ticket sales through the website have also been phenomenal – the highest ever for a Commonwealth Games – approximately 65 per cent of tickets have been sold via the Internet.

Ground-breaking achievements

The inclusion of elite athletes with a disability in the mainstream sports programme at the 2002 Games has earned high praise from the International Paralympic Committee's director of sport, David Grevenberg: "I don't think people yet realise just how

ground breaking the achievements in Manchester are," he said during a recent visit. "For a multi-sports event to record the performances of disabled athletes and have the medals won count towards the nations total... you are in totally uncharted territory." The Paralympics are not new, but the Sydney 2000 Paralympics was unique. They set a standard that the

"...to record the performances of disabled athletes and have the medals won count towards the nations total, you are in totally uncharted territory"

Commonwealth Games have met fully, including 10 events across five sports for elite athletes with a disability in the programme.
"The IPC is really looking to Manchester as an example for future Commonwealth Games," said Grevenberg. "This is the start of something very good within the Commonwealth movement.... We are looking to take what we learn forward to Melbourne 2006. "We are in the exciting position of being able to see for the first time the full inclusion of disabled athletes within the existing Games and this meets the IPC's objectives in terms of providing a catalyst for developing disabled sport within developing nations through the Commonwealth Games Associations. "We will have a full team of delegates here in the summer and we will be observing everything closely so that we can transfer the knowledge on to other events," he concluded.

Jamie Squire (Allsport)

News and views

Commonwealth Games goodies

There's a whole host of top quality merchandise and collectibles that Games fans can get their hands on. In fact, you name it, you can probably buy it! You'll be able to get cuddly toys of the Games' mascots, which are bound to be a hit with younger fans. There's also key rings, fridge magnets, height charts, stickers and model cars to keep smiles on little faces. For older fans, there's glass-ware, coasters, cuff links, tie slides, business card holders, hip flasks (could come in handy!) and pre-paid telephone cards. You'll also be able to buy special commemorative mobile phone ring tones and logos.

Anyone wanting to dress themselves up Games-stylee will be able to choose from rugby jerseys, polar fleeces, jackets, t-shirts, sweats, tops and bottoms. Then when the sun goes down you can kit yourself out in towelling robes, after you've rubbed yourself down with a Games towel of course! To add to all of that, there are stamps, balloons, paper towels, postcards, tea towels, interactive CDs and a whole host more. The range includes classic brand names such as car collectables from Corgi, towels from Christy Towels and replica product from Puma.

There's even an A-Z pocket map to help spectators to find their way round the city and makes an excellent pocket map.

There really is something for everyone and your contribution supports Manchester 2002, the Commonwealth Games and the athletes of the Commonwealth. There are stores in the Trafford Centre, Arndale Centre and the Airport. You can also order online at: www.commonwealthgames .com/merchandise, or by mail order catalogue (phone 0845 608 2002).

Manchester's mad about mascots

You may have noticed the two mascots that seem to be cropping up everywhere in preparation for this year's event. First up there's Kit, who is the official mascot of the 2002 Commonwealth Games. He made his first public appearance at a media lunch for journalists in Kuala Lumpur and became an instant hit when 500 million people worldwide watched him dance with Wira, the mascot for the KL Games, during the Closing Ceremony in Malaysia. Tony Hill, marketing manager for the Games Office, says: "Everybody who meets Kit falls in love with him. He's very Mancunian – young, vibrant, friendly, dynamic, a little bit mischievous and lots of fun." That description could also be used for Mad Ferret, the other mascot for the Games. Mike Hales, communications director of the Games explains why: "Mad Ferret is a play on the Manchester phrase 'mad fer it!' and he's a rodent on the fringe. He's almost like an anti-mascot," he says. "He's slightly anarchic and cocks a snook at convention! He's very impish and displays the humour that Manchester people have. He looks cool too, with his sneakers and cap on back to front. He's basically there to cause havoc!" You have been warned!

GO KIT ...Go!

How well do you know the Games?

So you think you're a Commonwealth Games expert? Now's your chance to prove it. Just answer the questions below and you could be the proud winner of one of five Commonwealth Games goodie bags. Send your answers on a postcard to the address below and the best of luck.

1. How many venues are being used for the sports at the 2002 Manchester Commonwealth Games?
(a) 15 (b) 10 (c) 25

2. In what year were the first Commonwealth Games held?
(a) 1914 (b) 1930 (c) 1952

3. How were the Games originally known?
(a) Sporting Style Games (b) British Empire Games
(c) Her Majesty's Games

4. Where were the last Games held in 1998?
(a) Malaysia (b) New Zealand (c) Canada

5. Where did Kit, the mascot for the 2002 Commonwealth Games, first make an appearance?
(a) Kuala Lumpur (b) Calgary (c) London

6. How many bedrooms are there at the Commonwealth Games Village? (a) 1,250 (b) 2,480 (c) 3,340

7. How are the Games universally known?
(a) The Professional Games (b) The Friendly Games
(c) The Stamina Games

8. Complete the line-up – Africa, The Americas, Asia, Europe, Caribbean and....?
(a) Latin America (b) Oceania (c) The Orient

9. How many people live within a two-hour drive of Manchester? (a) 12 million (b) 33 million (c) 80 million

10. What percentage of athletes at the 2002 Commonwealth Games will be female?
(a) 21% (b) 31% (c) 41%

Please send a postcard marked with a return address to:
The Editor, Commonwealth Games Competition, CWC, 4 Holford Yard, Cruikshank St, London WC1X 9HD

facts

1. A total of 5,250 athletes and team officials from 72 nations and territories will participate in 17 individual sports and three team sports at the Games – more than ever before.
2. 200 athletes with a disability are fully integrated, with 5,000 athletes participating in eight events and five sports.
3. Nine venues are within 15 minutes drive of the Athletes' Village in Manchester and five are within a 30-minute drive.
4. The total project expenditure to stage the Manchester 2002 Games is £207.8m.
5. BBC Television are the host broadcaster, ensuring that the projected cumulative TV audience of one billion will receive pictures of the highest quality.
6. Approximately 4,500 new jobs have been created.
7. Forty hectares of land was reclaimed for Sportcity, which is a catalyst for a regeneration programme in East Manchester.

Manchester 2002
THE XVII COMMONWEALTH GAMES

REGATTA
GREAT OUTDOORS ™

www.regatta.com

It's as good as it gets. Largo shirt in 100% cotton Cool Weave fabric with button-down collar and chest pocket **£16**, Terrain shorts in advanced Expe-tech fabric with Teflon stain resistant and water repellent finish, belt and reinforced seat **£25**. Direct customer line 0161 749 1313.

Hulton Getty

The British Empire Games in Sydney, Australia, 1938 – the Welsh runner JW Alford (pictured here running in third place, with Scotland's R Graham in first and Australia's F Barry Brown in second), scored an easy victory in the first heat of the mile race – his time of four minutes and 17 3/10 seconds was a record in New South Wales

QUEEN VICTORIA STILL HAD

a decade to reign when the idea of a gathering of sportsmen from throughout the British Empire was first proposed. Yet it took another 20 years before there was a response of any kind and almost twice that amount of time was to elapse before a Games worthy of the name was held.

It was in 1891 that J Astley Cooper wrote an article in the magazine, *Greater Britain*, about his ambition "to provide a platform for the expression of individual opinion upon events connected in the colonial and Indian Empire". He envisaged a sort of Grand Pan-Empire Exhibition, involving sporting,

military, literary and even what he called "moral" activities. Later that year, he tested wider public opinion on the matter in a suitably conventional manner for an English country gentleman – he wrote a letter to *The Times*.

Curiously, what might have seemed a project ideally suited to the Imperialist mood of the era never materialised. The reasons for this can only be guessed at, except that a visionary French educationalist, Baron Pierre de Coubertin, had much greater success during those last few years of the 19th Century in persuading the major powers that a revival of the Ancient Olympic Games was an attractive proposition.

Let the games commence

Bob Phillips, the author of _Honour of Empire, Glory of Sport_, takes you on a tour through the 72-year history of the Commonwealth Games, from Hamilton 1930 to Manchester 2002

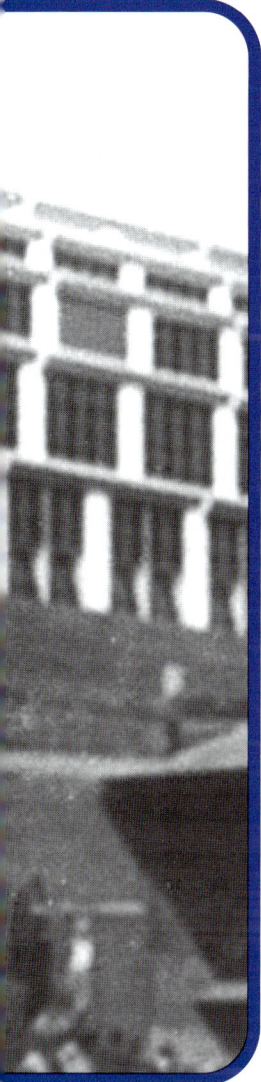

It was in all probability believed that one such meeting every four years was quite enough – even though one of the strongest advocates for an Empire Games during the first years of the 20th Century was the influential Richard Coombes, for 35 years President of the Amateur Athletic Union of Australia.

The first games

To celebrate the coronation of King George V in 1911, an "Inter-Empire Championships" was held at the Crystal Palace Grounds in London. Teams from Australia (managed by Coombes), Canada and South Africa took part, but the impressively-titled undertaking involved only five athletics events, two swimming races, boxing and wrestling. There is no evidence that Astley Cooper's writings of 20 years before provided the inspiration, the standards of competition were modest and there was no great public interest.

Even so, athletes from the British Empire had figured strongly at the Olympics from their inception in 1896 and the greatest impulse to competition among the Empire's member nations was provided by a series of matches against the USA which began after the 1920 Games. When a British Empire team met the Americans in 1928, the Canadian team-manager,

MM ("Bobby") Robinson, put forward the idea that an inaugural Empire Games should be held in his home town of Hamilton, Ontario, two years later.

Robinson already had the backing of his national officials, and his industriousness and enthusiasm overcame the indifference of the establishment in Britain. At a time of worldwide economic depression, he persuaded his city fathers to put up $30,000 to help visiting teams with their travelling expenses. He was rewarded by the presence of 11 countries and some 450 competitors, taking part in six sports – athletics, bowls, boxing, rowing, swimming, wrestling – even though the English contingent, for example, took nine days to reach Hamilton by sea and train.

The pioneering teams at those first Games came from Australia, Bermuda, British Guiana (now Guyana), Canada, England, Ireland, Newfoundland, New Zealand, South Africa, Scotland and Wales. The only sport for women at the time was swimming.

Bobby Robinson would have been delighted beyond his wildest dreams to learn that the 17th such Games would be held more than 70 years later and that in 1998 there would be 70 countries, 16 sports and 3,683 participants

Ancient Olympia

TM@ATHOC 2002

Unique Games on a Human Scale

Games of the XXVIII Olympiad   13-29 August 2004   www.athens2004.com

The Olympic Games are returning to Greece, their ancient birthplace, and to Athens, the city of their revival. In 2004, athletes from all nations will unite in Greece to engage in noble competition.

The Athens Olympics will combine history, culture and peace, with sports and Olympism. The people of Greece shall host a Unique Games on a Human Scale, inspiring the world to celebrate Olympic Values.

TM©

ATHENS 2004

A history in pictures (clockwise from top): The "Inter-Empire Championships" celebrated the coronation of King George V in 1911; Frank Sando, Peter Driver and Jim Peters at the British Empire Games in Vancouver (Canada); L Barnes (USA) at the British Empire v America Games at Stamford Bridge in 1928

Hulton Getty

involved. Astley Cooper, who had imagined an exclusively Anglo-Saxon assemblage, would have been astounded to discover that an Asian city, Kuala Lumpur, had proved to be such a sumptuous venue – and that athletes from independent nations in Central Africa and the Caribbean had already long since been prominent among those providing champions and record-breakers.

Those original 1930 Games were deservedly hailed as a resounding success and London provided the next setting in 1934 (though the cycling events were actually held at the Fallowfield track, in Manchester). The following celebrations in 1938 in Australia and in 1950 in New Zealand severely tested the resolve and the resources of the prospective visitors, and at a time when athletics was very largely still purely amateur, there were many would-be competitors who could not afford the unpaid time off from work to travel such long distances.

The great race

Despite these handicaps, there were two influencing factors that ensured the continued viability of the Games. Bobby Robinson had originally expressed the hope that the Games would be "free from both excessive stimulus and the babel of the international stadium" and that spirit prevailed. Then, when the Games returned to Canada in 1954, a single race captured the imagination of a public far beyond the confines of the old Empire. Roger Bannister, the Englishman who had become the first man to run a sub-four-minute earlier that year, met John Landy, the Australian who had improved that record the following month, and in a magnificent contest, Bannister passed Landy entering the final straight – a defining moment in sport forever captured in a famous photograph – and won the gold medal.

Four years later, the Games were held in Cardiff and the number of competing countries increased from 24 to 35, while the number of competitors almost doubled to 1,122. Another legendary miler, Herb Elliott, won that event and the 880 yards. Spectacular world records were set by a South African, Gert Potgieter, in the 440 yards hurdles and by a Polish-born Australian, Anna Pazera, in the women's javelin, and though athletics was then – as it still is now – the pre-eminent sport of the Games, there were other great deeds. Among those responsible were yet more all-conquering Aussies in the swimming-pool; a future world champion from the valleys named Howard Winstone in the boxing-ring;

the title had been pragmatically changed to suit altering political circumstances: from "British Empire Games", as it had been until 1950, to "British Empire & Commonwealth Games" from 1954 to 1966, and then "British Commonwealth Games" in 1970 and 1974, and finally plain "Commonwealth Games" from 1978 onwards. Still, mere nomenclature could not hold the growing Commonwealth family together for ever, as some of the infant nations rightly demanded their say.

Controversy

South Africa had pulled out of the Commonwealth after 1958 and a proposed rugby-union tour by the Springboks to New Zealand finally brought the apartheid problem to focus on the eve of the 1986 Commonwealth Games in Edinburgh. Virtually all of the African and Caribbean nations withdrew, leaving the Meadowbank athletics programme to go ahead without the great Kenyan and Tanzanian distance-runners or the Jamaican and Trinidadian sprinters.

Surprisingly, it was still a very good Games, with the likes of Ben Johnson (before his fall from grace), Steve Cram, Daley Thompson, Liz Lynch (later Mrs McColgan) and Tessa Sanderson scoring memorable wins in track and field events. In the 1990s, with South Africa welcomed back to the fold, the threat to the ongoing prosperity of the Games was a very different one. Forty years earlier, a group of Auckland businessmen had organised a whip-round to raise the £50,000 needed to underwrite their local Games, but now was the era of big business, with sponsors to entice and mass TV audiences to satisfy. Athletics had at long last recognised the economic facts of life and become more professional – with the other major sport, swimming, to follow – and there were alternative engagements on offer for the star performers. Grand Prix meetings could provide them with a healthy income and some of them could hardly be blamed for wanting to run for gold in the bank rather than a gold medal round their necks.

Somehow, over the years, a compromise has been reached, even if it meant that in 1994, Linford Christie flew off back to Europe immediately after winning the 100 metres at the Games in Canada in order to run a lucrative Continental race – in his absence a depleted England team only came third in the 4x100 metres relay. Four years later, Colin Jackson controversially declined to defend the 110 metres hurdles title in Kuala Lumpur – which he had twice before won for Wales – and raced in Tokyo instead, but Ato Boldon cheerfully won the Commonwealth 100 metres for Trinidad & Tobago and went on to the same meeting in Japan afterwards.

The last decade of the 20th Century saw the Games steadily expand in each of its three gatherings, growing to beyond 50 countries and 2,000 competitors in 1990, beyond 60 countries and 2,500 competitors in 1994, and then to 70 countries and almost 3,700 competitors in 1998. For the last event, in 1998, the Malaysian organisers took a bold step and invested in a marvellous array of new venues, including stadia for athletics, swimming, squash and hockey, all within walking distance of each other. The latter was one of four team sports contested for the first time and such was their success – the others being cricket, netball and rugby-

Winning ways (top to bottom): British cyclist Ray Booty winning the 120 miles road race during the Empire Games in Cardiff, 1958; Daley Thompson of Great Britain – pictured here at the 1984 Olympic Games in Los Angeles – is one of the many formidable athletes who have made the Games what they are today

and a lanky, bespectacled Englishman, Ray Booty, winning the cycle road-race by almost three minutes.

The Friendly Games

By 1966, the scope of the Games had scarcely changed – 34 countries, 1,143 competitors – but there was a revolution in cultures. The chosen venue was Kingston, Jamaica, and so for the first time the organisation had moved out of the grasp of the old colonial powers. The arrangements were often ramshackle, but the concept of the "Friendly Games" was born to the lilting sounds of the reggae beat, and the creators of that amiable ambiance themselves had something to cheer about when the majestic Louis Martin won the 13th gold-medal of his world-beating weightlifting career. It mattered little that Martin had left his home shores 10 years before to settle in England.

Now, as the Games moved onward into the 1970s and 1980s, a different challenge had to be faced. Over the years,

Hulton Getty; Tony Duffy (Allsport)

Leading the UK to sporting excellence

UK Sport's job is to lead the UK to sporting excellence by supporting:

Winning athletes

UK Sport invests over £25 million of Lottery funding each year in the country's top sportsmen and women through the World Class Performance Programme.

In addition, the UK Sports Institute co-ordinates a network of expertise delivering tailored solutions to individual sports and athletes.

World class events

UK Sport co-ordinates and supports bids to bring world class events to the UK. Since 1997, the Lottery-funded World Class Events Programme has supported over 70 events of World, European and Commonwealth status. The 2002 Commonwealth Games will showcase not just Manchester, but the UK's ability to successfully host major sporting events now and in the future.

Ethically fair and drug-free sport

UK Sport carries out over 5,000 drug tests each year as part of the UK's anti-doping programme. UK Sport has been contracted by Manchester 2002 to test athletes across every sport – the largest anti-doping operation ever at a Commonwealth Games.

UK Sport would like to wish everyone competing in Manchester the very best of luck.

For further information please visit www.uksport.gov.uk

uk sport

   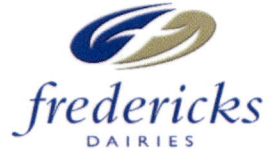

LAMINEX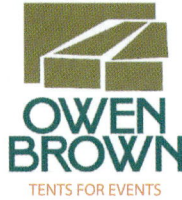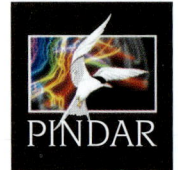

   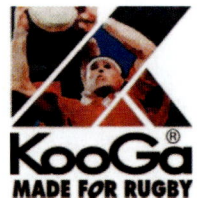

shared out among 23 different countries and that almost half of the competing teams – 34, to be precise – each won at least one medal of some kind. For some of these winners, the impact their successes made back home was as great as that of all those of the conquering Aussie hordes.

For example, Thabiso Moqhabi became the first ever Commonwealth champion from the southern African nation of Lesotho when he won the 1998 marathon. His team manager (who had himself twice run in the Games marathon in past years) proudly stated afterwards that "this victory is so important for our country".

The women's 800 metres triumph by Maria Mutola was no great surprise – she had already been world and Olympic champion – but it was an historic first Games gold for her country of Mozambique, newly-elected to the Commonwealth. Marcus Stephen, from the tiny Pacific island of Nauru (8.2 square miles in size and 9,000 population), won all three gold medals in his weightlifting division.

Manchester in 2002 holds high hopes for all these nationalities and many more besides. Maybe the emerging star this time will be someone like Françoise Mbango, who four years ago won the women's triple-jump silver medal behind England's Ashia Hansen to celebrate Cameroon's first appearance in the Games.

Maybe it will be a little known boxer from some unheralded faraway place who will bring honour to his homeland – after all, 21 different countries in all five continents of the world won boxing medals four years ago.

Whatever the destiny of the titles, these Commonwealth Games could never have been envisaged by J Astley Cooper, writing to *The Times* more than a century ago, or Bobby Robinson, realising his dearest ambition 40 years later. Yet if that intangible spirit of the "Friendly Games" is preserved, these pioneering spirits will surely rest easy.

union sevens – that it seemed surprising that such traditional Commonwealth pastimes had not appeared before.

Dominant forces

Despite the emphasis on friendly competition, gold-medal tables have inevitably occupied the minds of the media and there is no doubt as to which nation has been the most successful over the years. Australia has won more titles than any other country at every Games since 1970, with the exceptions only of 1978 (Canada) and 1986 (England).

In 1998, their domination was as great as ever – 80 gold medals and 198 medals in all, to England's 36 golds and 136 medals and Canada's 30 golds and 99 medals. The free-spending Malaysian hosts were rewarded for their investment by placing fourth in the rankings, with 10 gold medals and 36 medals in total. It is perhaps rather more significant that the 213 gold medals on offer at the 1998 Games were

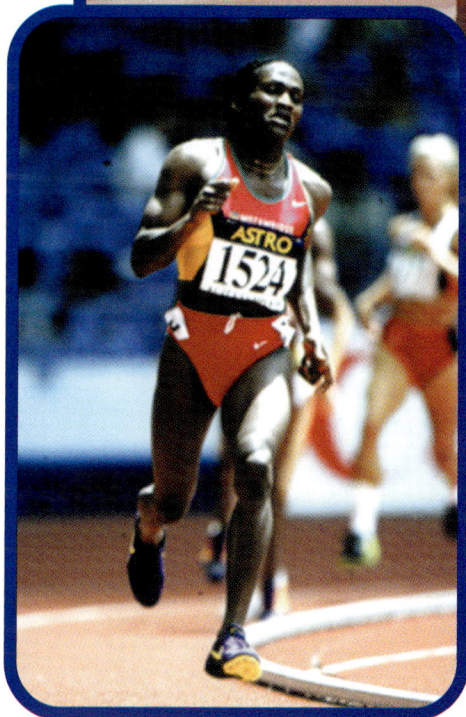

The Games today (top to bottom): The UK's Linford Christie on his way to victory in the men's 100m semi-final at the 1994 Games; Maria Mutola's 1998 victory in the women's 800m was the first Games gold for her home country of Mozambique

Games facts & figures

Over the decades, the popularity of the Games has been apparent to all who take part – here are some figures that illustrate their phenomenal growth:

year	venue	# sports	# competitors	# officials
1930	Hamilton	6	c. 400	c. 50
1934	London	6	c. 500	c. 100
1938	Sydney	7	464	43
1954	Vancouver	9	662	127
1966	Kingston	9	1,050	266
1970	Edinburgh	9	1,383	362
1978	Edmonton	10	1,519	481
1990	Auckland	10	2,073	700
1994	Victoria	10	2,557	914
1998	Kuala Lumpur	16	3,638	1,398

Manchester 2002
THE XVII COMMONWEALTH GAMES

Martin Rickett (PA)

The man with the plan

David Moffett, chief executive of Sport England, speaks about his excitement and enthusiasm for the Commonwealth Games. Interview by Nick Keith

THE 2002 COMMONWEALTH

Games in Manchester have been a glittering prospect for some time now and no-one was more eagerly awaiting the action than David Moffett, the new chief executive of Sport England. He was excited at the thought of all the Commonwealth Games events this summer – particularly athletics, rugby, netball, swimming and cycling.

"This is my first ever Commonwealth Games and I am looking forward to it immensely," he says. "I think these Games are going to be extraordinarily successful. They are an opportunity to put Manchester in the spotlight and raise awareness of it round the world."

Sporting chance

David Moffett and Sport England rate the 2002 Games as "the biggest multi-sports event ever held in Britain". Working with Manchester 2002 Ltd (the organising company), Manchester City Council and other national and regional agencies, Sport England set aside a fund of £165 million for the Games. Sport England's objectives for the Games are as follows:

● To contribute to the organising and staging of a successful international sporting event;

● To help to provide a lasting sporting legacy for Manchester, the North West region, and the whole country, and;

● To support English Sports Governing Bodies and their teams of athletes in their preparations for the Games. English-born, Australian bred David Moffett has been chief executive of Sport England since January 2002. He was "sitting at home minding my own business" when he was asked if he would be interested in the CEO's job at Sport England. He requested more information, one thing led to another and he landed the position.

He returned to England at the start of the year, leaving his wife and grown-up children (a son and a daughter) in Australia and it has been a happy homecoming for him. "I was born in Doncaster, although now I have the strangest Yorkshire accent," he jokes genially in his dry Aussie tones. "I have always retained a deep interest in English sport." In Australia, he says, he has been "privileged to have been involved with international sporting organisations and this has in turn allowed me to work with English officials in different sports. I've had the chance to observe some of the issues they face and to compare these with issues faced in other countries."

New Sport England chief executive David Moffett (above and at right), on a visit to the National Cycling Centre in Manchester, the venue for the cycling events at the 2002 Commonwealth Games – Sport England is the UK's leading sports development agency and a distributor of lottery funds to sport

Moffett is at the hub of what he considers to be "a vital programme for English sport" – as he explains: "I am English. I was born here and I want to see England win at everything. We have to embrace sport and active recreation as important to all of us and good for us. We want to encourage everyone to take an active part, from the grassroots to the elite athletes at the top. This idea is not new – it's always been around – but we have got to make it happen."

As the country's leading sports development agency and a distributor of lottery funding, Sport England's work is based around its mission "to foster a healthier and more successful nation through increased investment in sport and active recreation." Challenges for Moffett include managing a £300 million budget, maintaining Sport England as a strategic influencer of sport development and enabling sport both nationally and at a regional level.

The Commonwealth Games give Sport England the chance to increase awareness of its programmes. Its efforts are enshrined in new core values, framed by the acronym "SPORT" (Service, Passion, Outcome focused, Respect and Teamwork).

"In some ways, these things are obvious," Moffett says, "and they're what Sport England is going to live by. Each one is important, but, for me, respect is probably the biggest of all.

The significance of respect in sport came home to me when I was discussing what made an All Black with the then New Zealand captain, Zinzan Brooke, who said simply, 'An All Black has to show the right amount of respect.'

"When I thought about it, I realised that this is what defines the All Blacks and makes them so successful – their respect for their tradition, for their culture and for the opposition." Moffett is sure that the people who succeed at the Commonwealth Games will have the right qualities of passion, outcome focus, respect and (where

Martin Rickett (PA)

A fresh perspective on banking and investment

PRIVATE BANKING

With a reputation for excellence, Brown Shipley provides a wide range of financial services for private and corporate clients. From a network of regional offices, our specialist managers and advisers work with you to achieve your financial objectives.

INVESTMENT MANAGEMENT

PENSIONS

From discretionary and advisory portfolio management to personal and group pensions, corporate finance and management of global and specialist collective funds, Brown Shipley provides focused, high quality professional advice and service.

FUND MANAGEMENT

CORPORATE FINANCE

For further information please contact Rae Major on 0161 214 6701

BROWN SHIPLEY

KBL GROUP european private bankers

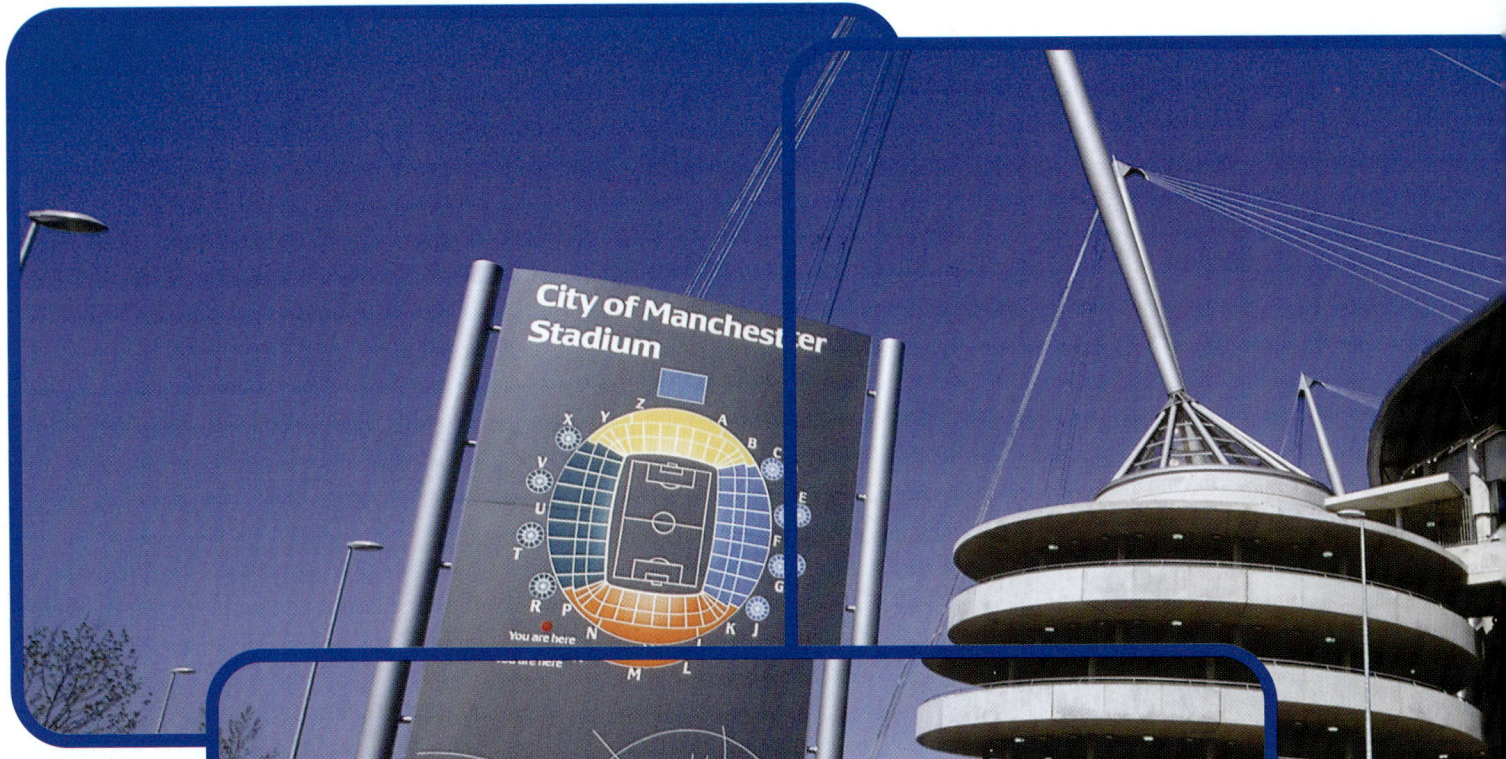

A general view (outside and in) of the City of Manchester Stadium the main venue for the 2002 Games in Manchester

appropriate) teamwork – and service will come from the army of volunteers. Having attended the Olympics in Sydney – albeit only as a spectator – he is delighted that "a lot of the good lessons learned in Sydney are being applied in a Commonwealth Games context by the Manchester organisers. Just as in Sydney, where volunteers did outstanding work, I have seen for myself that the Manchester team is doing a similar job. "There are some 15,000 volunteers from all parts of the community – including the long-term unemployed, which is very encouraging. There are good signs that the whole population of Manchester is doing what it takes to make

these Games an outstanding experience. There is no doubt that the sense of ownership, commitment and excitement increased as the Games grew closer. The Queen's Jubilee Baton Relay, for instance, was one of the events that created a focus for the Games. These Games will leave behind some large stadiums and other important sporting equipment for the city of Manchester and for the local community."

The business of sport

A successful businessman in Australia, David Moffett owned and sold Pacific Waste Management, one of Sydney's largest commercial and industrial waste management companies. In the last decade, he has turned to sports administration and a succession of key jobs have made him one of the top sporting administrators in the southern hemisphere.

Alex Livesey (Getty Images)

A general view of the interior of the City of Manchester Stadium, which offers athletes and officials alike an exceptional venue for the Commonwealth Games 2002

The legacy of the Games, he concludes, will be to provide opportunities to open up and regenerate the East Manchester area; to install facilities and equipment for future use; and to create a community of enthusiastic volunteers. "In the period leading up to the Games, there is euphoria and a high level of expectation – and then people will wonder, 'Why can't life always be like this?' One of our challenges is to keep that will-power and joie de vivre going long afterwards."

First, he was executive director of the New South Wales Rugby Union and, within three years, he had freed the Union of $6 million in debt and was trading at profit. Then he was appointed chief executive of South African, New Zealand and Australian Rugby (SANZAR), where he negotiated international television contracts and supervised the establishment of the Super-12 competition.

In 1996, he became the first "foreign" chief executive of New Zealand Rugby Football Union (the All Blacks), seeing it through the giant leap from amateur status to professionalism and, in the process, becoming one of the country's top 200 companies. Until recently, he has been chief executive of the National Rugby League of Australia, overseeing two years of huge changes as the game moved to a 14-team competition.

Moffett negotiated long-term sponsorship and television agreements, which brought significant financial stability, and he saw the need for major structural changes in the game's administration.

A direct, plain-speaking, clear-sighted man, David Moffett personifies the virtues of Australians and Yorkshiremen. He hopes the Games will provide a focus for promoting English national spirit. After the Games are over, he believes that spirit will help to keep the momentum going and ensure there is a positive outcome for the people of Manchester and for England in sporting, recreational, health and social terms.

factfile on david moffett

BORN: Doncaster, England, 1947. Spent his early life in Kenya before his family emigrated to Brisbane, Australia, in 1963.

BUSINESS: Range of jobs before owning and selling Pacific Waste Management, one of Sydney's largest commercial and industrial waste management companies.

SPORTS ADMINISTRATION:
● 1992, executive director, New South Wales Rugby Union.
● 1995, chief executive, South African, New Zealand and Australian Rugby (SANZAR).
● January 1996, chief executive, New Zealand Rugby Football Union.
● November 1999, chief executive, National Rugby League, Australia.
● January 2002, chief executive, Sport England.

Manchester 2002
THE XVII COMMONWEALTH GAMES

Gary M Prior (Getty Images)

British Waterways

BREATHING NEW LIFE INTO THE NORTH WEST OF ENGLAND

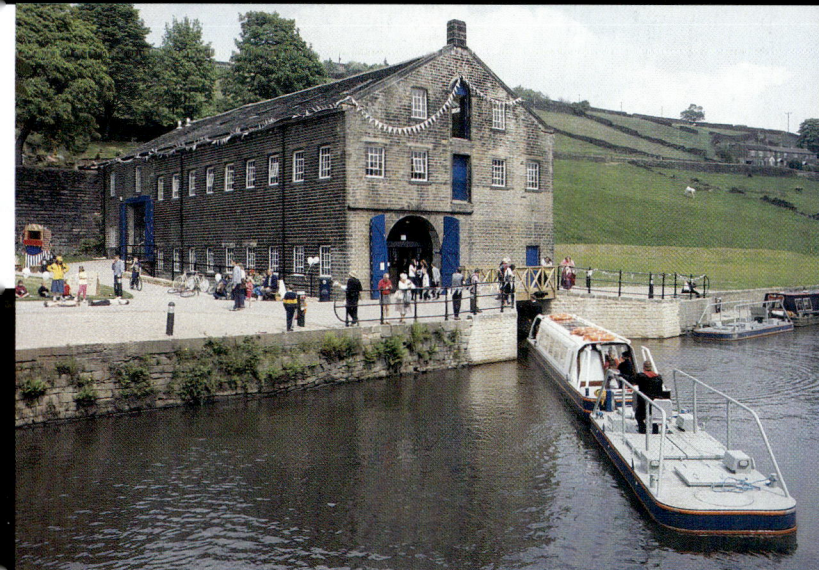

BRITISH WATERWAYS
- Breathing new life into the North West of England

In the North West British Waterways cares for nearly 600 miles of canals and inland waterways. We are currently restoring canals at a faster rate than they were built in the canal heyday of the 1790's.

Canal restoration brings:

- urban and rural regeneration

- jobs

- environmental improvements

- new leisure opportunities

- social inclusion

British Waterways are creating a virtuous circle of canal regeneration - attracting inward investment - creating sustainable growth - fostering local pride.
By the end of 2002, this formula will have worked in all of these projects:

Huddersfield Narrow Canal
- £30 million project
- Major improvements to Stalybridge
- Creation Standedge Visitor Centre, Marsden

Millennium Ribble Link
- £6 million project
- First new canal link for more than a century
- Investment and tourism opportunities for Preston

Rochdale Canal
- £23.8 million restoration
- Urban regeneration and tourism opportunities
- Re-energising East Manchester

Ashton Canal
- "Gateway to the Games"
- Creation of 2 canal rings
- Establishing local ownership

Anderton Boat Lift
- Restoration of the world's first boat lift
- Landmark structure for Cheshire
- Modern methods and Victorian ingenuity

We are now working on the following schemes:
- Northern Reaches of the Lancaster Canal
- Manchester, Bolton and Bury Canal
- Leeds and Liverpool Canal extension

British Waterways • North West Regional Office • Navigation Road • Northwich • Cheshire • CW8 1BH
Tel: 01606 723800 Fax: 01606 871471 Web: www.britishwaterways.co.uk

Let the fun and games Begin.

Manchester's number one radio station is proud to support the Commonwealth Games by launching a station for the nations. 87.7 The Games will bring the event alive with a mix of top sports action and light hearted fun. Locals and visitors to the city can tune in for today's best music, competitions, ticket offers and where to go in the evenings. We'll be on air 24 hours a day from July 17th to August 6th.

the games
87.7fm
powered by
❊**KEY103**

Capital of the North

Manchester represents everything great about Great Britain – it's a diverse, multicultural melting pot that has been at the heart of the country's great cultural, industrial, social and sporting advances. Janet Reeder salutes the city

TO ITS POPULATION

(around 2.5m at the last count) Manchester is the coolest place on the planet. It's been "Cottonopolis", "Madchester" and even, "Gaychester". The city has revolutionised politics, music and science – and it has the most famous football team in the world in Manchester United. It also has a knack for re-inventing itself, sometimes against the odds, which is why it remains one of the most defiantly modern cities on earth.

In the 19th Century, the city was at the fiery heart of the Industrial Revolution, the champion of Free Trade and the birthplace of the Labour movement. It could be argued quite forcibly that if it wasn't for Manchester, the UK would be a very different place than it is now. After all, in 1948 Manchester became the site of the first ever computer, affectionately called "Baby" by inventor Tom Kilburn and a team that included the brilliant mathematician Alan Turing.

"Baby" wouldn't be recognisable today, as it filled an entire room but was only capable of storing the amount of information that can now be included on a microchip.

From Halle to Haven

The Bee Gees, Joy Division, Simply Red, New Order, The Smiths, Stone Roses, Happy Mondays, 808 State, Lisa Stansfield and latterly, Badly Drawn Boy, Doves and Haven are just some of the acts that have emerged from the city's thriving music industry.

In the 1980s, the city was "Mad For It" – but mad for what exactly? The most original sounds in pop, a baggy-trousered rave revolution and the supercharged nightlife that evolved around the Hacienda nightclub. Music is still far and away one of the most important aspects of Manchester life with Oasis, Badly Drawn Boy, Haven and Doves all recently

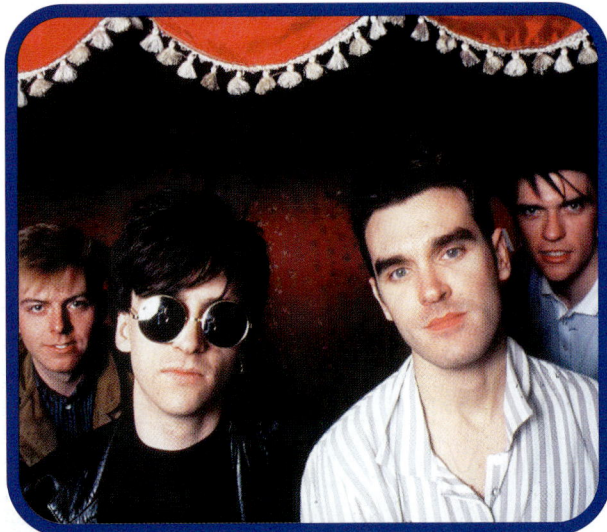

Creating a beautiful noise the Manchester way (clockwise from top): The Smiths, one of a multitude of celebrated bands originating in Manchester; the Royal Exchange Theatre has played host to an endless range of talent, from Vanessa Redgrave to Kate Winslett; mad for it – Oasis' Liam Gallagher

in the charts. In addition, *24 Hour Party People* – easily the best music-related movie since *Spinal Tap* – romps through the rise and fall of the notorious Factory Records empire (home of the Madchester early-1990s madness, including Happy Mondays and Stone Roses) and is destined to become cult viewing. Let's not forget that the city also has a fine heritage in classical music, with the Halle Orchestra founded by Sir Charles Halle in 1858, the BBC Philharmonic and the Manchester Camerata, the best freelance orchestra in the country.

Theatrical roots

Step into the Royal Exchange Theatre for the first time and you'll begin to understand something else about Manchester. This is one of the finest examples of how the city has been able to preserve its own old industrial past without compromising on innovation. Built in 1914-21, its proud boast was as the largest place of assembly for trades around the world. Now, beneath its large central dome, there's a modernist theatre that can only be described as looking like a luna module that's docked amidst the marble pillars. The stars who've appeared there are too numerous to mention, although the cream of the crop include Vanessa Redgrave, John Thaw, Bob Hoskins, Helen Mirren and Kate Winslett.

Older still are the Palace Theatre, the Opera House and the Library Theatre, while The Green Room and the Contact are the venues to check out cutting-edge alternative shows.

Home is where the art is

You can't miss the Urbis, the glass ski-slope designed by Manchester architect Ian Simpson – it towers over the city skyscape. Descend through its galleries and you will learn something about the city's urban development.

After a break of almost three years undergoing refurbishment, Manchester has got its City Art Gallery back, with a new £35m extension by Sir Michael Hopkins, doubling the space for exhibits, adding a new cafe and a children's gallery. The city also has a penchant for groundbreaking art – hence the concrete wall in the re-vamped Piccadilly Gardens, the work of Japanese architect, Tado Ando, and the controversial "Touchstone" sculpture outside the Halle's Bridgewater Hall home, by Kan Yasuda.

Student heaven

Manchester derives its young, upstart attitude in part from the 58,000 students who live in the city. Anna Ford, now

Linden

Prices from £104,950 to £500,000

Prices correct at time of going to press

01625 415415
www.lindenhomes.co.uk

Homegrown not mass produced

Individual homes. Innovative designs. Imaginative layouts. Some of the best locations in Cheshire and South Manchester. These are just some of the characteristics that differentiate a Linden home and make it special.

Our homes are not mass produced; each is a Linden original. Our passion for design is fuelled by our desire to create homes that people not only want to live in but are proud to live in. Linden homes are available in the North West in:

Cheshire: Nantwich, Chester, Audlem, Bollington, Great Warford, Cuddington.

South Manchester: Sale, Hale, Cheadle Heath and Lymm.

Although pre-eminent in Cheshire and South Manchester we also operate throughout the country in Berkshire, Bristol, Buckinghamshire, Gloucestershire, Hampshire, Hertfordshire, Kent, Oxfordshire, Surrey and West Sussex.

2001 WHAT HOUSE? AWARD
Sponsored by
THE SUNDAY TIMES

LINDEN

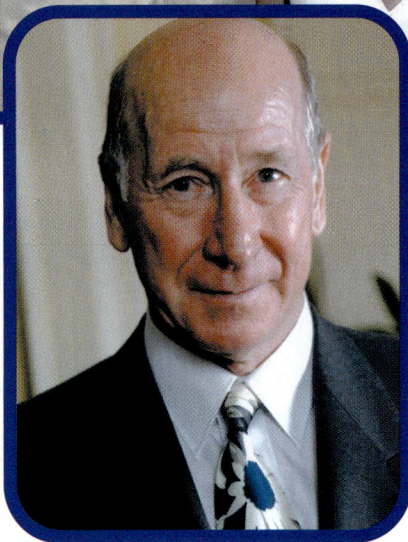

Fleet of footie (top to bottom): Alderley Edge residents, Manchester United's David Beckham with his wife, Victoria – his popularity has increased the sport's fame worldwide; Manchester United's Bobby Charlton – possibly one of England's greatest midfield maestros

a renaissance as a residential area. Currently, it's undergoing another transformation as the home of the Imperial war Museum North (Daniel Libeskind's magnificent creation, embodying symbols of both war and peace in its design). A fabulous bridge links it to the Lowry, which opened in 2000 and houses the world's largest collection of paintings by the Salford-born painter of matchstick men, from which it takes its name.

Travel further out of the city and you'll come to Alderley Edge. the north west home of England football captain David Beckham and wife Victoria, or "Posh 'n' Becks" as they are known. Cheshire also has some magnificent stately homes such as Lyme Hall, where Colin Firth (as Mr Darcy in the BBC TV adaptation of Jane Austen's Pride and Prejudice) famously emerged in a wet shirt .

Sporting legends

Go anywhere in the world and say you're from Manchester, and you'll be greeted with the names Bobby Charlton or David Beckham. You can't escape Manchester United – and let's not forget City. The Blues' fortunes have been a lot more mixed, but no less a cause for celebration. Manchester also has a velodrome, though nobody outside the sports world knew what it was until Jason Queally came on the scene and cycled his way to victory at the Sydney Olympics. The city's cycling track has made hopefuls of rising stars such as Dave Heald and Julie Paulding, among others. Local talent has been making use of the Olympic-sized swimming pool at the University, though James Hickman is the most recognised.

Big on the boxing circuit is undefeated welterweight Ricky "Hitman" Hatton, as well as Anthony Farnell and Michael Gomez. Sport is in the region's blood and there's nowhere better to spend a few hours on a sunny summer afternoon than Old Trafford cricket ground. A place of legend in a city well-equipped to create legends. What more could you want from a city – the Commonwealth Games? Well, we've got those too...

Chancellor of Manchester University, chose to become a student here after a chance meeting with The Beatles at Granada TV. Property developer Tom Bloxham honed his entrepreneurial skills as a student selling posters at the University and has made his millions turning the city's old warehouses into ultra-modern loft apartments.

Other luminaries of Manchester's universities and colleges include Victoria Wood, Rik Mayall, Ben Elton, the Chemical Brothers and the King of Norway.

The University started life as Owens College on Quay Street in the early 1850s. As one observer described it: "The entrance was guarded by a very Scylla and Charybdis of disreputable licenced houses... the Dog Inn, a fully licenced house with singing room, at the back of which shocking scenes were enacted. On the other hand there was a beer house of equally dangerous character."

By 1858, the Manchester Guardian had written the college off as a "mortifying failure". What did they know?

The biggest feat of engineering in Victorian times was the Manchester Ship Canal, but when industry declined, so did the city's waterways. Today, Salford Quays has had

five fab facts

1. Top of the Pops was first recorded at the BBC's studios on Dickenson Road, Manchester.
2. Presumably, Bee Gee Maurice Gibb (above) has fond memories of growing up in Manchester because he recently bought his former childhood home on Keppel Road, Chorlton.
3. In the 1930s, the city had its own film industry (Mancunian Films), featuring world famous stars of the time Gracie Fields and George Formby.
4. In 1991, less than 1,000 people lived in Manchester's city centre, but now with hundreds of new apartments being built, that figure is expected to rise to at least 10,000 by the end of this year.
5. Manchester Town Hall and Manchester University were the work of architect Alfred Waterhouse.

Manchester 2002
THE XVII COMMONWEALTH GAMES

Richard Young, Gillian Shaw (Rex Features)

EVERYTHING.
And everything else.

With 200 stylish shops, all the top High Street names and the fabulous 800 seater FoodChain Food Court - enjoy the best shopping experience in Manchester. All under one roof, open 7 days a week.

ARNDALE
centre of manchester
Everything. And everything else.

22nd July to 4th August. Open till 9pm Mon - Sat (11am - 5pm Sundays).

1902
Ashanti territory incorporated into the Gold Coast

1908
New Zealand first referred to as a Dominion

1909
Canberra chosen as the site of the Australian capital

1914-18
World War I: 1,115,000 UK and the British Empire troops killed

1921
The Irish Free State is created

1926
Dominions are given autonomy

1930
Nehru declares Indian independence

1939-45
World War II: 370,000 troops from the UK and the British Empire killed

1947
India and Pakistan become independent

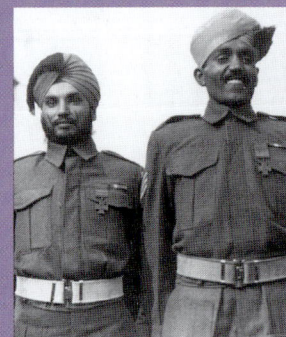

Family ties

A quarter of the world's population belongs to the Commonwealth. Despite this vast membership, surprisingly few people know about its history and purpose. Dr David Griffiths offers some answers

FOR MOST OF THE

19th and 20th Centuries, the British ruled over a colossal territorial empire, extending over a large part of North America, much of the Caribbean region, great tracts of Africa south of the Sahara, the whole of the Indian subcontinent and Australasia, territories in South East Asia and the Pacific, and for a time, much of the Middle East.

Throughout this empire, the British disseminated their institutions, language and culture, including sport. As a result, in varying degrees, British influences can be detected in systems of government, religious adherence, patterns of education, cultural tastes, sports and pastimes around the world to this day.

As the British colonisers spread around the globe, they took their sporting interests with them. These games were played in their spare time, but in due time the colonists encouraged local people to take up these sports – including cricket, rugby, soccer, golf and hockey.

The Commonwealth Games as we know them today began as the British Empire Games. The inaugural Games were held in 1930 in Hamilton, Canada. A field of 400 athletes from 11 countries competed in 1930; in Manchester 2002, 72 nations will take part.

The roots of today's Commonwealth can be found in the relationship between Britain and the self-governing colonies – the so-called "white dominions". In 1926, it was agreed that Canada, Australia, South Africa and New Zealand should manage their own foreign relations – and the Commonwealth evolved from this decision.

After World War II, many colonies swiftly won their independence and the Commonwealth adapted to ensure that emphasis was placed both on equality and on the voluntary basis of membership. The Commonwealth Secretariat took over the running of the Commonwealth in 1965 and has its headquarters at Marlborough House in London. There have been only four secretary-generals of the Secretariat: Arnold Smith of Britain (1965-75), Shridrath Ramphal of Guyana (1975-90), Emeka Anyaoka of Nigeria (1990-2000) and Donald Mckinnon of New Zealand, the current secretary-general.

Today's Commonwealth is a voluntary association of sovereign states, the majority of which are republics. There are 16 constitutional monarchies under HM Queen Elizabeth II, where, with the exception of Britain, a governor-general represents the Queen. Five others – Brunei Darussalam, Lesotho, Malaysia, Swaziland and Tonga have national, indigenous monarchs. The Queen, as a symbol of

1948
Ceylon and Burma become independent

1949
Ireland leaves the Commonwealth

1950
India becomes the first Commonwealth republic

1957
Ghana gains its independence

1960
Cyprus and Nigeria become independent

1961
South Africa leaves the Commonwealth

1962
Sierra Leone, Jamaica, Trinidad and Tobago, Uganda gain independence

1963
Kenya and Zanzibar gain independence

1965
Malta and Malawi become independent

Flying colours (clockwise from top left): The flags of the Commonwealth fly outside Parliament in Westminster, London; Queen Elizabeth II with members of the Commonwealth celebrating her Silver Jubilee in 1977; citizens celebrate India's independence from British rule in the streets of Calcutta on 21 August 1947

the free association of member states, is head of the Commonwealth. Only independent states are members, but the Commonwealth also includes about six million people living in self-governing states and dependencies of member nations, such as the Falkland Islands and the Cook Islands. The Commonwealth has no formal charter or requirements for membership, but there are unwritten conventions associated with entry:

● 1994: A commitment to the core values and principles of the Commonwealth as set out in the Harare Declaration.

● 1995: Acceptance of Commonwealth practices, including the use of English as the medium of communications and Commonwealth relations.

● 1996: Acknowledgement of the Queen as the head of the Commonwealth.

The members of the Commonwealth gather every two years at the "Commonwealth Heads of Government Meeting". In 1991, the meeting at Harare set out the principles of Commonwealth membership, which are still upheld today:

● We believe that international peace and order, global economic development and the rule of international law are essential to the security and prosperity of mankind.

● We believe in the liberty of the individual under the law, in equal rights for all citizens regardless of gender, race, colour, creed or political belief, and in the individual's inalienable right to participate by means of free and

1966
Botswana, Guyana and Lesotho become independent

1967
Aden gains independence

1968
Mauritius and Swaziland gain independence

1972
Bangladesh breaks away from Pakistan

1973
Bahamas becomes independent

1974
Grenada gains its independence

1975
Papua New Guinea becomes independent

1976
Seychelles gains independence

1978
Dominica achieves its independence

1979
Kiribati gains its independence

1980
Zimbabwe and Vanuatu gain independence

1981
Belize becomes independent

Andrew Dunsmore, Bill Orchard (Rex Features)

We want Heroes, Not just Winners

The World Anti-Doping Agency wants the world to Play True.

Without rules, sport doesn't exist. The fun of sport is being great, scoring and playing within the rules.

The World Anti-Doping Agency (WADA) came to existence in 1999 from the desire of the Olympic Movement, governmental agencies and especially, clean athletes to promote healthy, doping-free sport by ending the misuse of performance enhancing substances. In order to prevent doping there needs to be a clear understanding of the complex nature of the problem and the comprehensive mix of strategies needed to succeed.

As an independent organisation, WADA is working to implement one single anti-doping code, harmonise legislation and coordinate a worldwide anti-doping testing programme. WADA will also focus on developing education and prevention programmes, while also establishing research programmes relating to the detection of doping and the protection of athletes' health.

WORLD ANTI-DOPING AGENCY

play true

To learn more about WADA's vision and activities for a world that values and fosters doping-free sport:

www.wada-ama.org / info@wada-ama.org

The Logo Story
The concept "Play true" summarises and stands for the universal spirit of sports practised without deception and in full respect of the established rules. The "equal sign" expresses equity and fairness. The "square" represents the customs and the rules that must be respected. The mark is dynamic, yet simple, as is the nature of sport. Black evokes neutrality and is the traditional colour for the referee. Green evokes health and nature and is the usual colour of the field of play.

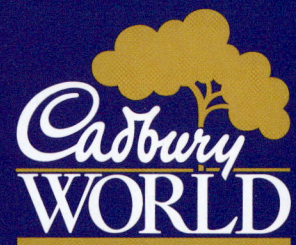

● Democracy, democratic processes... the rule of law and the independence of the judiciary;

● Fundamental human rights, including equal rights and opportunities for all citizens, regardless of race, colour, creed or political belief;

● Equality for women, so that they may exercise their full and equal rights;

● Provision of universal access to education.

Compared with many other international organisations, the Commonwealth is very new. Although the British empire dated from the 16th Century and self-rule for some dominions began in the mid-19th Century, the modern Commonwealth only really began with the creation of the Commonwealth Secretariat in 1965 and the issuing of the Singapore Declaration of Commonwealth Principles in 1971. Compare this with the dates for the founding of the European Union (the Treaty of Rome was signed in 1957) and the United Nations (founded 1945).

Today, the Commonwealth is an association of 54 independent states spread across the world, sharing ideas and experiences, skills, know-how and a common language. The Commonwealth Games reflect that commitment to unity and we welcome all the participants.

● The largest country in the Commonwealth is India, with a population of a billion people.
● The members with the smallest population are Nauru and Tuvalu, each with a population of 10,500 people.
● There are over 1.7 billion people in the Commonwealth.
● Half of the Commonwealth is under 18-years-of-age.
● Commonwealth Day is celebrated on the second Monday in March, chosen because all children are in school that day.
● Thirty Commonwealth countries are islands or parts of islands.
● The next Commonwealth Games will be held at Melbourne, Australia, in 2006.

2002 Manchester
THE XVII COMMONWEALTH GAMES

Celebrating diversity (clockwise from top left): An observance for Commonwealth Day 2001; Emeka Anyaoka of Nigeria, secretary-general of the Commonwealth from 1990-2000; the current secretary-general, New Zealander Donald Mckinnon; the Queen at a Commonwealth Day reception on 14 March 2000

democratic political processes in framing the society in which he or she lives.

● We recognise racial prejudice and intolerance as a dangerous sickness and a threat to healthy development, and racial discrimination as an unmitigated evil.

● We oppose all forms of racial oppression and we are committed to the principles of human dignity and equality. The Commonwealth also committed itself to the protection and promotion of the following values:

1982 Falklands War	1987 Fiji leaves the Commonwealth	1997 Hong Kong returned to China
1984 Brunei gains its independence	1994 Multi-racial elections in South Africa	2000 Tuvalu joins the Commonwealth
1984 Britain imposes sanctions over South Africa	1995 Nigeria is suspended from the Commonwealth	2002 Commonwealth Games held in Manchester

Welcome to Melbourne

Melboune will be the host of the 2006 Commonwealth Games and as they say in Australia's second city, with sport, it's not just a game; it's a passion.

AS HOST OF THE 2006

Commonwealth Games, Australia's events capital will share its infectious enthusiasm for competition, proving that it loves nothing more than to pack a stadium, cheer from a grandstand or witness the roar of engines trackside.

An experienced event host, Melbourne boasts some of the nation's biggest sporting events and a calendar of festivals, exhibitions, carnivals, parades and games. Whether it's high-octane Formula One action when Melbourne hosts the annual Foster's Australian Grand Prix or a battle of the world's best at the Australian Open tennis championship, Melbourne loves the heat of combat.

The 2006 Commonwealth Games will see 4,500 athletes from 72 nations compete over 12 days. Melbourne's existing collection of world-class venues will host the majority of sporting events. Most of these venues are concentrated around the Games Precinct, at the centre of which is the legendary Melbourne Cricket Ground. The MCG will be the venue for the Opening and Closing ceremonies, just as it was for the 1956 Melbourne Olympics.

Arts capital

With a population of more than 3.5 million, Melbourne is the second largest city in Australia and is renowned for its cosmopolitan atmosphere. Melbourne is recognised for excellent music and culture, quality fresh food, superb restaurants and entertainment venues, beautiful parks, gardens, architecture and shopping.

Melbourne has a proud record of arts and culture, producing international talent like Barry Humphries, Kylie Minogue, Geoffrey Rush, Cate Blanchett and George Miller. Melbourne is also a hub for both the visual arts and major stage shows. A cultural programme will be coordinated alongside the 2006 Commonwealth Games to showcase acts from Australia and other Commonwealth countries.

Must-see attractions include Melbourne Museum, Queen Victoria market, Melbourne Zoo, Melbourne Aquarium and Federation Square, which boasts the nation's finest collection of Australian art. Visit Melbourne for the 2006 Commonwealth Games and enjoy not only a sporting feast, but the chance to explore one of the world's most vibrant and intriguing cities.

Tourism Victoria

YOU SHOULD SEE OUR
PLAYING FIELDS

VISIT MELBOURNE'S PLAYGROUNDS AT THE 2006 COMMONWEALTH GAMES

Melbourne's playgrounds are some of the most spectacular arenas in the world. There's the Great Ocean Road with its world famous 12 Apostles, the acclaimed Yarra Valley wine region, and the breathtaking Grampians National Park. Oh and our sporting venues aren't bad either! To find out what you can look forward to at the Melbourne 2006 Commonwealth Games, inside the arena and out, **visitmelbourne.com/2006games**

You'll love every piece of Victoria

me!bourne
australia

Baton convoy (above): The Queen's Jubilee Baton Relay, on its 137 day journey through the Commonwealth – pictured here, the nominated runner is supported by an eager team of local followers in Scarborough, Tobago in March 2002 – before arriving on 25 July, 2002 at the opening ceremony for the Commonwealth Games

THE REPUTATION OF THE

Commonwealth Games as "the Friendly Games" has been given a unique physical expression in the countdown to the opening ceremony.

A specially-designed baton began its global journey at Buckingham Palace on 11 March. It was exchanged between runners as they passed through a bewildering variety of Commonwealth countries – from Canada to Tanzania, South Africa to Australia and New Zealand to India – a total of 23 countries in 87 days – before returning for a 50-day tour taking in all corners of the United Kingdom. This epic journey has seen the baton travel 59,000 miles across the Commonwealth, before arriving back on these shores. Once it arrived back in the UK, 5,000 runners carried it for ten hours a day over the course of 50 days, arriving in

time for the Opening Ceremony of the XVII Commonwealth Games in Manchester. There, the baton was handed back to Her Majesty The Queen, who will no doubt be relieved to find her opening address to the massive worldwide audience still sealed inside it.

The whole concept of a worldwide baton relay is an ambitious undertaking and was organised for this event by Australian Di Henry, a veteran of the Olympic torch relay at the 2000 Sydney Olympics.

"The philosophy behind the Queen's baton relay is for it to be a curtain raiser to the Commonwealth Games," she explains. "Around the world, they've really caught on to the idea, they've been very enthusiastic about seeing the baton. Some places, Africa and the Caribbean for example, had lots of baton carriers. Others have had official receptions.

Greg Garay

Message in a baton

When the Queen reads her opening address at the Commonwealth Games, it will mark the climax of the Queen's Jubilee Baton Relay, a four-month odyssey that has seen the baton pass through 23 countries, bringing diverse groups from the Commonwealth together. Anwar Brett follows its path

Pretty much every country it's gone to, we've seen the Head of State greet it officially.

"It's been out on some wild trips – on naval boats, on race courses, everything you can think of. The other thing we wanted to do was make it a once in a lifetime opportunity for the runners, so that they have a fantastic time holding the baton and help us get it to the opening ceremony with the message from the Queen that will open the Games."

Each of the 5,000 runners in the UK will carry the baton about 500 yards, far enough to provide a lasting memory, but not so far that it will require months of training. As well as athletes and celebrities, this unprecedented pool of runners has been drawn from each of the many diverse areas that the baton passes through. These are people who have made a notable contribution to life in that community, who have been nominated as deserving of this singular honour. People like 18-year-old Joanna Strycharczyk from Carlisle, who has demonstrated an acute awareness of other peoples' needs in various ways. She organised Operation Christmas Child at her school, where classmates filled shoeboxes with Christmas presents for needy children, and also became actively involved in Age Concern's Winter Campaign.

In addition, she is heavily involved in the Duke of Edinburgh's Award Scheme.

Nominated by a teacher, Strycharczyk had no idea she was "in the running" until she heard that she had been accepted. "It was a complete surprise," she says, beaming. "I was delighted when I found out, but I didn't know much about it before that. They sent me the uniform and an information pack, and that's when I really learned that they were running through hundreds of towns, with a big evening celebration planned at the end of each day."

Manjula Baul Sood was equally surprised to find out that she had been selected. The Leicester councillor is a diligent representative, a tireless worker for womens' rights and equal opportunities. This is why she was nominated by Secretary of State for Trade & Industry Patricia Hewitt.

Sood took on her council seat when her husband – a much loved local politician – suffered a tragic, premature death. She was the first Hindu woman councillor in the city. The bond that evidently exists between her and the people of Leicester is a source of pride, but Sood thinks the honour of carrying the baton reflects the people she represents as much as it acknowledges her own achievements.

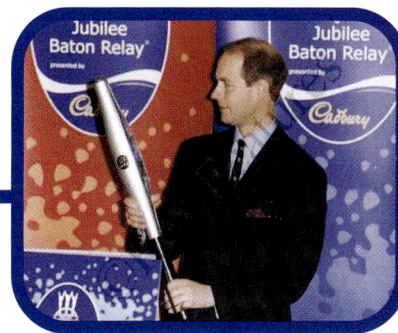

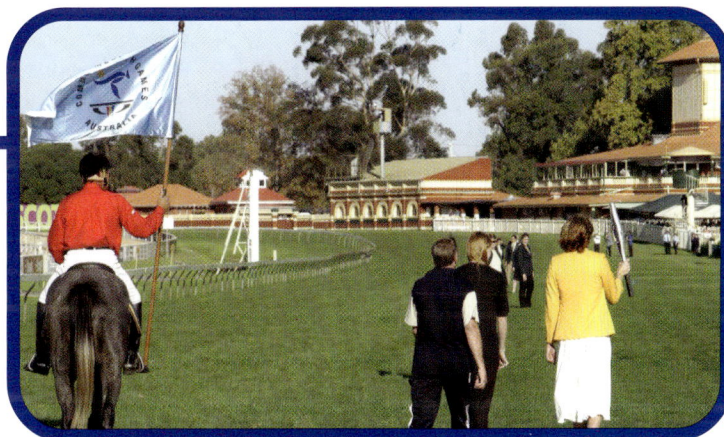

Greg Garay

Spread the word (clockwise from top left): With the famous Twin Towers in the background, British High Commissioner Bruce Cleghorn carries the Baton proudly in Kuala Lumpur, Malaysia; the baton in Barbados; Prince Edward and the Queen make a royal inspection; Christine Stanton (gold medalist – high jump) carries the Baton down the straight at Ascot race course between races on the Baton's first day in Perth, Australia; President John Kuffour carries the Baton through the grounds of The Castle, the President's residence, in Accra, Ghana

"The love that Leicester people have given me has meant that my soul has become very strong," says Sood. "I was very touched and honoured to be nominated, especially as the Commonwealth Games is a place where people come together." The logistical problems that inevitably arise from such an epic undertaking as the Queen's Jubilee Baton Relay have, for Henry and her team, been eased a little by her experience in the Sydney Olympics. Not that it was a total cakewalk.

"When I came over here initially, I had less than 18 months to pull it off," she recalls. "The weather was cold and wintry, and if I was ever going to turn it down, that was the time. What I really needed was to get a couple of key people who already knew how to do certain things on board. Things to do with the logistics and the administration, the computer programming that would decide the order of the runners – stuff like that.

"Otherwise, we've trained all the British people we've employed and to be honest it's gone like a dream. Everyone has been really understanding and helpful, and Cadbury has been a great

sponsor. Of course, it is easier doing it for the second time because we made our mistakes on the first one. We hope we've been able to perfect what we were aiming to do.

"If anything, the difference in this one is that the Sydney Olympics was the main game in town, so everyone wanted to play. Here it's a much bigger market, with a lot more people and a lot of events going on. It's been a lot of work to sell it, but it's gone great," adds Henry.

Where the Olympic torch is a live flame, the Queen's Jubilee Baton behaves in a slightly different way. Designed by Ideo, it is made from machined aluminium, weighs 1.69kg, is 710mm tall and measures between 42.55mm to 85mm in diameter. The really clever bit is happening inside though, as a series of sensors detect and monitor each runner's pulse rate, creating – through a series of light emitting diodes – a pulsating, artificial "flame".

This truly represents the beating heart of an event for and by the people of the Commonwealth.

Thorpedo time

Ian Thorpe is the most famous swimmer in the world and possibly the greatest of all time (though he'd never admit it). Craig Lord, swimming correspondent of *The Times*, meets this shy swimming superstar

THE TARGET SET FOR

Ian Thorpe in Manchester appears to be a Spitzean seven gold medals, which would make the man recently voted the World's Most Outstanding Athlete also the most titled swimmer in the history of the Commonwealth Games.

"My ambitions don't revolve around gold medals and winning," says the 19-year-old from Sydney. "I can't control what other people do and what they are capable of doing. In everything I do, I never try to compare myself with others. I try to satisfy my own expectation, as opposed to doing what other people want me to do. I train to be the very best I can be and when I race, I'm only satisfied if I know I gave it my best. It would be terrible for me to win knowing I could have swum better."

A slight tendency to shyness is the only hint that Thorpe, now 6ft 4in, 15 stone and the owner of those famous size 17 feet, is a teenager – albeit a very talented one. As Duncan Armstrong, the 1988 Olympic 200m freestyle champion once said: "He marries grace with power. He caresses the water, but when it's time to be brutal, he's like a raging bull. When his musculature matures, he will be unstoppable."

Thorpe's worth to Australian sport is summed up by Bill Sweetenham, the Australian who heads British swimming: "The day that Thorpe came along, Australian swimming got down on its knees, looked heavenward and said, 'Thank you God'. He is a gift, a once in a lifetime. You can only pray for such talent to come, you can't make it."

That said, the right type of training is paramount. Of his relationship with Doug Frost, his 58-year-old coach, Thorpe says: "We have a great deal of respect for each other and admiration too. We have been on a long journey together."

At 14, Thorpe won 10 gold medals at New South Wales age-group championships. At Perth, Western Australia, in January 1998, he became the youngest male world swimming champion, winning four gold medals later the same year at the Commonwealth games in Kuala Lumpur. To date, he has established 17 world records over 200, 400 and 800 metres freestyle, and relays. In Sydney, he became Olympic champion over 400m freestyle before moving into a league of his own in Japan last year, when he won the world titles over 200, 400 and 800 metres freestyle.

Thorpe has relished the prospect of the Games in Manchester for some time now: "I'm excited about it. I can't wait to race in the Manchester pool – it's going to be a great competition."

THE HARDWARE.

THE SOFTWARE.

The XVII Commonwealth Games will be the biggest sporting event ever held in the UK. It will also be the first international multi-sport event to run on a single, common platform – Microsoft Windows.® Microsoft has created a software and service solution that will keep everything running smoothly throughout the 10 days of the Games. Microsoft Windows® will be managing results and data from 17 venues involving over 5,200 athletes and officials, covered by 4,500 media people and watched by more than 1 million spectators in person, as well as over a billion on TV. Competitors from around the world will be striving to realise their potential. With Microsoft providing the infrastructure to ensure 100% system reliability, they can concentrate on achieving the best results, while we concentrate on sending those results around the world. Visit www.microsoft.com/uk/cwg2002 or www.msn.co.uk/games2002 to find out more about what Microsoft is bringing to the XVII Commonwealth Games.

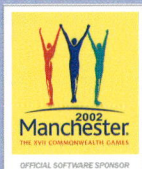

Manchester 2002
THE XVII COMMONWEALTH GAMES
OFFICIAL SOFTWARE SPONSOR

Microsoft. Proud to be the official software sponsor of the 2002 Commonwealth Games.

Microsoft®

Fitz the bill

Sarah Fitz-Gerald has won almost every squash title, including a silver in 1998. Is she going for gold at Manchester? Nick Cheek finds out

THERE ARE FEW ATHLETES

who can match the achievements of Sarah Fitz-Gerald. The 33-year-old world squash champion has snared almost every major competition – in fact, only one title eludes her, the Commonwealth gold. Hers has been a glittering career, which she capped in 2001 by taking home top honours at the Australian Sports Awards and winning 11 out of the 12 tournaments in which she competed, including British and World Opens. Like many athletes, she started young and her road to the pinnacle of sporting achievement has been paved with triumph, struggle and even a career-threatening injury.

When did you start playing squash?

I started at six-years-old, so my mum tells me. Mum, Judith (Tissot) Fitz-Gerald was four time Australian and three time Victoria champion, then managed a squash centre in Melbourne (Mordialloc). She went on to coach and manage the Australian women's and Victorian women's and junior teams. My introduction to the game was obviously through her and I had access to facilities as well as top notch coaching.

You won 11 out of 12 tournaments in 2001 and took top honours at the Australian Sport Awards. Do you think 2002 will be as successful?

This year started with a bang [when I took] the British Open again and so convincingly – it was my first tournie back after a month out with a calf tear. If I can win the gold, my year will already be on a major high. To top it off with the World Open title (and team title) would be amazing, as it would put me in the record books for having won more World Open and World Tour titles than any other player. These achievements are definitely personal goals. However, I play for the love of the game, not for medal and accolades. Having been awarded the Dawn Fraser and Female Athlete Awards was a huge honour and it is wonderful to be acknowledged in the sport of squash.

Do you feel any pressure, as favourite to win the gold medal in this year's Games?

The only pressure I feel is the pressure I put on myself. I know I am capable of winning the gold medal – as long as I have faith in my ability, I can win. I do feel the weight of expectation as many people believe it is a foregone conclusion, but everyone must remember (me too) that I still have to work hard to win my matches and maintain my form until July.

How have you prepared yourself for the Games?

I [was] in the USA playing events, which I [was] training through. If I win the events, that only adds to my confidence – as well as reminding my opponents of the effort required to beat me.

What's your training regime like?

I basically train seven days a week, which is not always recommended by trainers, but it works for me. I spent a lot of time on court playing games with men, [working on] skills and other squash specific routines, as well as gym work, massage and hanging around positive people.

Who are your nearest challengers from the other Commonwealth countries?

There are plenty of challengers. Leilani Joyce [New Zealand] is returning from an achilles tear, Carol Owens [New Zealand], Cassie Campion [England],the former world No 1 and 1999 world champion, and Tania Bailey, British Open runner-up. All tough and all very definitely chasing my tail.

What do you love about squash?

I love the speed, individuality and chess-like aspects of the game. It is the only racket sport not in the Olympics and with our history and the number of countries it is played in... it deserves to be in all games. Squash is not a mainstream media sport, so the people involved are passionate, social and the players are down-to-earth.

Mike Hewitt (Allsport); Alex Livesey (Getty Images)

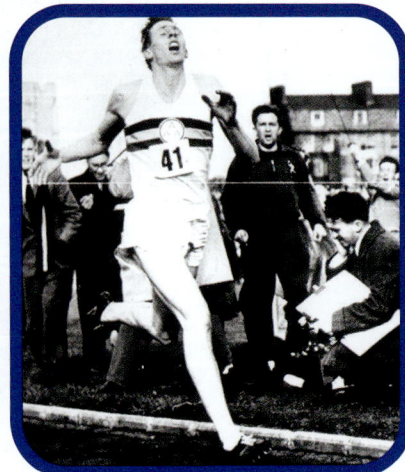

Famous faces (clockwise from top left): Canadian Percy Williams, the sensation of the 1928 Olympic Games at Amsterdam; Daley Thompson of England at the 1986 Commonwealth Games (Edinburgh, Scotland); Mary Peters, Great Britain, in 1970, clearing the bar in the high jump; Roger Bannister of Great Britain crosses the line to become the first person ever to run a mile in under four minutes, in 1954; Raelene Boyle of Australia at the 1970 Commonwealth Games in Scotland; Filbert Bayi of Tanzania rounds the bend during the 5,000m event at the AAA Championships in Crystal Palace, London, in 1978; England's Precious McKenzie wins the flyweight weightlifting class in the 1974 Games

Bettmann (Corbis): Steve Powell, Tony Duffy (Allsport); Hulton Getty/Getty Images

The hall of fame

Since its inception in 1930, the Commonwealth Games have produced more than their fair share of astounding moments and great athletes. Nick Keith opens the Commonwealth Games Hall of Fame

IN ANY LIST OF GREAT

competitors, the most interesting names are often those who are omitted. The compiler's choice is difficult enough in any major world event, such as the Commonwealth Games, and it is made harder by having to limit the numbers of stars while including a broad range of different competitive eras and disciplines.

These considerations have also counted against some of the modern gold medallists – on the basis that their stories are more familiar.

Let us start with an apology for the omission of some of golden heroes and heroines, such as:

Philip Adams (Australia); Charles Asati and Mike Boit (both Kenya); Angela Chalmers (Canada); Linford Christie, Steve Cram, and Sally Gunnell (England); Dawn Fraser and Cathy Freeman (Australia); Murray Halberg (New Zealand); Jon Konrads and Pam Kilborn (Australia); Anita Lonsborough and Linda Ludgrove (England); Syed Modi and Padukone Prakash (India); Mark McKoy and Milt Ottey (Canada); Adrian Moorhouse, Judy Oakes, Howard Payne, Steve Redgrave, and Tessa Sanderson (all England); and finally four heroic Scots, Ian and Lachie Stewart (5,000 and 10,000 metres in Edinburgh, 1970), David Wilkie, and Allan Wells (three sprint golds, including a dead heat).

8 Greats

Percy Williams (Canada)

Canadian Percy Williams, the double Olympic sprint champion for 1928, took the oath of allegiance at the inaugural British Empire Games ceremony in Hamilton in 1930.

Already the world record holder at 100 metres (10.3 seconds), he set a long-standing Commonwealth Games record of 9.6 secs in the 100 yards heats, and in the final seemed sure to break the world record of 9.5 secs. However, he pulled a thigh muscle at 70 yards and battled through the agony barrier to take gold in 9.9.

Roger Bannister (England)

The so-called "Miracle Mile" between Bannister and John Landy on 7 August 1954 was one of the key moments in putting the Commonwealth Games on the world sporting map. The story even reached the front page of the respected, but American-oriented magazine *Sports Illustrated*. In the battle between the only two men who had already broken the four-minute mile, Bannister (now Sir Roger) won in 3 mins 58.8 secs, with his Australian rival second in 3:59.6. Landy said later: "I looked over my left shoulder to see where he was on the final turn. When I looked back, he was ahead of me."

Mike Wenden (Australia)

One the great Aussie swimmers, Wenden won 9 golds, three silvers, and one bronze medal at the Commonwealth Games between 1966 and 1974. He also won two Olympic golds and set six world records. As a youngster, he had preferred ball games and only took up swimming at the age of 14 to help him recuperate after breaking a leg. Two years later, he was involved in his first world record swim (in the 4x220 yard relay at the 1966 Commonwealth Games). In the 1974 Christchurch Games, he was given a commemorative shield for his contribution to world swimming.

Precious McKenzie (England and New Zealand)

The South African-born McKenzie won four successive weightlifting golds from 1966 to 1978 representing first England and then New Zealand. After a tough childhood – his father was killed by a crocodile and his mother sent him to a foster home – McKenzie became a top weightlifter in South Africa, but was not allowed to compete for his country because of Apartheid. He moved to England, won golds for his adopted country in 1966, 1970 and 1974. At the 1974 Games in Christchurch, he fell in love with New Zealand, stayed on and represented them in the 1978 Games when the Queen was in the audience to see him win his fourth gold.

National Museums & Galleries on Merseyside

Merseyside Maritime Museum

the Walker

Museum of Liverpool Life

Conservation Centre

Sudley House   HM Customs & Excise National Museum

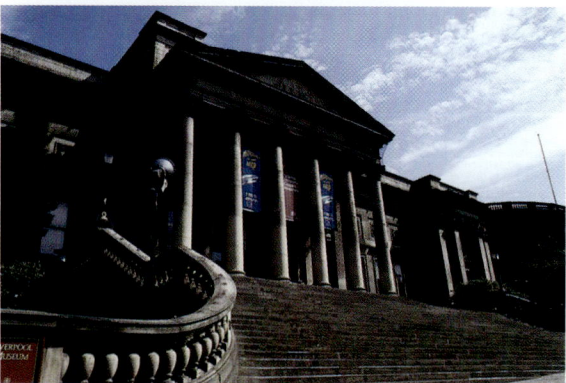

Liverpool Museum

Lady Lever Art Gallery

FREE for ALL

Liverpool's Cultural Heart

Telephone 0151 207 0001

www.nmgm.org.uk

LIVERPOOL 2008 EUROPEAN CAPITAL OF CULTURE BID

NATIONAL MUSEUMS & GALLERIES ON MERSEYSIDE
NMGM
NATIONAL MUSEUMS & GALLERIES ON MERSEYSIDE

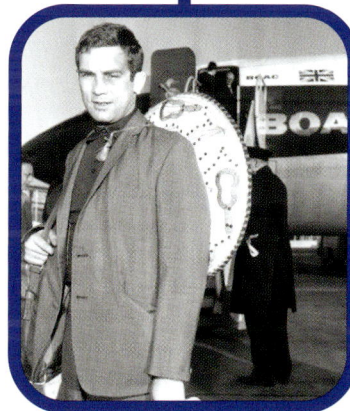

Talent on display (clockwise from top): Jack Lovelock of New Zealand during the 1,500 metres event at the 1936 Olympic Games in Berlin; Mataika Tuicakau at the Games in 1950, winner of Fiji's only gold; Welsh featherweight, Howard Winstone in 1967

Raelene Boyle (Australia)

In 1968, Raelene Boyle won a silver at the Mexico Olympics while a schoolgirl. Two years later, the great Australian sprinter took her first Commonwealth double while still in her teens and repeated the feat in 1974. In 1978, she was recovering from a tendon injury and had to be content with a silver in the 100m (she did not contest the 200).

Boyle was back in business again four years later when she carried the Queen's Baton into the QEII Stadium in Brisbane and later won the 400m in 51.26 secs. Following the race, she described the race as "a nice way to finish".

Mary Peters (Northern Ireland)

The warm and engaging smile of Northern Ireland's Mary Peters won many friends in a wonderful career that brought three Commonwealth golds and a silver, and triumph in the 1972 Olympic pentathlon at the age of 33. After Commonwealth silver in the shot in 1966, the Belfast heroine's first Commonwealth golds were in the shot and the pentathlon in 1970. In 1974, the pentathlon went down to the final event, the 200m event, where Mary had to run within a second of her main rival, Nigeria's Modupe Oshikoya, to retain her title – and she did.

Filbert Bayi (Tanzania)

An elite 1,500m field in 1974 was eclipsed by Filbert Bayi, who set a new world record in a memorable final. For sheer depth of quality, this was the greatest 1,500m race ever. The front-running Bayi, who hailed from a small village on Mount Kilimanjaro, took an early lead and, in a desperate finish, held off John Walker (New Zealand) and Ben Jipcho who won both the 5,000m and the Steeplechase. Bayi's time was 3 min 32.2 secs, which clipped nine tenths of a second off Jim Ryun's 1967 world record. Roger Bannister called it "the greatest run I have ever seen."

Poetry in motion (clockwise from left): New Zealand's Yvette Williams, winner of the women's shot putt at the 1954 Commonwealth Games in Vancouver (BC), Canada; Australia's World Record sprinter, Marjorie Jackson (left) and Indian sprinter Maty D' Souza in a practice run at the Olympic Village before the 1952 Olympiad; Peter Snell of New Zealand wins the 1,500m race at the 1964 Olympic Games in Tokyo; Ghulam Raziq of Pakistan, in action in 1958; South African Daniel Bekker wins at the 1960 Olympics

Daley Thompson (England)

Always the ultimate competitor, Daley Thompson was undoubtedly the outstanding all-round athlete of his generation and one of the greatest of all time.

He won a remarkable 19 out of 31 competitive decathlons, including two Olympic golds, three Commonwealth titles, two European crowns and a world championship. He competed in his first decathlon at the 1976 Olympics and finished a not terribly impressive eighteenth. However, in 1977, everything began to change and his true talent emerged. He twice scored 8,000 points (while still a teenager) and gave notice that he had arrived in 1978 when, at the age of 20, he won gold at the Commonwealth Games with the second highest ever score. Thompson is the son of a Nigerian father and Scottish mother. He was born in London and christened Adodele, but was called Daley by his friends.

Memorable moments

The first modern athlete

Jack Lovelock carried the New Zealand flag at the opening ceremony in London in 1934 and proceeded to beat the field on a sodden track. A prolific note-taker, Lovelock was called the "first modern athlete" by Roger Bannister, and he went on to win 1,500m gold at the Berlin Olympics. He died mysteriously in a New York subway train accident in 1949.

Five times a lady

Decima Norman of Australia was renowned for the elegance of her running. "Dashing Dess" won five golds for Australia in 1938, including a sprint double, the long jump and two relays – "You performed for your team's good, not for yourself," said Norman before the 1982 Brisbane Games where she was the first carrier of the Queen's Baton.

Hulton Getty

Hulton Getty

The big Fijian

The popular ever-smiling Mataika Tuicakau won Fiji's only gold, in the shot putt in 1950, and also took silver in the discus. He discarded a bandage from his injured throwing arm before each round of competition so as not to give himself an unfair advantage.

Multi-tasking to Gold

Yvette Williams, the multi-talented athlete from New Zealand, won gold in the long jump and silver in the javelin in 1950. This New Zealand field star won Olympic gold in 1952 and three more golds in the 1954 Commonwealth Games in Vancouver, where she had to compete in the discus and javelin almost at the same time because of the programme schedule, as well as repeating her long jump success.

All for love

Australia's Marjorie Jackson was one of the stars of athletics in the 1950s. She won seven Commonwealth titles, two Olympic golds and set 13 world records. When she retired young, the modest Australian said that her marriage was more important to her than athletics – and that her most lasting sporting friendships were those developed during the Commonwealth Games.

Middle-distance marvel

Aussie Herb Elliott was one of the silkiest middle distance runners of all time, the Australian legend won the 880 yards and the Mile in the 1958 Games. He remained undefeated at the mile or 1,500m between 1958 and 1961, and then he retired at the age of 22.

Welsh wonder

Howard Winstone, from Merthyr Tydfil, was aged 18 when he won the 1958 bantamweight final in Cardiff. He beat a hard-hitting Aussie Ollie Taylor (whose brother Wally got revenge by outpointing another Welshman Dave Collins at featherweight). As a pro, Winstone lost three world title fights at featherweight to Vicete Saldivar of Mexico before winning the crown at the Albert Hall in 1968.

On the move (top to bottom): Don Quarrie on the run with a handful of medals in 1978; Debbie Brill of Canada jumps the bar during a women's high jump event

Five-star South Africans

Heavyweight bronze medallist at the 1956 Olympics, the southpaw Daniel Bekker was one of the South African stars in the ring in 1958 when they won five boxing titles. Another was Henry Loubscher, who won Olympic bronze in Melbourne, followed by Commonwealth gold in the light-welterweight division.

Snell's pace

Another great New Zealand specialist in the Blue Riband events, Peter Snell was disappointed that he could not prove himself against the retired Herb Elliott in 1962. He took 1.7 secs off Elliott's Games record in the 880 yards (where he pipped Jamaica's George Kerr, who won the 440 yards), and Snell also won the mile. He later achieved the 800 and 1,500m double at the 1964 Olympics.

Jumper, hurdler, winner

Ghulam Raziq of Pakistan started as a high jumper (bronze in 1958) and reached two Olympic semis. Then he persuaded the Pakistani team managers to allow him to switch to hurdling and won the 120 yards final in 1962 at the age of 30.

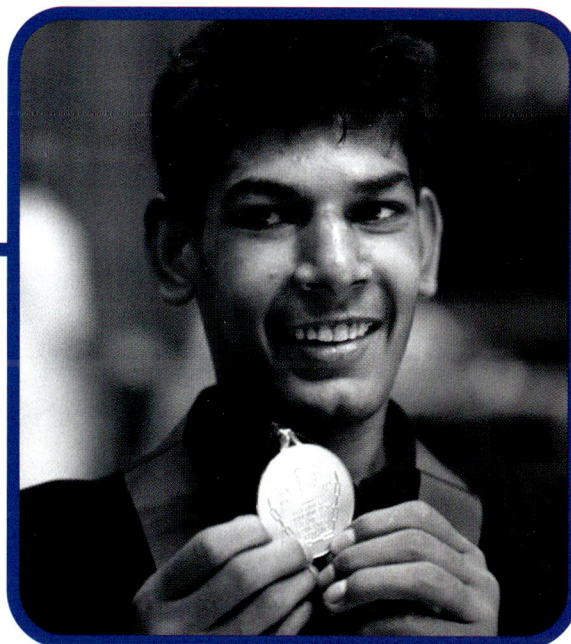

Victory and defeat (clockwise from top left): West Indies-born Frankie Lucas stands over the fallen Zambian, Julius Luipa at the 1974 Commonwealth Games; Indian wrestler Ved Parkash in 1970, displaying his gold medal for the light flyweight event at the Games; Yvonne Gowland of Australia, the only woman entrant at the smallbore rifle shoot for the 1974 Commonwealth Games

"At last I have achieved it [his lifelong ambition] – after 12 years of trying," he said

Hill climbing

The 1970 Games marathon had the greatest field possible with the four fastest runners in the world. Gold went to England's Ron Hill in 2:09.28, who broke three records. He lowered the Games record by nearly 12 seconds and set new British and European times.

He was followed home by the defending champion, Jim Alder (Scotland), with no medals for the early leaders and pre-race favourites Derek Clayton (Australia) and Jerome Drayton (Canada).

Double dealing

Like Raelene Boyle, Jamaica's Don Quarrie completed a double sprint double in 1974, changing his shoes just before the final to get more grip on the track.

He won the Olympic 200m gold and 100m silver in 1976, and one last Commonwealth gold at 100m in 1978, where he had revenge over Hasley Crawford (Trinidad), his Olympic conqueror. Unfortunately, a slightly pulled muscle in the 200m final relegated Quarrie to fifth place and prevented him from achieving a treble sprint double.

Brill-iant

The Canadian Debbie Brill was the first woman high jumper to win a major title using the Fosbury flop – the backward method pioneered by Dick Fosbury, gold medallist in the 1968 Olympics. Brill won the event twice, but her successes were separated by 12 years, from 1970 to 1982, with a silver in between in 1978.

Just desserts

Born in the West Indies, Frankie Lucas lived most of his life in England, but in 1974, when he was left out of their boxing team for the Games, he chose to represent his birthplace, the tiny island of St Vincent. On the way to the middleweight title, Lucas narrowly beat his England usurper Carl Speare in the semis and won the final by a knockout.

Girl power

The only female competitor in the 1974 shooting events, Australia's Yvonne Gowland, a 30-year-old housewife, made a name for herself by beating 24 men to gold in the smallbore event. In a difficult wind, she lost only six points out of 600, finished three ahead of Scotland's Alister Allen (who won the gold in 1978 and two more in 1982) and Bill Watkins of Wales.

Young blood

Only 14 when winning a light flyweight wrestling gold in 1970, Ved Prakash of India had to get permission to attend the Edinburgh Games both from his mother and from the International Wrestling Federation.

Kenya feel it

Kip Keino came to the 1996 Games after twice beating the legendary Ron Clarke and set two world records. Keino duly won the Commonwealth mile and three mile titles that year. He won the 1,500m at the 1968 Olympics and again at the 1970 Commonwealth Games, where he also took bronze at 5,000m. He rounded off a brilliant career by winning the 3,000m steeplechase at the 1972 Olympics, so he had

Hulton Getty

over the world, including the world title in 1983 and the 1986 Commonwealth gold.

The Clones cyclone

Only 17 when he took part in the 1982 bantamweight boxing competition, Barry McGuigan was the underdog in the final and was twice knocked down. He bounced back to beat the hard-hitting Tumat Sogolik from Papua New Guinea narrowly, but with guts and panache. He turned pro and three years later became WBA world featherweight champion.

Bull's eye babe

A paraplegic for 13 years, New Zealand's Neroli Fairhall won the women's archery gold from a wheelchair in the event's only appearance at the Commonwealth Games in 1982. With a bull's eye on her final shot, she came from behind to beat Janet Yates, a 17-year-old Belfast student.

Runaway winner

India's Chandersekaran Raghavan ran away from school as a young man, joined the railway in Madras and was introduced to weightlifting by work colleagues. Then he won three golds as a teenager in 1990, when he broke a Commonwealth Games record set in 1974 by 17.5kg. The original record was set by Precious McKenzie, who was on hand to present the medals.

Action Jackson

Welsh wonder Colin Jackson was a world force in sprint hurdling in the 1990s and he won Commonwealth Gold in 1990 and 1994. World record holder when he won his second gold, on each occasion Jackson recorded identical times at 13.08 secs and beat England's Tony Jarrett (who won gold in 1998).

taken major titles at every distance from 800 to 10,000m. He was also the first Kenyan athlete to appear on the cover of *Sports Illustrated*.

Hot Ottey

The glamorous and graceful sprinter form Jamaica, Merlene Ottey first made her mark in 1978 when she won the 200m in a wind-assisted 22.19 seconds. World 200m champion in 1989, she achieved a Commonwealth sprint double the following year.

Mighty marathon man from Melbourne

Australia's Rob de Castella caused a sensation in the 1982 Commonwealth Games by overhauling a huge lead established by Tanzania's Jum Ikanangaa. Although de Castella never took Olympic gold, he won marathons all

Right on target (clockwise from top left): Neroli Fairhall goes for gold during the 1982 women's archery event at the Commonwealth Games; Colin Jackson of Great Britain in action in the 110m hurdles at the 2000 Olympic Games in Sydney, Australia; Merlene Ottey of Jamaica in action in the women's 200 metre event during the 1995 World Championships in Sweden

Hulton Getty; Mike Powell, Clive Mason (Allsport)

commonwealth crackers

The Force failed him: Dave Prowse, English weightlifter in 1958 who was eliminated after four failed attempts at a lift, later starred as Darth Vader in Star Wars.

Ring legends: Boxing golds were won in 1954 by Englishman Brian Harper, who went on to box professionally as Brian London; and in 1986 by Lennox Lewis, then from Canada and now the world heavyweight champion.

Always the bridesmaid: Ron Clarke, Australia's world record long distance runner, managed only four silvers between 1962 and 1970.

Family fortune: Malcolm and Sarah Cooper, an English married couple, won shooting gold together in 1982.

Manchester 2002
THE XVII COMMONWEALTH GAMES

Actress Suranne Jones, better known as Coronation Street's Karen McDonald (top left) helped launch the crew uniforms for the 2002 Commonwealth Games – volunteers will help keep things running smoothly, both inside the Manchester Stadium and out

"WHEN I SAW THE GAMES WERE

coming to Manchester, I marched straight out to sign up as a volunteer. I think it's a once in a lifetime opportunity to get involved with an event like this."

Desmond Pastore's enthusiasm for the Commonwealth Games can be found in all the volunteers who have given their time and effort to make the event a success. Unlike the other volunteers, Pastore is 87 years-old, though he's got as much energy as someone a quarter of his age. He can be found dishing out information on rugby, a topic on which he has a lifetime's experience – "I played rugby for Sale from the age of 17-39 and still play at least once a week." Although Pastore will be putting in the hours like every other volunteer,

he admits the Games will be a chance to catch up with some old friends from far-flung places: "I've played some of the people coming over for the Games, as I've been on a number of rugby tours. It's going to be great seeing all those players and having them play in Manchester. It's going to be more like a wonderful social occasion than work for me."

It's partly due to this that he's willing to spend his own time making sure the Games are special. He admits, "I want the world to see that when Manchester does something, it does it well. I want Britain to be the best country to have ever hosted the Games and I'm very proud that it's coming to the UK. I can't wait for Manchester to become really multi-cultural. There will be a million people coming to Manchester from all over the world and it'll be great seeing them in the pubs and clubs, and out and about in the city."

He's a rock

For other volunteers, the Games will be a great learning experience. Mark Adeji-Kumi lives a couple minutes from the stadium and seeing it being built made him want to get involved. He is currently studying for a degree in Youth and Community Studies and has been a volunteer on a number of youth projects before.

Adeji-Kumi took part in a Pre-Volunteers Programme, which he says was incredibly valuable: "We were taught all about the history of the Commonwealth Games and taught a lot about customer service. We learned communication skills,

Unsung heroes

Caroline Blight introduces those people who'll be at the very heart of the Commonwealth Games 2002, the hardy souls who have volunteered to help make the Games a roaring success

Adecco

first aid, health and safety, skills that will be useful in the future. It's given me a practical insight into the things I'm learning at University." He'll be helping the team from Gibraltar, which he admits will be exciting in itself, because he's never visited the country.

"It's been fascinating speaking to people who live there. I'm helping them around the athletes village and I'll still be there after the Games end for anyone who's staying on a bit for a holiday, showing them around Manchester," he smiles. "The whole thing has just been a great experience and it's really opened my eyes to the world."

An unbeatable buzz

Some of the volunteers will go back to their normal lives after the Games, happy that they have been part of an historic event, but for others, this has changed their lives for good. Alberta Barton thought she didn't have a chance of becoming a volunteer when she saw an ad on television.

"The next day, I sat up at my computer at eight in the morning because I thought, if I was the first person to send in an application, I might be allowed to volunteer." It worked – she bagged the job. "I've really got a buzz for this kind of thing now. I don't know what I'll do when the Games are over – I've loved working on them so much," she admits. Before being accepted onto the programme, Barton was working at a local company while completing her NVQ in customer service. She was ready for a change and knew the Games would be it.

"I've done so many jobs, from stuffing envelopes and checking that all the seats in the stadium have the correct numbers on them, to interviewing people for jobs. Every day is different and I've met some wonderful people."

It's the new friends she's made that she'll be keeping in touch with – "We've already decided we'll have a reunion every Commonwealth anniversary." Barton loved the experience so much, she'll also be working on the clear-up operation.

"I'll help get everything back the way it was – painting, tidying, the lot. It's been a fantastic experience and if they need volunteers in Athens or Melbourne, they can just give me a call and I'll be on the next plane. My sons think I'm mad, but they're happy for me."

They aren't just happy, they're incredibly proud – Barton's youngest hugged her, telling how proud he was of all her hard work, "although he did think I was crazy when I took the Queen's baton, which I had the honour of looking after, to bed with me."

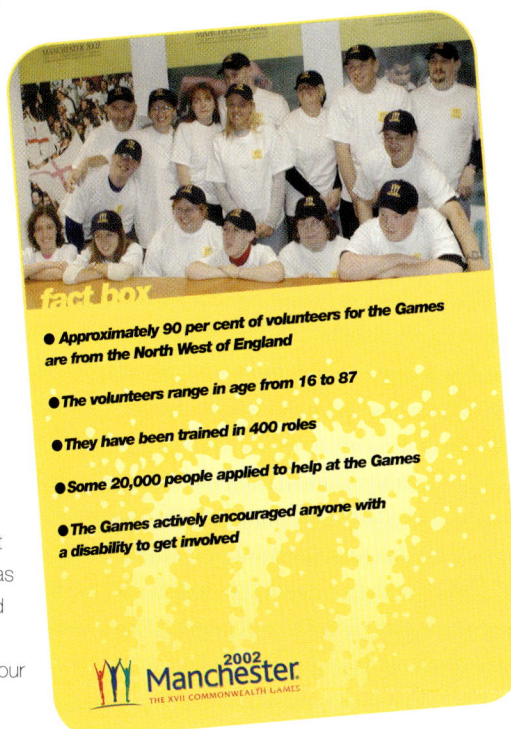

fact box

- Approximately 90 per cent of volunteers for the Games are from the North West of England
- The volunteers range in age from 16 to 87
- They have been trained in 400 roles
- Some 20,000 people applied to help at the Games
- The Games actively encouraged anyone with a disability to get involved

Manchester 2002
THE XVII COMMONWEALTH GAMES

Nyree Lewis, 21, is based in Manchester. She has cerebral palsy, but has not let her disability get in the way of an incredible swimming career. She arrives at the training facility, looking relaxed and happy: "Manchester has a disability high performance centre, which means there are lots of athletes in training and it's a really good laugh."

Nyree Lewis runs through her training programme with Emma Patrick, who has coached her since 2000 and was with her at the Sydney Paralympic Games.

Lewis limbers up and stretches before plunging into the pool. She's been swimming since the age of five. Initially, the need for physio brought her to the pool – but the will to win has kept her there.

At the Sydney Paralympics in 2000, Nyree Lewis won silver in the 100m backstroke as well as two bronzes in the 100m breaststroke and the 4x50 medley relay. She says that her best career moment was "winning the silver – it was great, people thought I'd won it, but it was just on the touch."

Training day

Nyree Lewis will be carrying Welsh hopes in the EAD 100 metres freestyle in Manchester. We reveal what it takes to make it to the Games

Stewart Darby

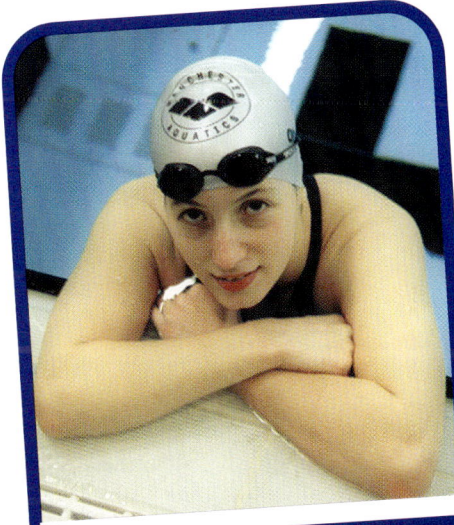

Her ambitions for the Games are to "get somewhere, not necessarily a gold medal, but definitely to get somewhere" – Wales will be right behind her.

The Commonwealth Games are the first wholly-inclusive multi-sport event – for the first time ever, medals won by Elite Athletes with a Disability (EAD) will count toward the final medal tally. Lewis says that "everyone is pleased that they're letting us in. It's great step forward. It would be even better if there was a full disability programme."

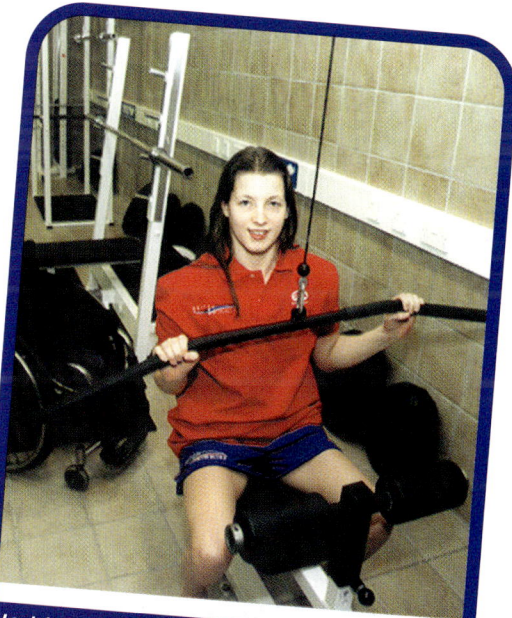

Lewis knows that the competition for Commonwealth gold will be fierce: "Danielle Campbell from Canada may be the biggest threat, but it's difficult to assess." She's hoping that all her hard work will give her that extra yard and bring her gold.

Her training routine is gruelling, to say the least. She has seven or eight sessions in the pool – with two hours for each session. She follows this with one hour in the gym three times a week. She doesn't just work with weights, she also works on core stability and reaction drills. Before the Games, she rests down with some lighter weights.

Stewart Darby

Mind the gap (clockwise from bottom left): Shirley Page, at the 1998 Commonwealth Games in Kuala Lumpur, with her lawn bowls bronze medal; the UK women's Lawn Bowls team for the 2002 Commonwealth Games in Manchester, including (from left to right) Jean Baker, Lynne Whitehead, Amy Cowshall, Gill Mitchell, Ellen Alexander, Carole Duckworth and Shirley Page; former European table tennis champion Jill Hammersley-Parker, mother of table tennis star Katy Parker; Katy Parker displays her phenomenal touch at table tennis

Don Morley (Empics)

The generation games

A 16-year-old table tennis prodigy and a 56-year-old lawn bowls veteran make an odd couple, but Nikki Racklin has found that the Commonwealth Games brings all sorts of talented individuals together

THERE MAY BE FOUR DECADES between them, but lawn bowler Shirley Page and table tennis player Katy Parker have struck up an unlikely friendship, which should stand them in good stead during the excitement of this year's Commonwealth Games.

Not many people can lay claim to meeting at Buckingham Palace, but that's exactly where 16-year-old Parker and 56-year-old Page first became acquainted.

"I was recently invited to Buckingham Palace on the occasion of Golden Jubilee Year," Page explains, "but no other members of my team seemed to be going. At the gates of the Palace, I bumped into Don Parker, former England international table tennis champ, who I met at the Commonwealth Games in Kuala Lumpur four years ago. He brought along his daughter Katy, who was also invited to Buckingham Palace in her capacity as a table tennis player. Don asked me if I'd mind accompanying Katy during the visit. In the meantime, Don went to while away a couple of hours in the pub!"

"It was wonderful," adds Page, who has been bowling for 20 years. "We met with Prince Charles, the Queen, the Duke of Edinburgh and Sophie Wessex, who was particularly interested in table tennis. Katy and I were at the palace for at least two hours and we were so glad to have shared the experience."

Parker agrees: "It was great fun. Neither of us knew anyone else there, so it was good that we met up!"

Parker, whose mother is Jill Hammersley, former European table tennis champion, is thrilled to be competing in Manchester.

"If we get a good draw, we've been told we could do really well, but being a first timer at the Commonwealth Games, I don't honestly know what the standard will be like."

By no means the only teenager in town, Parker says the younger competitors are treated in the same way as the veterans: "One of the other table tennis girls is actually younger than me. There's another place to fill and it will probably be somebody my age."

Likewise, Page has noticed a drop in the age of her fellow bowlers since she started competing: "The game has changed and become much more competitive. There's much more of a younger element in the game." No doubt Page's wealth of experience will see her through this year's long-awaited Manchester gathering. Despite the differences in age and perspective between the two women, there is sure to be plenty of inter-generational conferring in the Village.

You barely have time to read this ad.

Do you have time to teach an advisor your business?

www.kpmg.co.uk

The less your professional advisors understand about your business coming in, the more you'll have to teach them. And the longer it will be before they'll have anything useful to contribute. But KPMG has chosen to focus on key industry sectors. So when you call us in, we'll bring deep vertical knowledge with us. Putting you one important step closer to the kind of informed advice you're looking for. For further information please **contact Peter Brown, Office Senior Partner on 0161 246 4776 or email peter.brown@kpmg.co.uk.**

understanding @ **KPMG**

Get your kit on

Geoff Wightman of Puma UK talks about the joy and pain of being the official provider of sports apparel to Team England at the Games

Statistics:
There are 17 sports at the Games, with 641 Team England members and 148 different apparel styles. Each athlete will have: tracksuits; rainsuits; eight t-shirts; four polo shirts; five pairs of shorts; 10 socks; one cap; one sunhat; sandals; sunglasses; a wheeled holdall; two luggage tags; 20 pin badges; three towels; one back pack; one blazer and a separate outfit for the ceremonies, plus the kit for their individual sport. There will also be three permanent seamstresses, 20 Puma staff seconded to the project at different times and nine members of the Team England athletes clothing committee

IMAGINE, FOR A

moment, the difficulty you have deciding what to wear for a night out. Now, think about having to organise the sartorial needs of 641 of the world's premier athletes who will be in front of the entire world in one of the biggest sporting celebrations England has ever seen – a daunting prospect, isn't it? This is exactly what Puma UK had to do as official provider of sports apparel to Team England for the Commonwealth Games. "When Puma was first approached," says Geoff Wightman, marketing manager at Puma UK, "we batted the idea around for a while before realising that this was something that fitted in with us as a performance brand. Not only did we feel it was essential for us to be part of this world class event, we had the vision to see that the Games would be a great success." However, an undertaking of this magnitude isn't to be taken lightly and there were a multitude of obstacles and hurdles to overcome, as Wightman explains.

"First, we don't produce kits and product for all the sports. So we had to work with a number of other brands on certain events – for example, we worked with Speedo on the Aquatics, with Milano in Gymnastics and also have worked with Slazenger on a couple of events.

"We also had to search out the best fabrics, materials and products from around the world. Some of the products have come from as far afield as the Far East, New Zealand, Venezula, Canada as well as several countries in Europe. Some events finalised their teams early, giving us a long lead time, but most weren't finalised until June – so we had to over order to compensate for team sizes that were not known." If over ordering took care of the size issue, how has Puma taken the march of science and technology into account? "Even in the past four years, sportswear has moved on in leaps and bounds. For example, a simple singlet may now have additional panels, which are there to provide comfort and get rid of moisture.

"This posed another challenge. We were sourcing items in some sports that we've never dealt with before – these are cutting-edge high-tech outfits. For example, the weightlifting unitards have built-in support panels to protect the lifter's back in addition to their own belts. It's definitely been an education." The line was launched on 28 May at PUMA's new Concept Store and the design of the kit harks back to the golden era of English sport of the 1980s.

Wightman believes the style, "successfully blends the influences from sport, lifestyle and fashion that also reflects the spirit of Puma."

After all the hard work that Puma has done, what effect does Wightman think the kit will have on Team England? "It's often said that if the kit is doing its job, then it shouldn't be noticeable, like the referee in a football game. However, we believe that when you're kitting out the best at the biggest sport event the country's seen for years, you have to go that extra mile. These athletes are going to be feeling like a million dollars and we want them to look like it too."

All the right moves

Ato Boldon shocked the athletics world with the stunning time he set in the men's 100m event at the 1998 Games. Duncan Mackay of *The Guardian* finds out if Boldon can do it all again in Manchester

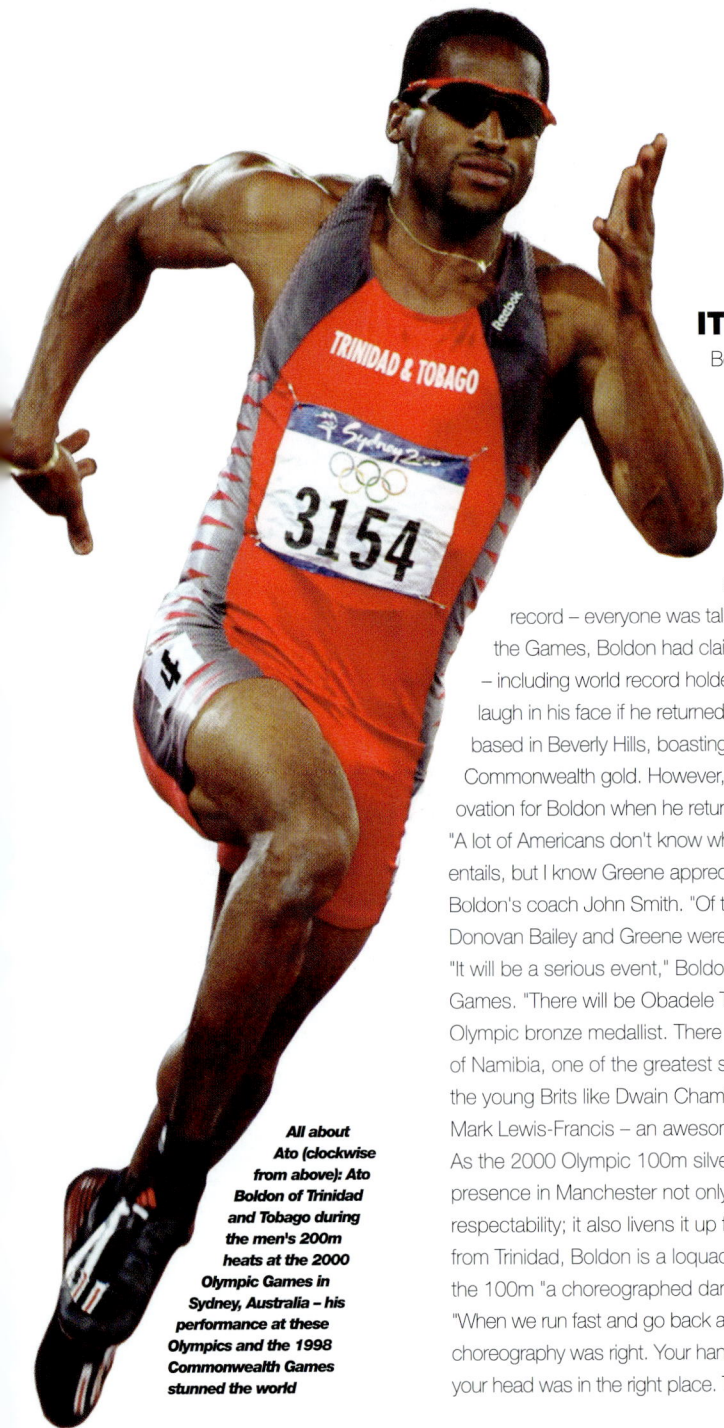

IT WAS ATO

Boldon's performance in Kuala Lumpur that made the world sit up and take notice of the 1998 Games. By the time he had sped down the track to win the 100m in 9.88sec – the blink of an eye away from the world record – everyone was talking about the event. Before the Games, Boldon had claimed that his training partners – including world record holder Maurice Greene – would laugh in his face if he returned to the US, where he is based in Beverly Hills, boasting about winning Commonwealth gold. However, Greene led a standing ovation for Boldon when he returned from Malaysia. "A lot of Americans don't know what the Commonwealth entails, but I know Greene appreciated the 9.88," says Boldon's coach John Smith. "Of the big players, only Donovan Bailey and Greene were missing in Kuala Lumpur."

"It will be a serious event," Boldon says of the Manchester Games. "There will be Obadele Thompson of Barbados, the Olympic bronze medallist. There will be Frankie Fredericks of Namibia, one of the greatest sprinters ever; and of course, the young Brits like Dwain Chambers, Darren Campbell and Mark Lewis-Francis – an awesome crop of sprinters." As the 2000 Olympic 100m silver medallist, Boldon's presence in Manchester not only gives the Games added respectability; it also livens it up for the media. Originally from Trinidad, Boldon is a loquacious livewire – he calls the 100m "a choreographed dance routine".

"When we run fast and go back and look at the tape, the choreography was right. Your hands were in the right place, your head was in the right place. There are seven other guys

out there – one wrong step and you're eighth." Boldon is deep into statistics, videos – anything he can find about 100m running. He was mocked for doing so much homework, but you would not expect anything less of an engineering graduate from the University of California. Now, he says, his rivals admit that he might have something. "I'm a thief when it comes to sprinting," admits Boldon. "I've stolen things from these guys and they don't even know it. I've taken what they do and given it my own flavour and personality."

All about Ato (clockwise from above): Ato Boldon of Trinidad and Tobago during the men's 200m heats at the 2000 Olympic Games in Sydney, Australia – his performance at these Olympics and the 1998 Commonwealth Games stunned the world

ato boldon

AGE: 28
BORN: Port of Spain, Trinidad
PERSONAL BESTS: 100m – 9.86 (1998 & 1999), 200m – 19.80 (1996)
MAJOR HONOURS:
● Olympics: silver medal for the 100m in 2000, bronze medal for the 100m in 1996, as well as for the 200m in 1996 and 2000
● World Championships: gold medal for the 200m in 1997; bronze medal for the 100m in 1995 and for the 4x100m relay in 2001
● Commonwealth Games: gold medal for the 100m in 1998

Manchester 2002
THE XVII COMMONWEALTH GAMES

Nick Wilson, Adam Pretty, Ezra Shaw, Stu Forster (Allsport)

Second to none

Bernard Lagat is one of the quickest men in the world over 1,500m, but a significant win has proved to be elusive for the Kenyan. Will he finally bag a gold in Manchester? Duncan Macay finds out

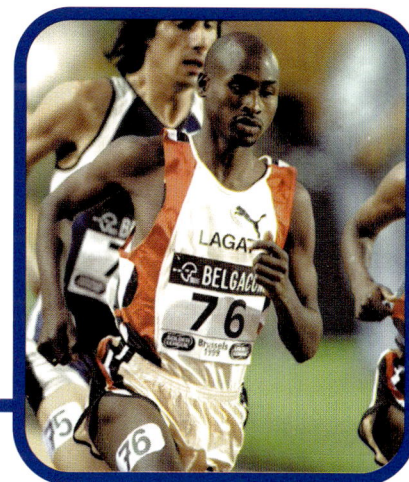

Let's go Lagat (left to right) Kenya's Bernard Lagat (#43) comes in second after Noah Ngeny (#45) in the 1,500m at the 16th IAAF Grand Prix Final in Doha, Qatar in 2000; Lagat in action in the 1,500m event during the IAAF Golden League Van Damme Memorial at Stade Roi Baudoin in Brussels, Belgium.

BERNARD LAGAT IS A MASTER

at running fast in big races. It is coming first that has proved elusive for the 27-year-old Kenyan, who has yet to win a major race at the international level. Lagat became the second fastest 1,500m runner in history last August, when he ran 3min 26.34sec at the Van Damme Memorial in Brussels, when he finished second behind Morocco's Hicham El Guerrouj. Lagat has broken 3:32 in the 1,500m on 11 occasions in the past three seasons, but the 2000 Olympic bronze medallist placed second or third in each of those races, including the 2001 World Championships in Edmonton, where he took silver. He has special reason to want to step out of the shadow of countryman Noah Ngeny and El Guerrouj in Manchester. Lagat, known as Kip after the legendary Kip Keino, has improved dramatically since the last Commonwealth Games, when he was ranked only 26th in the world and did not even make his national team. He realised that he had to make some changes to become one of the world's elite. First, he needed to alter his running mechanics – a shorter stride with a quicker turnover was required to excel in the fast-paced 1,500m. Second, he needed to work on his mental preparation for running against stars such as El Guerrouj and Noureddine Morceli of Algeria.

"I had a tendency to be in awe of them because they were so fast," says Lagat. The work paid off in 1999, when he beat Morceli, who later approached him and told him that he had a "very, very good future".

Running fast is in the genes of the Lagat family – he is the fifth of ten children and his sister, Mary Chepkemboi, and one of his brothers, William Cheseret, also became world-class runners. Lagat is also a brilliant student. Passing up the opportunity to attend Harvard on a scholarship, he went to Washington State University instead, where he graduated in management information systems.

One of Lagat's goals is to beat his team-mate Ngeny at the Games. When the two were discussing Manchester last season, Lagat said he encouraged Ngeny to make the trip: "I told him, 'It's always fun to run with you' – it would be even more fun beating him!"

bernard lagat

AGE: 27
BORN: Kapsabet, Kenya
PERSONAL BESTS:
- 1,500m – 3:26.34 (2001),
- Mile – 3:47.28 (2001)
MAJOR HONOURS:
- Olympics: bronze medal in the 1,500m in 2000
- World Championships: 2001 silver medal in the 1,500m

Manchester 2002

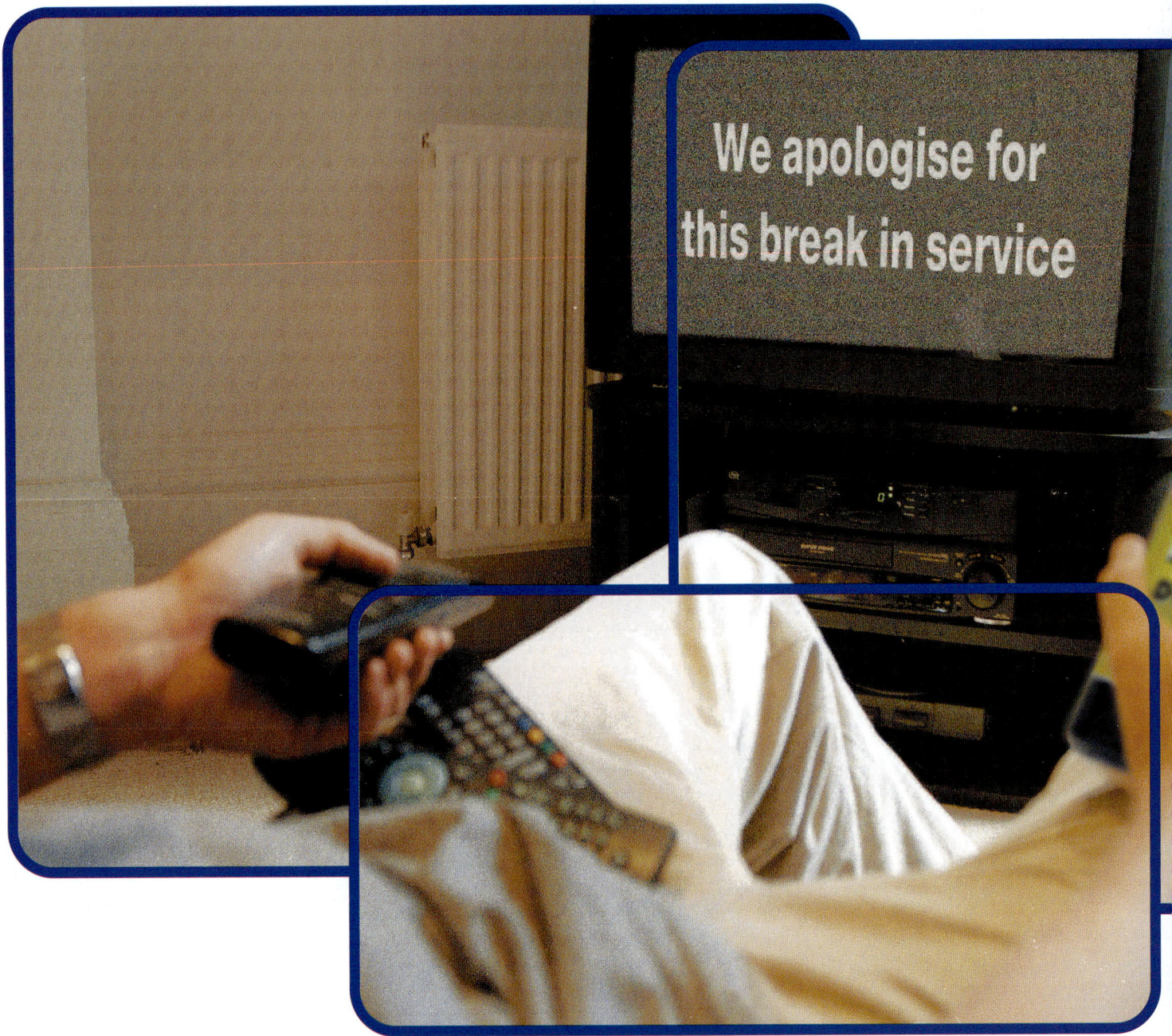

We apologise for this break in service

FROM 25 JULY TO 4 AUGUST,

BBC SPORT broadcasts live coverage of the Commonwealth Games daily across BBC ONE and TWO. Digital TV viewers have a choice of live coverage streams while favourite entertainment, factual and CBBC programmes reflect the colour of the Games. BBC Manchester's Commonwealth Games desk, within *North West Tonight*, and the dedicated radio on 97.7FM plus BBC GMR's regular Games-related news and features can all be accessed in Greater Manchester.

BBC Radio Five Live provides coverage and a flavour of the Arts Festival, which complements the sporting feast. The BBC SPORT website includes a dedicated site at bbc.co.uk/commonwealthgames and BBCi Manchester, at www.bbc.co.uk/2002, has all the details of the Queen's Jubilee Baton Relay and the 72 countries taking part.

Thursday, 25 July

1630 - 1800	*Commonwealth Games Grandstand*	*BBC 2*
2050 - 2300	*Commonwealth Games Grandstand*	*BBC 1*

Friday, 26 July

1030 - 1300	*Commonwealth Games Grandstand*	*BBC 1*
1300 - 1535	*Commonwealth Games Grandstand*	*BBC 2*
1345 - 1730	*Commonwealth Games Grandstand*	*BBC 1*
1730 - 1800	*Games Today*	*BBC 2*
1800 - 2230	*Commonwealth Games Grandstand*	*BBC 1*
2240 - 2330	*Games Today*	*BBC 1*
2330 - 0100	*Commonwealth Games Grandstand*	*BBC 1*

Saturday, 27 July

0900 - 1715	*Commonwealth Games Grandstand*	*BBC 1*
1600 - 1835	*Commonwealth Games Grandstand*	*BBC 2*
1835 - 2055	*Commonwealth Games Grandstand*	*BBC 1*
2055 - 2215	*Commonwealth Games Grandstand*	*BBC 2*
2300 - 0100	*Commonwealth Games Grandstand*	*BBC 1*

Sarah Lee

A couch potato's guide to the Games

If you can't make to the Games, just kick back with a cold one and watch the Commonwealth's finest from the comfort of your living room, all courtesy the BBC team

Sunday, 28 July

0750 - 1300	Commonwealth Games Grandstand	BBC 1
1145 - 1850	Commonwealth Games Grandstand	BBC 2
1850 - 2215	Commonwealth Games Grandstand	BBC 1
2315 - 0100	Commonwealth Games Grandstand	BBC 1

Monday, 29 July

0900 - 1300	Commonwealth Games Grandstand	BBC 1
1300 - 1345	Commonwealth Games Grandstand	BBC 2
1345 - 1730	Commonwealth Games Grandstand	BBC 1
1730 - 1800	Games Today	BBC 1
1800 - 1855	Commonwealth Games Grandstand	BBC 2
1855 - 2030	Commonwealth Games Grandstand	BBC 1
2035 - 2230	Commonwealth Games Grandstand	BBC 2
2240 - 2330	Games Today	BBC 2
2330 - 0100	Commonwealth Games Grandstand	BBC 2

Tuesday, 30 July

0900 - 1300	Commonwealth Games Grandstand	BBC 1
1300 - 1345	Commonwealth Games Grandstand	BBC 2
1345 - 1730	Commonwealth Games Grandstand	BBC 1
1730 - 1800	Games Today	BBC 1
1800 - 2230	Commonwealth Games Grandstand	BBC 2
1955 - 2100	Commonwealth Games Grandstand	BBC 1
2240 - 2330	Games Today	BBC 1
2330 - 0100	Commonwealth Games Grandstand	BBC 1

Wednesday, 31 July

0900 - 1300	Commonwealth Games Grandstand	BBC 1
1300 - 1345	Commonwealth Games Grandstand	BBC 2
1345 - 1730	Commonwealth Games Grandstand	BBC 1
1730 - 1800	Games Today	BBC 1
1800 - 2230	Commonwealth Games Grandstand	BBC 2

1900 - 2120	Commonwealth Games Grandstand	BBC 1
2240 - 2330	Games Today	BBC 1
2330 - 0100	Commonwealth Games Grandstand	BBC 1

Thursday, 1 August

0900 - 1300	Commonwealth Games Grandstand	BBC 1
1300 - 1345	Commonwealth Games Grandstand	BBC 2
1345 - 1730	Commonwealth Games Grandstand	BBC 1
1730 - 1800	Games Today	BBC 1
1800 - 2230	Commonwealth Games Grandstand	BBC 2
2240 - 2330	Games Today	BBC 1
2330 - 0100	Commonwealth Games Grandstand	BBC 1

Friday, 2 August

0900 - 1300	Commonwealth Games Grandstand	BBC 1
1300 - 1345	Commonwealth Games Grandstand	BBC 2
1345 - 1730	Commonwealth Games Grandstand	BBC 1
1730 - 1800	Games Today	BBC 1
1800 - 2230	Commonwealth Games Grandstand	BBC 2
2240 - 2330	Games Today	BBC 1
2330 - 0100	Commonwealth Games Grandstand	BBC 1

Saturday, 3 August

0900 - 1900	Commonwealth Games Grandstand	BBC 1
1400 - 2215	Commonwealth Games Grandstand	BBC 2
2300 - 0100	Commonwealth Games Grandstand	BBC 1

Sunday, 4 August

0750 - 1300	Commonwealth Games Grandstand	BBC 1
1200 - 1730	Commonwealth Games Grandstand	BBC 2
1355 - 1500	Commonwealth Games Grandstand	BBC 1
1600 - 1930	Commonwealth Games Grandstand	BBC 1
2050 - 2300	Commonwealth Games Grandstand	BBC 1

THE COMMONWEALTH GAMES'

opening and closing ceremonies in 2002 will definitely raise the bar, establishing the Games as a very 21st Century event. "They're going to set a new standard for the Games because they are going to be more similar to the standard of the Olympic ceremonies," says Julie Brooks, executive producer for the opening and closing ceremonies.

David Zolkwer, the artistic director for the ceremonies, believes the productions in Manchester will still be considered revolutionary long after the Games are finished: "I don't think anything like it will have been seen before in this country." The ceremonies will be totally multimedia in the way that they use lighting, lasers, pyrotechnics and sound in combination.

"I think the most important thing for us is that when we started developing the ceremonies, we looked at what had been done before – what was missing was that they didn't have much to do with Manchester or England or the 21st Century. We have looked at all the components, challenged them and reinvented them for our ceremonies."

The Sydney connection

Julie Brooks worked as an associate producer on the opening and closing ceremonies for the Sydney Olympics, and was headhunted to be executive producer for the Manchester event. She has brought in international talent from Australia and the US for creative and production purposes.

Tony Marshall (Empics)

Show stoppers

It takes a lot to stage a huge sporting event, and even more to introduce it in the right way and send it off with style – but the opening and closing ceremonies for the Games were always destined to be special. Graham McColl attends the biggest parties of the year

"At Sydney, we cracked it as far as giving a feel for the country and the people in the country," she comments. "I think it showed the world the nature of Australians: that we can laugh at ourselves, that we are very much a tongue-in-cheek society and don't take ourselves too seriously. We now want to reflect what Manchester is about and what England is about."

The Australian opening and closing events were stunning, but Manchester was not intended to be a mere copycat. "We're doing it our way," says Brooks, "and that's the most important point, even though we have huge respect for previous ceremonies."

David Zolkwer came away from Sydney inspired by the show: "No ceremony has captured the warmth and personality of a city in the way Sydney did," he says, "and that's what I took from them. They did it their way."

New horizons

Fireworks and a cast of thousands performing inside the City of Manchester Stadium are just two of the traditional aspects of the opening and closing ceremonies for the 2002 Games, but they have been augmented by radical departures as Manchester ventures into uncharted territory.

"With our special effects, we are taking risks and doing things that common sense says, 'Don't go there!'" explains Zolkwer gleefully, imagining public reaction to the spectacle. "It's a bit like working with children and animals – you are not supposed to do it, but we're challenging preconceptions with the things we're doing in our ceremonies."

The production team couldn't discuss the exact contents of the opening and closing ceremonies before the event, but glimmers of detail still slipped through in their conversation. The stadium itself, for example, has a leading role (elements of the ceremonies involve interaction with the stadium), while the athletes play a more active part than the traditional parade around the track in their uniforms.

"We have a very exciting new way of doing the athletes' part in the opening ceremony," explains Julie Brooks. "We are engaging the athletes to show their youthfulness, exuberance and enthusiasm."

"I think the biggest challenge," Brooks says, "is staging a theatrical event in an athletics stadium. You see rock and pop concerts in stadiums quite a lot, but you don't often see theatrical events. We have 7,500 cast members coming on and off the stage, which makes for a huge logistical

The exceptional opening ceremony begins at the National Sports Complex in Bukit Jalil, for the 16th Commonwealth Games in Kuala Lumpur, Malaysia, 1998

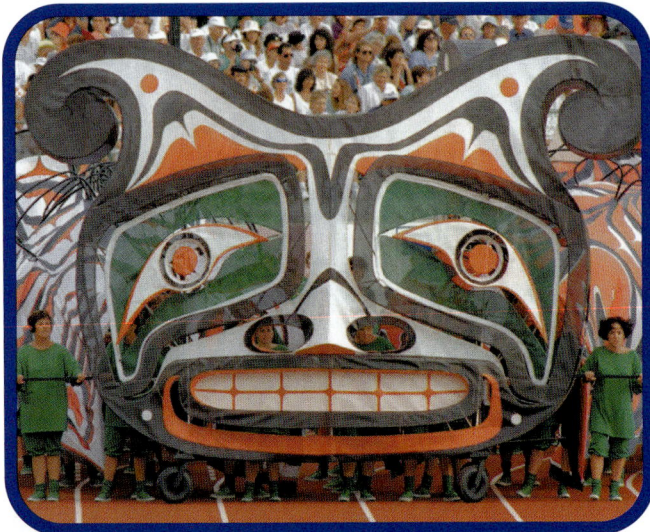

Familiar faces (clockwise from above): The opening ceremony in Victoria, BC (Canada) added a touch of native flavour to the Games; fireworks aplenty at the Bukit Jalil stadium, during the opening of the 1998 Games in Kuala Lumpur; athletes meet their public – Scotland's Dougie Walker, carrying the Scottish flag at the opening ceremony in 1998

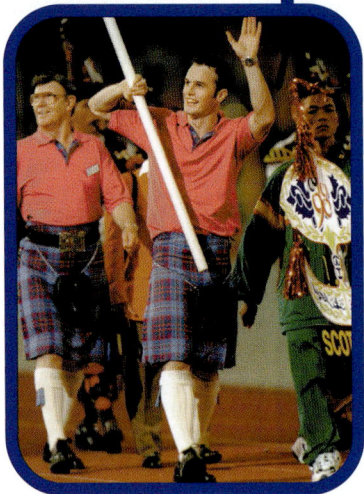

enterprise – and a sports stadium is not exactly conducive to theatrical atmosphere."

Brooks overcame that difficulty by harnessing the drive and passion of her team: "We've got a great show. We've got so much talent. We've got West End talent, rock 'n' roll designers, traditional theatrical designers and the music of Manchester will be heard throughout the ceremonies.

"One of the large areas of the show that people take for granted is the huge job of the music directors. Each element of the show has its own piece of music to reflect its theme and the musical supervisor, Max Lambert, has come from Sydney for that purpose," she says.

"What we are trying to do is inject the ceremonies with great moments," Zolkwer adds, "so that even the protocol has some topicality and has some focus to it, and making sure each scene in the ceremony informs the next scene. We're actually approaching it like a piece of theatre and making the show flow."

Regal progress

Additional pressure comes from the fact that history is being made in Manchester, with the Queen attending both the opening and closing ceremonies. It is the first time in Commonwealth Games history that she will be present at both and the closing ceremony was designed as the culmination of her Golden Jubilee celebrations. The ceremonies acknowledge her presence in a witty, warm, but informal manner.

"The way we've incorporated the royal moments into the show is special and even a bit radical," says Zolkwer. "If you take the royal family as human beings with a sense of humour, compassion and history, then you can engage the public in it. If part of the task of the Golden Jubilee is to get the Queen closer to the community, then our task is to bring the community closer to the Queen. It's fun and it might even be a little bit irreverent and have a few laughs. People expect the English Games to be a bit formal and a bit tight, but we may surprise them."

It is appropriate that the Queen watch over a ceremony that promises to be a genuine reflection of the now more relaxed, informal Commonwealth Games – Prince Charles and Princess Anne helped unbutton the ceremonials back in the Swinging Sixties. At Jamaica in 1966, the Queen's children – then young adults – represented royalty and were persuaded to dance along to West Indian sounds as the closing

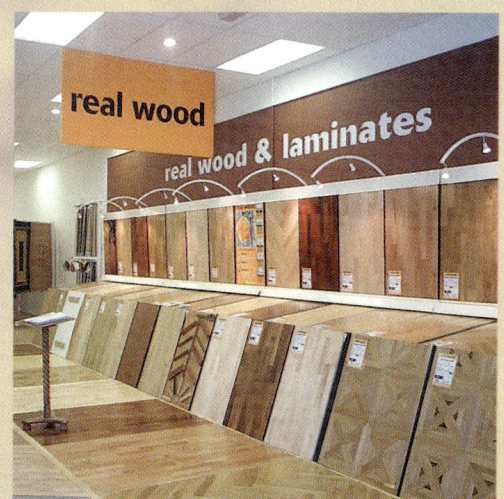

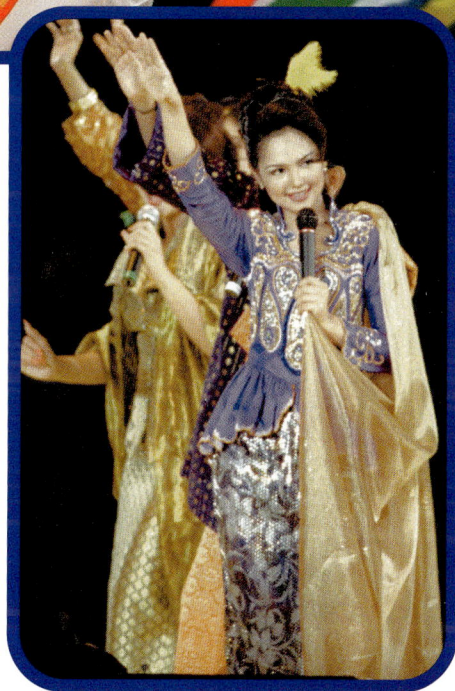

Celebrating nations (top to bottom): Flags fly at the opening ceremony of the Games in 1994; Malaysian women perform at the closing ceremony in Kuala Lumpur – the Games bring people together while providing a stage on which the host country can celebrate its own contribution and culture

An audience of millions across the Commonwealth is expected to tune in to the televised coverage of the ceremonies and Manchester will take this in its stride.

"We've been working very hard to make a show that's all about Manchester, of the moment and that doesn't owe anything to the past," says Zolkwer. "We have the arrival of the baton and the Queen's speech, but we're doing it the Manchester way. It's all about keeping the atmosphere of the place.

"The whole city has been re-energised over recent years, but the common denominator is the people. It's a city with lots of opinion," continues Zolkwer. "It's always got something to say about itself and that's reflected in the ceremony. Mancunians don't take themselves very seriously, but they're passionate about the city and that's a great combination."

A wealth of entertainment

At the time work began on the opening and closing ceremonies early in 2001, the stadium was a building site, so the production team for the ceremonies had to make operational decisions even before the stadium had been erected. Gradually, things began to take shape as thousands of volunteers from every secondary school in Greater Manchester were enlisted to reflect the fresh face of the city.

"I did say to my brother after Sydney, 'Shoot me if I do one of these again',"says Julie Brooks. "It takes over your life and it takes time to get back to normal, but there's nothing like that adrenaline rush of walking into a stadium and seeing all these people having a fantastic time and being entertained by a production that you have played a part in staging. We are, after all, in the entertainment business."

David Zolkwer is confident that each ceremony will be more rivetting than any previous Commonwealth Games offerings. He has some succinct, very British advice for viewers who are planning to take in the ceremony at home: "We are keen to avoid those moments where it's OK to go and put the kettle on – so have a pot ready before the ceremony begins!"

ceremony dissolved into a spirit of friendliness and fun. There have been other informal touches in recent years. In Victoria, Canada, in 1994, Myriam Bédard brought in the Queen's baton on roller skis, though that ceremony was otherwise traditional and included a fly-past by the Canadian Air Force, as well as a riding display by the Royal Canadian Mounted Police. The opening and closing ceremonies in Manchester promise to be the least formal that the Queen has yet seen.

Commonwealth aims

"Manchester is a microcosm of the Commonwealth," says Zolkwer. "Most of the Commonwealth is represented here and Manchester seems very good at absorbing and changing without being precious about it."

The theme, in a word, is "inclusivity", according to Zolkwer: "The whole show is about Manchester, England and the Commonwealth, and what's relevant today, what matters about the Commonwealth today. The ceremonies reflect what is best about the Commonwealth – on a good day, what is the best we can be?"

ceremonial statistics

There are 8,058 people taking part in the opening and closing ceremonies – 2,044 of them are children

A 350-strong team of volunteers provides back-up to the various performers throughout the Games

The creative/production team totals 70 and they have been putting the ceremonies together since May 2001

There are 72 countries participating in the Athletes' Parade

Exactly 6,736 athletes take to the track in the stadium for the opening and closing ceremonies

The oldest performer is 63 and the youngest performer is 12

Manchester 2002 THE XVII COMMONWEALTH GAMES

FRIEND OF **2002**
Manchester®
THE XVII COMMONWEALTH GAMES

akeler

Allied
London Properties Limited

amec

ARUP

BAXI
POTTERTON

BNFL

C²C
Management Ltd

CERIDIAN CENTREFILE
THE HR & PAYROLL COMPANY

EMERY
Forwarding

The
Fairhursts
Design Group

GP Georgia-Pacific

GRANADA
TELEVISION

GVA Grimley
International Property Advisers

HENRI LLOYD

JRK

Lambert Smith
Hampton
an ATKINS company

LAING
Construction

m|a|c|e

N Brown
Group plc

pets
at home
No.1 for fins, feathers, paws and claws.

PORTFOLIO
HOLDINGS

vita

British Vita PLC

A Dean, mean fighting machine

Dean Macey is England's brightest decathlon star. He finished fourth in Sydney, he took bronze at the World Championships, and now he's got the Commonwealth gold in his sights, as Nikki Racklin discovers

Born in Essex in 1977,

Dean Macey made his international decathlon debut in 1995. By 1999, he'd already produced the second highest score ever by a British athlete, bettered only by the great Daley Thompson. He went on to a brilliant silver medal at the World Championships in 1999, where he achieved a best ever total score of 8,556 points and set six individual event personal bests.

Macey's progress continued, taking him to fourth place in the Sydney 2000 Olympics, before he secured a heroic bronze medal in the World Championships 2001, despite several injuries. After setbacks and triumphs, it looks like Macey very well be the next Daley Thompson – did he look up to the great man as a young decathlete?

"It was drummed into me from a very early age that one in 4,000 people become professional sportsmen, so I never bothered making an icon out of any particular player or team – I just thought, 'It's not going to happen to me.' There are a lot of people I respect, but no one I've really ever wanted to be like."

Macey keeps his approach to the sport straightforward: "There is so much technology available now, but I just take a stopwatch and a bottle of water over to the track and that's me done. The simpler I can make my life, the better.

"I do three months of conditioning, two or three months of lactic endurance and a couple of months of speed work just before the season. During the season, it's out and out high quality work. I probably cover the whole decathlon in a six day training week. It's tough going, but I enjoy training as much as competing, if not more.

"The running events [in the decathlon]

are both the easiest and the hardest, purely because of the amount of effort and dedication it takes to get out there and bust a gut every single day. "On the other hand, the more technical events are very finicky – if a little thing goes wrong, it can throw everything off."

He's delighted that this year's Commonwealth Games are being held on home soil, although he thinks the fact that the European Championships start just nine days later is unfortunate.

"I'm 100 per cent dedicated to the Commonwealth Games this year, and if I'm fit enough afterwards, I'm going to have a go at the Europeans as well. If I'm only ever going to do one Commonwealth Games, then it's going to be this one in my own country and I want to make it worthwhile." He reckons his chances of bringing the Gold home for England are pretty good: "Nothing's a dead cert, but if I finish and I'm in decent shape then..." – he wisely doesn't tempt fate.

Of his challengers in Manchester, Macey says: "Look out for anyone in an Australian vest because they always seem to pull it out in the Commonwealth year. The Jamaican and the Canadian athletes could also be a threat."

"Decathlon takes a lot more hard work than any other event – you're prone to more injuries and you don't earn as much," Macey points out. "The satisfaction you get once you've completed a decathlon or done a hard training session is second to none. It is awesome – just the best feeling."

Dean Macey competing during the 8th IAAF World Athletics Championships, Edmonton, Canada – he eventually took the bronze medal

Andy Lyons, Stu Forster (Allsport)

Taking everything in his stride

Jonathan Edwards has won virtually every top title in athletics, but top honours at the Commonwealth Games have eluded him. Will he strike gold when he touches down in the sand pit at the City of Manchester stadium? Amy Sollitt rates his chances

AT 35 YEARS OLD,

world record holder, world champion and Olympic gold medallist Jonathan Edwards is a veteran triple jumper. He is widely expected to take the gold medal at the Commonwealth Games, but he doesn't expect it to be easy. Edwards smashed the triple jump world record in 1995 and took the World Championship gold in Gothenberg, and since then has established himself as the man to beat – only adding to his prestige with his gold at the Olympic Games in Sydney 2000. As a result, he has been under the constant scrutiny of the sporting media. The fact that he has never won a Commonwealth gold, his age (he is one of the oldest athletes in his field) as well as his status as a home favourite will only increase the press attention in Manchester. How will he cope? "I've had this kind of pressure for the last seven years," he says, "so you do get rather used to it and I tend to just ignore it." He also draws strength from the support of the public, his family and his religion: "I am doing it to serve God, which is a strong motivation in my life."

He's also looking forward to competing on home turf: "I've participated in many competitions abroad, where home athletes have received tremendous support, which has made a big difference to them. I'm really looking forward to competing in front of the home crowd."

As Edwards well knows, "it's probably my last chance to win a Commonwealth gold." He freely admits that "each year gets harder and harder", but as long as he enjoys the sport he sees no reason to retire – plus he is still in good shape. At the Brisbane Goodwill Games in September 2001, Edwards jumped 17.26m – eclipsing his nearest rival by over 30cm. "There's still work to be done, training wise, but by the time the Commonwealth Games come round, injury permitting, I'll be raring to go," he says.

With so much experience under his belt, the support of the nation, his family and his religion not to mention his consistent success, this is an athlete at ease with himself. Keep an eye on Edwards – whatever the result, his performance at the Games will be memorable in the least.

A Sporting Chance –

extra time for England's historic sports venues

England is a great sporting nation, with a large majority of the population involved with sports, from playing or watching and from designing, building and maintaining sports facilities through to the manufacture and sale of sports equipment. English Heritage began work in January 2002 on a study of England's sporting heritage.

We chose Manchester and its immediate environs for our pilot study, as the area has made a great contribution to the nation's sporting history. Over the past 200 years it has been at one time or another a leading centre for archery, crown green bowling, cycling, lacrosse, greyhound racing, real tennis, speedway racing, water polo and football. This contribution to our sports history continues with the 2002 Commonwealth Games.

Our pilot work has included not only a wide ranging study of sport and its history in Manchester, but also an opinion survey to find out what people in Manchester think about sporting heritage. The preliminary findings will be discussed at a conference in Manchester in June 2002.

To continue the sporting theme, we are re-enacting a number of historic sports across our historic properties this summer. If you want to find out more about our work on historic sports in Manchester or our wider programme of events and re-enactments at our properties, please contact our Customer Services Department on 0870 333 1181 or alternatively visit our website at
www.english-heritage.org.uk

Period games and pastimes

Victoria Baths, Manchester

Bellevue Greyhound Stadium, Manchester

Medieval Jousting

Join today!

As a member of English Heritage, you will be entitled to free admission to many of our events and a wide range of other benefits:

- free entry to over 400 properties
- full colour property guide plus map
- copies of our quarterly magazine, *Heritage Today*, packed with lively features to keep you up to date with projects we are working on
- half price admission to historic attractions in Wales and Scotland
- most importantly, you will be making a personal contribution to help conserve England's heritage

Please call our Membership Department on **0870 333 1181** for further details on joining, or visit our website at **www.english-heritage.org.uk** Alternatively you can join at any of our staffed properties.

The Spirit of Friendship
Festival
THE 2002 COMMONWEALTH GAMES

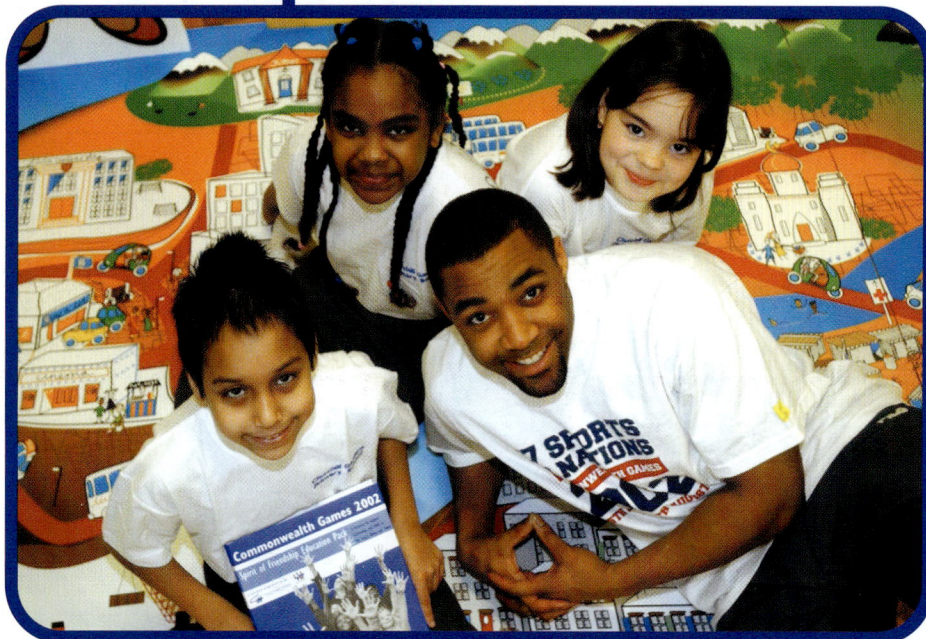

Touch of colour and competition (clockwise from above): Bringing a bit of the carnival spirit to the Festival; on your marks, get set – as part of the SOFF, youngsters will get a chance to find out what it's like to take part in the Commonwealth Games; fireworks and fun – "AquaFest" culminates in Manchester during the Games with a fireworks and water Spectacular; Pulse showcases a range of musical styles from opera to sitar, jazz to world music, and adds to the multi-cultural, multi-talented events of the Spirit of Friendship Festival; Darren Campbell, one of many English hopefuls at this year's Games, has also taken part in the SOFF

THIS YEAR'S GAMES

in Manchester welcome thousands of athletes from 72 nations, participating in a remarkable sporting spectacle – the largest multi-sport event ever to be hosted in Britain – but the Games are extra special for a number of reasons. They are the culmination of festivities marking Her Majesty The Queen's Golden Jubilee, and both the Games and the Jubilee reflect the many traditions and cultures within the Commonwealth – the core themes are Friendship, Diversity and Inclusion. The Spirit of Friendship Festival (SOFF) is the most ambitious cultural programme ever to run in parallel with the Games, designed to ensure that the widest possible audience enjoys the Games experience, spanning four strands of Sport, Education, Arts and Culture, together with Community Celebrations – representing more than 2,000 events.

The programme is concentrated in the four month build to the Games, culminating in Festival Live during Gamestime. Jo Hartley, the National Festival Director for SOFF, is thrilled to be involved: "You've got ten days of sporting spectacular in the Games, while the Festival is essentially 150 days of marking and celebrating the diversity of the modern Commonwealth across four strands. We're also helping to build a legacy for the next generation." The £3 million sport programme was launched in April 2002 by Sport England Chairman, Trevor Brooking, Ian Botham and his son Liam. It puts 10,000 young athletes with the potential to become Commonwealth stars of the future (in track and field, in rugby and swimming) through a programme of Active Sports Talent Camps. Participants learn what it takes to be a committed athlete. The residential programme sets these aspiring performers on the path to success. While the sports

The Spirit of Friendship Festival

Jo Hartley, the National Festival Director for The Spirit of Friendship Festival, speaks with Jane Crowther about this remarkable event and its power to take the message to the public

strand extends into local community sports activity – from an under-40s Rugby 7s competition with a Commonwealth theme to a Pool Championship in Shetland, and even Pigeon Racing. SOFF has also produced a £2 million programme in conjunction with the Department of Education and Skills, the Youth Sport Trust and The Commonwealth Institute. A Commonwealth Games Spirit of Friendship Education Pack has been issued to every school in the country, enabling teachers and their pupils to explore citizenship, culture and tradition, and to gain an understanding of what it means to be an elite athlete. The Youth Sport Trust's TOP-Link scheme enables 75,000 young people in the UK to hold their own mini-Commonwealth Games Festival, from the planning stage to execution – "It's a really tangible way to put sport back on the curriculum and help children feel closer to the Games, whether or not they come to Manchester," says Hartley "Hopefully, they'll remember this as a special summer of sport and acquire new skills in leadership." Under the banner of "CultureShock" and as part of a £3.5 million investment by the Arts Council, North West Arts Board and other Regional Arts Funders, more than 170 productions are planned in theatres, museums and galleries. The first ever Commonwealth Film Festival took place in early July, while

60 leading writers from around the world participated in the Literatures of the Commonwealth Festival in late June. A two-week season of rhythm at Manchester's Bridgewater Hall, *Pulse* showcases a range of musical styles from opera to sitar, jazz to world music and features a constellation of stars, including Dame Kiri Te Kanawa and Wynton Marsalis. The rest of country hasn't been left out – some 30 productions take place beyond the North West. *Spirit* is an open-air production in Cannon Hill Park, Birmingham, with a line-up of Commonwealth performers. In addition, West Yorkshire Playhouse's production of *Carnival Messiah* brings together local and professional actors from various backgrounds. SOFF has also formed partnerships with British Waterways – "AquaFest" culminates in Manchester during the Games with a Fireworks and Water Spectacular. English Heritage has also picked up the theme and is staging a variety of sports from a bygone era – jousting, archery and other medieval pastimes. "We seem to have captured the imagination," Hartley explains. "The Spirit of Friendship festival is about broadening the base. The legacy of these Games is a bright, innovative, very different sort of Festival, unprecedented in scale and celebrating our many cultures and traditions."

ANGUILLA

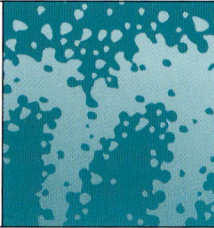

CAPITAL: THE VALLEY
AREA: 91 sq km
POPULATION: 12,132
CURRENCY: EAST CARIBBEAN DOLLAR
LANGUAGE: ENGLISH
THE PEOPLE/CULTURE: ANGUILLA'S WEST INDIAN CULTURE IS A BLEND OF BRITISH AND AFRICAN INFLUENCES

Island life

Anguilla is a small island east of Puerto Rico, located in the Caribbean Sea. It is the most northerly of the Leeward Islands in the Lesser Antilles. In 1650, the island was colonised by English settlers from St Kitts. Early in the 19th Century, the island was made part of a single British dependency, together with St Kitts and Nevis. Anguilla became a separate British dependency in 1980. In economic terms, Anguilla is heavily dependent on the tourism and offshore banking sectors, because the island has little in the way of natural resources. The island is approximately half the size of Washington DC.

Kuala Lumpur 1998 was a very special games for Anguilla, since it was the first time they had ever sent a team to the Commonwealth Games. It is hoped they will send a five member team to the Commonwealth Games in Manchester. US-based athletes Desiree Cox and Shyrone Hughes will compete in the 100m and 200m events respectively. Cox, who competed in 1998, will also compete in the long jump. Three cyclists, the Allen brothers (Charlie and Ronnie), along with Kris Pradel, will also compete in Manchester. Pradel is considered the pick of the bunch.

ANTIGUA AND BARBUDA

CAPITAL: SAINT JOHN'S
AREA: 442 sq km (ANTIGUA 281 sq km; BARBUDA 161 sq km)
POPULATION: 66,970
CURRENCY: EAST CARIBBEAN DOLLAR
LANGUAGE: ENGLISH (OFFICIAL), LOCAL DIALECTS
THE PEOPLE/CULTURE: A MIXTURE OF AFRICAN, BRITISH, PORTUGUESE, LEBANESE, SYRIAN

Bats at the ready

The islands of Antigua and Barbuda are situated in the Caribbean Sea, east-southeast of Puerto Rico. Together, they were declared an independent state within the British Commonwealth of Nations on 1 November 1981. As with most Caribbean economies, tourism is paramount, accounting for more than 50 per cent of GDP. Offshore banking had been a burgeoning economic sector, but unfortunately this has been hit by financial sanctions imposed by the US and the UK as a result of local legislation, which in effect relaxed controls on money-laundering. However, the government has attempted to fall in line with international demands in the hope that these sanctions will eventually be lifted.

Antigua and Barbuda sent a 25 strong team to the Commonwealth Games in Malaysia four years ago. Being a Caribbean nation, not to mention the birthplace of cricketing legend Vivien Richards, the cricket tournament in Kuala Lumpur was followed closely back home. They had mixed fortunes, with a drawn match against India, a defeat to Australia and a victory over Canada. With cricket not on the agenda for the Games in Manchester, perhaps athletics will become the focus of national interest.

Premium Financial Services

Dedicated Executive Banking Managers

Now you can enjoy a truly personal financial service, which gives you access to an excellent package of financial products and wealth management services. And, best of all, you'll have one to one attention with your own dedicated Executive Banking Manager.

So you can pick up the phone and talk to someone who knows you well - and deals with your request straightaway. You can see them whenever, wherever you want.

It's exactly the kind of financial relationship that could guide you through your different needs at the various stages of your life.

For more information call our Executive Banking Managers at The Chancery, Spring Gardens, Manchester, on **0161 832 1972** or e-mail:
adrian.blythe@eu.nabgroup.com
lee.gilmore@eu.nabgroup.com

www.YBonline.co.uk

Yorkshire Bank
Tailored Financial Solutions

EC121d

Silhouette ®

A New Definition in Sunwear

www.silhouette.com
For your nearest stockist call
020 8889 9997

AUSTRALIA

CAPITAL: CANBERRA
AREA: 7,682,300 sq km
POPULATION: 19.5 MILLION
CURRENCY: AUSTRALIAN DOLLAR
LANGUAGE: ENGLISH, ABORIGINAL LANGUAGES (PLUS NUMEROUS OTHER EUROPEAN, ARABIC AND ASIAN LANGUAGES)
THE PEOPLE: EUROPEAN, ASIAN AND ABORIGINAL

Out from under

Australian Aborigines, the original inhabitants of the country, have a history dating back to the last Ice Age. It is believed that the first of these peoples crossed the sea from Indonesia some 70,000 years ago. In the 16th Century, Europeans began to take an interest in Australia – first Portuguese navigators, then Dutch explorers. In 1770, Captain James Cook sailed the eastern seaboard. Upon rounding Cape York, he laid claim to the continent on behalf of the British Crown, founding New South Wales in the process.

It is well documented that in the early days of British colonial rule, Australia's history as a penal colony came about when one Joseph Banks, who had been a naturalist on Cook's voyage, suggested that overcrowding problems in British prisons could be alleviated by transporting convicts to New South Wales. Prisoners sent there faced unforgiving conditions and a constant battle against disease and starvation.

The Gold Rush of the 1850s brought a huge influx of immigrants. Aborigines were unceremoniously driven from their tribal homelands as white settlers looked to farming and mining as ways to make a living. Back in Britain, as the Industrial Revolution became greedier in its consumption of raw materials, Australia's exploitation of agricultural and mineral resources expanded to meet this demand. Sadly, though many other aspects of Australian life and society have changed, many Aborigines continue to live in extreme poverty.

Since WWII, waves of non-British European immigrants have turned Australia into a multi-cultural society; large numbers of Asian refugees have been admitted in recent decades. However, Australia still has to come to terms with her position and role within Asia. Other issues include republicanism, refugee policies and a push for an official government apology for the injustices suffered by the stolen generation of Aborigines.

FABULOUS FACTS

Australia officially became a nation when federation of the separate colonies took place, on 1 January 1901.

Australia Day falls on 26 January and Aussies around the world celebrate the day with pride.

Australia is the only nation on the planet to occupy an entire continent.

Australia is the sixth largest country in the world after Russia, Canada, China, USA and Brazil.

In 1984, Advance Australia Fair was officially designated the National Anthem for the country.

AT THE 1998 COMMONWEALTH GAMES IN KUALA LUMPUR, AUSTRALIA TOPPED THE MEDAL TABLE. IN THE HISTORY OF THE COMMONWEALTH GAMES, AUSTRALIA HAS WON 1,476 MEDALS – MORE THAN ANY OTHER COUNTRY, AS WELL AS TAKING HOME THE GREATEST NUMBER OF GOLD MEDALS (564 IN TOTAL). THE COUNTRY HAS BEEN BUOYED BY ITS SUCCESS HOSTING THE 2000 SYDNEY OLYMPICS, WHICH MANY DEEMED TO BE THE MOST IMPRESSIVE SPORTING EVENT OF MODERN TIMES.

Stu Forster (Allsport)

IN SYDNEY, THERE WAS NO DOUBT THAT THE DARLING OF THE AUSTRALIAN TEAM WAS THE ABORIGINAL 400M SPRINTER, CATHY FREEMAN. WHEN SHE WON THE GOLD MEDAL, SHE BECAME A NATIONAL ICON, SYMBOLISING THE MULTI-CULTURAL REALITY OF AUSTRALIA TODAY. IT IS HOPED SHE WILL RECOVER FROM INJURY IN TIME TO COMPETE IN MANCHESTER, WHERE SHE WILL BE A VERY HOT FAVOURITE TO TAKE THE GOLD. AUSTRALIANS WILL ALSO BE CHEERING ON IAN "THORPEDO" THORPE IN THE SWIMMING POOL. THIS INCREDIBLE YOUNG MAN WITH THE FLIPPER-SIZED FEET WILL BE OUT TO REPEAT THE REMARKABLE FEATS HE PULLED OFF TWO YEARS AGO IN SYDNEY.

Mark Dadswell (Getty Images); Al Bello, Mike Powell (Allsport)

FABULOUS FACTS

Scientists have discovered Aboriginal rock carvings and paintings that date back at least 30,000 years.

At 3.6km long and 348m in height, Uluru (formerly known as Ayers Rock) is perhaps Australia's most memorable landmark.

In the Great Barrier Reef, Australia boasts one of the world's natural wonders. It is the largest reef in the world.

Australia is the leading sporting nation in world cricket, rugby league, rugby union, swimming and cycling.

World famous Australians include the pop icon Kylie Minogue and Hollywood actors Mel Gibson and Nicole Kidman.

AUSTRALIA IS COMPETITIVE ACROSS THE WHOLE RANGE OF SPORTS IN MANCHESTER. JUDO, MAKING ITS SECOND SHOW AT THE GAMES, WILL PROVIDE MEDAL OPPORTUNITIES FOR MARIA PECKLI, WHO TOOK BRONZE IN THE 52-57KG DIVISION AT THE 2000 OLYMPICS. CARLEY DIXON FROM NEW SOUTH WALES IS ALSO A FAVOURITE. POSITIVE NOISES ARE ALSO COMING OUT OF THE TABLE TENNIS CAMP. AUSTRALIA'S TOP FEMALE PLAYER, MIAO MIAO – WHO FINISHED FIFTH IN THE DOUBLES TOURNAMENT IN SYDNEY – SHOULD BE A CONTENDER IN MANCHESTER. WILLIAM HENSELL IS ALSO A MEDAL PROSPECT. THE CURRENT AUSTRALIAN CHAMPION IN SINGLES AND DOUBLES HAS PLAYED IN THE EXTREMELY COMPETITIVE SWEDISH LEAGUE FOR THE LAST SIX SEASONS. HE SHOULD BE WELL PREPARED FOR MANCHESTER.

Clive Brunskill, Nick Wilson (Allsport)

BAHAMAS

CAPITAL: NASSAU
AREA: 13,940 sq km
POPULATION: 297,852
CURRENCY: BAHAMIAN DOLLAR
LANGUAGE: ENGLISH, CREOLE
THE PEOPLE/CULTURE: AFRICAN DESCENT, WHITE, ASIAN AND HISPANIC

History

The Lucayans, a tribe of the Arawak Indian group indigenous to the Bahamian archipelago, were a peaceful people. The arrival of the Spanish conquistadors in this network of islands, following hard on the heels of Columbus, spelled doom for the Lucayan people. They were wiped out through a combination of enslavement and disease. Little of the Lucayan culture is in evidence today.

During the 17th Century, the British Crown sponsored privateers to patrol the waters in and around The Bahamas, enhancing the careers of scores of pirates. This state of affairs lasted until 1714, when Britain signed the Treaty of Utrecht, which removed royal patronage and made the pirates outlaws.

At the beginning of 20th Century, less sinister invaders began to flood the island – tourists. By the end of World War II, hoards of wealthy Americans and Canadians were visiting the islands, attracted by sunny climes and the presence of the the the Duke and Duchess of Windsor, who governed the islands.

Since gaining independence from the United Kingdom in 1973, The Bahamas has exploited its proximity to the USA in the development of the tourist industry, and international banking and investment management. Traditional Bahamian culture is not so easily found in the highly American-influenced urban centres of Nassau and Freeport. Rather, one needs to do a little exploring to dig out the true culture of the archipelago, but with 700 islands and 2,500 cays, plus mangrove forests and coral reefs, there is certainly plenty to explore.

FABULOUS FACTS

Sidney Poitier, a Bahamian, was the first black actor to win a Best Actor Oscar, for *Guess Who's Coming to Dinner*.

In 1513, Juan Ponce de Leon went looking for the fabled Fountain of Youth. All he found was the fast-moving Gulf Stream.

Goombay, local Bahamian music, is a mix of calypso, soca and English folk songs.

Junkanoo is without a doubt the most famous Bahamian festival. It draws crowds of up to 20,000 people.

Two Bonds films were shot in the Bahamas: *Thunderball* and the remake, *Never Say Never Again*.

IN THE LAST COMMONWEALTH GAMES, THE BAHAMAS WON 15 MEDALS, FOUR OF WHICH WERE GOLD, AN AMAZING ACHIEVEMENT CONSIDERING THAT THE TEAM ONLY HAD 28 MEMBERS. AT THE SYDNEY OLYMPICS, THE BAHAMIAN WOMEN'S TEAM WON GOLD IN THE WOMEN'S 4X100M RELAY. CHANDRA STURRUP, CURRENT 100M COMMONWEALTH CHAMPION, WILL BE TRYING TO RETAIN HER TITLE; COMPATRIOT SAVATHEDA FYNES WILL PUSH HER HARD. AVARD MONCUR WON THE MEN'S 400M AT THE WORLD CHAMPIONSHIPS IN EDMONTON; HE SHOULD BE FAVOURITE TO TAKE THE TITLE IN MANCHESTER.

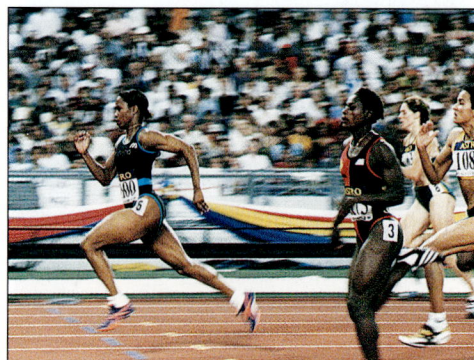

Andy Lyons (Allsport)

BANGLADESH

CAPITAL: DHAKA
AREA: 143,998 sq km
POPULATION: 129 MILLION
CURRENCY: TAKA
LANGUAGE: BANGLA, ENGLISH
PEOPLE/CULTURE: BENGALI, BIHARI AND VARIOUS TRIBES

Deep running

Looking out over the Bay of Bengal, Bangladesh is nestled between India and Myanmar. Bangladesh was formerly part of British India until independence in 1947. When India was partitioned, Bangladesh became part of Pakistan. After the development of a strong nationalist movement, Bangladesh declared its independence from Pakistan in 1971.

Fertile arable land accounts for approximately 60-70 per cent of Bangladesh and agriculture is by far the largest employment sector, accounting for two-thirds of the population. The climate of the country is subtropical and tropical. Essentially, there are three main seasons: the monsoon season, from the end of May to early October; the cold season, from the middle of October to the end of February, and; the hot season, from the middle of March to the middle of May. Incredibly, more than 90 per cent of the country is less than 10m above sea level, and, as a consequence, the country suffers repeated bouts of severe flooding.

Like India and its former partner, Pakistan, Bangladesh takes its cricket very seriously, recently achieving test status. Four years ago in Kuala Lumpur, Bangladesh gave a good account of themselves, even in defeat. This time around, of course, there is no cricket tournament, which means the Bangladeshi fans will need to look elsewhere for national glory. They could do worse than look to Fawzia Huda Jui and Havilder Ilias Uddin. The pair were given cash awards by the National Sports Council in recognition of their respective performances at the Eight Nation International Athletics Competition in Pakistan in 2000. Huda Jui won a gold medal in the 100m and bronze in the high jump; Ilias Uddin won bronze in the 5,000m.

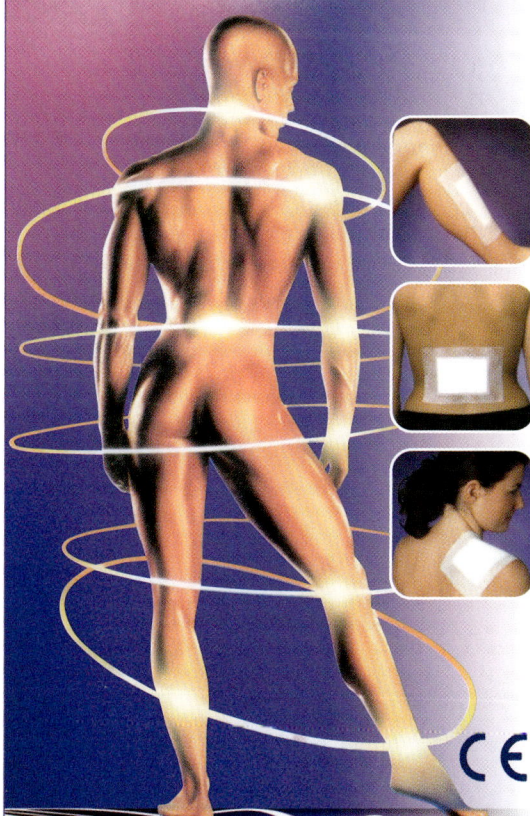

BARBADOS

CAPITAL: BRIDGETOWN
AREA: 430 sq km
POPULATION: 264,000
CURRENCY: BARBADIAN DOLLAR
LANGUAGE: BAJAN, ENGLISH
THE PEOPLE/CULTURE: AFRICAN, BRITISH

Cricket's capital

Barbados is located in the Caribbean, 2,585km south-east of Miami and 860km north-east of Venezuela. The west coast has white-sand beaches and calm turquoise waters. Coral reefs surround most of the island. After England claimed the uninhabited islands in 1625, the colonists established plantations, resulting in a booming sugar crop. The sugar industry grew immeasurably during the next century. In 1834, emancipation was granted to slaves on the island, but their living conditions improved only marginally.

Barbados gained internal self-government in 1961 and became an independent nation five years later.

As the sugar industry declined after World War II, tourism became progressively more important to the island's economy. By the early 1990s, it was the largest sector.

Barbados has been widely exposed to British culture for most of the last 400 years. In spite of its Spanish name, Barbados is often referred to as the "Little England" of the Caribbean. This could have something to do with the stone Anglican churches in every parish, the horse racing that takes place every Saturday and portraits of Queen Elizabeth II on walls all over the island. Then again, it could the national obsession with that most English of sports, cricket. Sir Frank Worrell, a national hero of Bajan cricket, appears on the face of the Barbadian five dollar bill.

FABULOUS FACTS

The lucky people of Barbados have very little need for umbrellas: the island boasts 3,000 hours of sunshine per year.

The Calypso artist Mighty Gabby hails from Barbados. The singer is well known throughout the Caribbean.

Star of Barbadian cricket Sir Garfield Sobers claimed a world record by hitting six successive sixes in a single over.

Portuguese explorer Pedro a Campos named the island Los Barbados ("the bearded ones") after the island's fig trees.

In 1627, Captain Henry Powell landed with a party of 80 settlers and ten slaves, establishing the first European settlement.

IN THE 1998 COMMONWEALTH GAMES IN KUALA LUMPUR, THE BARBADIAN TEAM GAINED A CREDITABLE NINE MEDALS. STAR OF THE TEAM WAS ANDREA BLACKET, WHO TOOK GOLD IN THE WOMEN'S 400M HURDLES, SETTING A GAMES RECORD IN THE PROCESS. OBADELE THOMPSON IS ANOTHER NAME TO LOOK OUT FOR. THOMPSON WON A BRONZE IN THE 100M AT SYDNEY, BECOMING THE ISLAND'S FIRST OLYMPIC MEDAL HOLDER AND A NATIONAL HERO OVERNIGHT. THE PRIME MINISTER AT THE TIME SAID: "IT MAY HAVE BEEN A BRONZE MEDAL FOR OBA, BUT IT WAS A GOLDEN MOMENT FOR BARBADOS."

Scott Barbour (Allsport)

BELIZE

CAPITAL: BELMOPAN
AREA: 22,966 sq km
POPULATION: 256,062
CURRENCY: BELIZEAN DOLLAR
LANGUAGE: ENGLISH (OFFICIAL), SPANISH, MAYAN, GARIFUNA (CARIB), CREOLE
THE PEOPLE/CULTURE: MESTIZO, CREOLE, MAYA, GARIFUNA

Beautiful Belize

Belize borders the Caribbean Sea and sits between Guatemala and Mexico. Formerly known as British Honduras, Belize became independent in 1981. Due to a series of disputes with the UK prior to independence, Guatemala did not recognise Belize as a new state until 1992.

The essentially privatised economy is, for the most part, based on tourism, construction, and agriculture. Sugar is the main agricultural crop, accounting for close to 50 per cent of overall exports, while the banana industry is the largest employer in the country. Tourism has also become increasingly important to the local economy, as people from Europe and both North and South America have discovered the country's beauty and its welcoming atmosphere.

Inevitably, given the historical influences, sporting interests in Belize tend to reflect those of Britain and the USA. This accounts for the popularity of football, cricket, basketball and baseball. Boxing has had a following in Belize for several decades and a number of Belizeans, such as Ludwig Lightburn and Fitzroy Giuseppi, have become known throughout the world. Cycling is also popular and there are annual road races that can cover distances of 150km.

FABULOUS FACTS

Independence Day, 21 September, is a National Holiday in Belize.

The legal system in Belize is still based on English Law.

Belize has the second-largest barrier reef in the world. At 290km long, it is the longest in the Western hemisphere.

Belize is home to a vast rainforest and an abundance of wildlife.

The Belizean people are internationally renowned for their hospitality.

IN THE 1984 OLYMPICS IN LOS ANGELES, BELIZE TOOK ITS FIRST BOW AS AN INDEPENDENT COUNTRY. IN THE PAN AMERICAN GAMES OF 1987, BELIZE WON A BRONZE MEDAL IN THE WOMEN'S SOFTBALL COMPETITION. FOUR YEARS AGO, BELIZE TOOK A TEAM OF SEVEN TO THE COMMONWEALTH GAMES, BUT THEY WENT HOME EMPTY-HANDED. THIS TIME AROUND THEY WILL BE RELYING ON A PAIR OF ATHLETES WHO GAINED INVALUABLE EXPERIENCE IN THE 2002 SYDNEY OLYMPICS. JAYSON JONES, THE 25-YEAR-OLD SPRINTER WHO RAN IN THE 200M IN SYDNEY COULD BE IN THE BELIZEAN TEAM FOR MANCHESTER; AS COULD EMMA WADE, WHO COMPETED IN THE 100M IN SYDNEY AT THE TENDER AGE OF 18, AN EXPERIENCE THAT SHOULD PREPARE HER FOR ANYTHING MANCHESTER HAS IN STORE.

where students come first

STOPWATCH

for more information on how to challenge your mind to achieve your personal best call **0870 126 2000**

The North West Regional Assembly has declared its intention to become an elected Regional Government for the North West at the earliest opportunity. The North West of England is a region of 6.9 million people – a population bigger than Scotland, Wales and Northern Ireland with an economy bigger than that of 4 EU member states.

Leading the field...

Working in partnership with local government, business organisations, public sector agencies, education and training bodies, trade unions and co-operatives together with the voluntary sector, the North West Regional Assembly works to promote the economic, environmental and social well-being of the North West of England.

North West Regional Assembly

FOR FURTHER INFORMATION PLEASE CONTACT:

Phil Robinson, Director of Corporate Affairs, North West Regional Assembly, Coops Building, Dorning Street, Wigan, WN1 1HJ.

Tel: 01942 737910 Fax: 01942 737927 Email: phil.robinson@nwra.gov.uk

Send money home from your Post Office™ branch* and send them a smile.

Thousands of international money transfers a day.
Call free on 00800 8971 8971

MoneyGram
International Money Transfers

*from selected branches only.

BERMUDA

CAPITAL: HAMILTON
AREA: 53 sq km
POPULATION: 62,912
CURRENCY: BERMUDIAN DOLLAR
LANGUAGE: ENGLISH (OFFICIAL), PORTUGUESE
THE PEOPLE/CULTURE: AFRICAN, EUROPEAN, NATIVE AMERICAN

Bermuda bound

The Bermuda islands were discovered by Spaniard Juan de Bermudez in 1503. In 1609, the ship of Sir George Somers, an English admiral, went down near the islands during a hurricane. The castaways established a colony called Somers Islands and settled in what is now St George's Parish. Somer's crew convinced King James I of England to award a land grant to the Virginia Company so the islands could be colonised. The first permanent inhabitants of Bermuda were 60 Englishmen, who landed in 1612 and established St George as the capital (it moved to Hamilton in 1815). Near the end of the 17th Century, the British Crown took over the administration of the islands, but ties between the US and Bermuda grew close during the 18th Century. Bermuda had large reserves of gunpowder and, when George Washington asked the islanders for assistance in his fight against the British, hungry Bermudians broke into Bermuda's Fort William and provided the Americans with much-needed ammunition – and the US Continental Congress voted to send Bermuda provisions for an entire year. As a consequence, the British began to provide for Bermuda more fully, ensuring the islands' loyalties. The links between the US and Bermuda did not end there, however. Prohibition in the US brought droves of Americans to the islands – effectively the beginning of an influx of tourist money that would change the island forever. In addition, a 99-year lend-lease agreement was established between Britain and the United States in 1940, providing the US with approximately one-tenth of the land area of Bermuda for military bases – the islands were invaluable during WWII as a site for British intelligence operations trapping German spies. In the following decades, Bermuda became a popular location for offshore corporate operations. International business is now a prime player in Bermuda's economy.

FABULOUS FACTS

Early navigators called Bermuda "Isles of the Devil" due to various strange events occurring in the area.

Tourism has replaced farming and the onion trade as the second most important industry in Bermuda.

Bermuda is host to both the Caribbean music festival, SOCA, and the Bermuda Reggae Sunsplash.

The islands are one corner of the infamous Bermuda Triangle (the other points are Puerto Rico and Florida).

Gombey dancing mixes West African tribal music, Christian imagery and British military and Native American costumes.

THE BERMUDA ISLANDS HAVE WON A TOTAL OF FOUR MEDALS IN THE COMMONWEALTH GAMES. THE COUNTRY HAS COMPETITIVE TRACK AND FIELD STARS: TRIPLE JUMPER BRIAN WELLMAN PLACED SIXTH AT LAST YEAR'S EDMONTON WORLD CHAMPIONSHIPS.
CYCLIST KRIS HEDGES IS ALSO ON FORM – NATIONAL TEAM CYCLING COACH GREG HOPKINS SAYS HEDGES WILL HAVE THE SUPPORT TO DO WELL AT THIS YEAR'S GAMES. "WE'RE HOPING TO HAVE OTHER RIDERS WITH HIM," HE SAYS. "IT'S IMPORTANT TO GET YOUR ONE RIDER IN A POSITION TO FINISH WELL."

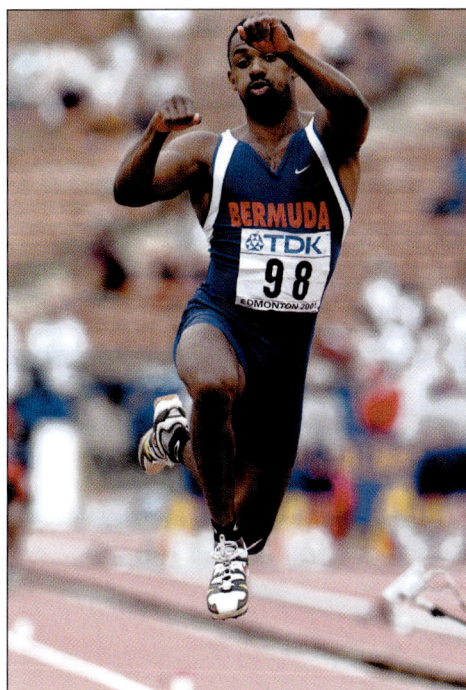

Empics

REGISTERED CHARITY NO. 297977

HIV Case study #D_45

SURNAME
[redacted],

FIRST NAME
[redacted]

MR/MS
MR

ADDITIONAL INFORMATION
[redacted] has been HIV positive for 12 years.

- [redacted] went to his family but his father threw him out of the house.
- [redacted] chose not to disclose his status to his employer but his Doctor broke client confidentiality and told his employer and told [redacted] that he shouldn't be working full st...

NOT UNTIL YOU'RE DIAGNOSED HIV POSITIVE DO YOU DISCOVER HOW SICK PEOPLE CAN GET.

Hate mail. Abusive phone calls. Even aggressive confrontations and physical attacks. This is how some people who are HIV positive are treated. And not just by strangers. By work colleagues, by former friends and sometimes even by close family. And it's not unheard of either for people with HIV to be discriminated against by medical professionals. Yet the fact is, there's no reason for them to be treated differently from anyone else. You can't contract HIV by working or socialising with someone who has it. And thanks to new treatments, it's possible for people with HIV to lead full and active lives. All that's stopping them is other people.

ARE YOU HIV PREJUDICED?

NAT

FOR 24 HOUR INFORMATION ON HIV, AIDS AND SAFER SEX CALL 0800 567 123 OR VISIT WWW.AREYOUHIVPREJUDICED.ORG

BOTSWANA

CAPITAL: GABORONE
AREA: 600,370 sq km
POPULATION: 1.6 MILLION
CURRENCY: PULA
LANGUAGE: ENGLISH, SETSWANA
THE PEOPLE/CULTURE: BATSWANA, BAKALANGA, BASARWA, BAKGALAGADI

A land of contrasts

Originally inhabited by the San people, Botswana was become a mixture of various tribes from the Khoi-Khoi (Hottentots) to various Bantu groups. It is a landscape of vast distances, with an extraordinary variety of natural settings that have become a part of the country's fabric – from the Chobe National Park to the vast plains of the Central Kalahari Game Reserve.

Botswana is a nation of sharp contrasts. It achieved its independence on 30 September 1966 – then almost immediately, three of the world's richest diamond mines were discovered within its borders. As a consequence, contemporary Botswana enjoys health, educational and economic standards that rival those found in South Africa. Nonetheless, most of the country remains largely a mixture of savannas, deserts and wetlands, with the population concentrated in the East.

The government of Botswana has gone to great lengths to maintain its natural resources, encouraging tourism that will not have a significant impact on the environment. The country is a republic, with members of the 40-seat National Assembly (parliament) directly elected and the majority party's leader taking office as President. There is a 15-member House of Chiefs, representing the major ethnic groups, that advises parliament on legislation pertaining to custom and tradition.

As for the judicial system in Botswana, it is independent of the government and comprises two branches. Cases involving customary law are heard in the Kgotla by local chiefs and headmen and statutory cases are heard in the Magistrate Court or the High Court.

FABULOUS FACTS

The San people (Bushmen) are believed to have inhabited Botswana for at least 30,000 years.

The Makoko and Dzucwa San people believe the Tsodilo hills in northern Botswana to be the site of creation itself.

Botswana's extraordinary Okavango Delta is the largest inland delta in the world.

Botswana offers every conceivable wildlife experience, from safaris on horseback to hiking in the Okavango Delta.

The ancient myths of the Botswana natives have been handed down orally for centuries – they were only recently transcribed.

BOTSWANA HAS PARTICIPATED IN SIX COMMONWEALTH GAMES SINCE ACHIEVING INDEPENDENCE IN 1966, WITH THE MAIN FOCUS ON ATHLETICS. THE COUNTRY SENT 33 ATHLETES TO PARTICIPATE IN THE 1998 GAMES IN KUALA LUMPUR – TSOSELETSO NKALA (HIGH JUMP) AND GABLE GARENAMOTSE (TRIPLE JUMP) DID WELL, THOUGH NEITHER BROUGHT HOME A MEDAL. TIYAPO AMOSA RAN IN THE SYDNEY OLYMPICS, WHERE HE WAS THE ONLY BOTSWANAN RUNNER IN THE MARATHON. HE LED FOR HALF THE RACE, BUT COULDN'T MAINTAIN THE PACE. PERHAPS AMOSA WILL HAVE BETTER LUCK IN MANCHESTER.

Matthew Stockman (Allsport)

BRITISH VIRGIN ISLANDS

CAPITAL: ROAD TOWN
AREA: 153 sq km
POPULATION: 19,610
CURRENCY: UNITED STATES DOLLAR
LANGUAGE: ENGLISH (OFFICIAL)
THE PEOPLE/CULTURE: AFRICAN DESCENT, NORTH AMERICAN, ASIAN

Virgin territory

The British Virgin Islands – situated some 60 miles east of Puerto Rico in the Caribbean – are made up of 50 or so islands, grouped around the Sir Francis Drake Channel. The first inhabitants on the islands were the Ciboney Indians from the Americas, followed by the Arawak Indians from South America and then the Carib Indians.Christopher Columbus discovered the islands in 1493, naming them "Las Once Mil Virgines". The Spaniards invaded in 1555, defeating the Caribs and claiming the territory. During the 16th and 17th Centuries, the islands remained largely uninhabited, too small for colonising – though this didn't stop French settlers (they made money by selling barbecued beef – called "boucons" – to sailors). The Spaniards eventually drove the French off the islands, but instead of fleeing, they became "Buccaneers" and targeted Spanish ships. As Spain declined as a colonial power, ownership of the islands shifted about until the Dutch established a settlement on Tortola in 1648. The defeat of the Spanish Armada (assisted by the Buccaneers) stabilised the area and many pirates settled in the territory. Their influence lives on, as many of the islands bear their names – Norman was named after a French pirate, Thatch was named after Edward Thatch (better known as Blackbeard) and one of the islands was immortalised in literature, Treasure Island. The English ousted the Dutch in the late 17th Century and, by the mid-1900s, there was a growing movement for independence from British control – this was achieved in 1967.

In 1998, the islands sent four athletes to the Games in Kuala Lumpur, including Tahesia Harrigan (she ran second in the 2002 Big Ten Conference, the women's 100m/200m) and Dion Crabbe (he ran second in the SEC Conference 200m and fourth in the 100m). We wish all the BVI athletes luck this year!

BRUNEI

CAPITAL: BANDAR SERI BEGAWAN
AREA: 5,765 sq km
POPULATION: 330,689 (2000 ESTIMATE)
CURRENCY: BRUNEIAN DOLLAR
LANGUAGE: MALAY IS THE OFFICIAL LANGUAGE, BUT ENGLISH AND CHINESE ARE ALSO SPOKEN WIDELY (ENGLISH IS ALSO USED FOR OFFICIAL PURPOSES)
THE PEOPLE/CULTURE: THE POPULATION IS MADE UP PREDOMINANTLY OF MALAY AND CHINESE

Small is beautiful

From the 15th to the 17th Centuries, the Sultanate of Brunei's control extended over coastal areas of northwest Borneo and the southern Philippines. It went into subsequent decline as a consequence of internal strife over royal succession, colonial expansion by various European countries as well as an ongoing threat of piracy.

Brunei became a British protectorate in 1888 and achieved independence on 1 January 1984. Executive authority within Brunei is held by the Council of Ministers, which is presided over by the Sultan of Brunei and by the chief minister, or mentri besar, who is responsible to the sultan. The same family has now ruled in Brunei for over six centuries.

Brunei benefits from extensive petroleum and natural gas fields, the source of one of the highest per capita GDPs among the less developed countries. The Sultanate has a small but wealthy economy, comprising foreign and domestic entrepreneurship, government regulation and welfare measures, and village tradition. Exports of crude oil and natural gas account for over half of GDP, while substantial income from overseas investment supplements income from domestic production. Brunei served as chairman for the 2000 APEC (Asian Pacific Economic Cooperation) forum, confirming the importance of its role in the region, while plans for the future include upgrading the labour force, reducing unemployment, strengthening the banking and tourist sectors, and a further widening of the economic base beyond oil and gas.

In 1998, Brunei sent 18 athletes (all men) to Kuala Lumpur. The Sultanate has yet to bring home a medal, but its athletes will be challenging all comers at badminton and squash, and perhaps this will be the year when they break through.

IMPERIAL LEATHER

Official Sponsors of the Commonwealth fun and Games.

releasethelather.co.uk

CAMEROON

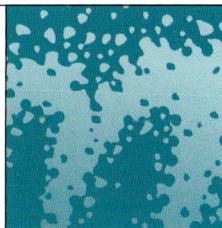

CAPITAL: YAOUNDE

AREA: 475,442 sq km

POPULATION: 15,891,531

CURRENCY: COMMUNAUTE FINANCIÈRE AFRICAINE (CFA) FRANC

LANGUAGE: THERE ARE 24 MAJOR AFRICAN LANGUAGE GROUPS, WHILE ENGLISH AND FRENCH ARE THE OFFICIAL LANGUAGES. ABOUT 240 LANGUAGES ARE SPOKEN IN CAMEROON, NEARLY 100 OF WHICH HAVE SOME WRITTEN FORM

THE PEOPLE: SOME 200 GROUPS, THE LARGEST OF WHICH ARE THE FANG, BAMILEKE, FULANI AND PAHOUIN (BETI)

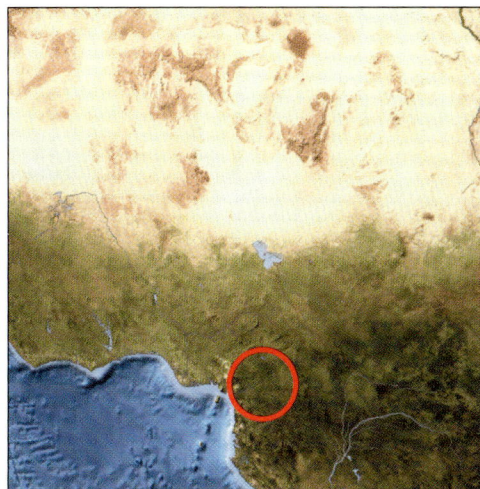

Clearly Cameroon

The earliest inhabitants of Cameroon were probably the Pygmies – they still inhabit the forests of the South and East Provinces. Bantu speakers from equatorial Africa were among the first groups to invade, followed by the Fulani, an Islamic people of the western Sahel. The Portuguese arrived on Cameroon's coast in the 1500s, though significant settlement was limited by malaria until the late 1870s (when quinine first became readily available). From the late 1880s, Cameroon and parts of several of its neighbours became the German colony of Kamerun. Following World War I, this colony was partitioned between Britain and France. In 1955, the outlawed Union of Cameroonian Peoples (UPC) began an armed struggle for independence in French Cameroon – and finally achieved this goal in 1960, becoming the Republic of Cameroon. In 1961, the northern half of British Cameroon voted to join Nigeria while the southern half voted to join with the Republic of Cameroon, forming the Federal Republic of Cameroon. The formerly French and British regions each maintained substantial autonomy.

Independence was achieved on 1 January 1960, from a United Nations (UN) trusteeship under French administration. Since the Republic of Cameroon was declared in 1972, Cameroon has had only two presidents: Ahmadou Ahidjo, a Northern Muslim, and then his southern Christian Prime Minister, Paul Biya. After attempted coups in 1983 and 1984, Biya dismantled the opposition. Bowing to domestic and international pressure, Biya instituted reforms in 1990, but unrest and strikes continued into 1991. Presidential and parliamentary elections, in which 32 parties contested seats, were held in 1992 but were boycotted in large numbers and the results were disputed. Biya retains his office as President.

FIVE FAB FACTS

The harmattan (winds that blow sand south from the Sahara, from December to February) can reduce visibility to 1km or less.

The Mt Cameroon Race (held in January) is a 27km (17mi) race up and down the 3,000m (10,000ft) mountain.

Cameroon is sometimes referred to as the "hinge of Africa" – between Equatorial Guinea and Nigeria.

Some of the 240 languages and dialects spoken include Ful, Pahouin, Bamiléké, Arabic, Penlil and Chadis.

Parc National de Korup, Cameroon's newest national park, enjoys 100 per cent humidity and waist-high pools.

DESPITE POLITICAL UNREST, SPORTS REMAIN A SIGNIFICANT FORCE IN THE COUNTRY, ESPECIALLY DURING THE COMMONWEALTH GAMES. AT THE 1998 KUALA LUMPUR GAMES, FOR EXAMPLE, CAMEROON TOOK TWO SILVER AND THREE BRONZE MEDALS (FRANÇOISE MBANGO, SILVER IN TRIPLE JUMP; HERMAN NGOUDJO, SILVER, BANTAM WEIGHT BOXING; MATAM DAVID, THREE BRONZES, 85KG SNATCH, CLEAN AND JERK AND THE COMBINED). GOOD LUCK TO ALL THE ATHLETES TAKING PART IN THIS YEAR'S GAMES.

Want to know how your business
can benefit from the
Commonwealth Games

?

Find out how at
www.nwbusinessclub.com

Register for **FREE** membership today and expand your business horizons.
FREE benefits include:

> Networking <
> Events <
> Business matching <
> Corporate hospitality <
> Seminars <

CANADA

CAPITAL: OTTAWA
AREA: 9,970,610 sq km
POPULATION: 31,330,255
CURRENCY: CANADIAN DOLLAR
LANGUAGE: BOTH ENGLISH AND FRENCH ARE OFFICIAL
LANGUAGES IN CANADA
THE PEOPLE/CULTURE: BRITISH ISLES ORIGIN, FRENCH ORIGIN,
OTHER EUROPEAN ORIGIN, INDIGENOUS PEOPLES

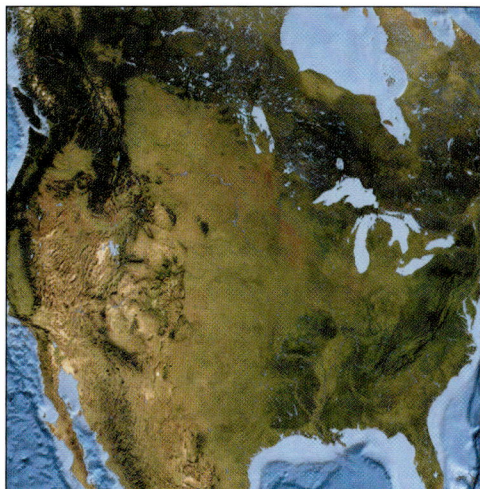

The history of Canada is rich and diverse. It is varied and dynamic, a mosaic of various cultures that complement its own heritage. Explored first by the French and then the English, Canada is a distinct mixture of both – to such an extent that both English and French are official languages.

The modern history of Canada began in 1 July 1867, when it was granted independence from the United Kingdom, with the union of the British Provinces into a new confederation. Canadians celebrate a national holiday (Canada Day) on this day each year. Canada is rich in a wide variety of natural resources – agriculture represents a significant contribution to the national economy.

Canadian amateur sport constitutes one of the longest-standing nationalist movements in the country. Canada has a long and impressive sporting history, stretching right back to Confederation in 1867, when the National Amateur Lacrosse Association was formed. This commitment to sport is reflected in the creation of the Commonwealth Games themselves.

The first Commonwealth Games – known as the British Empire Games – were held in 1930 in Hamilton, Ontario, Canada. Eleven countries with 400 athletes in total participated in the first Commonwealth Games and $30,000 was provided by the City of Hamilton to these nations to help cover travelling costs. Since then, Canada has played host to the Games four times, more than any other nation.

FABULOUS FACTS

Famous Canadians include: Jim Carrey, Leslie Nielson, William Shatner, John Candy, Linda Evangelista, Keanu Reeves.

Invented by Canadians: Superman (Joe Shuster, Jerome Siegel, 1938); the telephone (Alexander Graham Bell, 1874).

Sporting creations by Canadians: Basketball (James Naismith, 1892); five pin bowling (Thomas E Ryan, 1909).

Canada has won every Games gold medal in synchronised swimming since the sport joined the Games in 1986.

Not many people realise that the Canadian coastline is the longest in the world, an impressive 243,792 km in total.

KEN PEREIRA IS A TOP INTERNATIONAL HOCKEY PLAYER WITH MORE THAN 150 NATIONAL TEAM CAPS TO HIS CREDIT. HE SCORED THE WINNING GOAL IN A 1-0 WIN OVER ARGENTINA AT THE 1999 PAN AM GAMES TO GIVE CANADA AN AUTOMATIC BERTH FOR THE 2000 OLYMPICS. AN ACTIVE ATHLETE IN MANY SPORTS, INCLUDING 12 YEARS OF ICE HOCKEY, PEREIRA WAS DRAWN TO THE GAME BY A COUSIN WHO PLAYED ON TEAM CANADA. HE WOULD LIKE TO STICK AROUND UNTIL ATHENS 2004 AND PLAY A BIGGER LEADERSHIP ROLE FOR SOME OF THE YOUNGER PLAYERS ON THE TEAM.

Gary M Prior (Allsport)

Gloster
MADE FOR LIFE

www.gloster.com

Made for Life

CLAIRE CARVER-DIAS AND FANNY LETOURNEAU ARE HOT FAVOURITES FOR MEDALS IN SYNCHRONISED SWIMMING. THE DUO WERE PICKED FOR THE NATIONAL TEAM AFTER A STRONG PERFORMANCE AT THE CANADIAN CHAMPIONSHIPS 2002. CARVER-DIAS WON THE SOLO EVENT AND TEAMED WITH LETOURNEAU FOR A FOURTH STRAIGHT NATIONAL TITLE IN THE DUET. THE PAIR WERE THIRD IN DUET AT THE 1999 FINA WORLD CUP, FIFTH AT THE 2000 OLYMPICS AND THIRD AT THE 2001 WORLD CHAMPIONSHIPS. CARVER-DIAS WAS FIFTH IN SOLO AT THE WORLD CHAMPIONSHIPS LAST YEAR. BOTH WERE PART OF CANADA'S BRONZE MEDAL-WINNING TEAM AT THE 2000 SYDNEY OLYMPICS.

OLYMPIC MEDALLIST NICOLAS GILL LEADS THE CANADIAN JUDO TEAM, WHICH INCLUDES: DANIEL-GUILLAUME SIMARD, JEAN-FRANÇOIS MARCEAU AND KEITH MORGAN. SAYS GILL: "HAVING JUDO BACK AT THE COMMONWEALTH GAMES IS GREAT FOR THE SPORT. FOR THE ATHLETES, IT'S ALWAYS AN EXCEPTIONAL EXPERIENCE AT MAJOR GAMES TO MEET OTHER ATHLETES IN DIFFERENT SPORTS."

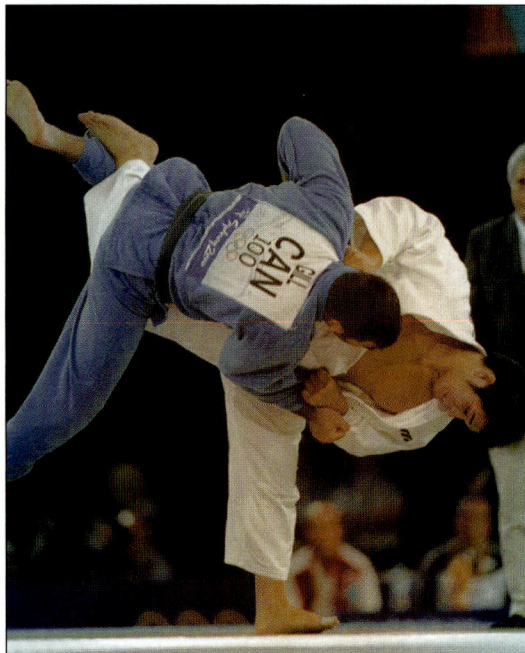

FABULOUS FACTS

Toronto's CN Tower stands at just over 553m and is the tallest freestanding structure in the world.

Canada is the second largest country in the world, after Russia. It covers an area of ten million sq km.

Life expectancy in Canada is 75.6 years for males and 81.7 years for females, which is the world's longest.

The Space Shuttle's Remote Manipulator System (RMS), or robot arm, was provided by the Canadian Space Agency.

Canada allegedly has more doughnut shops per capita than the United States, if not the entire world.

MORGAN KNABE DIDN'T MAKE THE TEAM FOR THE 1998 COMMONWEALTH GAMES, BUT AT THE GAMES TRIALS IN TORONTO, HE LEARNED SOME VALUABLE LESSONS. HIS IDOL IS THE LATE VICTOR DAVIS AND KNABE BROKE DAVIS'S 16-YEAR-OLD RECORD – THE SECOND OLDEST IN THE BOOKS AT THE TIME – AT THE 2000 OLYMPIC TRIALS IN THE MEN'S 100M BREASTSTROKE. HE HAS REDUCED HIS RECORD TIME AT ALMOST EVERY MAJOR MEET SINCE. HE WAS A WORKHORSE DURING THE 2000-2001 WORLD CUP SHORT COURSE SEASON: KNABE TRAVELLED TO ALL FOUR CORNERS OF THE GLOBE AND COMPETED AT EVERY MEET. HE TOOK HOME THE 50M AND 100M BREASTSTROKE WORLD CUP CROWNS, WHICH INCLUDED A 22-MEDAL HAUL.

Doug Pensinger, Michael Steele (Allsport)

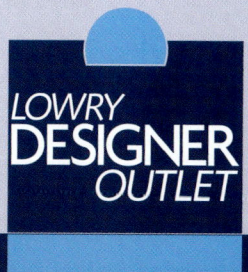

CAYMAN ISLANDS

CAPITAL: GEORGE TOWN
AREA: 259 sq km
POPULATION: 41,011
CURRENCY: CAYMANIAN DOLLAR
LANGUAGE: ENGLISH
THE PEOPLE/CULTURE: MIXED, WHITE AND BLACK

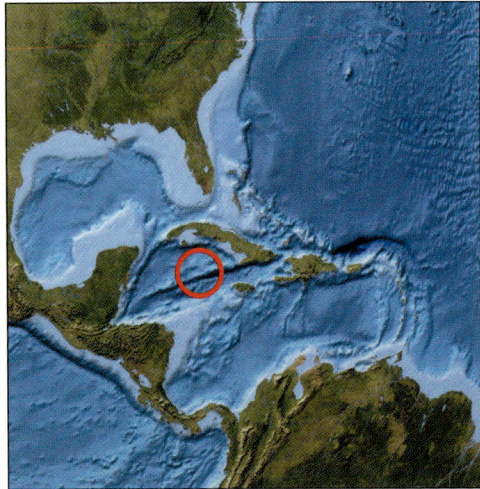

Discovering the Caymans

Christopher Columbus discovered the Cayman Islands in 1503, sighting Cayman Brac and Little Cayman when his ship was blown off course en route from Panama to Hispaniola. According to legend, they were first called Las Tortugas ("The Turtles") due to the remarkable numbers of tortoises/turtles found there. It wasn't until 150 years later that the islands finally came to be known, more or less, as the Caymans – or Caymanas, derived from the Carib word for the crocodile family, of which there were many.

When Jamaica was captured from the Spanish by Cromwell's army in 1655, the islands came under British control, becoming an official British territory when the Treaty of Madrid was signed in 1670.

Piracy limited the numbers of settlements on the islands until privateering (as piracy was known) officially came to an end with the Treaty of Utrecht (1713-14). France and Spain ceased hostilities toward Britain and permanent settlement was possible – records show permanent settlers in the Cayman Islands in 1734. The islands were formally annexed to Jamaica in 1863.

When Jamaica became independent in 1962, the Cayman Islands remained under British rule and power was transferred to the local Administrator and a new constitution was adopted in 1972.

The Cayman Islands are proud of their sporting heroes. One of their biggest heroes is Kareem Streete-Thompson – born in the USA, Streete-Thompson lived his first 18 years in the Cayman Islands. Originally he represented the Cayman Islands, then the USA and then, from 1999, the Cayman Islands again. He was NCAA Champion in 1995 for the long jump (he has also won the WUG 1993, the CAC Junior in 1990 and 1992) and came in second at the Pan American Games in 1999).

THE COOK ISLANDS

CAPITAL: AVARUA
AREA: 237 sq km
POPULATION: 20,407
CURRENCY: NEW ZEALAND DOLLAR
LANGUAGE: ENGLISH, MAORI
THE PEOPLE/CULTURE: POLYNESIAN, POLYNESIAN AND EUROPEAN, POLYNESIAN AND NON-EUROPEAN, EUROPEAN

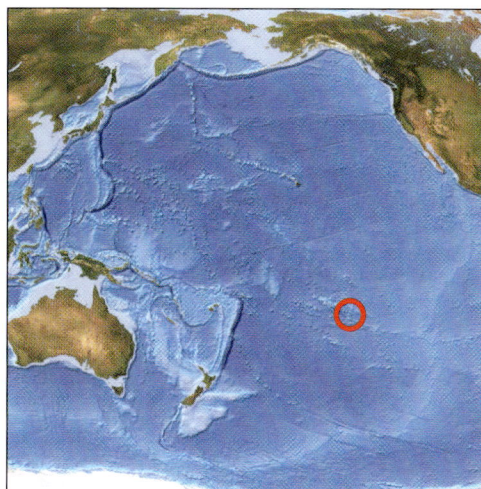

Ready, steady, Cook Islands

The first settlers to the Cook Islands were Polynesians who arrived around 800 AD from Raiatea, in what is now French Polynesia. Contrary to popular belief, James Cook was not the first European to sight the islands; that honour fell to the Spanish explorer Alvaro de Mendana. There is no record of further European contact for over 150 years, until Cook himself explored much of the group during his expeditions of 1773 and 1777. Cook set foot on just one island – tiny, uninhabited Palmerston – while overlooking Rarotonga, the largest. The first Europeans to sight Rarotonga were the mutineers on the HMS Bounty, who took control of the ship while sailing among the Cooks. Captain Cook named the southern group of islands the Hervey Islands in honour of a British Lord of the Admiralty, however a Russian cartographer renamed them 50 years later in honour of Cook himself. It wasn't until the turn of the century that both groups were united under the same name. The British took control of the islands in 1888, when they were declared a protectorate. However, by 1901, all the islands were annexed to New Zealand. The islands became internally self-governing in 1965, with foreign policy and defence left to New Zealand. In return, islanders received New Zealand citizenship and the right to come and go at will from both New Zealand and Australia. The Cook's first Prime Minister was Albert Henry, leader of the Cook Islands Party and a prime mover for independence. Today, the islands' Prime Minister is the Cook Islands Geoffrey Henry (Albert's cousin), who came to power in 1989.
Like its neighbours in the Oceanian region, Cook Islanders are mad about sport and have 28 sporting bodies affiliated to local or Olympic associations. In 1998, the Cook Islands brought 38 athletes to the Games. They'll be pinning their hopes on their powerful Rugby Sevens team.

CYPRUS

CAPITAL: NICOSIA
AREA: 9,251 sq km
POPULATION: 759,048
CURRENCY: CYPRIOT POUND
LANGUAGE: GREEK, TURKISH, ENGLISH
THE PEOPLE/CULTURE: GREEK, TURKISH

An isle divided

Cyprus has always been an important trading post between the empires of Europe, Africa and the Middle East, and throughout history someone has always wanted to take it off someone else. The Athenians, the Persians, the Egyptians, Alexander the Great and the Romans were the most important invaders during the ancient period, but after the partition of the Roman Empire in the 4th Century AD, the island became part of the Eastern Byzantine Empire. It was subsequently a casualty of the Arab invasions between 648 and 746 AD. During the Third Crusade, Richard I of England conquered Cyprus and installed Guy of Lusignan (previously King of Jerusalem), whose house ruled until the island passed to the control of Venice in 1489. From 1571, the Ottomans ruled Cyprus for over three centuries, before ceding it to Britain in 1878. Independence was achieved in August 1960, after a four-year military struggle between the UK and the guerrillas of EOKA (National Organisation of Cypriot Fighters), who sought union with Greece, which was anathema to the Turkish community.

In August 1960, Britain granted Cyprus its independence. A Greek, Archbishop Makarios, became president, while a Turk, Kükük, was made vice president. By 1964, Makarios was moving toward stronger links with Greece and intercommunal violence was on the rise. The United Nations sent in a peace-keeping force. In 1983, Turkish Cypriots proclaimed a separate state, naming it the Turkish Republic of Northern Cyprus (TRNC). Cyprus has been divided ever since.

FABULOUS FACTS

Cyprus may be an ancient land of myth, but Ayia Napa's thumping garage scene also draws the clubbing crowd.

Cyprus is the third largest island in the Mediterranean Sea, after Sicily and Sardinia.

Cyprus is said to be the birthplace of Aphrodite (or Venus), the Greek goddess of love.

The name Aphrodite, in fact, means "foam born". She was the oldest goddess in Olympus.

Lazarus, who was raised from the dead by Jesus, was Cyprus' first bishop and also the island's patron saint.

CYPRUS HAS WON TEN COMMONWEALTH MEDALS, COMPRISING FOUR GOLDS, THREE SILVERS AND THREE BRONZES. IN 1998, CYPRUS BROUGHT 29 ATHLETES AND TOOK HOME FOUR MEDALS. TWO ATHLETES MADE HISTORY FOR CYPRUS WHEN THEY WON THE MEN'S SKEET SHOOTING TITLE IN THE COMMONWEALTH GAMES IN LANGKAWI, MALAYSIA. COSTAS STRATIS AND ANTONIS NICOLAIDES WON THEIR GOLD MEDALS WHEN THEY SCORED 188, BEATING ENGLAND'S DREW HARVEY AND ANDREW AUSTIN BY JUST ONE POINT. OTHER MEDALLISTS IN MALAYSIA INCLUDED MICHALIS LOUCA, WHO WON SILVER IN THE SHOT PUT AND LIGHT FLYWEIGHT BOXER ROUDIK KAZANJIAN, WHO PICKED UP A BRONZE.

Mike Hewitt (Allsport)

DOMINICA

CAPITAL: ROSEAU
AREA: 750 sq km
POPULATION: 70,786
CURRENCY: EAST CARIBBEAN DOLLAR
LANGUAGE: ENGLISH (OFFICIAL), FRENCH PATOIS
THE PEOPLE/CULTURE: AFRICAN AND CARIB DESCENT

The nature island

Dominica has been called the Caribbean's "Nature Island" because of its lush mountainous interior of rainforests, waterfalls, lakes, hot springs and more than 200 rivers, many of which cascade over steep cliff faces en route to the coast.

Christopher Columbus sighted and named Dominica in 1493, but the indigenous Carib people successfully resisted early European attempts at colonisation. In 1632, the French gained a foothold on the island. They retained parts of it until 1763, when the Treaty of Paris assigned it to the United Kingdom. The British, however, did not assert full dominance over the French raiders and rebel slaves based on the island until 1805. Under British rule, Dominica became part of the Leeward Islands dependency in 1833 and was attached to the Windward Islands group in 1940. In 1967, it became an internally self-governing state associated with the United Kingdom.

Dominica attained full independence in November 1978 and subsequently joined the Commonwealth of Nations and the United Nations (UN). In 1980, Mary Eugenia Charles was elected Prime Minister, becoming the first female elected head of state in the Caribbean. The Caribbean's answer to Margaret Thatcher subsequently won three elections in a row, the last in May 1990, as head of the Dominica Freedom Party. The new Prime Minister is Pierre Charles who came to power in October 2000 at the age of 46 following the death of Mr Rosie Douglas.

In 1998, Dominica was represented by six athletes to the Games in Kuala Lumpur, so though small, Dominica will certainly have a presence in Manchester during the 2002 Games.

Great Deals for Summer at *Kodak* Express

Back the winning team and be sure of capturing all those moments you want to remember forever, with Kodak Express stores.

For all your photographic needs, visit your nearest store.

For more details contact www.kodakexpress.co.uk

Kodak, Kodak Ultra, Kodak Max, Advantix, Film for all Conditions and the Kodak Express logo are trade marks of Kodak

ENGLAND

CAPITAL: LONDON
AREA: 130,410 sq km
POPULATION: 49,495,000
CURRENCY: POUND STERLING
LANGUAGE: ENGLISH
THE PEOPLE/CULTURE: CAUCASIAN/EUROPEAN, INDIAN, PAKISTANI, WEST INDIAN AND AFRICAN

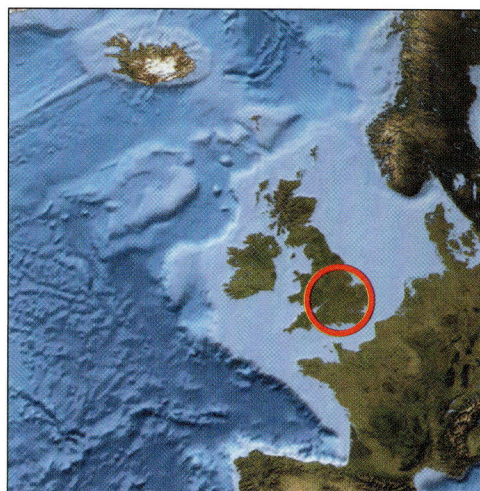

Little island, big history

The Romans conquered and settled the major part of the British mainland before the 5th Century AD. After their withdrawal (410-442 AD) the island was invaded by Jutes, Saxons and Angles. By the early 9th Century, Wessex had emerged as the dominant kingdom, spearheading resistance to the Danish invasions. In 1066, England fell under the Normans, lead by William (later King William I). English control and the territorial disputes were not settled until the end of the Hundred Years War in 1453. Between 1461 and 1485, two houses (the Yorkists and the Tudors) battled for control of the country, in what came to be known as the Wars of the Roses. The throne changed hands six times, until Henry VII (Tudor) finally defeated the Yorkist Richard III at the Battle of Bosworth. Tudor England (1485-1603) witnessed several important developments: centralised power, the break with Rome, overseas expansion, the union of England and Wales, and the growth of the power of Parliament. The latter came to a head during the English Civil War in the 1640s, ending with the execution of Charles I in 1649 and the establishment of a series of republics and protectorates during the English Revolution (1649-1660). In 1660, King Charles II was re-established as monarch. The reign of Victoria (1837-1901) was the greatest period of British conquest and overseas settlement – at the height of Empire, Britain ruled vast tracts of the globe. The 20th Century saw the end of colonial empires and two World Wars, while postwar years saw the emergence of the Welfare State in England, as well as the Swinging Sixties and the rise of Prime Minister Margaret Thatcher. Today, England is characterised as an economic powerhouse, a multi-cultural melting pot and breeding ground for artists of all kinds. In the 21st Century, it's a land where stiff upper lips are becoming just a little more relaxed.

FABULOUS FACTS

Some famous English inventions include: the telescope, the vacuum cleaner, the tank and the jet engine.

The Bank of England (founded 1694), the central bank of the UK, is known as the "Old Lady" of Threadneedle Street.

In 1966, England hit the pinnacle of sporting achievement, winning the World Cup final 4-2 against West Germany.

In 1066, King Harold and the English troops met William the Conqueror and the Norman invaders at the battle of Hastings.

Alfred the Great was crowned King of Wessex at the age of 22 and ruled until his death at 50-years-old.

AS HOST OF THE GAMES, ENGLAND WILL BE LOOKING FOR GREAT THINGS FROM ITS STAR ATHLETES. OUT OF 641 COMPETITORS, THERE ARE ENDLESS PROSPECTS FOR MEDALS. MARK LEWIS-FRANCIS IS A REAL PROSPECT FOR THE 100M GOLD MEDAL – THE 19-YEAR OLD BIRCHFIELD HARRIER RAN 9.97 SECS AT LAST YEAR'S WORLDS IN EDMONTON AND WAS VOTED BRITISH JUNIOR MALE ATHLETE OF THE YEAR (2000, 2001).
"I AM SO EXCITED ABOUT MY FIRST MAJOR CHAMPIONSHIP IN THE UK," SAYS LEWIS-FRANCIS. "I'M REALLY LOOKING FORWARD TO IT. I WANT TO COME BACK WITH MEDALS – GOLD MEDALS."

Michael Steele (Allsport)

MATTHEW SYED IS THE CURRENT COMMONWEALTH TABLE TENNIS CHAMPION AND THE 30-YEAR OLD FROM RICHMOND, SURREY LOOKS LIKE AN EXCELLENT BET TO GRAB GOLD IN MANCHESTER. HE RETAINED HIS TITLE IN FRONT OF A PARTISAN INDIAN CROWD, DEFEATING THE HOME NATION'S NUMBER ONE PLAYER, CHETAN BABOOR, IN A MATCH IN WHICH SYED HAD TO SAVE THREE MATCH POINTS AGAINST HIM. HE'LL DEFINITELY HAVE THE CROWD BEHIND HIM AS HE BIDS TO ADD THE COMMONWEALTH GAMES GOLD TO HIS LIST OF TRIUMPHS.

Be-Well Lifestyle Range

BE-WELL LIFESTYLE

The Be-Well Lifestyle Range was developed to help combat diet related diseases so abundant in today's society.

Be-Well also look after nutritional requirements of a squad of elite athletes including Paula Radcliffe and Ranulph Fiennes, to name but a few.

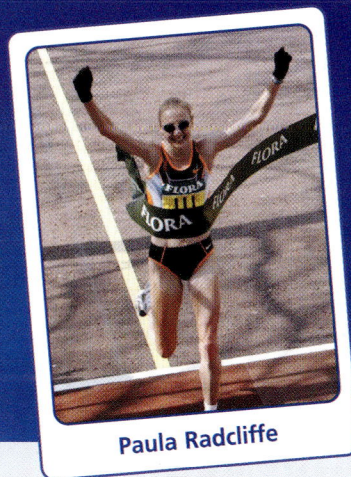

Paula Radcliffe

Ranulph Fiennes

Feminine Balance
Price £15.95

A dietary supplement made of naturally occurring isoflavones from Soya. Daily use helps to balance oestrogen levels leading to comfort at period times. Female athlete Paula Radcliffe has found Feminine Balance to be beneficial, enabling continuity in training at all times during the monthly cycle.

Isoflavones also show promise in the prevention of many serious diseases, which affect society.

1. Bone Health

Because of the chemical similarity between oestrogen and isoflavones, researchers suggest that isoflavones prevent bone loss. Therefore, the use of Feminine Balance represents a natural alternative to drug based therapies to prevent Osteoporosis.

2. Hormone Replacement Therapy

(HRT) can also alleviate such menopausal symptoms. However there is much controversy about the safety of HRT and for women who are nervous about taking a drug Feminine Balance is a natural way to alleviate such worries.

Breakthrough
Price £27.95

Breakthrough has been developed to provide the 'missing links' in our daily diet in the building of a strong immune system.

Breakthrough consists of a powerful antioxidant formula including isoflavones, bioflavonoids combined with organically complexed vitamin and minerals, and valuable amino acids.

Many case histories have been compiled by Be-Well on the affects of Breakthrough as a nutritional support system, with many top sports performers and also with less fortunate individuals who have succumbed to diet related illnesses including ME, Autoimmune Haemolytic Anaemia, Multiple Sclerosis, Ankylosing Spondylitis (arthritic condition) and so on.

Amongst the sporting performers who have been helped by Be-Well over the past six years or so include Paula Radcliffe, Denise Lewis and England Rugby Captain Martin Johnson.

Nutricol
Price £19.95

A nutritional drink mix designed for joint mobility. Active ingredients include Glucosamine, Methyl Suiphonyl Methane (MSM), Hydrolysed Collagen, containing amino acids and peptides together with a vitamin and mineral complex to allow joint repair, regeneration and quick recovery.

Nutricol provides not only the raw materials to repair and prevent cartilage and connective tissue damage, but assists greatly as we grow older or damage ourselves in sporting activities. By continuous use the symptoms decline after several weeks and with a regular daily dose do not readily return.

Nutricol was used by athlete Paula Radcliffe prior to the 2002 London Marathon to aid her recovery from a knee injury.

Sports nutrition products will also be available in Autumn 2002

BE-WELL FITNESS

How to Order:

by phone: 24 hours - 7 days +44 (0) 845 130 4559 by fax: +44 (0) 1778 560 872

by post: Be-Well (Health Dietary & Nutritional) Products Ltd, 20 King Street Industrial Estate, Langtoft, Market Deeping, Peterborough, PE6 9NF. Cheques made payable to Be-Well (Health Dietary & Nutritional) Products Ltd.

RITCHIE BARBER IS THE REIGNING WORLD CHAMPION AT 50M BUTTERFLY. HE ALSO WON THE SILVER AT THE 2000 PARALYMPICS AND GOLD AT THE EUROPEAN CHAMPIONSHIPS. HE HAS EVEN PICKED UP THE TITLE OF BBC NORTH WEST DISABLED SPORT PERSON FOR 2001. THE LOCALS AT THE NEW MANCHESTER AQUATICS CENTRE WILL BE ROARING HIM ON IN THE MEN'S EAD FREESTYLE EVENT.

CYCLIST JASON QUEALLY MBE WAS ONE OF ENGLAND'S GOLDEN BOYS IN SYDNEY 2000. IN FACT, NOT CONTENT WITH TAKING GOLD IN THE MEN'S 1KM TIME TRIAL, HE GRABBED SILVER IN THE SPRINT CYCLING EVENT. HE ALSO WON SILVER IN THE 1KM EVENT AT THE 1998 COMMONWEALTH GAMES. AMAZINGLY, THE 32-YEAR-OLD, BORN IN STAFFORSHIRE, DID NOT TAKE UP CYCLING UNTIL HIS MID-TWENTIES, BUT HE'S DEFINITELY MAKING UP FOR LOST TIME.

FABULOUS FACTS

The first test tube baby was English – Louise Joy Brown was born in Oldham General Hospital on 25 July 1978.

Born in England (though you might not know it): Kim Cattrall (Liverpool); Cary Grant (Bristol); Jerry Springer (London).

Heathrow is the world's busiest international airport with 53.2 million international passengers per year.

The Notting Hill Carnival, London's multicultural music and dance festival, is the second largest carnival in the world.

The first General Assembly of the United Nations was held in 1946 at Methodist Central Hall in Westminster, London.

KELLY HOLMES WON IN THE 1,500M EVENT IN VICTORIA, CANADA IN 1994 AND THE 800M BRONZE IN SYDNEY IN 2000, BUT THERE'S MORE TO COME FROM HOLMES.

"I FEEL VERY MOTIVATED FOR THIS YEAR AND, MORE IMPORTANT, I FEEL VERY RELAXED ABOUT MY ATHLETICS AGAIN," SHE SAYS. "EACH YEAR, YOU HAVE DIFFERENT GOALS AND AMBITIONS AND MINE THIS YEAR IS TO FOCUS ON THE COMMONWEALTH GAMES. I ALWAYS GO INTO A CHAMPIONSHIP AIMING FOR A GOLD MEDAL AND THAT'S WHAT I'LL DO THIS YEAR."

Jamie Squire, Adam Pretty (Allsport)

Weetabix *Generating energy for everyone*

FALKLAND ISLANDS

CAPITAL: STANLEY
AREA: 12,173 sq km
POPULATION: 2,826
CURRENCY: FALKLAND POUND
LANGUAGE: ENGLISH
THE PEOPLE/CULTURE: BRITISH

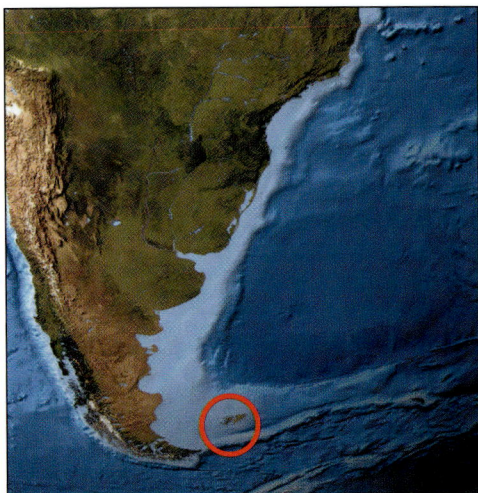

Distant relations

The Falkland Islands sit at the southernmost reaches of the South Atlantic Ocean and, though their nearest neighbours are Argentina and Antarctica, the Falklands are British through and through.

The first documented landing on the islands was made by a British expedition in 1690. The explorers claimed the islands for the Crown and named them after a British naval officer, Viscount Falkland.

In 1764 the French occupied the islands, but they were quickly ceded to Spain, which at the time ruled the adjacent territory in Latin America. The British occupation of East Falkland, which took place in 1765, was recognised by the Spanish, who were only established in West Falkland. The British declared full sovereignty over the Islands in 1833. However, newly independent Argentina refused to recognise the British occupation and has maintained a consistent claim to sovereignty ever since.

The sovereignty issue came to a head in April 1982, when Argentina invaded the Falklands and set up outposts in South Georgia and the South Sandwich Islands. Britain sent a naval task force to retake the islands and after 72 days, the war ended with Argentina's surrender. Since the war, relations between Britain and Argentina have warmed (except on the football field!) and a series of agreements have since been signed between the British and Argentinian governments covering fishing rights, oil exploration and other matters. Though small in size and population, the islands have sent a number of teams to the Commonwealth Games. In 1998, they sent a 10-strong team, including a shooting party that comprised of Graham Didlick (pistol), Dave Peck (pistol), and Henry McLeod (shotgun), who all achieved personal bests in their respective disciplines. The islands will be hoping to achieve the same success in Manchester.

FIJI

CAPITAL: SUVA
AREA: 18,376 sq km
POPULATION: 823,376
CURRENCY: FIJI DOLLAR
LANGUAGE: ENGLISH, FIJIAN, HINDUSTANI.
THE PEOPLE/CULTURE: FIJIAN, INDIAN, EUROPEAN, CHINESE

Totally tropical

Fiji has a unique history in the Pacific and today it is an interesting blend of Melanesian, Polynesian, Micronesian, Indian, Chinese and European influences. For nearly 50 years, until the military coup of 1987, the indigenous people of Fiji represented an ethnic minority in their own land.

Little is known of the islanders' history before the arrival of Europeans (an assortment of roving traders, missionaries and shipwrecked sailors) in the mid-17th Century. The first known European to sight the Fijian islands was Abel Tasman, who passed by on his way to Indonesia in 1643. James Cook was next to visit when he stopped at Vatoa in the Lau group in 1774. Relations between the indigenous community and the new arrivals were reasonably good, founded on mutually beneficial commercial activity, until the establishment of plantations in the 1860s destabilised the economy. In 1874, Fiji became a British colony.

After developing a greater political awareness following World War II, the country gained independence in 1970 and for the 17 years after independence, the moderate conservative Alliance party governed without interruption. Since 1987, the country has been the subject of a number of governmental upheavals that have left the political situation in this island paradise somewhat unstable.

FABULOUS FACTS

The first Lapita settlers settled in Fiji around 1 500 BC, coming mostly from other parts of Melanesia.

Fiji's biggest sporting name is golfer Vijay Singh. He reached his peak winning the US Masters tournament in 2000.

In 1921, a lightning bolt hit Government House and caused a fire that completely razed the Governor's residence.

William Bligh landed at Fiji under some duress, after the mutineers of the HMS Bounty set him and 18 crew adrift in a tiny boat.

The Tabua, a whale's tooth, is much prized in Fijian tradition. It is used as a symbol of peace, to settle disputes.

FIJIANS ARE SPORTS MINDED AND THEY LOVE RUGBY AND SOCCER. THE COUNTRY IS A WORLD FORCE IN RUGBY, PARTICULARLY SEVENS. THE TEAM WON THE RUGBY SEVENS WORLD CUP IN 1997 AND THEY WERE SILVER MEDALLISTS AT THE COMMONWEALTH GAMES IN KUALA LUMPUR. THE MAN TO WATCH OUT FOR IS WAISELE SEREVI, A TRULY DEVASTATING PLAYER. SEREVI DOMINATES EVERY TOURNAMENT IN WHICH HE PLAYS AND WILL COUNT HIMSELF UNLUCKY TO HAVE ONLY PICKED UP A SILVER IN MALAYSIA AFTER LOSING OUT TO JONAH LOMU'S KIWIS. THE FIJIAN CAPTAIN WILL BE LOOKING TO GO ONE BETTER IN MANCHESTER.

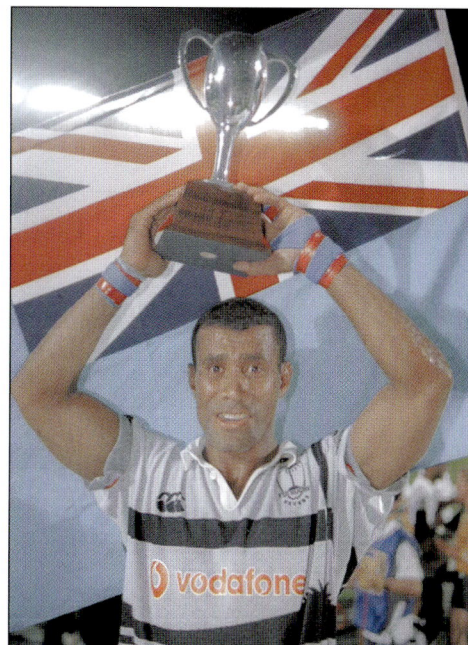

Darren England (Allsport)

GHANA

CAPITAL: ACCRA
AREA: 238,500 sq km
POPULATION: 19, 271,744
CURRENCY: NEW CREDI
LANGUAGE: ENGLISH IS THE OFFICIAL LANGUAGE, BUT AKAN, MOLE-DAGBANI, EWE, GA-ADANGBE AND OTHER AFRICAN LANGUAGES ARE ALSO SPOKEN
THE PEOPLE/CULTURE: BLACK AFRICANS (INCLUDING FANTI, ASHANTI, GA-ADANGBE, EWE, HAUSA, MOSHI-DAGOMBA)

Going, going, Ghana

There is evidence of settlements along the Ghanaian coast dating back some 40,000 years. However, a written history did not come into existence until the Portuguese arrived in the late 15th Century. The Portuguese first came in search of gold, which they found in abundance and began to build forts along what became known as the Gold Coast. They went on to make their money in the slave trade, attracting the attentions of the Dutch, British and Danes in the late 16th Century. During the next 250 years, all four nations competed fiercely to control the trade.

After the demise of slavery, the British took over the forts to use as customs posts, signing treaties with many of the local chiefs. In 1873, the British declared the Gold Coast a Crown Colony. Several years of violence with the Ashanti people of the interior followed until, in 1901, the whole of present-day Ghana became a British protectorate. Although, by World War I, the Gold Coast was the most prosperous colony in Africa, anti-British sentiments ran deep. Over the years following the war, various political parties dedicated to regaining African independence began to emerge, and in 1951 the Convention People's Party (CPP), under Kwame Nkrumah, won control of the Government. The CPP went on to win further elections in 1954 and 1956, and on 6 March 1957, Ghana won its independence.

FABULOUS FACTS

In 1957, Ghana became the first country in colonial Africa to win freedom from its colonisers.

The name "Ghana" was chosen after the name of the first great empire in West Africa.

The massive Kujani Game Reserve is Ghana's largest protected area and is known for its wildlife.

Britain's first black professional footballer, Arthur Wharton, was Ghanaian. He came to the UK in 1882.

One of Ghana's oldest games is Oware. It is a game for two people, played with 24 stones on a wooden board.

GHANA HAS PERFORMED WELL IN THE GAMES IN THE PAST, WINNING A TOTAL OF 46 MEDALS OVER THE YEARS. ANDREW OWUSU TOOK SILVER IN THE TRIPLE JUMP IN KUALA LUMPUR 1998 AND GHANA ALSO WON THREE BOXING MEDALS: RAYMOND NARH TOOK GOLD IN THE LIGHTWEIGHT CATEGORY, JAMES TONY TOOK BRONZE IN LIGHT MIDDLEWEIGHT AND ALORYI MOYOY TOOK BRONZE IN SUPER HEAVYWEIGHT. LEONARD MYLES-MILLS IS GHANA'S HOT PROSPECT FOR TRACK AND FIELD – HE MADE IT TO THE SEMI-FINALS OF THE 100 METRES IN THE SYDNEY OLYMPICS, FINISHING IN NINTH PLACE.

Jamie Squire (Allsport)

CAPITAL: BANJUL
AREA: 11,295 sq km
POPULATION: 1,381,496
CURRENCY: DALASI
LANGUAGE: ENGLISH (OFFICIAL), MANDINKA, WOLOF, FULFULDE, FRENCH
THE PEOPLE/CULTURE: MANDINKA, FULANI, WOLOF, JOLA, SERAHULI

GAMBIA

Go, go, Gambia

The Gambia is Africa's smallest nation, only 15 to 30 miles wide and extending inland from the ocean 180 miles. As early as 500 AD, towns and villages were dotted across the West African region. The Gambia's first contact with Europeans came in 1456, when navigators landed on James Island. The first European settlement in The Gambia was made by Baltic Germans, who built a fort on James Island in 1651. Ten years later, they were displaced by the British, who were themselves ever under threat from French ships, pirates and the mainland African kings. Britain declared the River Gambia a British Protectorate in 1820 and for many years ruled it from Sierra Leone. In 1886, The Gambia became a crown colony and the following year, France and Britain drew the boundaries between Senegal (by then a French colony) and The Gambia. In 1965, The Gambia became independent (although Britain's Queen Elizabeth II remained as titular head of state), and without any official explanation the "The" was added to its name. In 1970, The Gambia became a fully independent republic. Troubles in the 1980s began with falling groundnut prices (groundnuts are one of The Gambia's biggest sources of income), while the government of President Dawda Jawara did little to diversify the economy. Several coup attempts were quelled with the assistance of Senegalese troops, who were integrated with Gambian troops in 1982 as the Senegambian Confederation. The army seized power in 1994 and Yahya Jammeh declared himself head of state, but a new 1996 constitution and presidential elections, followed by parliamentary balloting in 1997, have completed a nominal return to civilian rule. In sport, Gambians are mad about football and athletics. In Manchester, they'll be hoping to improve on their all-time medal tally of one bronze and we wish them luck in their endeavours.

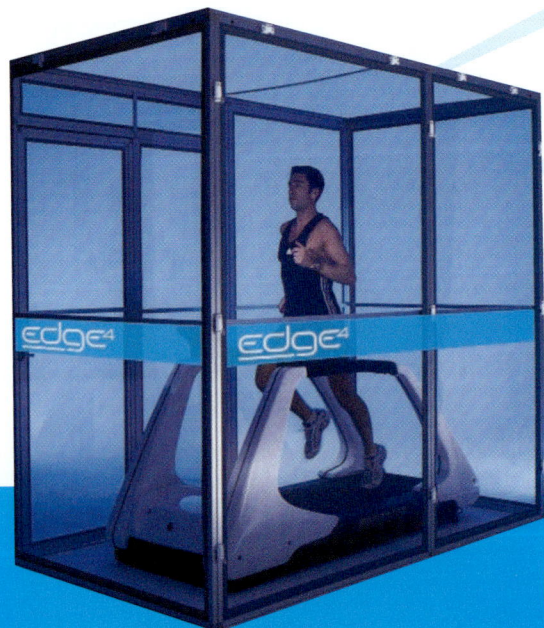

GIBRALTAR

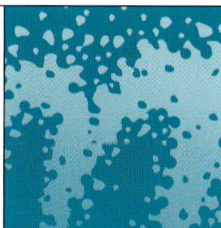

CAPITAL: GIBRALTAR
AREA: 6.5 SQ KM
POPULATION: 29,272
CURRENCY: GIBRALTAR POUND
LANGUAGE: ENGLISH, SPANISH, ITALIAN, PORTUGUESE, RUSSIAN
THE PEOPLE/CULTURE: SPANISH, ITALIAN, ENGLISH, MALTESE
AND PORTUGUESE

Rock and roll

To the ancient Greeks and Romans, Gibraltar was one of the two Pillars of Hercules, set up by the mythical hero to mark the edge of the known world. The other pillar was the coastal mountain Jebel Musa in Morocco. The Muslim governor of Tangier, Tariq Ibn Ziyad, landed at the Rock of Gibraltar in 711 AD, to launch the Islamic invasion of the Iberian Peninsula. The Rock has borne his name ever since: Jebel Tariq (Tariq's Mountain). In 1462, Gibraltar was taken from the Muslims by Castilla. Later, in 1704, an Anglo-Dutch fleet captured Gibraltar during the War of the Spanish Succession. Spain ceded the Rock to Britain in 1713 and Britain developed it into an important naval base. Gibraltar has been a source of tension between the Spanish and British ever since. In fact, during the Franco period, from 1967 to 1985, Gibraltar's border was closed. In 1969, Gibraltarians voted by 12,138 to 44 in favour of British rather than Spanish sovereignty, and a new constitution gave Gibraltar domestic self-government. Today, Spain offers Gibraltar autonomous-region status within Spain, but Britain and the Gibraltarians continue to reject any compromise over sovereignty.
The majority of the Rock is limestone – it is 426m-high and has over 140 caves. The Rock's most famous inhabitants are its colony of Barbary macaques, the only wild primates in Europe. Legend has it that when the apes (probably introduced from North Africa in the 18th Century) disappear from Gibraltar, so will the British. Gibraltar signals the position of the Strait of Gibraltar, the narrow neck that separates Europe from Africa and provides the only link between the Atlantic Ocean and the Mediterranean Sea.
In 1998, the island sent nine competitors to the Kuala Lumpur Games; 15 names have been confirmed for Manchester. There will be three triathletes coming: Chris Walker, Sigund Haveland and Richard Muscat, six swimmers and six shooters, including air rifle specialist Heloise Manasco.

GRENADA

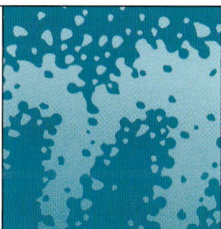

CAPITAL: ST GEORGE'S
AREA: 344 SQ KM
POPULATION: 97,913
CURRENCY: EAST CARIBBEAN DOLLAR
LANGUAGE: ENGLISH, FRENCH-ENGLISH-AFRICAN PATOIS
THE PEOPLE/CULTURE: AFRICAN DESCENT, EUROPEAN AND EAST INDIANS

Grenada the Great

The history of Grenada began in 1498, when Christopher Columbus sighted the island on his third voyage to the so-called New World. However, the first European settlement was not attempted until 1609. In 1650, Governor Du Parquet of Martinique "purchased" Grenada from the Caribs for a few hatchets, some glass beads and a couple of bottles of alcohol. Grenada remained under French control until it was eventually ceded to the British in 1783. It remained under British rule until independence, though animosity lingered between the British colonialists and the minority French settlers, with violence erupting periodically.
In 1877, Grenada became a Crown colony and, in 1967, became an associate state within the British Commonwealth. Grenada and the neighbouring Grenadine Islands of Carriacou and Petit Martinique adopted a constitution in 1973 and became an independent nation on 7 February 1974.
The Carifta Games in the Bahamas over the Easter Holidays provide a good indicator of contenders to watch out for at the Commonwealth Games. Out of the competing countries from Central America and the Caribbean, Grenada managed to win 22 medals, despite only entering half the number of athletes the competition allows. The outstanding Grenadian athletes at the Carifta Games included Shamir Thomas, winning her second consecutive gold for the discus, and Alleyne Left, who won gold in the heptathlon. Kendall Smith also won two distance medals and Jackie-Ann Moran won the 400m hurdles bronze medal. Grenada's biggest hope for the Commonwealth Games is Alleyne Francique, the 400m specialist and collegiate champion.

GUERNSEY

CAPITAL: SAINT PETER PORT
AREA: 194 sq km
POPULATION: 64,080
CURRENCY: GUERNSEY POUND
LANGUAGE: ENGLISH
THE PEOPLE/CULTURE: THE POPULATION IS PREDOMINANTLY
OF UK AND NORMAN-FRENCH DESCENT

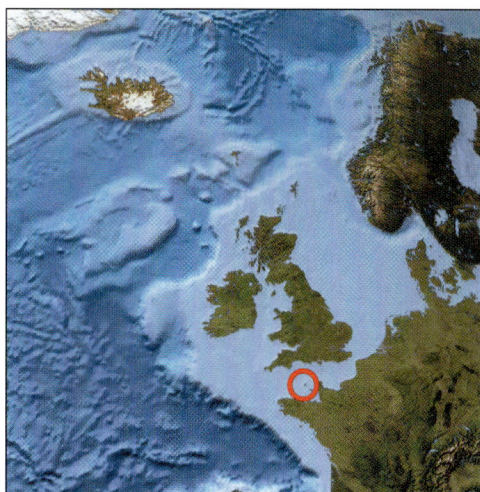

Island hopping

The island of Guernsey and the other Channel Islands represent the last remnants of the medieval Dukedom of Normandy, which held sway in both France and England. The island became part of the Norman realms in 933 AD following the treaty of St Clair-sur-Epte. In 1066, William Duke of Normandy became King William the First and his Duchy of Normandy included the Channel Islands. Some 138 years later, King John lost most of the Duchy of Normandy, but Guernsey and the other Channel Islands remained loyal to the English Crown. In World War II, Guernsey became the only British soil to be occupied by the Germans. Guernsey was occupied for nearly five years, with, at one point, some 13,000 Wehrmacht troops on the island. However, this more than anything further anglicised the island. Thousands of islanders were evacuated to the UK and of the remaining inhabitants – some 2,000 Guernsey people – were imprisoned in Germany. Relics of the occupation, such as the Cobiere Tower on the south coast, are open to the public today.
The Bailiwick of Guernsey consists of four main islands: Guernsey, Alderney, Sark and Herm. It has its own constitution, making it almost a self-governing member of the Commonwealth. However, Guernsey's legislation occasionally has to be approved by the Queen in Council before it can be enacted locally. The island's main income is derived from its finance industry, thanks to the low rate of taxes and other advantages. The island has an all-time medals tally of six, including one gold in 1990 claimed by Adrien Breton in the Rapid Fire Pistol. This year, they are sending a total of 30 athletes, including a 10-strong lawn bowls team and four swimmers (Ben Lowndes, Ian Powell, Gail Strobridge, Jonathan Le Noury). They will also have competitors in athletics, badminton, cycling, squash and shooting.

GUYANA

CAPITAL: GEORGETOWN
AREA: 214,969 sq km
POPULATION: 703,399
CURRENCY: GUYANESE DOLLAR
LANGUAGE: THE OFFICIAL LANGUAGE IS ENGLISH BUT HINDI, URDU, NATIVE AMERICAN
DIALECTS ARE ALSO SPOKEN. CREOLESE, AN ENGLISH-BASED CREOLE, IS WIDELY USED
AS A LANGUAGE OF INFORMAL COMMUNICATION
THE PEOPLE: THE COUNTRY IS MADE UP OF EAST INDIANS, BLACK AND MIXED RACES,
NATIVE AMERICANS, EUROPEANS AND CHINESE

Great Guyana

The aboriginal inhabitants of the Guyanese coast were Carib Indians. Although Christopher Columbus had sailed off the coast of Guyana in 1498, it wasn't until a century later that European settlement was first attempted. Sir Walter Raleigh visited the territory in 1595 and this was followed by several unsuccessful attempts to establish permanent settlements. The first permanent European settlement was not established until 1615, when the Dutch West Indian Company built a fort and depot on the lower Essequibo River and went on to build up large sugar plantations. While the coast remained firmly under Dutch control, the English were also establishing sugar and tobacco plantations west of the Suriname River. So much so, that by 1796 Britain had become the major power in the area. Guyana's early history is reflected in the many Dutch and French place names throughout the country, and in many words commonly used. Its history is also reflected in traces of Roman-Dutch law in the legal system of the country. Slavery was abolished in 1834, so the British began shipping indentured workers over from India. From 1846-1917, almost 250,000 labourers entered Guyana, dramatically transforming the country's demographic balance. The name Guyana is derived from an Amerindian word meaning "land of many waters", but is often referred to as the "land of six peoples", reflecting the multi-ethnic composition of its population. Guyana achieved independence from the UK on 26 May 1966 and, four years later, became a co-operative republic within the Commonwealth.
Sports remain important to Guyana's people. Track athlete Aliann Pompey is at the top of the list for the Commonwealth Games, with several others attracting substantial attention, including Nicolette Fernandes and Luke Fraser (squash), Marian Burnette (athletics) and Theophilous Blue and Rudolph Fraser (boxing).

INDIA

CAPITAL: NEW DELHI
AREA: 3,165,596 sq km
POPULATION: 1,017, 645,163
CURRENCY: INDIAN RUPEE
LANGUAGE: THERE ARE AT LEAST 300 KNOWN LANGUAGES IN INDIA, 24 OF WHICH HAVE ONE MILLION OR MORE SPEAKERS. 40 PER CENT OF THE POPULATION SPEAK THE NATIONAL LANGUAGE, HINDI. THE CONSTITUTION ALSO RECOGNISES 17 OTHER LANGUAGES, INCLUDING BENGALI, TELUGU, MARATHI, TAMIL AND URDU
THE PEOPLE/CULTURE: INDO-ARYANS AND DRAVIDIAN

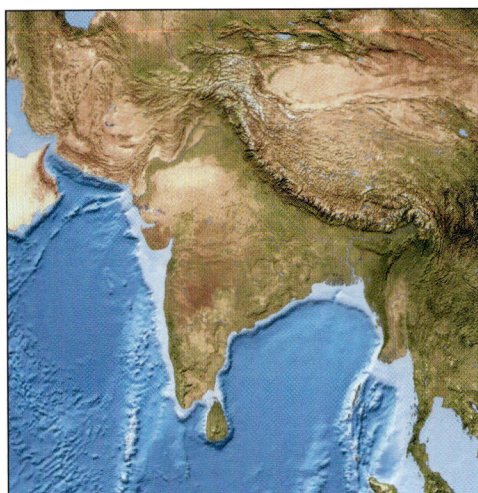

A land of many faces

The Indus Valley civilisation, one of the oldest in the world, goes back some 5,000 years. Aryan tribes from the northwest invaded about 1500 BC, while Arab incursions began in the 8th Century and were followed by the Turkish in the 12th Century. European traders, including Portuguese, Dutch and French, invaded in the late 15th Century. By the early 19th Century, Britain had assumed political control of virtually all Indian lands. It was not until the turn of the 20th Century that opposition to British rule began to flourish. The "Congress", which had been established to give India a degree of self-rule, began to push for the real thing. In 1915, Mohandas Gandhi and Jawaharlal Nehru – key protagonists in the fight for independence – adopted a policy of passive resistance, or satyagraha, to British colonialism. However, within India itself, there was significant division among the Muslims and Hindus as the large Muslim minority realised that an independent India would be Hindu-dominated. The British, under Viceroy Mountbatten, reluctantly decided to divide the country. The subcontinent was thus divided into the secular state of India and the smaller Muslim state of Pakistan, with the Republic of India gaining independence from the United Kingdom on 15 August 1947.
However, when the dividing line was announced, the greatest exodus in human history took place as Muslims moved to Pakistan and Hindus and Sikhs relocated to India. More than 10 million people changed sides and even the most conservative estimates calculate that 250,000 people were killed. On 30 January 1948, Gandhi, deeply disheartened by the partition, was assassinated by a Hindu fanatic.
A third war between the two countries in 1971 resulted in East Pakistan becoming the separate nation of Bangladesh. Clashes between Hindus and Muslims still remain an integral part of Indian life today.

FABULOUS FACTS

India has the largest reserve of coal in the world.

The Taj Mahal was built in 1631 by Emperor Shah Jahan in memory of his second wife.

India is the birthplace of the Hindu, Buddhist, Jain and Sikh religions.

Links between Greece and India go back to 975 BC. The first Olympic sports were common to both countries.

Polo, chess, wrestling, archery and hockey are all believed to have originated in India.

CONSIDERED BY MOST AS THE TEST EVENT BEFORE THE COMMONWEALTH GAMES IN MANCHESTER, THE FOURTH COMMONWEALTH SHOOTING FEDERATION CHAMPIONSHIPS IN SEPTEMBER 2001 CLEARLY DEMONSTRATED INDIA'S STRENGTH IN THIS FIELD. INDIA TOPPED THE MEDAL TABLE: 13 OF THE COUNTRY'S 27 MEDALS WERE GOLD.

Mark Dadswell (Allsport)

CHAMPION
food...

for a **winning** combination of **savouries** and **sandwiches** sprint along to your **local** Greggs, where the **food** is always **freshly** **made** in the shop **everyday**.

unbeatable winners from **::: GREGGS**

great taste ▪ great value

for details of your nearest shop: tel: **0191 281 7721**

ONE INDIAN STAR TO LOOK OUT FOR IS
CHETA PANDURANGA BABOOR, WHO
IS RANKED AS ONE OF THE TOP FIVE
TABLE TENNIS PLAYERS IN THE WORLD.
CHETA, A SPECTACULAR DEFENSIVE
PLAYER, WON THE COMMONWEALTH
SILVER MEDAL IN NEW DELHI 2001 AND
IS A REAL FAVOURITE FOR THE
COMMONWEALTH TITLE.

Al Bello, Shaun Botterill (Allsport)

ISLE OF MAN

CAPITAL: DOUGLAS
AREA: 572 sq km
POPULATION: 73,117
CURRENCY: MANX POUND
LANGUAGE: ENGLISH, MANX, GAELIC
PEOPLE/CULTURE: MANX (NORSE-CELTIC DESCENT) AND UK DESCENT

Standing in the isles

The Isle of Man is steeped in history. Farming was first introduced in the fourth millennium BC; the island then went on to experience the Manx Iron Age from 500 BC to 500 AD, the Celtic traditions, through to Christianity and Viking rule in the 9th Century. During this time, it formed part of the Norwegian Kingdom of the Hebrides, until it was ceded to Scotland in the 13th Century. However, this situation was tenuous and during the mid-13th to early 15th Centuries, sovereignty passed frequently between Scotland and England, with occasional incursions from Ireland.

By the 18th Century, it had become a major centre for the smuggling trade. To prevent this, the British government introduced a new law in 1765 – the Re-Vestment Act – and managed to purchase the Island for just £70,000. Since 1765, the Isle of Man has remained under the British Crown.

The Isle of Man will be represented by its biggest ever team of at least 31 sportsmen and women at the Commonwealth Games in Manchester. For the first time, they are entering a lawn bowls team, with Pauline Kelly and Maureen Payne in the women's pairs. The Isle of Man also has competitors in badminton, husband and wife team Steve and Cal Partington taking part in the race walking, a number of competitors in the shooting disciplines, such as Charlie Kennish and Steven Watterson, swimmers such as Alan Jones, Fane Harrop and S12 category disabled swimmer, Ian Sharpe. The island also has a strong cycling squad, including the experienced Rob Holden and multi-Island games medallist Andrew Roche, plus a competitive high jumper, in the shape of Island Games champion Martin Aram.

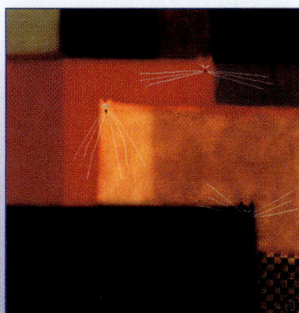

RINGTONES & LOGOS

Easy SMS ordering with just 1 text message

The ultimate in ringtone quality

Tune	UK Top Ten	SMS Order
H & Claire - Dj		tune dj
Pink - Don't Let Me Get Me		tune dontletmeg
Enrique Iglesias - Escape		tune escape
Nigal & Marvin - Follow Da Leader		tune followdale
Sugarbabes - Freak Like Me		tune freaklike
Ronan Keating - Tommorrow Never		tune iftommorrow
Milk Inc.- In My Eyes		tune immyeyes
Liberty X - Just A Little		tune justlittle
Puretone - Addicted to bass		tune kisskisss
S Club Juniors - One Step Closer		tune stepclose

Tune	SMS Order
Eminem - Without Me	tune withoutme
Jay-Z feat. U.G.K. - Big Pimpin'	tune bigpimpin
Brandy - What About Us	tune whatboutus
Vangelis - Chariots Of Fire	tune chariotsof
Theme from 'Beverly Hills Cop'	tune axelf
Linkin Park - In The End	tune intheend
Kylie Minogue - Out Of My Head	tune cantgetyou
Lasgo - Something	tune something
Shakira - Whenever Wherever	tune whenever
Nickleback - You remind me	tune thisishowy

Tune	SMS Order
Shaggy & Ali G - Me Julie	tune mejulie
Gareth Gates - Unchained Melody	tune unchainedm
William Young - Evergreen	tune evergreen
Ja Rule - Always On Time	tune alwaysonti
Enrique Inglesias - Hero	tune hero
Theme from Knight Rider	tune knightri
PPK - ResuRection	tune resurectio
Bubba Sparxxx - Ugly	tune ugly
Puretone - Addicted to bass	tune addictedto
Fat Joe - What's Luv?	tune whatsluv

Tune	SMS Order
Rank 1 - True Love Never Dies	tune truelove
Soft Cell - Tainted Love	tune taintedlov
Usher - You Remind Me	tune uremindme
Yakety Saxs (Benny Hill)	tune bennyhil
R Kelly - The World's Greatest	tune theworldsg
Theme from 'The Simpsons'	tune simpsons
Pink - Get The Party Started	tune getthepart
Daniel B - Gotta Get Thru This	tune gottagetth
Theme from Mission Impossible	tune mission
Theme from Only Fools & Horses	tune onlyfoolsa

Tune	SMS Order
Busta Rhymes - Break Ya Neck	tune breakyanec
Westlife - World Of Our Own	tune worldfour
Outkast - The Whole World	tune wholeworld
Theme from 'The Great Escape'	tune greatescap
Mis-Teeq - B With Me	tune bwithme
Bang! - Shooting Star	tune shootingst
Theme from 'Rocky'	tune rockytheme
Usher - U-Turn	tune uturn
Christina Milian - AM To PM	tune amtopm
So Solid Crew - 21 Seconds	tune 21seconds

Tune	SMS Order
P.O.D. - Alive	tune alivepod
Bad Religion - American Jesus	tune americanje
RHCP - Around The World	tune aroundthe
Cosmic Gate - Back To Earth	tune backtoeart
X-Press 2 - Lazy	tune lazy
Ram Jam - Black Betty	tune blackbetty
Treble Charger - Brand New Low	tune brandnewlo
Project Pat - Chickenheads	tune chickenhea
Scooter - Chinese Whispers	tune chinesewhi
The Offspring - Defy You	tune defyyou

Get one of our exclusive logos !

logo elvis2	logo winniethepooh	logo simplysexy
logo dragon	logo sg	logo england
logo angel	logo pacman2	logo 2lovebears
logo runawaydog	logo alig	logo owls
logo hallow14	logo toes	logo hearts
logo tigger	logo dancingpenguins	logo angry
logo candleeyes	logo indian	logo pooh4
logo nofear	logo worldcup	logo hearts6

JAMAICA

CAPITAL: KINGSTON
AREA: 10,991 sq km
POPULATION: 2.6 MILLION
CURRENCY: JAMAICAN DOLLAR
LANGUAGE: ENGLISH, JAMAICAN PATOIS
PEOPLE: AFRICAN DESCENT, AFRO-EUROPEAN, EUROPEAN, EAST INDIAN, MIDDLE EASTERN AND A MIXTURE OF CHINESE AND AFRO-CHINESE

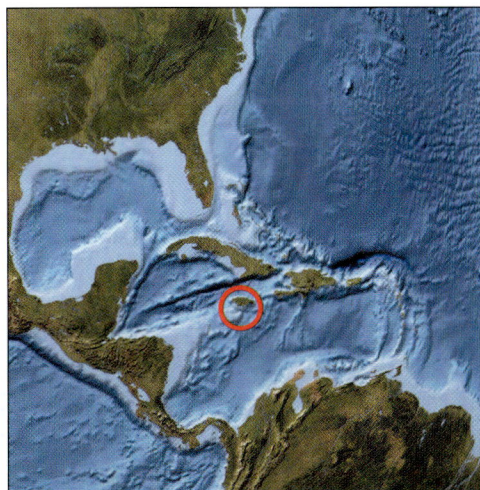

The fairest of them all

Christopher Columbus arrived in Jamaica in 1494. He described the island as "the fairest isle that eyes beheld". In the mid-17th Century, England took control of the island. Most of Jamaica's money came from sugar plantations, where slaves toiled in appalling conditions – slavery was finally abolished on 1 August 1834. Jamaica gained its independence from England in 1962 and post-independence politics were led by Alexander Bustamante of the Jamaica Labour Party, and Norman Manley of the People's National Party. Manley's son Michael led the PNP in the mid-1970s. The US government, hostile toward Manley's socialist direction and ties with Cuba, planned to topple the government. Overseas businesses pulled out and tourism suffered, leading to severe economic decline.

Jamaican culture is as varied as its people – even down to its language. Patois is a mixture of English peppered with African, Spanish and Portuguese terms. Although English is the national language, visitors to the island consider Jamaica bilingual because patois is spoken by most people. Music is everywhere on the island. From beach parties at the various hotels scattered across the island to house parties, clubs and "dancehall" street parties, Jamaica vibrates to the beat of reggae, calypso, soca and R&B. Earlier genres of music include ska and mento, a calypso type of folk mixed with Cuban influences.

Arawak, African, Spanish, British, Indian, Middle Eastern and Chinese food have their places in the island's cuisine. The national dish of ackee and saltfish is said to be addictive. The most popular delicacy is "jerk" – any type of meat or fish marinated in scorching hot spices and barbecued slowly in a pit over a fire of pimento wood.

FABULOUS FACTS

Jamaica's Blue Mountain coffee is considered one of the best in the world; 90 per cent is exported to Japan.

In 1988, Jamaica's bobsled team entered the Winter Olympics. The film *Cool Runnings* was based on this event.

During the 1930s and 1940s, Navy Island (off the coast of Port Antonio) was Errol Flynn's secret hideaway.

Jamaica hosts two of the biggest reggae festivals in the Caribbean: Reggae Sunsplash and Reggae SunFest.

The colours of the flag of Jamaica are black, green and gold – not red, green and gold, as many erroneously believe.

THE JAMAICAN NETBALL TEAM IS RANKED TOP TEN IN THE WORLD. ACCORDING TO MOLLY RHONE OF THE JAMAICAN NETBALL ASSOCIATION: "I AM EXPECTING THE TEAM TO DO WELL IN THE COMMONWEALTH GAMES AND I AM EXPECTING A MEDAL." TRACK & FIELD IS WHERE THE JAMAICAN ATHLETES EXCEL, WINNING MORE MEDALS PER CAPITA THEN ANY OTHER COUNTRY. OLYMPIC WOMEN'S 400M HURDLES RECORD HOLDER DEON HEMMINGS IS CERTAINLY FANCIED TO PICK UP GOLD. AS FOR THE MEN, GREGORY HAUGHTON LOOKS LIKE A GOOD TIP FOR A 400M MEDAL AFTER WINNING A BRONZE IN SYDNEY 2000.

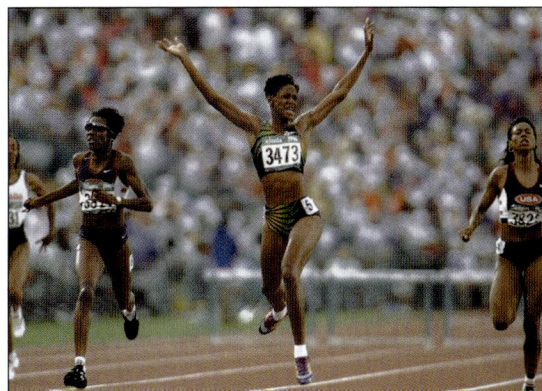

Scott Barbour, Mike Hewitt (Allsport)

Jersey an hour away...

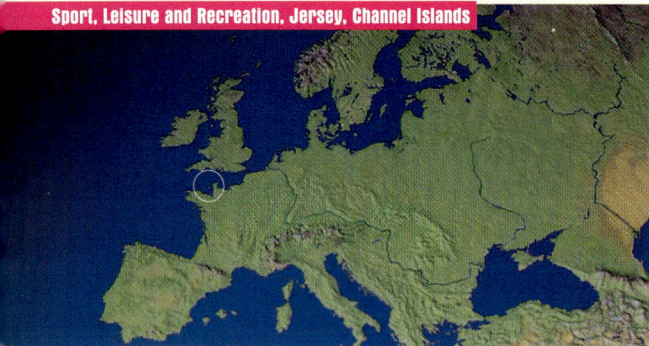

Jersey is less than an hour away from both the United Kingdom and mainland Europe. The Island's charming blend of British and French influences, breathtaking coastlines and country lanes create the perfect setting for sporting and corporate events. Presenting a fantastic portfolio of hotels and leisure facilities, Jersey offers exceptional choice for your event. The Island boasts 5 golf courses and water sports in abundanceas as well as many award winning restaurants from town bistros to clifftop brasseries, you will be spoilt for choice.

Sport, Leisure and Recreation have three main facilities in Jersey; Fort Regent Leisure Centre, Les Quennevais Sports Centre and Springfield Stadium. Together they offer the best sporting and fitness facilities in the Island.

...but a world apart

Fort Regent – dominating the St. Helier Skyline

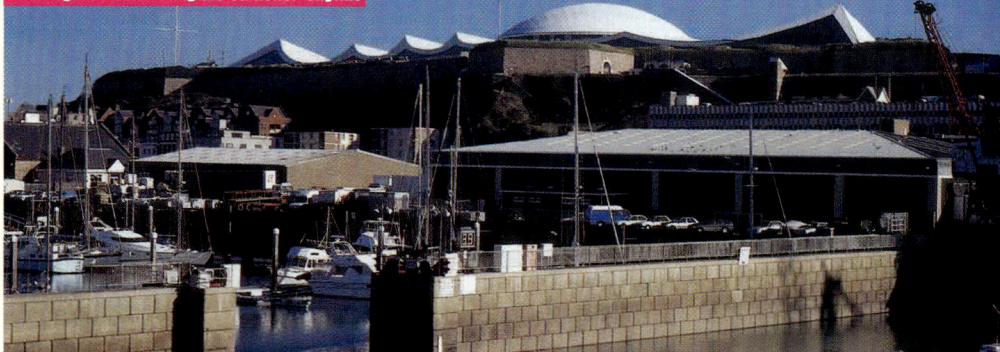

Fort Regent
Leisure Centre

Fort Regent is a truly unique venue, originally a napoleonic fortress dating from 1806, this multi-purpose leisure centre houses the Island's largest gymnasium, furnished with all the lastest equipment. The Fort also has two swimming pools and caters for a vast range of indoor sports and fitness classes, all supervised by highly qualified staff and instructors. The Fort operates creche facilities and hosts one of the largets childrens Soft Play Areas in Europe.

The Fort also incorporates two large conference, meeting rooms and a lecture theatre, allowing for a variety of functions such as concerts, conferences, trade shows and sporting events. The rampart areas situated around both halls give spectacular panoramic views of the Island.

Les Quennevais
Sports Centre

Les Quennevais Sports Centre is in the north of the Island and has just completed an extension to their already well equipped gym as well as a new dance studio. The Centre is bright and modern and offers more than 25 fitness classes every week.

Les Quennevais has a main pool and a childrens pool and is ideal for a strenuous workout or a day of family fun.

Springfield
Stadium

Springfield Stadium is Jersey's premier football venue with grandstand seating for 960 and a totaal capacity of 7,000. The large concourse area has a cafeteria and a bar.

Springfield also has a large multi purpose sports hall and also has seminar and meeting rooms.

Largest Gymnasium in Jersey

Fitness Classes

International size pool

The latest Gym Equipment

Springfield Stadium

- weights & fitness
- swimming
- badminton
- table tennis
- squash
- aerobics
- aquaerobics
- indoor bowling
- basketball
- volleyball
- netball
- racketball
- softball
- short tennis
- cricket
- hockey
- yoga
- five-a-side football
- circuit training
- toddlers gym
- gymnastics
- roller skating
- trampolining
- martial arts
- archery
- shooting
- fencing
- snooker
- bars & cafes
- conference facilities
- concert halls
- football stadium

Sport Leisure and Recreation
J E R S E Y

Sporting event enquiries please contact Derek de la Haye on Tel. 01534 500004 Fax. 01534 500225 e-mail d.delahaye1@gov.je.

www.slr-online.com

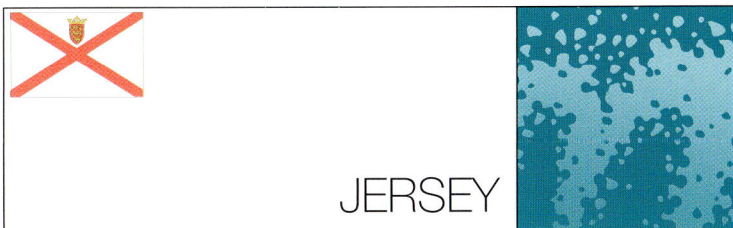

JERSEY

CAPITAL: ST HELIER

AREA: 14.5km X 8km

POPULATION: 87,000

CURRENCY: POUND

LANGUAGE: ENGLISH, FRENCH, NORMAN-FRENCH IS SPOKEN IN COUNTRY REGIONS

THE PEOPLE: PEOPLE ARE OF UNITED KINGDOM AND NORMAN-FRENCH DESCENT

An island like no other

Jersey is a small island in the England Channel. It is a mixture of English and French cultures, as a consequence of its history as well as its geographical location. During the 9th Century, Viking pirates from the north came to the Channel Islands to plunder while en route to and from the coasts of England and France. In the treaty of 911 AD, the French King, Charles the Simple, realised that the only way to stop the pirate chief Rollo from terrorising his subjects was to make a bargain with him. Rollo agreed to keep the peace in exchange for the area around Rouen, known as Normandy today. Rollo's son, William, incorporated the Channel Islands into the duchy when he became Duke of Normandy, so from 933-1204 AD, Jersey was ruled from Normandy.

St Helier, after whom the capital is named, was from Belgium and he came to Jersey in about 540 AD. It is said his original name was Helibert, but when he was cured of paralysis at the age of seven by a Christian missionary, he was given the name Helier (which means pity, because God had taken pity on him).

William the Conqueror and his descendants, who were also Kings of England, ruled Jersey until war broke out in the 13th Century. King John lost all his French possessions and in 1204, the islanders elected to give their allegiance to England, breaking their ties to France.

Despite being demilitarised by Sir Winston Churchill, Jersey was invaded by Germany in 1940 and was occupied for five years. German occupation ended on Liberation Day, 9 May 1945, which is a public holiday. A thanksgiving service is held on every anniversary of Liberation Day in the Royal Square, where the news was first announced.

FIVE FABULOUS FACTS

Jersey has given its name to a kind of jumper, a breed of cattle, a potato, a state in the US and the beautiful Jersey lily.

In the 16th and 17th Centuries, people who rebelled against Calvinism in Jersey were called witches and burnt alive.

Jersey's court of justice hears criminal and civil cases that are too serious to be dealt with by the magistrate's court.

Jersey's internal affairs are not administered by Westminster – only large issues are handled by the Queen and Privy Council.

Dolphin species have been observed around Jersey, including the Common Dolphin and White-Beaked Dolphin.

JERSEY'S ATHLETES ARE MOSTLY KNOWN IN THE SPORTS OF SHOOTING AND LAWN BOWLS. IN THE 1990 COMMONWEALTH GAMES IN NEW ZEALAND, COLIN MALLETT WAS THE MEN'S FULL BORE RIFLE SHOOTING CHAMPION. IN 1998, IN KUALA LUMPUR, DAVID LE MARQUAND BEAT NEAL MOLLET OF GUERNSEY IN THE MEN'S SINGLES IN LAWN BOWLS. THE JERSEY GAMES TEAM HAS BEEN PRACTISING HARD IN THE HOPES OF BRINGING HOME A MEDAL. IN PRACTICE MATCHES HELD IN THE RUN UP TO THE GAMES IN MANCHESTER, DEREK BOSWELL, A MEMBER OF THE TEAM, BEAT THE CURRENT BRITISH CHAMPION.

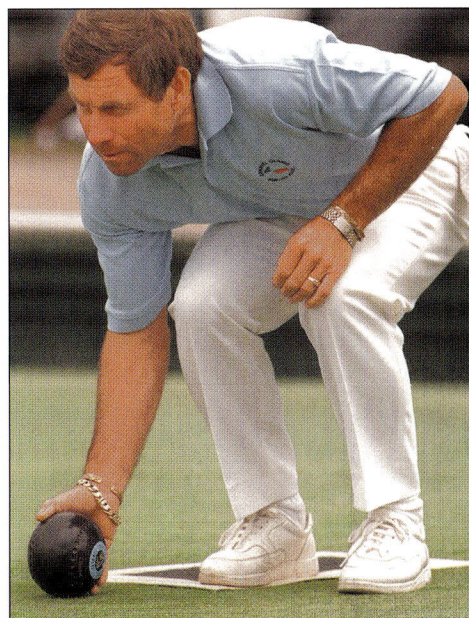

Tony Pike

KENYA

CAPITAL: NAIROBI
AREA: 583,000 sq km
POPULATION: 29.2 MILLION
CURRENCY: KENYAN SHILLING
LANGUAGE: ENGLISH, KISWAHILI AND OTHER MAJOR
TRIBAL LANGUAGES
THE PEOPLE/CULTURE: AFRICAN, ASIAN, ARABIC AND EUROPEAN

Kenya feel it?

As a consequence of the Leakey family's discoveries of several hominid skulls in Kenya, the Rift Valley, which runs through the country, has been established as the "cradle of humanity". The first set of people were the nomadic Cushitic-speaking people from Ethiopia, around 2000 BC. The rest of Kenya's various tribes date from 500 BC to 500 AD. From the 8th Century, Muslims and Shirazis began to visit the East African coast. The Portuguese arrived sometime in the late 15th Century and Kenya was under colonial rule for the next 200 years. By the middle of the 19th-century, Europeans were showing interest in Kenya.

Kenya achieved independence on 12 December 1963. Jomo Kenyatta of the Kenya Africa National Union was President until 1978 and, under his rule, Kenya became one of Africa's most prosperous and stable countries. Kenya's main industry is agriculture, exporting tea, coffee and tobacco, among other products. Kenya's capital Nairobi is a lively, cosmopolitan city with a population of around 1.5 million. It is now the largest city between Cairo and Johannesburg, but it was a swampy watering hole until the late 19th Century. Nairobi National Park is only a few kilometres from the city centre; it is the oldest park in the country (it was created in 1946). Leopard, cheetah, gazelle, onyx, lion, zebra, giraffe and buffalo are all seen regularly in the park, with Jomo Kenyatta International Airport serving as an incongruous backdrop. Although safaris offer amazing views of Kenya, they also cause major environmental problems. A recent survey found that each of the camps around the Masai Mara uses about 100 tonnes of firewood per year.

Benga is the modern dance music of Kenya today, which originated from the Luo people of Western Kenya. Nyama Choma, barbecued goat's meat, served with plantain, is the country's most popular dish.

FABULOUS FACTS

One of Kenya's best geological features is the Great Rift Valley, which extends nearly 5,000km down to Mozambique.

The equator divides Kenya into hot and dry zones in the north and humid, temperate and tropical zones in the south.

The Masai live in huts built by the women of the village. They are made of branches, grass, cow dung and urine.

In July and August, Kenya's most spectacular annual event is the migration of millions of wildebeest.

Mombasa is the largest port on the East African coast, with a history that dates back to the 12th Century.

SINCE THE 1960S, KENYA HAS PRODUCED MORE WORLD CLASS ATHLETES, MORE OLYMPIC MEDALLISTS AND MORE WORLD RECORD HOLDERS IN LONG DISTANCE RUNNING THAN ANY OTHER COUNTRY. IN THE 1996 OLYMPICS, KENYA TOOK HOME BRONZE MEDALS IN THE 800M AND THE 1,500M, SILVER IN THE 5,000M AND 10,000M, AND ANOTHER SILVER IN THE MARATHON. WITH RUNNERS LIKE NOAH NGENY AND RUEBEN KOSGEI, WHO WON TWO GOLD MEDALS IN THE 2000 OLYMPICS IN SYDNEY, KENYA WILL UNDOUBTEDLY BE ONE OF THE COUNTRIES TO WATCH OUT FOR IN THE MEDALS RACE.

Nick Wilson (Allsport)

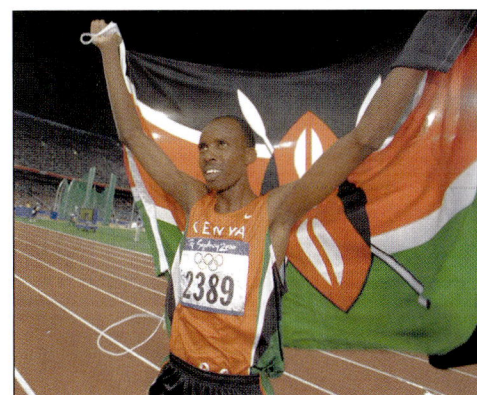

IN BOXING, KENYA'S NATIONAL TEAM HAS BEEN GIVEN
THE DAUNTING MONIKER OF THE "HIT SQUAD". KENYA HAS
PARTICIPATED IN FIVE OLYMPIC BOXING EVENTS AND WON A
TOTAL OF SEVEN GOLD MEDALS. BOXER EVANS OURE IS THE
REIGNING WORLD BOXING ORGANISATION MIDDLEWEIGHT
CHAMPION, WINNING HIS TITLE IN JUNE 2001 IN DENMARK.
TABLE TENNIS PLAYERS VICTOR OUKO AND PARIT SHAH ARE
ALSO EXPECTED TO BE ON TOP FORM AT THE GAMES THIS
YEAR. OUKO WAS THE OVERALL WINNER AT THE NATIONAL
TRIALS, FOLLOWED BY SHAH FROM MOMBASA (HE HAS
LOST ONLY A SINGLE MATCH TO OUKO).

Jed Jacobsohn, Hamish Blair, Michael Steele, Andy Lyons (Allsport)

KIRIBATI

CAPITAL: TARAWA
AREA: 810 sq km
POPULATION: 87,000
CURRENCY: AUSTRALIAN DOLLAR
LANGUAGE: ENGLISH, GILBERTESE
THE PEOPLE/CULTURE: MICRONESIAN, TUVALUAN MINORITY

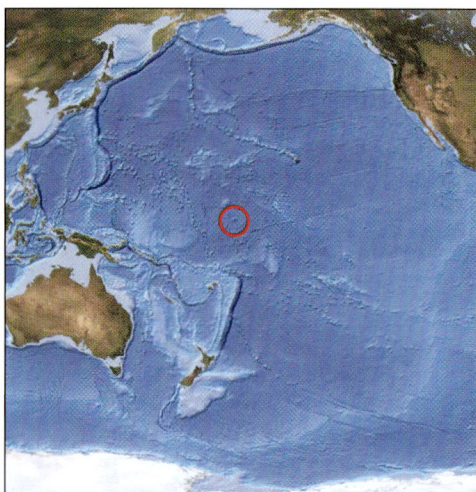

Idyllic islands

The Republic of Kiribati, located in the Pacific, comprises three groups of islands: the Gilbert, Line and Phoenix Islands. The capital, Tarawa, is not one single town but a group of islands linked by a causeway and inter-island boats. Spanish explorer de Quiros came to Butaritari in 1606, yet evidence shows that indigenous people were on the island 2,000 years earlier. Fijians and Tongans arrived in the 14th Century.

In the 1850s, missionaries arrived on the islands and the Reverend Hiram Bingham, an American, was the first missionary to live in Kiribati. By 1892, Britain claimed the group of islands as a protectorate and annexed Banaba in 1900. Other islands, including Kiritimati, Tabuaeran and Teraina became a part of the group later in the century. Islanders were given an "advisory" role in their own government and were finally granted full independence on 12 July 1979.

The people of Kiribati are very religious; there are reported to be about 40,000 Roman Catholics and about 28,000 Protestants. However, traditional customs and beliefs still survive – the power of magic and the existence of ghosts are widely accepted.

Three athletes participated in the Commonwealth Games in Kuala Lumpur in 1998. Unfortunately, none took home a medal. At the time of writing, it was unclear whether a larger contingent would be sent to Manchester.

LESOTHO

CAPITAL: MASERU
AREA: 30,355 sq km
POPULATION: 2.1 MILLION
CURRENCY: LOTI
LANGUAGE: SESOTHO, ENGLISH
THE PEOPLE/CULTURE: BASOTHO, NGUNI, SAN, GRIQUA AND OTHER GROUPS

The kingdom in the sky

The Khoisan people were the original inhabitants of Lesotho (originally Basutholand). Europeans arrived in the early 19th Century and in 1868, the British government annexed Basutholand. After being defeated by the Boers, the British signed control over to the Cape Colony in 1871. Yet another war in 1880 saw the land again shuttled back to British control. In 1910, the Basutholand National Congress was established and by the 1950s, it was requesting self-governance. The Basutholand National Party won the 1960 elections and demanded independence from Britain, which it gained in 1966, becoming the new Kingdom of Lesotho. Moshoeshoe II was crowned king and Chief Leabua Jonathan was named Prime Minister.

Lesotho is surrounded by South Africa and is known as the "kingdom in the sky" because the entire country is more than 1,000m above sea level. When people in Lesotho greet each other they often ask, "How do you live?" or "How did you get up?" The usual answer is, "I live well" or "I got up well".

Lesotho has had recent success in the Commonwealth Games. Thabiso Moqhali picked up a gold medal in the marathon in Kuala Lumpur in 1998. He followed this up with a win in the Belgrade Stark Marathon. In second place was fellow countryman Persy Sephooa. Welterweight Mosolesa Tsie and light flyweight S'busiso Ketetsi are well known boxers from Lesotho.

MALAWI

CAPITAL: **LILONGWE**
AREA: 118,484 sq km
POPULATION: 11.1 MILLION
CURRENCY: MALAWI KWACHA
LANGUAGE: ENGLISH, CHICHEWA
THE PEOPLE/CULTURE: CHEWA, NYANJA, TUMBUKO, YAO, LOMWE, SENA, TONGA, NGONI, NGONDE, ASIAN, EUROPEAN

A land with heart

Malawi is a country landlocked by Zambia, Tanzania and Mozambique. Between the 14th and 18th Centuries, the Bantu tribes migrated to Malawi. The Yao invaded southern Malawi, killing or capturing the inhabitants and selling them into slavery. Simultaneously, Zulus settled in central and northern Malawi, and became known as the Angoni or Ngoni. In the mid-19th Century, explorer David Livingstone encouraged missionaries to come to Central Africa to spread the holy word and try to suppress the slave trade.

In the 1950s, the Nyasaland African Congress was formed, led by Hastings Banda. Malawi became independent in July 1964 and Banda was made president in 1966 when Malawi became a republic. Banda declared himself president for life when opposition threatened to topple him from power. Under Banda's rule, several books were banned – including medical textbooks – for being indecent. The 1990s brought extreme opposition to his president-for-life rule and, in 1992, Catholic bishops called for a change. In 1993, a multi-party political system was introduced.

Malawi is dubbed the "warm heart of Africa" because of the beauty of the country and the warmth and friendliness of its people. It has a large number of protected wildlife areas, though poaching was rife in the 1980s and early 1990s.

Major industries include tobacco, tea, cassava, sorghum, goat farming and cement. The country's main trading partners are the UK, USA, South Africa, Germany, Japan and Zimbabwe.

Dance and music are important in Malawian tradition and social functions. Most tribes have their own dances and music. The Chewa tribe's Gule Wamkulu is the most notable traditional dance in Malawi.

FABULOUS FACTS

Lake Malawi, which is the third largest lake in Africa, takes up an astonishing 20 per cent of Malawi's total area.

Malawi is well known for its fish. Lake Malawi has 500 species, more than any other inland body of water in the world.

There are Muslims in north Malawi, however the majority of the citizens are Christians.

Settlements of humans dating back 100,000 years have been found on the shores of Lake Malawi.

Tobacco is a major export for Malawi. A sign on the wall of the main tobacco auction hall reads, "Thank you for smoking".

MALAWI'S SWIMMING TEAM HAS BEEN WORKING VERY HARD FOR THESE COMMONWEALTH GAMES, INCLUDING A WEEK'S TRAINING CAMP AT A RESORT IN MANGOCHI. THE COACH SAID THAT SHE WANTED THE SWIMMERS TO STEP UP THEIR TRAINING TO A NEW LEVEL, SO THEY WILL BE ABLE TO PERFORM AT THEIR VERY BEST. IT WAS REPORTED THAT THE TEAM WAS FULL OF NEW DETERMINATION AND ENTHUSIASM. AS WELL AS ATHLETICS, EXPECT TO SEE THE MALAWI NATIONAL NETBALL TEAM IN ACTION. THE TEAM DID WELL IN THE SOUTHERN AFRICA NETBALL ASSOCIATION TOURNAMENT.

Scott Barbour (Allsport)

MALAYSIA

CAPITAL: KUALA LUMPUR
AREA: 329,750 sq km
POPULATION: 22 MILLION
CURRENCY: MALAYSIAN RINGGIT
LANGUAGE: BAHASA MALAYSIA, ENGLISH, CHINESE DIALECTS, TAMIL AND INDIGENOUS DIALECTS
THE PEOPLE/CULTURE: MALAY, CHINESE, INDIAN, PLUS INDIGENOUS TRIBES SUCH AS ORANG ASLI AND IBAN

Getting there first

Orang Asli ("original people") is the name given to the first people to settle on the Malay peninsula, 10,000 years ago. The Cambodian-based Funan, the Sumatra-based Srivijaya and the Java-based Majapahit empires ruled the peninsula until the Chinese arrived in Melaka in 1405. The introduction of Islam came about in Melaka at about the same time. The Portuguese arrived and took over Melaka in 1795, having established a port in Penang in 1786.

Malaya was occupied by the Japanese during WWII. Communist guerrillas initiated an armed struggle against British rule in 1948. Malaysia eventually achieved independence in 1957. Sarawak, Saba and Singapore combined with Malaya to form the Federation of Malaysia in 1963. However, two years later, Singapore withdrew from the confederation. Indonesia and the Philippines each had territorial claims on East Malaysia. Riots broke out between Malays and Chinese in 1969.

Prime minister Dr Mahathir Mohamad led Malaysia from 1981 to 1997. In 1998, Malaysia hosted the 16th Commonwealth Games. During that time, students and citizens protested the unfair firing and imprisonment of deputy prime minister, Anwar Ibrahim.

Malaysia has a strong tradition of dance. Music is based mainly around the gendang (drum). Other artistic forms include silat (a stylised martial art) and shadow puppets. Malaysia is also famous for beautiful batik.

Kuala Lumpur is Malaysia's largest city. The city's most impressive buildings are the twin Petronas Towers, built in 1996. The towers are constructed of stainless steel and glass, with a bridge linking them at the 44th floor – as immortalised in the film *Entrapment,* starring Sean Connery and Catherine Zeta-Jones.

FABULOUS FACTS

The major festival in Malaysia is called Hari Raya Puasa and it marks the end of Ramadan.

The Malaysian jungle is 120 million years old. There are 8,000 species of flowering plants in Peninsular Malaysia alone.

Georgetown, the capital of Penang, was named after George IV, as the island was acquired on his birthday.

The elusive, nocturnal tapir sports hoofed feet and a trunk-like snout. It is one of Malaysia's strangest animals.

Wayang Kulit is the musical shadow puppet theatre that originated in Indonesia and continues to this day.

THE MALAYSIANS ARE STRONG IN THE HOCKEY ARENA. SUHAIMI IBRAHIM WAS THE YOUNGEST MALAYSIAN HOCKEY PLAYER AT THE KUALA LUMPUR COMPETITION, AT JUST 18 YEARS OF AGE. IBRAHIM ALREADY HAS A SILVER MEDAL FROM THE LAST COMMONWEALTH GAMES AND HE'LL DEFINITELY BE AIMING FOR A GOLD IN MANCHESTER THIS YEAR. WITH THE MALAYSIAN CAPTAIN, MIRNAWAN MAWAWI – KNOWN AS "THE DRIBBLE KING" – AND IBRAHIM ON THE SAME TEAM, MALAYSIA LOOKS LIKE A STRONG CONTENDER FOR A HOCKEY MEDAL IN MANCHESTER 2002.

Stanley Chou (Getty Images)

IN DECEMBER 2001, THE MALAYSIAN WOMEN'S HOCKEY TEAM WAS IN DISPUTE OVER WHETHER TO TAKE PART IN THIS YEAR'S GAMES, AS THE TEAM DID NOT ACTUALLY QUALIFY AND WAS A REPLACEMENT FOR JAMAICA, WHO WITHDREW. THE TEAM HAS SINCE DECIDED TO PARTICIPATE AND IT IS GROUPED ALONGSIDE DEFENDING CHAMPIONS AUSTRALIA, SCOTLAND AND SOUTH AFRICA.
BOXERS SUCH AS ZAMZAI AZIZI MOHAMAD, ADNAN YUSOH, ZAINUDIN SIDI, SUHAIRI HUSSAIN AND RAKIB AHMED ARE TRAINING HARD FOR MANCHESTER, KEEN TO REPEAT THEIR SUCCESSES AT THE SEA GAMES LAST YEAR.

Stanley Chou (Getty Images)

CAPITAL: MALE
AREA: 185 sq km
POPULATION: 310,000
CURRENCY: RUFIYAA
LANGUAGE: DHIVEHI
THE PEOPLE/CULTURE: SINHALESE, DRAVIDIAN, ARAB, AFRICAN

MALDIVES

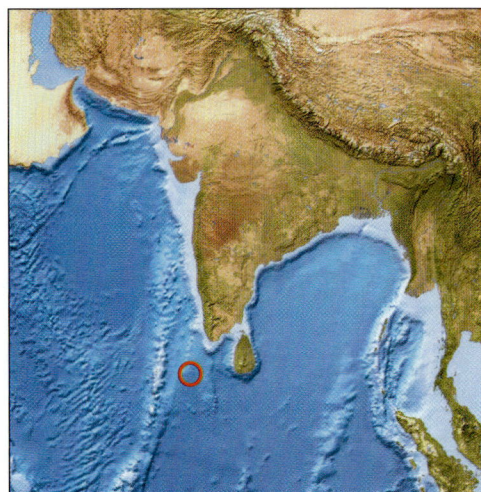

The last paradise on Earth

A popular tourist destination, the Maldives consists of 1,190 coral islands, which form an archipelago of 26 major atolls. Only 200 islands are inhabited. Tourism is the main industry, contributing almost 20 per cent of the GDP. The first inhabitants probably arrived in the archipelago from Sri Lanka and southern India before 500 BC. In 1153 AD, the islanders converted to Islam. The Maldivian king at the time was sold on Islam and Abu Al Barakat, a visiting North African Arab, later became the first sultan. In the 17th Century, the Maldives came under the protection of the Dutch and in 1887, it became a British protectorate administered from Ceylon (now Sri Lanka). In 1965, the Maldives achieved independence as a sultanate and in 1968 the people voted to establish a second republic.

Maldivians are very keen on sports, football being the most popular. Two athletes were sent to last year's World Athletics Championships. Naseer Ismail ran the 800m and his fellow Maldivian Shamaa Ahamed ran the women's 100m – they both competed in the Sydney Olympics two years ago.

You may also recall the swimmer Fariha Fathimath, who made history as the youngest competitor in the Sydney Olympics in 2000. Aged 13 at the time, she broke the national record (34.06 seconds) for 50m freestyle, which she did in 32.36 seconds. Although she was seven seconds slower than the Olympic record, this was no mean feat when you consider that she stood around a foot shorter than her rivals and weighs only 86 pounds. You may spot Fariha Fathimath, Naseer Ismail or Shamaa Ahamed on the streets of Knutsford come July, as Knutsford Council has offered its hospitality to the Maldivian team as part of the Games' "Adopt a Nation" programme.

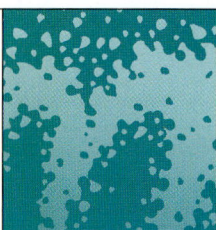

CAPITAL: VALLETTA
AREA: 200 sq km
POPULATION: 383,285
CURRENCY: MALTESE LIRA
LANGUAGE: MALTESE ENGLISH
THE PEOPLE/CULTURE: MALTESE, BRITISH, SICILIAN, FRENCH, SPANISH AND ITALIAN

MALTA

Maltese falcons

Malta gained independence from Britain on 21 September 1964 and a constitutional republic was established. The head of government is the Prime Minister (currently Eddie Fenech Adami), who is appointed by the President from the members of parliament.

Thanks to its position halfway between Gibraltar to the west and Alexandria to the east, and between Sicily and Tunisia, Malta has always attracted both invaders and traders to its shores. The island's oldest legacy is the megalithic temples that date from as far back as 3800 BC.

Normans, Ottomans, the Order of St John and the British have all ruled here, while today, Malta Freeport considers itself one of the Mediterranean's largest container ports. It's not surprising that 90 per cent of the population lives in its many walled-cities – they offered protection from enemy forces in the past and people have now settled in them to work as traders.

Sport is very important to Malta. It is a leading light in the Games for the Small States of Europe: the island played host in 1993 and is due to do so again in 2003. Last year saw great success in the San Marino Games; in particular the women's judo and athletics outfits, which both took home a brace of gold medals. Names to look out for include Laurie Pace and Natalie Galea, both of whom will be taking part in the judo. Perhaps they can translate last year's successes in the San Marino Games to Manchester this summer and then to even greater heights on their home soil for the Small States Games in 2003.

RUSSIAN PILOT
NASA TECHNOLOGY
NO LIFT-OFF

X-static
THE SILVER FIBER

SHOCK ABSORBER

COOL
YOURSELF TOGETHER

TWININGS
Iced Tea
Peach
Best Served Chilled

Cool yourself together with a harmonious blend of refreshing fruit juice, purified water and ice cool Twinings Tea

There's more to tea with **TWININGS**

MAURITIUS

CAPITAL: PORT LOUIS
AREA: 1268 sq km
POPULATION: 1,196,000
CURRENCY: MAURITIAN RUPEE
LANGUAGE: ENGLISH
THE PEOPLE/CULTURE: INDIAN MAURITIAN, CREOLE, CHINESE MAURITIAN, FRENCH MAURITIAN

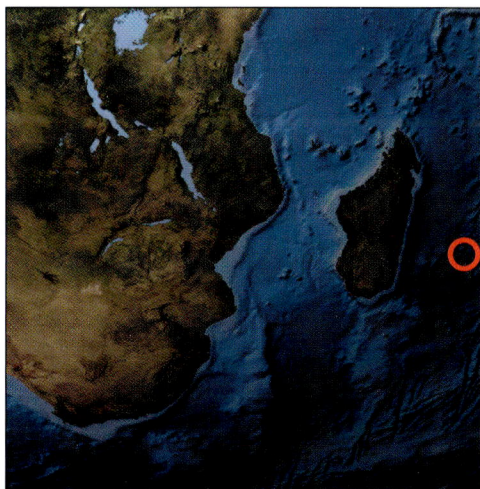

Moreish Mauritius

An island to the east of Madagascar, Mauritius' prime resource was for a long time sugar. However, in 1979, Cyclone Claudette virtually wiped out the sugar industry and, since then, Mauritius has diversified its agriculture to include staples such as maize and potatoes, while the fishing industry has also grown. Tourism is another significant contributor to GNP.

Mauritius gained independence from Britain on 12 March 1968 and Sir Seewoosager Ramgoolam became the nation's first Prime Minister. In 1992, the country became a republic, although it remains in the Commonwealth. The country has practically no army and has been politically stable since independence. Most governments have been coalitions. The 1991 elections returned Anerood Jugnauth to power, who first became Prime Minister in 1982. The Mauritian Social Democratic Party is governing the island at the moment.

The Mauritian team returned home from the 1998 Kuala Lumpur Games with one gold, one silver and one bronze medal. It was the first year that Mauritius achieved Commonwealth glory (it first sent a team to the Games in 1970), the boxing team winning all the medals. Now Mauritius is also establishing itself on the world stage of athletics – two to watch are Stephane Buckland and Eric Milazar. Both men put up their best performances at the World Championships in Edmonton last year – Buckland came sixth in the 200m and Milazar was fifth in the 400m. There are big hopes that they both make the podium in Manchester.

Their success has led to offers from other countries, offering them better training facilities and the opportunity to run under a different flag. Whoever Milazar and Buckland run for, Mauritians are sure to bask in some of that glory, too.

MONTSERRAT

CAPITAL: PLYMOUTH
AREA: 63 sq km
POPULATION: 5,000
CURRENCY: EAST CARIBBEAN DOLLAR
LANGUAGE: ENGLISH
THE PEOPLE/CULTURE: AFRICAN AND EUROPEAN ORIGIN

Jewel in the Caribbean crown

Montserrat is an overseas territory of the UK. A lush green and mountainous island, it lies in the Eastern Caribbean chain of islands, south west of Antigua. It is situated near the islands of Redonda, Nevis and St Kitts to the north and west, while Guadeloupe to the south can be seen from various points on the island. Known fondly as the Emerald Isle of the Caribbean, this pearl-shaped island rises in a series of dramatic mountain slopes to a high point of over 900m. The lushness of the island contributes to a rich and varied agriculture – its hot peppers and live plants are a popular export – and also to its attractiveness as a tourist destination.

However, Montserrat has been in the news for the wrong reasons over the last few years. Major volcanic activity, which started in 1995, has left the southern half of the island uninhabitable and it is now illegal to venture into the area. Even though half of the land is now uninhabited, the volcanic activity has actually increased the island's total surface area and the islanders never fail to jokingly refer to Montserrat's expanded size. Indeed, the most drastic effect on Montserrat has been the estimated halving of the island's population – from around 12,000 in the 1991 Census to current estimates of 5,000.

Competitive sports have naturally become less of a priority as the islanders seek to rebuild their lives on the remaining habitable parts of the island or on the neighbouring islands, which have generously extended sanctuary to those driven away by the explosive tendencies of the volcano. The audience in Manchester is sure to give the athletes who do make it the warmest of welcomes and support.

MOZAMBIQUE

CAPITAL: MAPUTO
AREA: 496,711 sq km
POPULATION: 19.6M
CURRENCY: METICAL
LANGUAGE: PORTUGUESE
THE PEOPLE/CULTURE: MOZAMBIQUE HAS 16 MAJOR ETHNIC GROUPS – THE MOST SIGNIFICANT ARE THE MAKUA AND MAKONDE IN THE NORTH, THE SENA IN THE CENTRE AND THE SHANAGAAN, WHO DOMINATE THE SOUTH

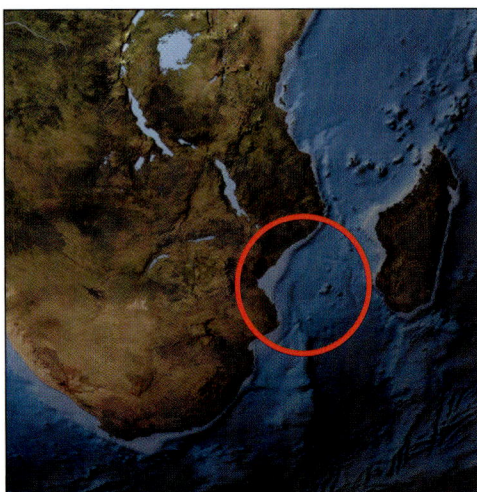

Magical Mozambique

Lying on the African coast between South Africa and India, Mozambique has always held a natural attraction for traders. Late in the first millennium, the Bantus (who had settled there) developed trading links to the rest of Africa, the Middle East and India.

The Portuguese explorer, Vasco da Gama came upon this vibrant trading area in 1498. Trading first in gold and ivory – and latterly in slaves – the Portuguese slowly moved inland, colonising Mozambique. Mozambicans were exploited during the rule, from 1932 to 1968, of Portugal's fascist ruler, Antonio Salazar. He introduced the cultivation of cotton and rice, insisting that all males over the age of 15 work on plantations. Famine and very limited access to education and healthcare – except for the colonists – led to peaceful demonstrations for proper representation. The Portuguese responded with force; one protest in 1960 ended with 600 people dead. In 1962, the Mozambique Liberation Front, Frelimo, was formed to free the country from Portuguese rule. The war lasted more than ten years and the independent Republic of Mozambique was proclaimed on 25 June 1975 – but even greater troubles lay ahead.

The Portuguese pulled out virtually overnight. Chaos ensued – the country lacked skilled professionals and an infrastructure, capital fled the country and the economy collapsed. Frelimo, now the governing party, turned to the Soviet Bloc for assistance. This antagonised relations with Zimbabwe and South Africa, which in turn sponsored a rebel force, Renamo, to overturn the new government – the result was 16 years of civil war. In the late 1980s, Mozambique gradually opened up to western assistance and peace was established between Frelimo and Renamo in 1992. Free and fair elections in 1994 saw Frelimo's Joaquim Chissano appointed as President.

FABULOUS FACTS

Mozambique is one of the newest members of the Commonwealth, having only joined in November 1994.

Two of Southern Africa's largest rivers flow through Mozambique, the Zambezi and the Limpopo.

A journalist once took refuge in Mabuto after covering the Boer War in South Africa – his name was Winston Churchill.

Mozambique's worst floods occurred in spring 2000, causing most damage in the Limpopo River valley.

Cashew nuts are a key crop in Mozambique. Settlers planted trees; they ended up growing wild along the coast.

MOZAMBIQUE WILL BE EXPECTING A REPEAT PERFORMANCE FROM MARIA (LURDES) MUTOLA, WHO WON THE WOMEN'S 800M GOLD IN KUALA LUMPUR. HER COMPATRIOT TINA PAULINO TOOK THE SILVER. THESE ARE THE ONLY TWO MEDALS WON BY MOZAMBIQUE IN ITS SHORT HISTORY OF PARTICIPATION IN THE COMMONWEALTH GAMES. MUTOLA WENT ON TO EVEN GREATER HEIGHTS, WINNING OLYMPIC GOLD IN THE WOMEN'S 800M IN SYDNEY AND LAST YEAR TAKING THE 800M TITLE IN THE WORLD CHAMPIONSHIPS IN EDMONTON. SHE WILL FACE TOUGH COMPETITION IN THE SHAPE OF GREAT BRITAIN'S KELLY HOLMES, WHO LOST TO MUTOLA IN BOTH KUALA LUMPUR AND SYDNEY.

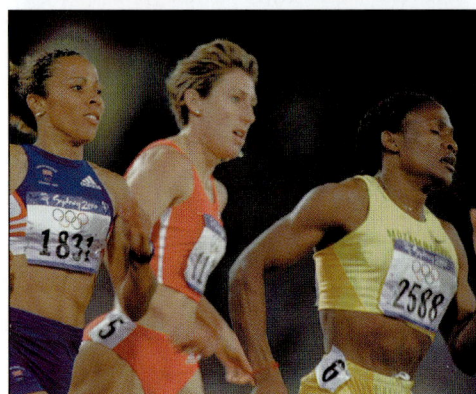

Ezra Shaw, Clive Brunskill (Allsport)

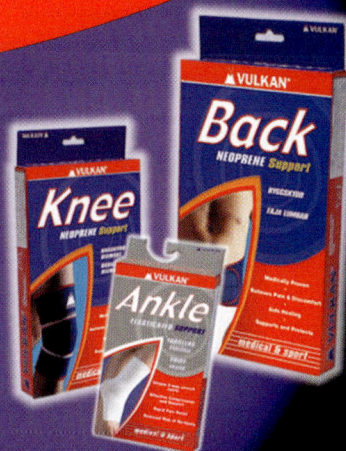

NAMIBIA

CAPITAL: WINDHOEK
AREA: 512,177 sq km
POPULATION: 1.67 MILLION
CURRENCY: NAMIBIAN DOLLAR
LANGUAGE: ENGLISH, GERMAN AND AFRIKAANS
THE PEOPLE/CULTURE: APPROXIMATELY 86 PER CENT OF THE POPULATION BELONG TO ABOUT 11 TRIBES. THESE INCLUDE THE OVAMBO AND THE KAVANGO GROUPS. OTHERS INCLUDE THE HERERO, DAMARA, NAMA, CAPRIVIAN, BUSHMEN, BASTER AND TSWANA

Namibia now

Namibia, situated on the South West coast of Africa between Angola and South Africa, was initially ignored by European explorers as they sought to establish and control territories in Africa and beyond. This changed in the late 19th Century, when the major European powers scrambled for colonial domination in Africa and the Germans took control from the indigenous tribes. Two of these tribes – the Nama and Herero – rebelled in 1908, but were put down by the Germans at the cost of 100,000 lives. The Germans were displaced by South Africa in World War I, which then gained a League of Nations mandate to administer the territory. Namibian history, from the foundation of the United Nations in 1945 to Namibian independence in 1991, was dominated by the repeated refusal of the South African government to convert its League of Nations mandate to administer the country into a UN trusteeship, or even to recognise that the UN had a legitimate interest in the region. South Africa also appropriated the best farming land into 6,000 lots, for whites only.

Efforts to introduce democracy to Namibia bore fruit in 1998, as both South Africa and Cuba agreed to withdraw troops from neighbouring Angola – a key nation in the proxy "Cold War" in Africa, which South Africa used to justify its presence in Namibia. In 1989, elections were held and SWAPO – South West Africa People's Organisation – swept to power. SWAPO's leader, Sam Nujomo, took office as the first President of Namibia in 1991 and he has been re-elected twice since, in 1994 and 1999.

The President has executive authority, while legislative authority is vested in the National Assembly, a body made up of 72 elected members and up to six appointed representatives, and the National Council, made up of two representatives from each of Namibia's 13 regional councils. There is also an independent judiciary.

FABULOUS FACTS

Southern Africa's earliest inhabitants – a nomadic tribe of hunters called the San – were the original settlers in Namibia.

Africa's earliest pottery was found in Namibia, the work of the Khoi-Khoi, who supplanted the San in Naimibia.

The Namib Desert, the world's oldest arid region, has been in existence for more than 80 million years.

In Namibia, you'll find seals on the coast, flamingoes in the north and elephants, zebras and giraffes in the desert.

The Germans influenced Namibian architecture and cuisine – the boerewors is a popular "farmers' sausage".

NAMIBIAN SPORT HAS BEEN DOMINATED BY ONE NAME OVER THE LAST DECADE: FRANKIE FREDERICKS. HAVING PICKED UP THE 200M GOLD AND 100M BRONZE IN VICTORIA IN 1994, AND THE 100M SILVER IN KUALA LUMPUR, FREDERICKS IS LOOKING FOR A MEDAL IN MANCHESTER. ACHILLES TENDON AND HAMSTRING INJURIES SAW HIM WITHDRAW FROM THE SYDNEY OLYMPICS AND LAST YEAR'S EDMONTON WORLD CHAMPIONSHIPS RESPECTIVELY, SO HE WILL BE LOOKING FOR A RETURN TO FORM. AS HE SAYS, "IF I CAN GET A MEDAL, IT WILL BE A MAJOR BONUS, BECAUSE THERE WILL BE SOME TOP COMPETITION."

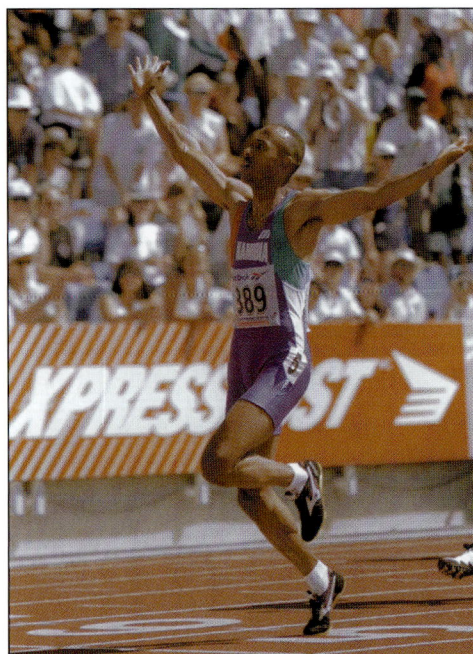

Mike Powell (Allsport)

NAURU

CAPITAL: YAREN
AREA: 13 sq km
POPULATION: 10,704
CURRENCY: AUSTRALIAN DOLLAR
LANGUAGE: NAURUAN (OFFICIAL, THOUGH ENGLISH IS USED IN GOVERNMENT AND COMMERCE
THE PEOPLE/CULTURE: NAURUAN, OTHER PACIFIC ISLANDERS, CHINESE, EUROPEAN 8 PER CENT

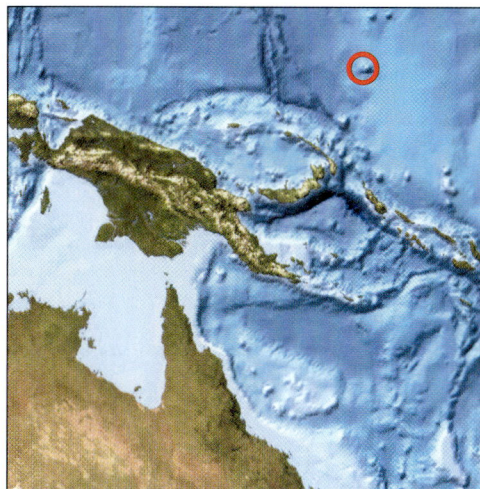

Mining for gold

Nauru came into little contact with Europeans until the 1830s, when whaling vessels and other traders visited. It was annexed by Germany in 1888. Nauru subsequently surrendered to Australian armed forces at the outbreak of World War I and was placed under British administration. It gained independence from its trustees on 31 January 1968.

Post independence, Nauru claims to be the smallest republic in the world – at 13 sq km. However, Nauru has a very high per capita income, thanks to the presence of phosphate on the island. Australia and Britain have mined Nauru's phosphate supply intensively and, until very recently, it was virtually the only output Nauru produced.

As the reserves of phosphate are coming to an end, it has been working hard to diversify into other areas – notably offshore banking. Earnings from phosphate exports and compensation for ecological damage caused by mining by Australia, Britain and New Zealand have funded this process. Global warming and rising sea levels also pose a significant threat to its coastline.

In much the same way as Nauru has relied for a long time on only one industry, it has also made its sporting name through one sport – weightlifting. Nauru first struck gold through the lifting exploits of Marcus Stephen back in the 1990s and, at one point, Stephen had won all seven of the Commonwealth Games medals taken for Nauru. Former Australian coach Paul Coffa then settled on the island and established weightlifting as the nation's one and only sporting pursuit. Nauru won three golds in Kuala Lumpur in 1998 – they'll hope to improve on that tally in Manchester.

Think Apples
Think enza

For the perfect healthy snack you can't beat **enza** apples from New Zealand. Crisp, sweet and juicy they are ideal after any sporting activity.

Enza would like to wish all competitors and spectators a wonderful Commonwealth Games. If you would like further information on supply of **enza** apples please contact us on www.worldwidefruit.co.uk

enza

WORLDWIDE *fruit*

NEW ZEALAND

CAPITAL: WELLINGTON
AREA: 268,680 sq km
POPULATION: 3.86 MILLION
CURRENCY: NEW ZEALAND DOLLAR
LANGUAGE: ENGLISH, MAORI
THE PEOPLE/CULTURE: NEW ZEALAND EUROPEAN, MAORI, PACIFIC ISLANDER, ASIAN

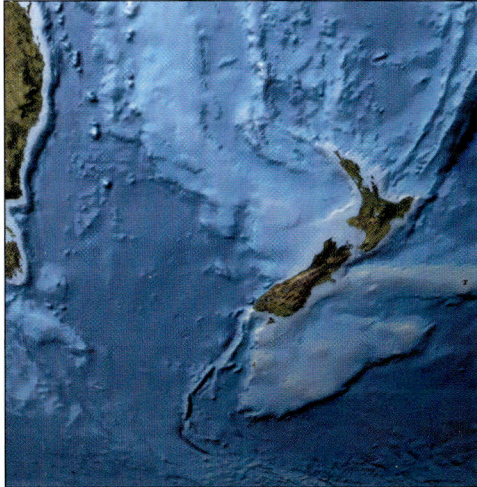

The cloud land

Polynesians were the first settlers in New Zealand. The navigator Kupe discovered New Zealand in 950 AD, when he saw an island covered by a white cloud that stretched as far as the eye could see.

In 1769, Captain James Cook explored the islands, claiming them for the British crown before heading for Australia. The British colonised the region extensively in the early 19th Century. The European presence led to problems: tensions over land ownership were tackled in the Treaty of Waitangi (1840), under which the Maoris accepted British rule in exchange for protection of their lands. However, tensions between settlers and Maoris remained, and this led to war in the 1860s.

The development of sheep farming and the discovery of gold contributed to a new prosperity and self-sufficiency. The nation introduced sweeping reforms, encouraging trade unions and women's suffrage: women were given the vote in 1895, some 25 years before the British.

New Zealand gained dominion status from the British Empire in 1907 and full autonomy in 1931. Full independence was proclaimed in 1947. By this time, New Zealand had fought as an ally of Britain in the Boer War, as well as both World Wars. Late 20th Century politics were characterised by Maori pressures for political reform. This led to "The Treaty of Waitangi Act", which enabled Maoris to initiate claims against the British Government. Financial reparations provided an opportunity for renewed investment and development within the Maori population, which now represents around ten per cent of the islands' inhabitants. Internationally, New Zealand has become an important regional force, with a firm anti-nuclear stance.

FABULOUS FACTS

The national bird of New Zealand is the Kiwi, while the national plant is the Pohutukawa.

The city of Auckland is built on an astonishing total of seven dormant volcanoes.

New Zealand's stunning, rugged landscapes provided the ideal location for the filming of *The Lord of the Rings*.

New Zealand was originally named Aotearoa (Land of the Long White Cloud) by the navigator Kupe, in 950 AD.

New Zealand is a similar in size to the UK, but it is one of the least populated countries in the world, with just four million inhabitants.

NEW ZEALAND IS A MAJOR FORCE IN THE COMMONWEALTH GAMES. IN 1998, IT WON EIGHT GOLDS, SEVEN SILVERS AND 20 BRONZE MEDALS AND IT IS DETERMINED TO BUILD ON THAT SUCCESS. THE RUGBY SEVENS EVENT WAS A HIGHLIGHT WHEN IT MADE ITS DEBUT IN KUALA LUMPUR. THIS YEAR, NEW ZEALAND HAS THE LIKES OF AMISIO VALENCE AND THE TEAM'S DREADLOCKED CAPTAIN, KING KARL TE NANA, TO TACKLE THE OTHER 15 NATIONS. IF THE TEAM'S SHOWING AT THE RECENT HONG KONG SEVENS IS ANYTHING TO GO BY, THE KIWI RUGBY SEVENS TEAM WILL BE HOT CONTENDERS IN MANCHESTER.

Stanley Chou (Allsport)

IT'S NOT WHERE YOU'RE FROM IT'S WHERE WE'RE GOING

POLICE OFFICERS – £25,953

after 18 weeks' initial training

London is a vibrant mix of cultures, languages and lifestyles. Like you, we want to create a Police Service that reflects and represents the diversity of the city. Become a Police Officer, and you will be making your community a safer place, enjoying a rewarding career, and earning £25,953 after training. In addition, you will benefit from free rail travel within a 70 mile radius of London. To apply visit our website or call the recruitment line on 0845 727 2212 Mon-Fri 8am-6pm (answerphone facility Sat).

Please quote Ref: GAM/01/02.

METROPOLITAN POLICE *Working for a safer London*

www.met.police.uk / 0845 727 2212

Nick Wilson, Brian Bahr, Phil Cole (Allsport)

IN SQUASH, FORMER AUSTRALIAN WORLD CHAMPION
CAROL OWENS IS AN EXCITING ADDITION TO THE SQUAD.
LIKE TEAMMATE LEILANI JOYCE, SHE WILL BE PLAYING
SINGLES, DOUBLES AND MIXED DOUBLES.
TRIATHLETES HAMISH CARTER AND KRIS GEMMELL HAVE
JOINED CRAIG WATSON IN THE CHASE FOR MEDALS, AS HAS
HEATHER EVANS, WHO QUALIFIED FOR THE GAMES NEARLY
A FULL MINUTE AHEAD OF HER NEAREST COMPATRIOT.
NEW ZEALAND'S HOCKEY SQUAD IS GOING FROM STRENGTH
TO STRENGTH; COACH KEVIN TOWNS WAS DELIGHTED WITH
ITS RECENT TOP TEN PERFORMANCE IN THE WORLD CUP,
BOASTING: "WE ARE CONFIDENT AND READY FOR THE
GAMES, AND FIRMLY BELIEVE WE ARE MEDAL PROSPECTS."

FABULOUS FACTS

New Zealand includes: the Antipodes Islands, Bounty Island, Campbell Island, Chatham Islands, and Kermadec Islands.

Mild earthquakes are a common natural hazard. New Zealand also has live and dormant volcanoes.

The largest lake in New Zealand is Lake Taupo. It is heart-shaped and the water is heated by volcanic activity.

Originally a British colony, New Zealand was granted autonomy in 1931 and declared independent in 1947.

New Zealand's natural resources are varied and include natural gas, iron ore, gold, timber and limestone.

IN SHOOTING, THE KIWI FULLBORE EXPERT MIKE COLLINGS HAS RECENT VICTORIES OVER ENGLAND AND AUSTRALIA TO HIS CREDIT.

SEVEN OF NEW ZEALAND'S CURRENT WORLD CHAMPIONS ARE IN THE BOWLS SQUAD. IT IS ANXIOUS TO REVERSE THE RESULTS FROM KUALA LUMPUR, WHEN MILLIE KHAN BROUGHT HOME A LONE BRONZE IN THE WOMEN'S SINGLES, AND THE MEN FAILED TO REACH THE MEDALS PODIUM FOR THE FIRST TIME EVER. CHIEF EXECUTIVE OF BOWLS NEW ZEALAND, KERRY CLARK, SAYS THERE IS GREAT OPTIMISM IN THE NATIONAL SQUAD AT PRESENT: "WE HAVE ENJOYED TWO YEARS OF UNPRECEDENTED SUCCESS ON THE INTERNATIONAL SCENE," SAYS CLARK, "INCLUDING TWO TRANS TASMAN WINS, THREE WORLD CHAMPIONSHIP GOLDS AND TWO BRONZE MEDALS, PLUS SERIES WINS AGAINST IRELAND AT HOME AND ENGLAND AWAY."

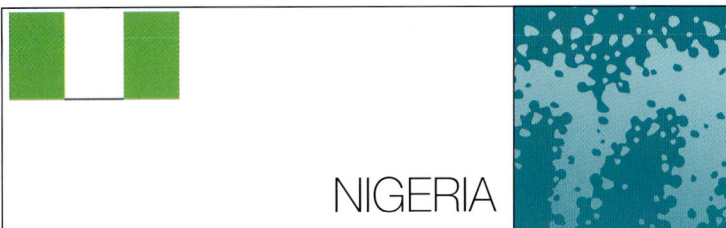

NIGERIA

CAPITAL: ABUJA
AREA: 924,000 sq km
POPULATION: 127 MILLION
CURRENCY: NAIRA (WHICH CONSISTS OF 100 KOBO)
LANGUAGE: EN, HA, YORUBA, IBO, FULANI, ENGLISH
THE PEOPLE: HAUSA, FULANI, YORUBA, IBO, IJAW, KANURI, IBIBIO, TIV

An ancient land

The earliest Nigerians were the Nok people, skilled artisans from around the Jos area. By the beginning of the second millennium, the Nok had virtually disappeared and the state of Kanem was flourishing. Between the 11th and 14th Centuries, Hausa Islamic empires flourished. In the 14th and 15th Centuries, a number of Yoruba Epries profited from important access to trans-Sahara trade. The Yourba states had a sacred monarchy, which ruled by a court system – the kings, or "Obas", still play an important role in Nigerian culture and ceremony. The Portuguese made contact with the Yoruba in the 15th Century, trading pepper and then slaves. At the same time that slavery was abolished in the early 19th Century, the British increased their political control, ruling through a system of local kings who helped raise taxes. This policy met with differing levels of success, but British involvement continued until after World War II, when demands for independence increased. The British developed a constitution designed to cater to the different needs of Muslim, Catholic and Yoruba areas. This led to increased regional competition, with localised systems of government in these areas, so that when the country gained independence in October 1960, Nigeria effectively consisted of three nations. Power struggles, domestic conflict and strikes in 1964 and 1965 led to a disputed election and then a coup in 1966. General Ironsi's rule lasted just months; he was replaced by Lieutenant Colonel Gowon. In the East, the military commander Lieutenant Colonel Ojukwu refused to accept the new head of state and announced the creation of Biafra as an independent state. A civil war ensued, at the end of which the Biafran forces capitulated. A series of coups in the 1970s and the 1980s further destabilised Nigeria. After nearly 16 years of military rule, Nigeria adopted a new constitution in 1999 and made a transition to civilian rule.

FABULOUS FACTS

Until his death in 1997, the world-renowned musician Fela Kuti was Nigeria's most famous musician.

The country has a population density of 133 per km and is the most populous country in Africa.

The ibej (twin dolls that are adorned with beads) are worn by Nigerians to bring good luck and prosperity.

Nigeria has 681 species of birds, as well as 274 identified species of mammals and 4,175 species of plants.

Nigeria's main export is petroleum and it is also a major exporter of cocoa and rubber around the world.

NIGERIA HAS A GREAT RECORD IN THE COMMONWEALTH GAMES HAVING TAKEN A TOTAL OF 107 MEDALS – 30 GOLD, 38 SILVER AND 39 BRONZE. NIGERIA'S HIGHEST PROFILE ATHLETE WAS GLORY ALOZIE, WHO WON A SILVER MEDAL AT THE SYDNEY OLYMPICS – HOWEVER, SHE WILL NOT BE AT MANCHESTER, HAVING TAKEN UP SPANISH CITIZENSHIP IN 2001. OTHER MEDALLISTS IN SYDNEY INCLUDED RUTH OGBEFO, WON TOOK SILVER IN THE WOMEN'S HEAVYWEIGHT WEIGHTLIFTING AND THE MEN'S 4X400M RELAY TEAM, WHO'LL DEFINITELY BE IN CONTENTION FOR A MEDAL IN MANCHESTER.

NIGERIA'S MARY ONYALI IS AN EXCITING
COMMONWEALTH GAMES PROSPECT,
A SEMI-FINALIST FROM THE 2001 WORLD
CHAMPIONSHIPS IN 100 AND 200 METRES,
AS WELL AS A 4X100 METRES RELAY FINALIST.
OFF THE TRACK, NIGERIA'S TABLE TENNIS STAR
LANRE JEGEDE IS DETERMINED TO REPEAT HIS
CONSISTENT FINE FORM AND INFLICT SOME
SHOCK VICTORIES ON THE FAVOURITES.

Andy Lyons, Craig Prentis, Mike Powell (Allsport)

NIUE

CAPITAL: ALOFI
AREA: 260 sq km
POPULATION:
CURRENCY: NEW ZEALAND DOLLAR
LANGUAGE: NIUEAN, ENGLISH. THE NIUEAN LANGUAGE CAN BE TRACED TO SAMOAN AND TONGAN ROOTS
THE PEOPLE/CULTURE: POLYNESIAN (WITH SOME 200 EUROPEANS, SAMOANS, AND TONGANS)

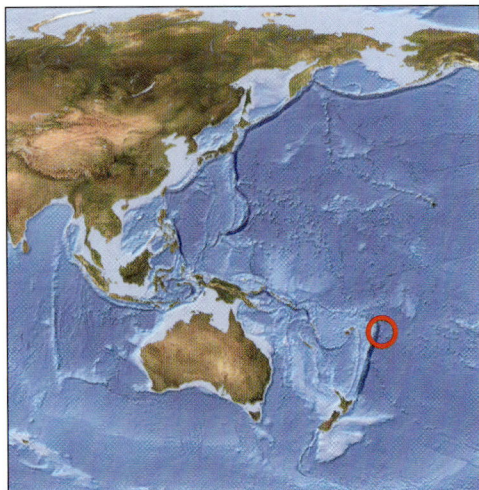

Coconut reef

Niue is the world's largest coral island – the islanders call it "the Rock", while its name means "Behold the Coconut". Migrants from Samoa, Tonga and other nearby islands are believed to be the first settlers of this remote island. In 1774, Niue was sighted by Captain Cook, who was not welcomed by the natives. His landing party was scared off by Niuean warriors, who performed a war dance and painted their mouths red. The friendly people of Niue had never seen pale-skinned people before, so they assumed them to be invaders from other islands covered in white war paint.

Christian missionaries from the London Missionary Society soon followed Cook's expedition and converted many of the island's inhabitants. One of the famous Niuean missionaries was Peniamina and Niue still celebrates his achievements each year with a public holiday.

In 1901, Niue was annexed to New Zealand as a colony of Great Britain. On 19 October 1974, Niue gained self-government, plus free-association with New Zealand. This free-association gave Niueans automatic New Zealand citizenship status. With its democratically-elected legislative assembly of 20 members, Niue is the world's smallest self-governing state.

Niue may be small, but they have some big athletes who'll be hoping to compete at this year's games. The country's Rugby Sevens team will definitely be mixing it up with their Southern hemisphere neighbours; other hopefuls include Speedo Hetutu and Hetesa Hetutu, both of whom are champion weightlifters.

NORFOLK ISLANDS

CAPITAL: KINGSTON
AREA: 35 sq km
POPULATION: 1,900
CURRENCY: AUSTRALIAN DOLLAR
LANGUAGE: ENGLISH AND LOCAL POLYNESIAN DIALECT
THE PEOPLE/CULTURE: AUSTRALIANS, NEW ZEALANDERS, POLYNESIANS

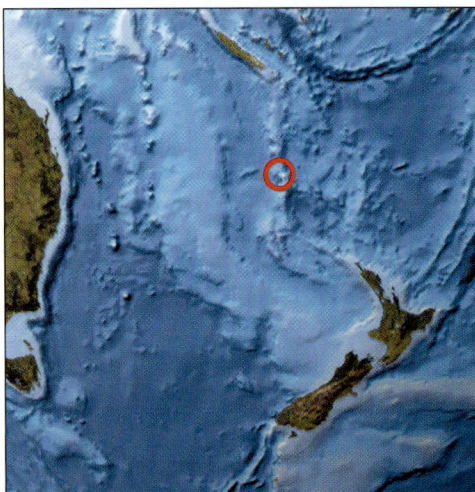

Beauty and the bounty

Norfolk Island is three million years old, the tip of an undersea mountain that rose above the water. Captain Cook discovered it in 1774 and described it as "paradise". In fact, many of the island's families have the same names as the Bounty mutineers, such as Christian-Bailey, Quintals, Evans. Nicknames make identification easier; the Norfolk Island phone book is the only telephone directory in the world that lists people under nicknames, such as Bubby, Diddles and Smudge.

The British made two attempts to establish a penal colony on the Norfolk Islands, first between 1788-1814 and then from 1825 to 1855. After the penal colony was closed, the descendants of the mutineers from The Bounty resettled the island. By the start of World War II, an airport had been completed for transmitting wartime aircraft.

In 1979, The Norfolk Island Act, a Commonwealth Act of Parliament passed into law, allowing the establishment of a Norfolk Island Legislative Assembly to assume responsibility for a wide range of functions previously handled by a Commonwealth-appointed administrator, with assistance from a locally-elected Advisory Council. The first assembly elected on 1 August 1979.

Incredibly for a country with a population of only 1,900, the Norfolk Islands took 21 competitors to the Kuala Lumpur games in 1998. Norfolk Island is particularly strong in Lawn Bowls and will provide some stiff competition for rival nations.

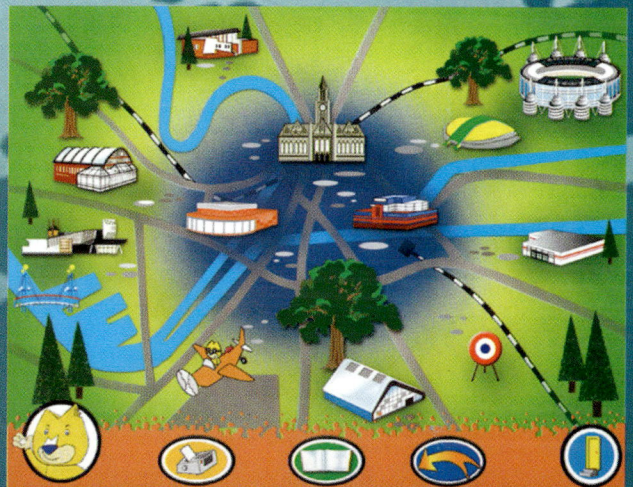

NORTHERN IRELAND

CAPITAL: BELFAST
AREA: 14,160 sq km
POPULATION: 1.54 MILLION
CURRENCY: ENGLISH POUND
LANGUAGE: ENGLISH, GAELIC IRISH
THE PEOPLE/CULTURE: BRITISH, IRISH

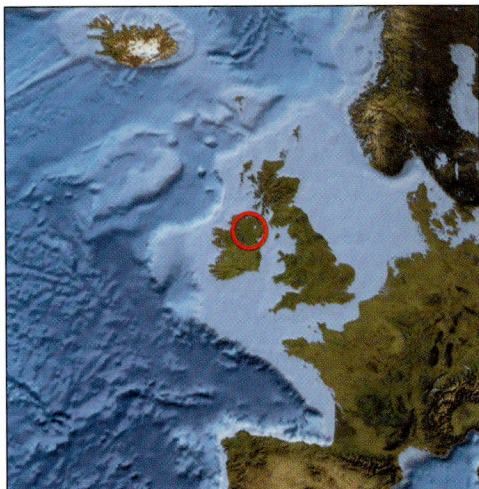

Turning over a new cloverleaf

Northern Ireland's history began in the 17th Century, when an Irish rebellion was suppressed and land confiscated by the British crown. It was given to Scottish and English settlers, who gave the Ulster region an identity that was typically more Protestant than the Catholic South. In 1886, British politician William Gladstone suggested Home Rule, which led to fears that the fate of the Protestant North would be determined by the Catholic majority in the South. In 1920, British Prime Minister Lloyd George passed the Government of Ireland Act, which created the province of Northern Ireland and allowed for Parliaments in both the North and the South. The Republic of Ireland, established in 1922, refused to recognise the partition. A boundary commission, established to reconsider the borders, collapsed in 1925 without reporting. Violence was a regular occurrence and the Republic of Ireland withdrew from the Commonwealth in 1948. Conflict between Protestants and Catholics, and the intensive terror campaigns of the Irish Republican Army, led in 1972 to the suspension of the Northern Ireland government and direct rule from Britain resumed. In 1973, a new government was formed in which Catholics and Protestants shared power, but British Direct Rule returned in 1974 until 1981. Bombings and attacks spread to Dublin and London. In 1985, an Anglo-Irish Accord laid the foundations for talks between Northern Ireland and the Republic. Terrorist groups declared a ceasefire in 1994 and peace talks began in 1995.

A peace deal for Northern Ireland was approved in 1998; the settlement was implemented in 1999, culminating in a multi-party government. Britain ended direct rule and David Trimble became head of the Northern Irish Government.

FABULOUS FACTS

The Gaelic name for the capital of Northern Ireland, Beál Feirste (or Belfast), refers to the River Farset.

Ireland's first settlers touched down near modern-day Belfast approximately 9,000 years ago.

Two thirds of Northern Ireland's population lives within a 50 mile radius of Belfast.

England's involvement with Ireland began in 1170, when the Earl of Pembroke intervened in a local dispute.

The doctor and poet, William Drennar, coined the phrase "The Emerald Isle" in 1795, in reference to Ireland.

NORTHERN IRELAND HAS WON A TOTAL OF 84 COMMONWEALTH MEDALS – 22 GOLDS, 23 SILVERS AND 39 BRONZES. IN KUALA LUMPUR, TWO OF NORTHERN IRELAND'S GOLD MEDALLISTS WERE MARTIN MILLAR AND DAVID CALVERT, WHO WON THE PAIRS FULLBORE RIFLE. THIS YEAR, HOPES WILL BE PINNED ON MIDDLE DISTANCE RUNNER GARETH TURNBULL, WHO IS JOINED BY TRACK COMPATRIOT JAMES MCILROY AND SHOT MEDAL HOPE EVA MASSEY. IN CYCLING, DAVID MCCANN IS A MAJOR PODIUM HOPE; THE BELFAST RIDER SAYS: "I WOULD BE DISAPPOINTED IF I DIDN'T BRING HOME A GOLD MEDAL."

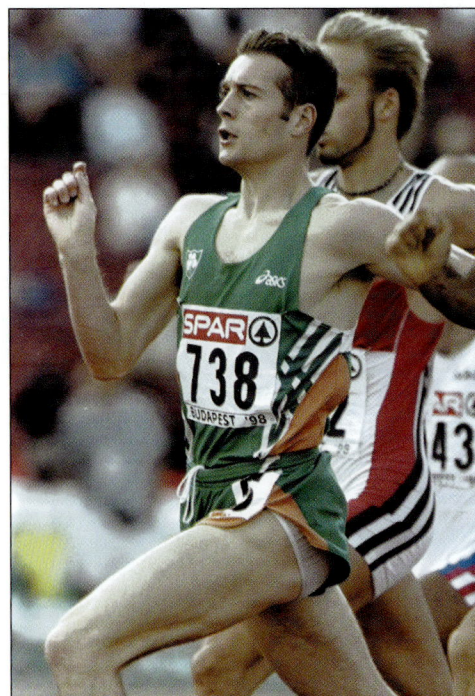

Michael Cooper (Allsport)

What do you do after breaking records and winning medals?

Relax

What better, after setting a few records or beating the best, than thinking about taking things a little easier. It's then that your thoughts should turn to holidaying in Ireland. Easy to get to (a mere hop, skip and jump away), where the people are friendly and the options to relax and enjoy yourself are plentiful. Outdoor sports, stunning countryside, cuisine and culture, it's all here waiting for you in Ireland.

Call now for your free holiday guide to Ireland

0800 917 2002
www.ireland2002.com

Ireland - the enchantment never ends

PAKISTAN

CAPITAL: ISLAMABAD
AREA: 796,095 sq km
POPULATION: 142 MILLION
CURRENCY: PAKISTAN RUPEE
LANGUAGE: URDU, PUNJABI, SINDHI, ENGLISH
THE PEOPLE: PUNJABI, SINDHI, PASHTU, BALOCH, MUHAJIR

Fighting for freedom

Pakistan occupies an area in which some of the earliest human settlements can be found. The foundations of ancient Pakistan were built by the Kushans, who at the height of their powers occupied an empire that stretched from eastern Iran to the Chinese border. During the 16th and 17th Centuries, the Moghuls held sway in the country. In 1906, the Muslim League was founded to demand an independent Muslim state, but it wasn't until 24 years later that a totally separate Muslim homeland was proposed.

After violence between Hindus and Muslims escalated in the mid-1940s, the British were forced to admit that a separate Muslim state was unavoidable. As a modern state, Pakistan dates from 1947, when the Indian sub-continent was partitioned at the end of British rule. In 1948, the first Governor General of Pakistan, Mujammed Ali Jinnah, died. Pakistan proclaimed itself an Islamic republic in 1956 and in 1958, General Ayyub Khan took control, declaring martial law. He became President in 1960. In 1970, a general election in East Pakistan for the breakaway Awami League led to considerable tension within West Pakistan. Attempts by East Pakistan to secede led to civil war the following year. India intervened, supporting East Pakistan, which eventually became Bangladesh. In 1973, Zufiqar Ali Bhutto became Prime Minister, a post he held until 1977, when General Zia ul-Haq staged a military coup. Zia became President in 1978 and maintained martial law. Benazir Bhutto, daughter of the Zufiqar Ali Bhutto, returned to Pakistan to win an election in 1988. Dismissed on charges of corruption, she again won an election in 1993, but was again dismissed in 1996. In October 1999, General Musharraf staged a coup, leading to Pakistan's suspension from the Commonwealth. Musharraf became President in June 2001.

FABULOUS FACTS

The Pakistan flag symbolises the nation's commitment to Islam, still very influential in the country to this day.

Stone Age relics around 500,000-years-old have been discovered in the Soan Valley of the Potahar region.

Gandhara Art, created from the 1st to the 5th Centuries AD, blends Indian, Buddhist and Greco-Roman traditions.

The Urdu language used throughout Pakistan derives mainly from both Arabic and Persian vocabularies.

Cricket is a national obsession in Pakistan. The team's greatest triumph came in the 1992 Cricket World Cup.

PAKISTAN HAS AN OVERALL COMMONWEALTH GAMES MEDAL TALLY OF 47, COMPRISING 20 GOLDS, 14 SILVERS AND 13 BRONZES. PAKISTAN WILL BE TAKING PART IN 13 DISCIPLINES AT THESE GAMES: ATHLETICS, BADMINTON, BOXING, CYCLING, GYMNASTICS, HOCKEY, JUDO, SHOOTING, SQUASH, SWIMMING, TABLE TENNIS, WEIGHTLIFTING AND WRESTLING. THE COUNTRY FINISHED FIFTH IN THE MEN'S HOCKEY 2002 WORLD CUP AND IT IS HOPING TO BUILD ON THAT SUCCESS. PAKISTAN IS ALSO HOPING TO EXCEL ON THE SQUASH COURT, LIKE LEGENDS OF THE PAST JANSHER AND JAHINGER KHAN.

Stanley Chou (Allsport)

The Commonwealth...

The Commonwealth Youth Programme salutes the athletes of the XVII Commonwealth Games.
Champions all! Just like the thousands of young men and women throughout the Commonwealth who are making a difference in their communities as volunteers, peer mentors, HIV counsellors, electoral observers, civil society leaders, small business entrepreneurs and more.

...championing youth,

With young people as our partners in development and democracy, the possibilities for a brighter today and tomorrow are limitless.

We are the first international organisation to ... have established a development arm focusing solely on young people. RT. HON DON MCKINNON, COMMONWEALTH SECRETARY GENERAL

As inheritors of the Commonwealth values of respect for diversity, economic and social development, democracy and good governance, young people must have a say about tomorrow's world today. Youth for the Future is a new pan-Commonwealth initiative to encourage young people's participation in national development.

championing the present and the future.

To find out more,
Tel: +44 (0) 207 747 6463, Fax: +44 (0) 20 7930 1647, Email: cyp@commonwealth.int, *or visit* **www.cypyouth.org**

COMMONWEALTH YOUTH PROGRAMME
COMMONWEALTH SECRETARIAT

PAPUA NEW GUINEA

CAPITAL: PORT MORESBY
AREA: 462,800 sq km
POPULATION: 4.6 MILLION
CURRENCY: KINA
LANGUAGE: 750 INDIGENOUS LANGUAGES, PIDGIN, MOTU
THE PEOPLE/CULTURE: MELANESIAN, POLYNESIAN, MICRONESIAN, CHINESE

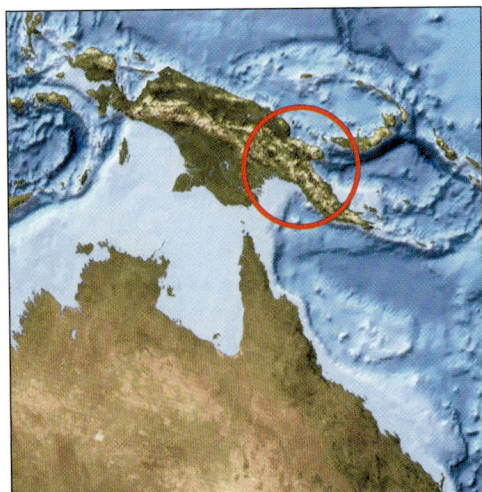

Lift your game

It is believed that Papua New Guinea was originally inhabited by Asian settlers more than 50,000 years ago. The first European contact, in 1526-27, was by the Portuguese explorer Jorge de Meneses, who named the island "Ilhas dos Papuas". The Spaniard Inigo Ortiz de Retes later called it New Guinea because he thought the people similar to those of Guinea in Africa. Further exploration followed, including landings by Bougainville, Cook, Stanley and John Moresby.

In 1824, the Dutch formalised their claims to sovereignty over the western portion of the island. Germany followed, taking possession of the northern part of the territory in 1884. Three days later, Britain declared a protectorate over the southern region; outright annexation occurred four years later.

In 1906, British New Guinea became Papua, and administration of the region was taken over by newly independent Australia. Post World Wars I and II, after various regions of the islands had fallen into German and Japanese hands, the eastern half of New Guinea reverted to Australia and became the Territory of Papua and New Guinea. Indonesia took control of Dutch New Guinea in 1963.

Papua New Guinea achieved independence in 1975, two years after it was granted self-governance. Troubles between Papua New Guinea and the island of Bougainville started soon after, with Bougainvilleans demanding succession. A ten-year war claimed 20,000 lives. It officially ended in 1998.

Papua New Guinea's overall Commonwealth Games medal tally is six, with one gold, three silvers and two bronzes. At Manchester, Papua New Guinea will be right behind Dika Toua, the weightlifter who competed in the 2000 Olympics in Sydney. The country will also be competing in the Rugby Sevens.

SAMOA

CAPITAL: APIA
AREA: 2,831 sq km
POPULATION: 235,302
CURRENCY: TALA
LANGUAGE: SAMOAN, ENGLISH
THE PEOPLE/CULTURE: SAMOAN, EUROPEAN AND ASIAN

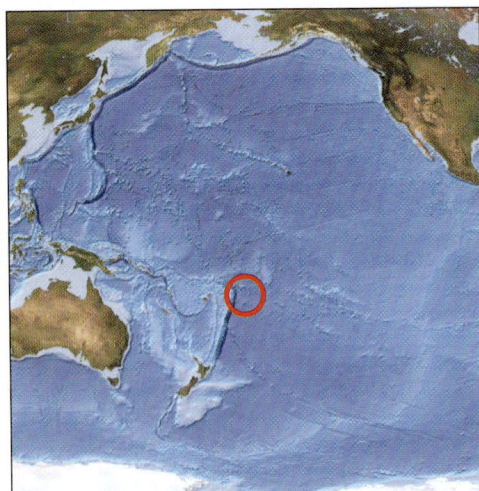

Same old Samoa?

Samoa belongs to a group of islands in the South Pacific and has great natural beauty, with white-sand beaches, rugged forested mountains and numerous waterfalls. Civilisation on the island can be traced back to 1000 BC, when Polynesians are said to have migrated here from the west. Today's society continues to reflect a distinctive Polynesian cultural heritage.

The island was first influenced by Europe after its discovery in 1722 by Dutchman Jacob Roggeveen. Later, in 1768, the French explorer, Captain Louis-Antoine de Bougainville named the group the Navigator Islands. By far the greatest impact on the island came with the Western missionaries of the late 19th Century. Their influence on Samoan life was lasting and the islanders continue to be a religious people, devoting much time to church activities. Among Samoa's past inhabitants is Robert Louis Stevenson, Scottish author of *Treasure Island*, who settled here with his family in the late 19th Century.

The Germans ruled Samoa following the signing of the Berlin Treaty in 1889. Britain persuaded New Zealand to seize control at the beginning of World War I. New Zealand administered the island until independence was sought in January 1962, when Samoa became the first independent island nation in the Pacific.

Samoa is one of the 16 nations competing for gold in the Rugby Sevens event. Several team members play for New Zealand internationally and will be proud to represent Samoa in the Commonwealth Games. Competition is tough and Samoa will be facing the likes of New Zealand, Fiji and Australia – medal winners in the Kuala Lumpur Games in 1998. They loo strong, however, having narrowly missed a victory over South Africa that would have won the team the World Series in New Zealand.

GOING FOR GOLD AT CHATSWORTH

A magnificent treasure house in the heart of the country

Twice winner of a gold award when voted 'Britain's favourite National Treasure', Chatsworth is only one hour from Manchester.

The home of the Duke and Duchess of Devonshire, its magnificent garden and waterworks, the farmyard and playground and a 1000 acre park offer something for every taste and every generation.

This year, for only the second time, Chatsworth is also open for a Christmas season, with special decorations, floodlighting and Father Christmas, from 9 November to 22 December 2002.

Everyone at Chatsworth wishes the Games well and looks forward to welcoming you here.

House, garden, farmyard and playground, shops and restaurant are open every day until 22 December 2002

Chatsworth, Bakewell*, Derbyshire
Telephone 01246 582204
www.chatsworth.org

*off the A6 via Stockport and Buxton

CHATSWORTH

SCOTLAND

CAPITAL: EDINBURGH
AREA: 244,110 sq km
POPULATION: 5,120,000
CURRENCY: POUND STERLING
LANGUAGE: ENGLISH (ALTHOUGH GAELIC IS STILL SPOKEN IN PARTS OF THE SCOTTISH HIGHLANDS AND ISLANDS)
THE PEOPLE/CULTURE: SCOTTISH, ASIAN AND AFRICAN

Borders patrol

Scotland's history can be traced back to the 1st Century AD, when Roman Emperor Hadrian built his wall in a bid to contain the fierce tribes of Caledonia (as Scotland was then known). Scotland took its name in the 10th Century from the Irish immigrants who settled there 500 years earlier – the Scots. In 1290, Margaret – the only heiress to the Scottish throne – died, making way for Edward I of England to proclaim himself king. He moved the ancient Stone of Scone, on which Scottish kings had long been crowned, to London's Westminster Abbey. This provoked a hostile response, as William Wallace and Robert the Bruce rose against the English to fight for their independence, formally recognised by Edward III in 1328.

However, border clashes with England continued and during the reigns of James IV and James V in the 16th Century, Scotland's monarchy faced additional challenges to its authority – first from wealthy barons and later from supporters of the Protestant Reformation as it swept through Europe. The latter culminated in the imprisonment and execution of Scotland's Catholic queen, Mary Stuart.

Queen Elizabeth of England died without an heir in 1603, leaving James VI of Scotland to inherit her throne. The two nations became united under a single king, but each remained a separate state with its own parliament and government until 1707, when the parliaments of both nations agreed to the Act of Union. This act merged the parliaments of the two nations and established the Kingdom of Great Britain.

During the second half of the 20th Century, many Scots began to demand a greater say over their political affairs. Eventually, a new Scottish parliament was established in Edinburgh in 1999, enjoying considerable power over education, health, the environment, economic development and the arts.

FABULOUS FACTS

The Scots use many terms derived from Gaelic – for example, the word for dull is dreich; a brae is a hill; a bairn is a baby.

Scotland is renowned for its malt whisky – uisge beatha, meaning the water of life – and it has over 150 distilleries.

Glasgow football fans are traditionally divided by religion: Rangers fans are Protestant; Celtic supporters are Catholic.

Scandinavian invaders alerted locals when one of them yelped in pain after stepping on a thistle; it is now the national emblem.

Scotland has produced a number of British Prime Ministers, such as: Tony Blair, WE Gladstone and Ramsay MacDonald.

ALISON SHEPPARD IS CURRENTLY RANKED NUMBER ONE IN THE WORLD FOR THE WOMEN'S 50M AQUATIC SPRINT EVENT. SHE TOOK SILVER IN THE KUALA LUMPUR GAMES IN 1988 AND IS AIMING FOR GOLD THIS TIME AROUND.
THE TRIATHLON MAKES ITS DEBUT AT THIS YEAR'S GAMES AND SCOTLAND OFFERS STIFF COMPETITION IN STEPHANIE FORRESTER, BRONZE MEDAL WINNER IN THE 1998 EUROPEAN CHAMPIONSHIPS. SHE SAYS: "I GET FEW OPPORTUNITIES TO WEAR SCOTTISH COLOURS. TO DO SO IN ONE OF THE BIGGEST SPORTS EVENTS IN THE WORLD WOULD BE EXTRA SPECIAL."

Brian Bahr, Jamie McDonald (Allsport)

Reaching New Heights

BANK OF SCOTLAND Scottish Team COMMONWEALTH GAMES 2002

To represent your country in your chosen sport is a magnificent achievement. It takes years of hard work, dedication and training. As well as being proud sponsor of the Scottish Commonwealth Games team, Bank of Scotland also provides support through several innovative sponsorships, including athletics, swimming, hockey and badminton. Indeed, this year alone, over 20,000 young people will take part in sporting events made possible by Bank of Scotland. To find out more visit **www.hbosplc.com**

BANK OF SCOTLAND ✳ Always giving you extra

SEYCHELLES

CAPITAL: VICTORIA
AREA: 454 sq km
POPULATION: 79,672
CURRENCY: SEYCHELLES RUPEE
LANGUAGE: CREOLE, FRENCH, ENGLISH.
THE PEOPLE/CULTURE: SEYCHELLOIS, INDIAN AND CHINESE

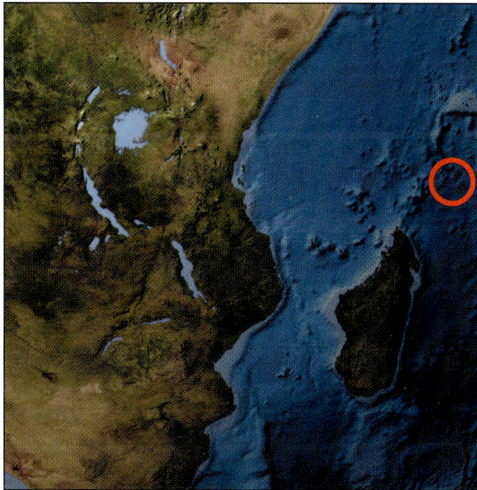

Simply Seychelles

Seychelles is a group of islands in the Indian Ocean, off the east coast of Africa, that were not inhabited until the late 18th Century. Having taken possession of the islands in 1742, the French landed on Ste Anne Island to start a permanent settlement in 1770.

Although the French were the first to settle here, it is thought that Arab traders were probably the first to have spotted Seychelles. During the 16th Century, the islands were also frequented by the Portuguese.

The first plantation industry in Seychelles was started in 1771 by Frenchman Pierre Poivre, in a bid to compete with the Dutch spice trade. It was at this time that Seychelles was also being used as a transit point for slaves from Africa, India and Madagascar. Slavery was abolished in 1835 and this became a key event in the history of the islands, along with the arrival of the Roman Catholic Church to the islands in 1853.

After 1794, the British challenged the French for the islands on several occasions; they changed hands no fewer than seven times. A series of sea battles in 1811 led to the British occupation of the islands. The 1814 Treaty of Paris formally put both Seychelles and Mauritius under British control, and a year later Seychelles became a dependent of Mauritius. In 1903, it became a separate British Crown colony in its own right. Seychelles gained independence from the United Kingdom on 29 June 1976 and became a member of the British Commonwealth of Nations.

FABULOUS FACTS

The unique culture in Seychelles mixes the characteristics of French settlers, African slaves and British sailors.

The islands were first sighted at the beginning of the 16th Century, by Vasco da Gama, a Portuguese navigator.

Louis XVII was allegedly taken to Seychelles during the French Revolution, to stop him claiming the throne.

As much of 46 per cent of Seychelles' land area is set aside for national parks and nature reserves.

The Seychelles islands are different geologically: the first group is low-lying coral, the second is mountainous granite.

SEYCHELLES HAS A SOMEWHAT BIZARRE COMMONWEALTH GAMES HISTORY. IT WON ITS FIRST MEDAL IN 1994, BUT THE CIRCUMSTANCES WERE A LITTLE PECULIAR. BOXER RIVAL CADEAU, A LIGHT-MIDDLEWEIGHT CHALLENGER, FAILED TO SHOW FOR HIS SEMI-FINAL AGAINST THE EVENTUAL CHAMPION, NORTHERN IRELAND'S JIMMY WEBB. REALISING THAT HIS ABSENCE WAS DUE TO A BREAKDOWN IN COMMUNICATION RATHER THAN ANYTHING MORE SINISTER, THE JUDGES AWARDED HIM A BRONZE MEDAL. IN 1998, SEYCHELLES GAINED TWO "GENUINE" SILVER MEDALS. LIGHT WELTERWEIGHT GERRY LEGRAS WAS BEATEN IN A TITANIC BOUT BY CANADA'S MIKE STRANGE, WHILE IN THE HEAVYWEIGHT DIVISION, ROLAND RAFORME EQUALLED HIS COMPATRIOT. BOXING MUST BE SEYCHELLES' TOP PRIORITY AND IT WILL BE GOING FOR GOLD IN MANCHESTER.

CAPTURED BY CHARITY NUMBER 297500

WE HOPE YOU ENJOY A CRIME-FREE COMMONWEALTH GAMES AND REMEMBER - IF YOU HAVE ANY INFORMATION ABOUT CRIMINAL ACTIVITY PLEASE CALL CRIMESTOPPERS ANONYMOUSLY ON

0800 555 111

Greater Manchester CRIMESTOPPERS
0800 555 111

CRIMESTOPPERS TRUST - THE ONLY CHARITY HELPING TO SOLVE CRIMES
TO MAKE A DONATION PLEASE VISIT CRIMESTOPPERS WEBSITE - WWW.CRIMESTOPPERS-UK.ORG

SIERRA LEONE

CAPITAL: FREETOWN
AREA: 71,740 sq km
POPULATION: 5,509,263
CURRENCY: LEONE (LE)
LANGUAGE: ENGLISH, KRIO, MENDE, TEMNE, OTHER INDIGENOUS
THE PEOPLE: BLACK AFRICANS, INCLUDING THE MENDE, TEMNE AND LIMBA; KRIO (CREOLES); LEBANESE

The pace of change

The country's name has a complex history, with origins going back as far as 1462, when a Portuguese explorer, Pedro da Cintra, sailed down the coast of West Africa and saw the long range of mountains of what is now the Freetown Peninsula. He called the lands "Sierra Lyoa" meaning "lion mountains".
In the 16th Century, an English sailor called it "Sierra Leoa"; by the 17th Century, it was "Sierra Leona" and by 1787, under the Sierra Leone Company, it became the first of several British Administrations. Following years of British Colonisation, Sierra Leone became the name by which the country is known today.
Throughout its period of British colonisation, Sierra Leone served as the seat of government for other British colonies along the West African Coast. During this time, the country earned itself the name "the Athens of West Africa" owing to its achievements in the fields of medicine, law and education. West Africa's first college for higher education, Fourah Bay College, was established in Sierra Leone in 1827.
Sierra Leone was for many years used as a slave trading outpost, until it was gradually phased out and later, in the 18th Century, it became a settlement for freed slaves, largely owing to the work of the English philanthropist Granville Sharpe, He was deeply concerned about the welfare of freed slaves and forced a move to bring them all back to Africa to settle.
Sierra Leone's recent history has been marred by a rebel war which began in 1991 and lasted until 7 July 1999, when a peace agreement was signed between the Government and the Revolutionary United Front (RUF) – the group that had been waging the war.

FIVE FAB FACTS

The main diamond and gold mining areas of Sierra Leone still form a large part of the country's export earnings.

Most people in Sierra Leone speak Krio – a mix of English, Yoruba and African – along with one of 15 ethnic languages.

The peninsula on which Freetown stands is a mountainous promontory, 300 feet above sea level in places.

The original local name for what is now "Freetown" was "Romarong", meaning the place of the "wailers".

Sierra Leone's capital, Freetown provides natural anchorage and berthing facilities for ships at the Queen Elizabeth II Quay.

IN 1998, SIERRA LEONE TOOK A SMALL TEAM TO THE GAMES IN KUALA LUMPUR, BUT STILL PUSHED FOR MEDALS – THEY FINISHED SIXTH IN THE MEN'S 4X100M RELAY, AT ONLY ONE AND HALF SECONDS BEHIND GOLD MEDALLISTS ENGLAND. IT HASN'T ALWAYS BEEN THIS GOOD, HOWEVER. IN 1994, HORACE DOVE-EDWIN, AN UNKNOWN SPRINTER, WON SILVER BEHIND LINFORD CHRISTIE IN THE 100M EVENT. UNFORTUNATELY, DOVE-EDWIN TESTED POSITIVE FOR DRUG USE AND HIS MEDAL WENT TO JAMAICA'S MICHAEL GREEN – SO, SIERRA LEONE STILL AWAITS ITS FIRST MEDAL. WILL MANCHESTER PROVIDE IT? ONLY TIME WILL TELL.

Blackpool
get set
to visit the winning resort

go!

Fun for all ages - Blackpool Pleasure Beach

Zipper Dipper - Blackpool Pleasure Beach

Vladimir - Eclipse Circus Musical

Blackpool Tower - Walk of Faith

Mooky the Clown - Tower Circus

Blackpool Tower - Jungle Jims

For an exciting short break or day visit, Blackpool has awarding winning shows and world beating attractions. With direct road & rail links to Blackpool from Manchester. **Now is the time to get on your marks!**

Pepsi Max Big One - Blackpool Pleasure Beach

CAPITAL: SINGAPORE
AREA: 648 sq km
POPULATION: 3,571,710
CURRENCY: SINGAPORE DOLLAR
LANGUAGE: CHINESE, MALAY, TAMIL, ENGLISH
THE PEOPLE/CULTURE: CHINESE, MALAY, INDIAN, EUROPEAN AND JAPANESE

SINGAPORE

Lion heart

The earliest recorded reference to Singapore is in a Chinese account, in which the island is referred to as Pu-luo-chung, or "island at the end of a peninsula". Having undergone several name changes, the island finally became commonly known by its Sanskrit name, Singapura (Lion City), by the end of the 14th Century. In the second half of the 18th Century, the British established trading posts in Penang (1786) and Singapore (1819), and captured Malacca from the Dutch (1795). They were expanding trade with China at the time and wanted somewhere convenient to protect their merchant fleet, while simultaneously forestalling any advance by the Dutch in the East Indies.

By 1826, the three ports had become known as the Straits Settlements under the control of British India (later a Crown Colony in 1867). By 1832, Singapore had become the centre of government for the three areas. By the late 19th Century, Singapore was a major port of call for ships trading between Europe and East Asia, and was experiencing unprecedented prosperity.

Singapore became a Crown Colony in 1946 and attained self-government in 1959. In 1963, following discussions of Singapore's merging with the Malaya Union (formed in 1948 and incorporating Penang and Malacca), Malaysia was formed and consisted of the Federation of Malaya, Singapore, Sarawak and North Borneo (now Sabah). The merger proved to be short-lived, however. Singapore was separated from the rest of Malaysia on 9 August 1965 and became a sovereign, democratic and independent nation.

Independent Singapore was admitted to the United Nations on 21 September 1965 and became a member of the Commonwealth of Nations on 15 October 1965. On 22 December 1965, it became a republic.

FABULOUS FACTS

Singapore's multiplicity of languages reflects its racial diversity. Most Singaporeans are bilingual or multilingual.

Buddhism, Taoism, Confucianism, Islam, Christianity, Hinduism and Judaism are all practised in Singapore.

The opening of the Suez Canal in 1869 and the advent of steamships led to an eightfold increase in trade in Singapore.

The five stars on the Singaporean flag represent democracy, peace, progress, justice and equality.

Hindus walk across red-hot coals in honour of the goddess Draupadi, in an annual ritual held in Singapore City.

SINGAPORE HAS SEVERAL OUTSTANDING ATHLETES, NOT LEAST TABLE-TENNIS STARS LI JA WEI AND JING JUN HONG, WHO ARE BOTH LOOKING FORWARD TO SUCCESS AT THESE GAMES. CURRENT COMMONWEALTH GAMES TITLE HOLDER JA WEI IS A WORLD TOP-20 RANKED PLAYER. JUN HONG HAS WON SINGAPORE'S SPORTSWOMAN OF THE YEAR THREE TIMES (MOST RECENTLY IN 2001) AND WAS A SEMI-FINALIST AT THE SYDNEY OLYMPIC GAMES. SHE IS RANKED TWELFTH IN THE WORLD. JUN HONG WILL CONTINUE TO CHALK UP HONOURS AND WOULD EVENTUALLY LIKE TO COACH THE NATIONAL TEAM.

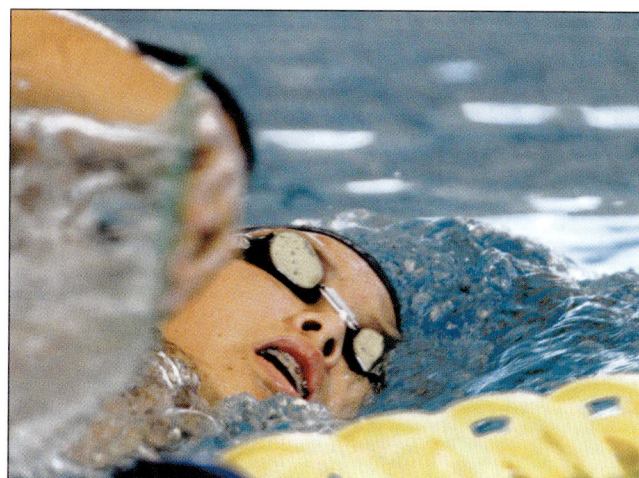

Stanley Chou (Allsport)

GNC LiveWell.
GENERAL NUTRITION CENTRES
Incredible Products
for an
Incredible Body
at
Incredible Prices
Welcome to the healthier world of GNC, the world's leading speciality retailer of nutritional supplements and self care products. Whether you're looking for vitamins, minerals or sports nutrition to aromatherapy products or special diet foods, GNC's the place for you! We put your health first and quality is our watch-word - it's got to be the best, or it's not in GNC!
20% OFF
when you join our fabulous
Gold Card Discount Scheme
Call 0845 601 3248 or log onto www.gnc.co.uk
for store details or to place an order.
GNC LiveWell.
GENERAL NUTRITION CENTRES

SOLOMON ISLANDS

CAPITAL: HONIARA
AREA: 27,556 sq km
POPULATION: 470,000
CURRENCY: SOLOMON ISLANDS DOLLAR
LANGUAGE: MELANESIAN PIDGIN, ENGLISH AND MORE THAN 80 INDIGENOUS LANGUAGES
THE PEOPLE/CULTURE: MELANESIAN WITH SOME 30,000 POLYNESIAN AND MICRONESIAN

Under the surface

The Solomon Islands lie in the Pacific Ocean and are made up of more than 990 islands, most notably Choiseul, Guadalcanal, Santa Isabel, San Cristobal, Rennell and Bellona, Malaita and New Georgia. Early civilisation on the islands has been traced back some 5,000 years, to the arrival of Austronesian immigrants, neolithic people from South-East Asia. The first documented European contact was made in 1568 by the Spanish explorer, Alvaro de Mendana, who discovered alluvial gold on Guadalcanal. According to legend, he believed he had found the source of King Solomon's great wealth and named the islands the "Isles of Solomon".

Great Britain declared a protectorate over the southern Solomon Islands in 1893, adding the Santa Cruz group in 1898 and 1899. The islands of the Shortland group were transferred by treaty from Germany to Great Britain in 1900. The Solomon Islands became a fully independent nation in 1978 and today, the country operates under a system of nine provinces.

Some of the worst naval battles of the Second World War were fought here and the wrecks have created artificial reefs, which attract masses of fish and an incredible variety of coral life. One of the most intact wrecks is that of the Toa Maru, a Japanese ship that was sunk by American bombers in 1943. A dive to the wreck reveals trucks, tanks, ammunition and even sake bottles.

The Solomon Islands may be small in size, but they're tough competitors and will be challenging in the wrestling and boxing events. We wish them luck.

REPUBLIC OF SOUTH AFRICA

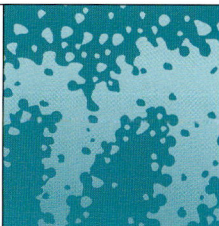

CAPITAL: PRETORIA (ADMINISTRATIVE), CAPE TOWN (LEGISLATIVE), BLOEMFONTEIN (JUDICIAL)

AREA: 1,219,090 sq km

POPULATION: 43,981,758

CURRENCY: RAND

LANGUAGE: SOUTH AFRICA HAS 11 OFFICIAL LANGUAGES: AFRIKAANS AND ENGLISH (EUROPEAN ORIGIN); ZULU, XHOSA, SISWATI AND NDEBELE (NGUNI LANGUAGE GROUP); SOUTHERN SOTHO, NORTHERN SOTHO AND TSWANA (SOTHO LANGUAGE GROUP); TSONGA; AND VENDA

THE PEOPLE: AFRICAN DESCENT, WHITE, MIXED AND INDIAN

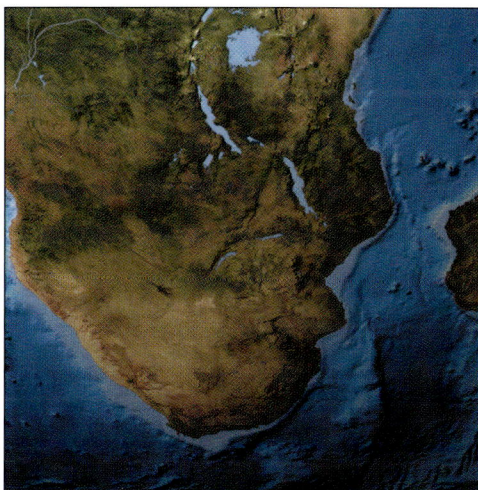

South of the border

The Dutch East India Company landed at the Cape of Good Hope in 1652. They were known as Boers or Afrikaners and developed the Dutch dialect, Afrikaans. British settlers arrived in 1814 and took possession of the Cape Colony. Following years saw the anglicisation of government and the freeing of slaves. Some 12,000 Afrikaners were forced into African tribal territory, where they established the Transvaal and the Orange Free State. The discovery of diamonds in 1867 and gold nine years later in these new republics led Cecil Rhodes, Prime Minister of Cape Colony to plot annexation. His plans failed and he resigned in 1895. A war with the Boers broke four years later (they were defeated in 1902). The Union of South Africa was established in 1910; comprising the two republics and the old Cape and Natal colonies. Louis Botha became the first prime minister and the African National Congress (ANC) was established in 1912. The country joined the UN in 1945, but wouldn't sign the Universal Declaration of Human Rights. Apartheid – racial separation – dominated domestic politics. South Africa became a Republic in 1961, cutting ties with the Commonwealth. The subsequent Nationalist government imposed rigid racial laws and, in 1967, Prime Minister Verwoerd was assassinated. His successor, Balthazar J Vorster, began reforms, followed by president FW de Klerk in 1989, who removed a ban on the ANC and released Nelson Mandela after 27 years of imprisonment. In 1991, Parliament dropped apartheid laws concerning property ownership and the Population Registration Act of 1950. In 1994, Mandela and his ANC enjoyed a massive election victory. Mandela retired in 1999 and was replaced by Thabo Mbeki on 2 June 1999.

FABULOUS FACTS

South Africa's vast Kruger National Park in supports the greatest variety of wildlife species on the entire African continent.

Johannesburg is the third largest African city, nicknamed "City of Gold" after gold was discovered there in 1886.

South Africa is often referred to as "The Rainbow Nation" due to its exceptionally multicultural population.

The 3,106-carat Cullinan is the world's biggest diamond and was discovered in Pretoria in 1905.

Notably, the Republic of South Africa has three capital cities: Pretoria, Cape Town and Bloemfontein.

HAVING WON THE WORLD SERIES RUGBY SEVENS TOURNAMENT IN NEW ZEALAND EARLIER THIS YEAR, EXPECTATIONS WILL BE RUNNING HIGH FOR THE SOUTH AFRICAN TEAM AT THIS YEAR'S GAMES. AMONG THE FAVOURITES ARE NEW ZEALAND (CURRENT COMMONWEALTH GAMES TITLE-HOLDERS), AUSTRALIA AND SAMOA (THE TEAM LOST NARROWLY TO SOUTH AFRICA IN THE NZ WORLD SERIES FINAL). COACH CHESTER WILLIAMS SAID OF THE SOUTH AFRICAN VICTORY: "IT FEELS VERY GOOD. MY INITIAL AIM WHEN I TOOK OVER WAS TO GET THE SIDE TO IMPROVE, BUT MY MAIN GOAL WAS FOR THE SIDE TO WIN A TOURNAMENT."

Stanley Chou (Getty Images)

drop anchor at
Albert Dock
...your quay to a great day out!

The Beatles Story

Merseyside Maritme Museum

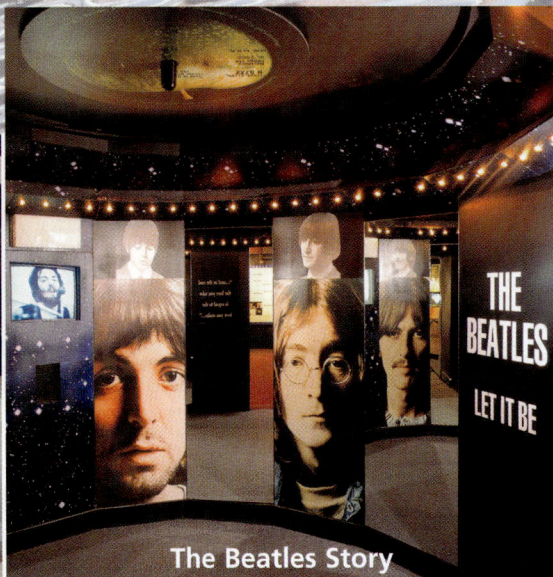

Tate Gallery

Tate Liverpool

speciality shopping

cafes

restaurants

bars

entertainment

dock tours

. THE ALBERT DOCK .
· L I V E R P O O L ·

Open EVERY DAY of the week from 10am
Bars and restaurants open until late

Enquiries: Albert Dock Tourist Information Centre
Tel: 0151 708 8854
Email: askme@visitliverpool.co

Visit the Albert Dock website: www.albertdock.com

*Stay at the Dock's own "Express by Holiday Inn" hotel.
New Premier Lodge Hotel opening 2003.*

The Room Store

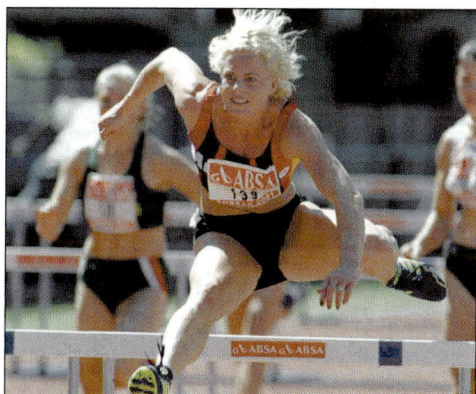

Stu Forster, Touchline Photo (Allsport)

SOUTH AFRICA WILL ALSO BE WELL REPRESENTED IN TRACK AND FIELD EVENTS, AND SHOULD COME AWAY WITH A GOOD NUMBER OF MEDALS. SURITA FEBBRAIO HAS HAD A VERY GOOD SEASON SO FAR AND, WITH A PERSONAL BEST OF 54.10 SECONDS, SHE WILL REPRESENT A SIGNIFICANT CHALLENGE IN THE 400M WOMEN'S HURDLES. MORNÉ NAGEL HAS ALSO HAD A GOOD SEASON, SETTING A PERSONAL BEST OF 20.10 SECONDS IN THE MEN'S 200M.

DISCUS THROWER FRANTZ KRUGER IS ONE OF SOUTH AFRICA'S BIGGEST MEDAL HOPES. "DOC" – KRUGER IS A MEDICAL STUDENT – TOOK BRONZE IN SYDNEY 2000, BEFORE BEATING THE OLYMPIC CHAMPION, VIRGILIJUS ALEKNA, AT THE 2001 GOODWILL GAMES.

FABULOUS FACTS

Durban is the location for the Juma Mosque, which is the largest mosque in the entire Southern hemisphere.

Adrenaline junkies don't have to go cold turkey in South Africa: try ostrich riding or the world's highest bungee jump.

Rock and cave paintings created by the San, South Africa's original inhabitants, date back 26,000 years.

South Africa is home to the ostrich (the world's largest bird) and also the Kori bustard (the world's largest flying bird).

Public holidays were renamed after the 1994 elections: Human Rights Day now commemorates the Sharpeville massacre.

JACQUES FREITAG SHOULD ALSO BE FLYING HIGH IN MANCHESTER. HE SET AN AFRICAN RECORD IN THE HIGH JUMP OF 2.33M IN FEBRUARY 2002; THE 21-YEAR-OLD LOOKS LIKE HE HAS A BRIGHT FUTURE.

Touchline Photo, Darren England (Allsport)

A wine for all seasons

Official Licensed Product
2002 Manchester.

Bonnievale
south africa

Bonnievale pinotage 2001
Bonnievale cabernet sauvignon 2001
Bonnievale merlot 2001
Bonnievale blush 2001
Bonnievale colombar 2001
Bonnievale sauvignon blanc 2001
Bonnievale chenin blanc 2001
Bonnievale chardonnay 2001

LIVERPOOL
the world in one city

On behalf of the people and the city of Liverpool, we wish you all a very successful 2002 Commonwealth Games.

The Games is great for Manchester, the North West and for sport. I am particularly proud that 25 athletes from Liverpool will be taking part. Most have come through the city council's Sports Development programme.

But the Games is about more than sport. It is about human endeavour, effort and excellence. And it is also about bringing people together. That's why Liverpool is supporting Manchester 2002 by taking part in the multi-cultural Spirit of Friendship programme.

Liverpool will be welcoming acts and events from all over the Commonwealth including Aboriginal artists, Africa Oye, the UK's only African Music Festival, and the 22-night Summer Pops, which this year boasts a truly international line-up of top class acts. We hope our involvement will add to the attractions which the thousands of visitors to the North West of England can enjoy this year.

So welcome, enjoy the Games and our rich culture. And have a great time!

Best wishes,

Mike Storey

Mike Storey, CBE
Leader, Liverpool City Council

SRI LANKA

CAPITAL: SRI JAYAWARDENEPURA (LEGISLATIVE), COLOMBO (ADMINISTRATIVE)
AREA: 65,610 sq km
POPULATION: 19,355,053
CURRENCY: SRI LANKAN RUPIYALA
LANGUAGES: SINHALA, TAMIL, ENGLISH
THE PEOPLE: SINHALA, TAMILS, MOOR

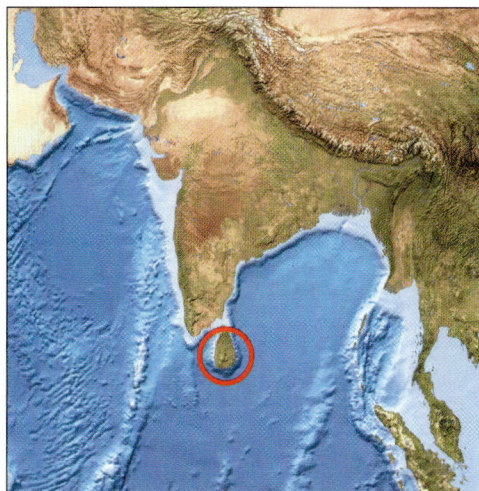

A beautiful teardrop

The Democratic Socialist Republic of Sri Lanka, an island covering 66,000 sq km located just off the south eastern tip of the the Indian peninsula, is a diverse island with a mix of culture, breathtaking beaches and hills, and a friendly, accommodating population.

Occupied by the Portuguese in the 16th Century and the Dutch in the 17th Century, the island was ceded to the British in 1802. As Ceylon, it became independent in 1948 and its name was changed in 1972. Since then, the country has established a sound democratic system. In 1977, the present constitution was introduced, including provision for a strong executive presidency.

Unfortunately for visitors to Sri Lanka, much of the country is off-limits to tourists. Civil War has raged in the country since 1983; southwestern Sri Lanka is the only area open to the tourist trade at the moment. However, relations between the Liberation Tigers of Tamil Eelam and the Sri Lankan government have recently eased somewhat.

Geographically, Sri Lanka is quite magical. There are endless expanses of idyllic beaches to the south of Colombo and in the cooler hill country, many of the hillsides are covered with tea plantations. There is a wide range of bird life native to the island and larger game in the shape of elephants and leopards. The island's principal industries are in the agricultural sector – they include the production of: rubber, tea, tobacco, rice, sugarcane, grains and pulses, oilseed, spices, beef and coconuts.

FABULOUS FACTS

From December to April, pilgrims from a variety of religions converge to climb a hill named Adam's Peak.

The village of Kitulgala was the location for Sir David Lean's 1957 film masterpiece, Bridge Over the River Kwai.

For Westerners, nodding your head means yes, while shaking it means no. It is the complete opposite in Sri Lanka.

The Dalada Maligawa is a temple housing Sri Lanka's most important religious relic – the tooth of Buddha.

Sri Lanka means "Resplendent Island". Marco Polo described it as the most beautiful island he'd ever seen.

ASIAN GAMES GOLD MEDALLIST SUGATH TILLAKARATNE (MEN'S 400M), ASIAN CHAMPIONSHIPS DOUBLE GOLD MEDALLIST ROHAN PRADEEP KUMARA (MEN'S 400M), COMMONWEALTH GAMES SILVER MEDALLIST SRIYANI KULAWANSA (WOMEN'S 100M HURDLES) AND ASIAN GAMES DOUBLE GOLD MEDALLIST DAMAYANTHI DARSHA (WOMEN'S 400M) HAVE BEEN IN INTENSIVE TRAINING FOR THE GAMES. SUSANTHIKA JAYASINGHE, KNOWN IN HER NATIVE LAND AS "THE DAZZLING GAZELLE" IS ALSO HOPING TO ADD TO HER MEDAL TALLY, AFTER WINNING A BRONZE IN THE 200M AT THE SYDNEY OLYMPICS.

Scott Barbour (Allsport)

ST HELENA

CAPITAL: JAMESTOWN
AREA: 410 sq km
POPULATION: 7,197
CURRENCY: ST HELENA POUND
LANGUAGE: ENGLISH
THE PEOPLE/CULTURE: AFRICAN DESCENT

An island fit for an emperor

The island of St Helena can be found in the tropical South Atlantic, 2,414 km to the north west of Cape Town. It is said that the Portuguese first came across the island in 1502, though conflicting evidence suggests that it may have been discovered on 30 July 1503 by a squadron under the command of Estavao da Gama. For more than 150 years, the island was used by Portuguese, Dutch and English mariners as a victualling station on their return passage from the East Indies. However, in the main, the island remained uninhabited.

St Helena was formally granted to the East India Company in 1673 after the Royal Navy captured the island from the Dutch, who had occupied it from January to May of that year. The Company's proprietorship of the island continued until April 1834, when St Helena was vested in the Crown by provision of the Government of India Act 1833, although the East India Company continued to administer the island until 1836. The island has been a colony ever since, although it is now more commonly described as a dependent territory.

Since the advent of air travel, St Helena, which to this day lacks an airport, has suffered – the only significant trade is in coffee, the export of fish and the sale of postage stamps.

St Helena is a predominantly rural community, where the inhabitants grow their own maize, potatoes and green vegetables; they also raise their own animals. The island is most famed for being home to Napoleon, who spent his final days on the island in exile, from 1815 to 1821.

In sporting terms, St Helena first became involved in international sport when it accepted an invitation from the Isle of Man in 1985 to take part in the newly organised Island Games, held in the Isle of Man that year. In 1998, the island took two athletes to the Kuala Lumpur Commonwealth Games. We look forward to welcoming a larger contingent in Manchester.

ST KITTS & NEVIS

CAPITAL: BASSETERRE
AREA: 269 sq km
POPULATION: 38,756
CURRENCY: EAST CARIBBEAN DOLLAR
LANGUAGE: ENGLISH
THE PEOPLE/CULTURE: AFRICAN DESCENT WITH SOME BRITISH, PORTUGESE AND LEBANESE

The sugar islands

St Kitts became the site of the first British colony in the West Indies in 1623. The following year, the French also settled in part of St Kitts. After they had killed off the native Caribs in a series of bloody battles, the British and French turned on each other and St Kitts changed hands between the two several times, before the 1783 Treaty of Paris brought the island firmly under British control.

Nevis has a similar history. In 1628, a British settlement was established on the western coast; Nevis went on to prosper, developing one of the most affluent plantation societies in the Eastern Caribbean.

In 1816, the British linked St Kitts and Nevis with Anguilla and the Virgin Islands to form a single colony. In 1958, these islands became part of the West Indies Federation. When the federation dissolved a mere four years later, the British positioned St Kitts, Nevis and Anguilla together as a new state.

In 1967, the three islands were given independence from the Crown as an associated state. In the same year, Anguilla withdrew from the union with St Kitts and Nevis, becoming first an independent republic then, at its own request, a dependency of the United Kingdom. St Kitts and Nevis jointly attained full independence within the Commonwealth of Nations in 1983 under its official name, the Federation of Saint Kitts and Nevis.

The inhabitants of Nevis went to the polls on 10 August 1998, to decide whether it should secede from St Kitts. The results revealed that 61.8 per cent of the electorate supported independence. This fell just short of the two-thirds majority required under the terms of the constitution of the two-island federation.

In 1993, St Kitts and Nevis was recognised by the International Olympic Committee and in 1998, entered the Commonwealth Games. Kim Collins, who competed with compatriot Velma Collins at the 2000 Olympics, will be coming to Manchester full of hope after narrowly missing out on the men's 200m final in Sydney.

Bolton

a great place to visit, in which to live, learn and do business.

Business

Bolton provides the infrastructure and support for businesses to prosper. It has already attracted over £300 million worth of investment since 1992 and operates an award winning business support network.

Visiting

Bolton is one of northern England's most vibrant towns, with a wealth of attractions and events all year round. 8 million visitors annually visit this cosmopolitan town, proud to be an official Commonwealth Games venue.

Living

Bolton has a huge programme of celebrations and multi-cultural activity. As 1 of 14 local authorities to pilot a Local cultural strategy, Bolton creates an environment that allows people to do their best.

Lifelong Learning

Bolton provides opportunities for everyone to fulfil their potential through learning. From formal education right through to gaining knowledge and skills from on the job training and working in the community.

Telephone 01204 394645 (24 hours)

Business Enquiries: business@bolton.gov.uk
Visitor Enquiries: tourist.info@bolton.gov.uk

www.bolton.gov.uk

BOLTON M·E·T·R·O

Manchester 2002

See it **live** in Bolton

bolton 2002 COMMONWEALTH GAMES OFFICIAL VENUE

Objective 2 European funding, assisting the local economy

THE ETHNIC MINORITIES BUSINESS SERVICE

HITACHI

SAINT LUCIA

CAPITAL: CASTRIE
AREA: 616 sq km
POPULATION: 158,178
CURRENCY: EAST CARIBBEAN DOLLAR
LANGUAGE: ENGLISH; FRENCH PATOIS
THE PEOPLE/CULTURE: 90 PER CENT AFRICAN; FOUR PER CENT EUROPEAN/ EAST INDIAN

Twin peaks

Archeological finds on the island indicate that St Lucia was settled by Arawaks between 1000 and 500 BC. Around 800 AD migrating Caribs conquered the Arawaks and established permanent settlements on the island. The first attempt at European colonisation came in 1605, when a party of English settlers was routed by the Caribs. A second attempt by British colonists from St Kitts was made in 1638, but the settlement was abandoned within two years, after most of the settlers were killed in attacks.

After the British left, the French laid claim to the island and in 1746, the French established the island's first town, Soufrière, and began developing plantations. The British successfully invaded in 1778 and established naval bases on the island. In1814, the island was ceded to the British.

St Lucia gained autonomy in 1967 and full independence, as a member of the British Commonwealth, in 1979. Since then tourism has boomed.

In spite of the recent resort developments, the rural areas in the south of the island are truly unspoilt. The island's two most impressive landmarks are also found in this area: the twin volcanic peaks of the Pitons cast an imposing shadow over the rest of the island.

In 1998, St Lucia sent six athletes to the Commonwealth Games and a similar number will be in Manchester. These will undoubtedly include pole vaulter Dominic Johnson, who is the current Central American and Caribbean men's champion. He will be joined by swimmer Jamie Peterkin, who represented the island in the 2000 Olympics and Zepherinus Joseph, the promising distance runner who may be an outside bet for a medal.

ST VINCENT AND THE GRENADINES

CAPITAL: KINGSTOWN
AREA: 389 sq km
POPULATION: 115,942
CURRENCY: EAST CARIBBEAN DOLLAR
LANGUAGE: ENGLISH (OFFICIAL), FRENCH PATOIS
THE PEOPLE/CULTURE: BLACK AFRICAN DESCENT, WHITE, EAST INDIAN, CARIB NATIVE AMERICAN

Rugged yet beautiful

St Vincent is a rugged and raw-edged backwater, while the 30 islands and cays that comprise the Grenadines are among the most popular cruising grounds in the Caribbean. The Grenadine islands stretch from St Vincent to Grenada and they are surrounded by coral reefs and crystal clear waters – perfect for diving and sailing. Less than a dozen of these islands are populated – even those that are have sparse, scattered populations and scant development.

The first full-time European settlers on the island were the French in the early 1700s. In 1783, the Treaty of Versailles recognised St Vincent as a British colony and plantation owners enjoyed great prosperity until 1812, when La Soufrière volcano erupted. A second eruption in 1902 resulted in the deaths of 2,000 inhabitants and destroyed what was left of the plantation economy.

In 1979, St Vincent and the Grenadines acquired full independence as a member of the Commonwealth. La Soufrière erupted that same year, spewing a blanket of ash over much of the island, necessitating the evacuation of 20,000 people. In 1984, Sir James F Mitchell was elected prime minister and his New Democratic Party was in power throughout the 1990s. In the 2001 elections, the Unity Party took control. Like their Caribbean neighbours, the people of St Vincent and The Grenadines are sports mad – cricket and football are played and watched with passion. The islands' most famous athlete is marathon runner Pamenos Avorsant Ballantyne, who will be hoping to make his nation proud as he pounds the streets of Manchester.

centre of attention

G·MEX
manchester
I·C·C

The Perfect Partnership

Major venue for the

Commonwealth Games 2002

englandsnorthwest

on your doorstep...

Take time to discover England's North West.

On your doorstep - ultra-chic cities where cultural treasures and breathtaking architecture rub shoulders with the stylish and the hip.

On your doorstep - rural escapes, combining laid back lifestyles with adrenaline infused outdoor pursuits.

On your doorstep - colourful landscapes and sights that stir the soul, a place where friendliness and warm welcomes are guaranteed.

englandsnorthwest - on your doorstep.

Call **0845 600 6040** or visit **www.englandsnorthwest.com**

SWAZILAND

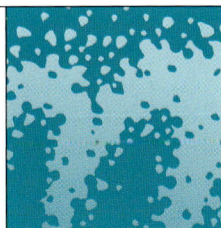

CAPITAL: MBABANE
AREA: 17,363 sq km
POPULATION: 1,004,072
CURRENCY: LLILANGENI
LANGUAGE: ENGLISH SISWATI
THE PEOPLE: AFRICAN, EUROPEAN

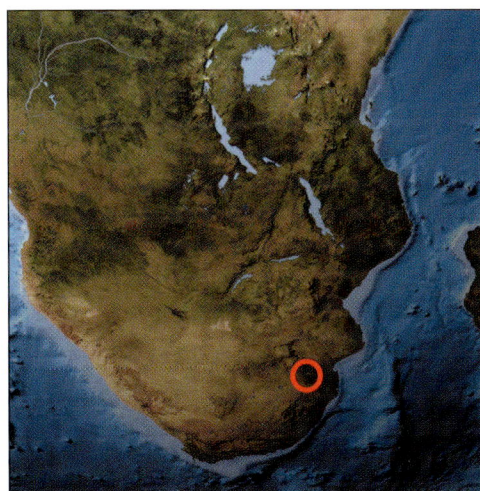

Small but perfectly formed

Swaziland is the smallest country in the Southern hemisphere and its people are some of the friendliest in the world according to those who have visited. In addition, it's a land with a rich and ancient history. In eastern Swaziland, archaeologists have discovered human remains dating back 110,000 years, but the Swazi people arrived only relatively recently. It wasn't until the middle of the 18th Century that a Dlamini king, Ngwane III, lead his people south to what is now southern Swaziland.

In 1877, the British annexed the nation, but the Swaziland Convention of 1881 guaranteed the nation's independence on paper, while considerably contracting its borders, and any real independence was short-lived.

In 1968, Swaziland achieved independence from Britain and King Sobhuza II, who had reigned since 1921, became the official head of the new state. Swaziland inherited a constitution largely the work of the British – though King Sobhuza II suspended it in 1973, on the grounds that it did not reflect Swazi culture. Four years later, Parliament reconvened under a new constitution that vested all power to the king. Sobhuza was followed in 1986 by King Mswati, who continues to maintain and represent tradition.

Swaziland will be bringing a good sized squad to the Games, including Bongiwe Mndzebele, who will run in the 800m and Siphesihle Mdluli, who is competing in the 10,000m. It will also have a 14-strong lawn bowls team, as well as competitors in weightlifting and boxing.

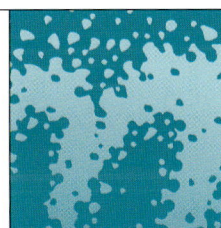

TONGA

CAPITAL: NUKU'ALOFA
AREA: 750 sq km
POPULATION: 109,959
CURRENCY: PA'ANGA
LANGUAGE: TONGAN AND ENGLISH
THE PEOPLE: TONGAN, EUROPEAN, POLYNESIAN

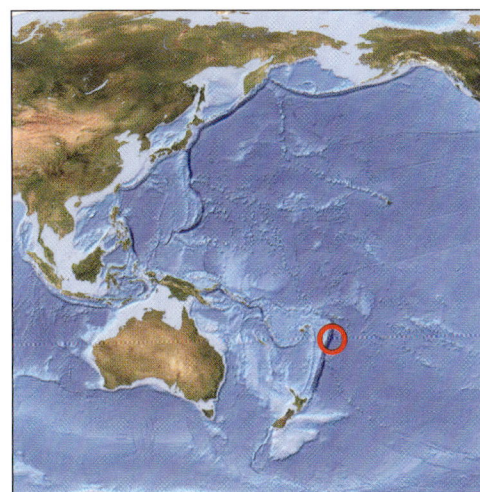

The friendly islands

Tonga, one of the many Polynesian islands that lie to the east of Australia, is known for its incredible beaches, the numerous coral reefs that surround the islands and tropical sunshine. The Dutch were the first Europeans to visit Tonga, in 1616. Captain James Cook came from England in 1773 and returned in 1777, naming Tonga "the friendly islands" because he was treated so well by the inhabitants.

Civil war erupted in the 1790s and continued until 1849, when the islanders were united into a kingdom by Chief Taufa'ahau Tupou. Tupou, chief of the Ha'apai, converted to Christianity in 1831 and renamed himself George IV, after the British King. In 1845, Topou proclaimed himself King George Tupou I and founded the dynasty that has ruled to this day. Tonga and the UK signed a treaty of friendship and in 1900, the United Kingdom made Tonga a protectorate. In 1970, Tonga became completely independent of the UK and joined the Commonwealth.

Tonga may be small in terms of area and population, but to coin a boxing phrase, they punch above their weight in the sports arena. They first participated in the 1984 Los Angeles Olympic Games in boxing, bringing just two officials and two competitors. Tongan superheavyweight boxer Paea Wolfgramm won the country's first Olympic medal – a silver – at the 1996 Olympic Games.

For this year's Commonwealth Games, Tonga will be sending its powerful and combative Rugby 7s team to challenge neighbours like Australia and Fiji, and Northern hemisphere rivals like England and Scotland. Also, watch out for Tongan athletes in the weightlifting and boxing events.

TRINIDAD & TOBAGO

CAPITAL: PORT-OF-SPAIN
AREA: 5,128 sq km
POPULATION: 1,169,682
CURRENCY: TRINIDAD AND TOBAGO DOLLAR
LANGUAGE: ENGLISH (OFFICIAL), HINDI, FRENCH, SPANISH, CHINESE
THE PEOPLE: AFRICAN DESCENT, EAST INDIAN, MIXED, EUROPEAN, CHINESE

Crusoe's island

Trinidad and Tobago epitomises the Caribbean's reputation as a melting pot of cultures, with a mix of people from virtually all the world's continents. Lying just 16 km from the Venezuelan coast, off the Orinico delta, it is the southernmost Caribbean island and was once connected to the South American mainland. This proximity has provided it with its vast gas and oil reserves.

Christopher Columbus discovered both islands in 1498, christening the larger of the two "La isla de la Trinidad" (Holy Trinity). Soon after, the original Amerindians became slaves for Spain's expanding empire in South America. However, it wasn't until 1597 that the Spaniards colonised Trinidad, establishing the settlement of San Josef. No attempt was made to colonise the smaller island of Tobago and in 1704 it was declared a neutral island, becoming a haven for pirates. The English wrested Trinidad from Spain in 1797, while Tobago came under English sovereignty in 1802; both islands became a single colony in 1889. African slaves worked the plantations until the abolition of slavery in the 1830s, when indentured labourers from China and India were brought in. Today, Indian influence is still strong in many Trinidadian villages, while African influences predominate in others. Trinidad and Tobago became independent on 31 August 1962. Although both islands are valued for their agricultural produce, including sugar, coffee and cocoa, another major export has also been the naturally occurring asphalt and crude oil, which has been the life-blood of the Trinidadian economy for the last hundred years. Discovered in the south of the island in the 1860s, it was first exported in 1900, and in the 1970s, the country experienced an oil boom (and became the third largest exporter in the world). Today, Trinidad and Tobago also has a flourishing tourist industry.

FABULOUS FACTS

Trinidad is the home of the Caribbean Carnival, with amazing celebrations that last more than two months.

The steel drum (Pan) was invented in Trinidad about half a century ago, using the hammered-out ends of old oil drums.

Pitch Lake in Trinidad is a 40ha lake of tar and is the world's biggest natural source of bitumen.

Trinidad and Tobago has 400 species of birds, 600 species of butterflies, 50 kinds of reptile and 100 different mammals.

It's believed that Tobago was the inspiration for Daniel Defoe's *The Adventures of Robinson Crusoe*.

ATO BOLDEN, THE 100M OLYMPIC SILVER MEDALLIST AND 100M GOLD MEDALLIST AT THE KUALA LUMPUR GAMES, IS THE MAN TO WATCH. HE CLOCKED A TIME OF 9.88SEC IN MALAYSIA, SMASHING THE COMMONWEALTH RECORD. TEAMMATE DARREL BROWN IS A RISING STAR AND, AT 16, BECAME THE YOUNGEST EVER MEDALLIST WHEN HE HELPED TRINIDAD AND TOBAGO SECURE THIRD PLACE IN THE 4X100M RELAY AT THE WORLD CHAMPIONSHIPS IN EDMONTON LAST YEAR. STEVE BROWN WON THE SILVER IN THE 110M HURDLES AND WENDELL WILLIAMS TOOK BRONZE FOR LONG JUMP AT KUALA LUMPUR. TRINIDAD ALSO HAS A GOOD PRESENCE IN NETBALL; THE COUNTRY IS RANKED SEVENTH IN THE WORLD.

Adam Pretty (Allsport)

The things I value.
SALLY GUNNELL | *athlete*

"NFU Mutual have individual insurance policies to suit me and my family.
I think they're the best at what they do. And that's something I've always valued."

NFU **Mutual**

insurance brought down to earth

0845 704 5031 www.nfumutual.co.uk

It's takes years of training
to prepare the perfect body.

Even beautiful bodies occasionally need some help. And if yours is unlucky enough to need an accident insurance claim, remember: it's your decision which body specialist you use, not your insurer's. The good news is the UK's most advanced Bodyshop, Blue Bell, is right on your doorstep. And as well as technology that's the envy of our competitors, we offer a free Accident Management Service – whatever the make and model of your car. From collecting your car within a 50 mile radius, to dealing with your insurer and providing you with a loan car, we'll take care of everything – from start to a perfect finish.

Call us on 0800 1380678 to receive your Blue Bell Accident Management Card, it's free, and as they say, don't leave home without it.

Blue Bell Bodyshop
Brooke Park
Lower Meadow Road
Handforth, Wilmslow
Cheshire SK9 3LP
Tel: 0800 1380678

www.bluebellbmw.co.uk

BMW Approved
Bodyshop

BMW

The Ultimate
Driving Machine

TURKS & CAICOS

CAPITAL: COCKBURN TOWN
AREA: 430 sq km
POPULATION: 18,122
CURRENCY: UNITED STATES DOLLAR
LANGUAGE: ENGLISH
PEOPLE: AFRICAN DESCENT

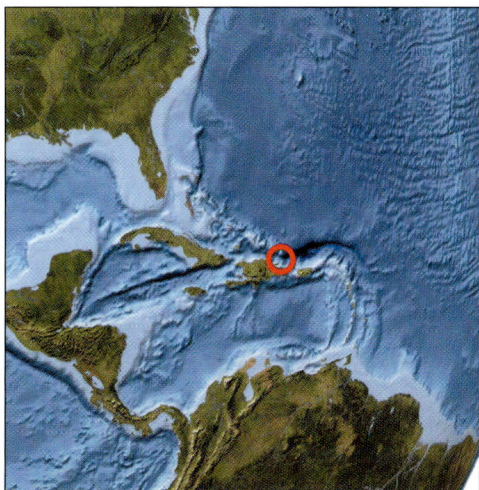

Isles of plenty

This island group lies 30 miles south of the Bahamas and boasts one of the longest coral reefs in the world, with vast white sandy beaches that cover a total area of 230 miles. The first inhabitants were the Taino Indians, who built ball courts similar to those that were found in the Mayan cities of Central America and also unearthed in Bermuda. However, the arrival of the Europeans spelled their doom and by the mid-16th Century, the culture had disappeared. The islands had for centuries been subjected to a tug of war between the French and British, but they remained uninhabited due to lack of resources and a dry climate that prohibited the growing of sugar cane. Eventually they were settled in 1678 by Bermudans, who extracted salt and logged timber. Salt traders created salt drying pans that still exist on some islands and supplied the cod-fishing industries of New England and Canada. In 1766, the Bahamian government extended its jurisdiction to cover the islands.

Following the American War of Independence, a wave of loyalists settled on the islands, bringing with them their African slaves, the descendants of whom now form the majority of the island's population.

In 1872, the islands were annexed to Jamaica until 1962, when they were passed back to the Bahamas. In 1973, the islands became a separate crown colony of Britain. Today, the islands attract tourists lured by the pristine beaches and superb diving. The islands also have a reputation for being a retreat for jet-setting millionaires, including the likes of Teddy Roosevelt III.

Like its neighbours, Turks and Caicos is wild about all sports, particularly football and netball. In 1998, the country sent four athletes to the Kuala Lumpur games.

TUVALU

CAPITAL: FUNAFUTI
AREA: 26 sq km
POPULATION: 10,730
CURRENCY: TUVALUAN DOLLAR; AUSTRALIAN DOLLAR
LANGUAGE: TUVALUAN, ENGLISH
PEOPLE: POLYNESIAN

The "Internet" islands

Formerly known as the Ellice Islands, Tuvalu recently hit the headlines when the Prime Minister declared that he was suing the industrialised nations over rising sea levels. Tuvalu is made up almost exclusively of coral and the islands are no higher than 5m above sea level at any point, so they are certainly at risk if sea levels continue to rise. With a population of just over 10,000, this small collection of Pacific islands to the east of Australia is also one of the smallest countries in the world.

Polynesians from Tonga and Samoa originally settled in Tuvalu in the 14th Century. In 1597, Don Alvaro de Mendana left Peru in search of a legendary land and discovered the Tuvalu islands. The islands were mapped in 1826 and were named the Ellice Islands after the English MP who owned the ship that first landed on Funafuti Atoll in 1819. In 1916, the islands became a crown colony; by 1978, Tuvalu was independent. Prior to the introduction of Christianity, Tuvaluans worshipped a number of island gods, placating them with offerings of food and possessions. Powerful priests called "vaka atua" acted as intermediaries between the people and the gods, and presided over special ceremonies. Today, Tuvaluans still adhere to a traditional way of life, including a deep respect for family, community and environment. In 1998, the Islands were named as the only nation above reproach for human rights violation.

A major source of income is derived from the licensing of its ".tv" internet domain name and also the sale of highly sought-after postage stamps.

Tuvalu brought two athletes to the Kuala Lumpur Games in 1998 and is expected to send a team of eight to this year's Games.

UGANDA

CAPITAL: KAMPALA
AREA: 241,038 sq km
POPULATION: 23,451,687
CURRENCY: UGANDAN SHILLING
LANGUAGE: ENGLISH, SWAHILI AND ARABIC
THE PEOPLE/CULTURE: GANDA, NYANKOLE, KIGA, SOGA, ITESO, LANGI, ACHOLI

Have a gander at Uganda

Legend has it that Uganda takes its name from a poor hunter who hunted to feed his family, but was so successful he was soon feeding his neighbours. Eventually he became Kimera, the first King of Buganda. Landlocked Uganda is made up of a complex range of tribes, speaking mainly Bantu and Nilotic languages. The 16th Century saw the emergence of various kingdoms, with the Bugandan people eventually becoming the dominant one. It wasn't until the 19th Century that contact was made with Arabs and European explorers; at this time there were three main kingdoms – Buganda, Kitara and Karagwe.

In 1857, the British explorers John Hanning Speke and Francis Burton set out on the expedition that would lead to Speke's discovery of Lake Victoria. He also found the source of the Nile on his return journey with Augustus Grant in 1862. Trade was established and Uganda formally became a British protectorate in 1894. Colonial rule was characterised by "indirect rule", whereby a civil service made up of the Baganda administered the colony. An oligarchy of Baganda chiefs received huge estates from the British and were able to accrue vast wealth, while the Acholi and Lango sought influence in the military. This policy would have far-reaching consequences in later years.

The recent history of Uganda, once described by Winston Churchill as the Pearl of Africa, has been one of tragedy and upheaval. Since 1962, when Uganda gained independence, there have been seven presidents and eight regimes, including the dictatorship of Idi Amin (1971-79). Amin was finally ousted by Milton Obote and in 1986, Yoweri Museveni became president, introducing democratic reforms. Uganda is now one of the world's fastest growing countries, with the modern, bustling Kampala at its hub.

FABULOUS FACTS

Uganda's capital city is built on 21 hills and takes its name from Kasozi Kampala, "The Hill of Antelopes".

The Kibale National Park, in the Ruwenzori Mountains, boasts one of the highest densities of primates in the world.

Jinja, on the shores of the Lake Victoria, is one of the places where Gandhi chose to have his ashes scattered.

Bwindi National Park is home to 320 Mountain Gorillas – half the world's surviving population.

Situated in the "Interlacustrine Region" of Africa, more than a sixth of Uganda is covered by open water.

UGANDA HAS PRODUCED SOME OUTSTANDING ATHLETES, NONE MORE SO THAN 400M RUNNER DAVIS KAMOGA, WHO WON THE BRONZE AT THE ATLANTA OLYMPICS IN 1996 AND THE SILVER AT THE WORLD CHAMPIONSHIPS IN 1997. ALEX MALINGA IS UGANDA'S HOPE IN THE MARATHON; HE IS ONE OF THE TEN ATHLETES EXPECTED TO MAKE THE TRIP. UGANDA WILL ALSO COMPETE IN SWIMMING, WEIGHTLIFTING, SHOOTING, TABLE TENNIS AND BOXING, WHERE LIGHT MIDDLEWEIGHT ISAAC "ZEDBRA" SSENYANGE AND WELTERWEIGHTS HAMZA WANDERA AND PAUL SSERUNJOGI WILL BE ROLLING WITH THE PUNCHES.

Gary M Prior (Allsport)

Northern Exposure

Expose yourself to one of the North West's most exciting & expanding locations

Blackburn with Darwen

BLACKBURN with DARWEN BOROUGH COUNCIL

LGC AWARDS — REWARDING EXCELLENCE IN LOCAL GOVERNMENT 2002 — Council of the Year 2002

Business is Booming!

"Blackburn is the most prosperous town for business in the North West… with the town emerging as the UK's 10th top location for industry and commerce."

National Survey by D&B Business Information Specialists, 2002.

Extensive Skills Base. Quality Site Availability. Active and Buoyant Private Sector. Committed and Professional Council. Beacon Business Support Expertise. Excellent Transport Links. Major Infrastructure Investment Programmes. Rapidly Growing Local Economy. Regeneration with Vision. Planning for Success.

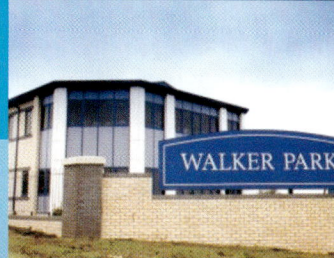

Lifestyle Blackburn with Darwen: a sub-regional centre at the top of the 'Quality of Life' Premier League.

Two Vibrant Urban Centres. Magnificent Countryside and Parklands. Quality Housing Stock. Beacon Primary and Secondary Educational Standards. Fascinating History, Heritage and Culture. Convenient Travel and Commuter Networks. Lively Arts, Entertainment and Nightlife Scene. Buzzing Town Centre and Shopping Areas. Close to the Lakes, Dales, Bronte Country and the Cities of Manchester, Liverpool and Leeds. Sporting Excellence and Exceptional Leisure Facilities.

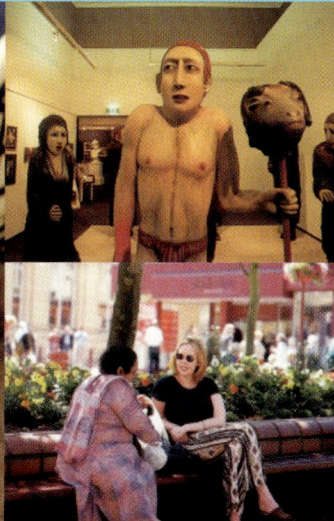

Services Blackburn with Darwen Borough Council is committed to providing a professional and pro-active support service tailored to your individual business needs.

Property / Land Acquisitions. Relocation. Inward Investment. Regeneration Initiatives. Small Business Employment Charter Grants. Public & Private Sector Partnerships. Recruitment & Training Advice and Support. Strategic Planning and Development.

Beacon Council
- Fostering Business Growth
- Fostering School Improvement
- Libraries as a Community Resource

To discover how Blackburn with Darwen can help to support your business success call: 01254 696869

LANCASHIRE – GATEWAY TO THE GAMES
Cycling events at Rivington between 27th & 3rd August

UNITED REPUBLIC OF TANZANIA

CAPITAL: DAR ES SALAAM
AREA: 945,100 sq km
POPULATION: 31,962,769
CURRENCY: TANZANIAN SHILLING
LANGUAGE: SWAHILI, ENGLISH
THE PEOPLE/CULTURE: AFRICAN, INDIAN, EUROPEAN AND ARAB

Land of the Serengeti

For many, Tanzania represents the wide-open spaces of Africa, with its abundant wildlife and the kind of dramatic scenery that simply takes your breath away. With the Serengeti, Ngorongoro crater and Mount Kilimanjaro, Tanzania's reputation as one of the world's best countries for spotting wildlife is well-deserved.

However, Tanzania is also a country of cities and trade. Zanzibar, the city that evokes romance and mystery, lies just off the Tanzanian coast. Indeed, most knowledge of the early history of Tanzania (formerly Tanganyika) centres on this coastal region. Masai warrior tribes originally migrated into Tanzania from Kenya. Neither Arab merchants nor slave traders would dare enter the Masai's territory until the middle of the 18th Century.

Trading between Arabia and the East African coast was established by the 1st Century and there are also indications of connections with India. The coastal trading centres were mainly Arab settlements. Arab interest in the region increased in the early 19th Century, with the expansion of the slave and ivory trades, to the extent that Sa'id bin Sultan moved his capital from Muscat to Zanzibar.

The first Europeans to show real interest in the region were the Germans, who started a programme of railway building around the turn of the century. After World War II, however, Tanganyika was mandated to the British. After WWII nationalist organisations emerged and took shape in 1954 under Julius Nyerere, founder of the Tanganyika African National Union (TANU). In 1964, the mainland united with Zanzibar and Pemba to form Tanzania.

FABULOUS FACTS

Each April, two million Wildebeest migrate from the 9,265 sq km Serengeti national park to new pastures in Kenya.

Zanzibar traded with a wide range of countries, but the Shirazi Persians and Omani Arabs had the biggest cultural impact.

Mount Kilimanjaro is Africa's tallest mountain (and its biggest active volcano), rising to a height of 5,893 m.

The Saleous Game Reserve has the world's largest concentration of elephant, buffalo, hippo and crocodile.

Fossils found at the world famous Olduvai Gorge disclosed some of the earliest evidence of human life.

TANZANIA HAS AN ENVIABLE RECORD IN THE COMMONWEALTH GAMES, HAVING PICKED UP A TOTAL OF FOUR GOLDS, SIX SILVERS AND SEVEN BRONZE MEDALS SINCE ITS DEBUT IN 1970. AT THE LAST COMMONWEALTH GAMES, WHERE THE NATION BROUGHT ONLY 21 ATHLETES, IT PICKED UP THREE MEDALS. SIMON BASILIGITWA WON SILVER AND ANDEA GEWAY SUJA WON BRONZE IN THE MARATHON, WHILE MICHAEL YOMBA TOOK GOLD IN THE BANTAMWEIGHT BOXING DIVISION. TANZANIA IS STRONG IN DISTANCE EVENTS AND, HAD IT NOT BEEN FOR THE EMERGENCE OF THE KENYANS, IT WOULD STILL ARGUABLY BE THE PREDOMINANT FORCE IN WORLD MARATHON RUNNING.

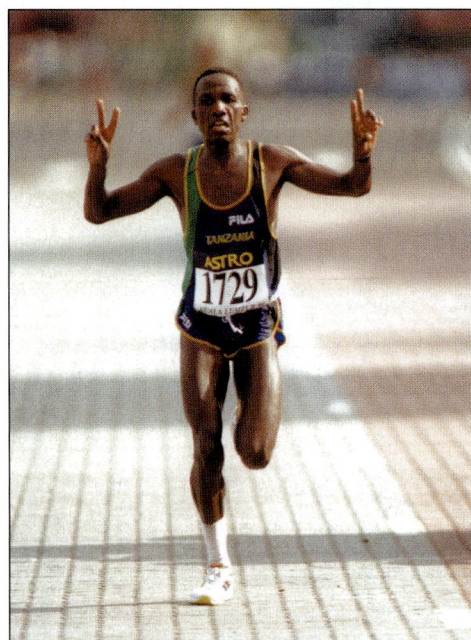

Empics

VANUATU

CAPITAL: PORT-VILA
AREA: 12,190 sq km
POPULATION: 192,848
CURRENCY: VATU
LANGUAGE: ENGLISH, FRENCH AND BISLAMA
THE PEOPLE/CULTURE: NI-VANUATU (MELANESIAN), EUROPEAN, VIETNAMESE, CHINESE, PACIFIC ISLANDERS

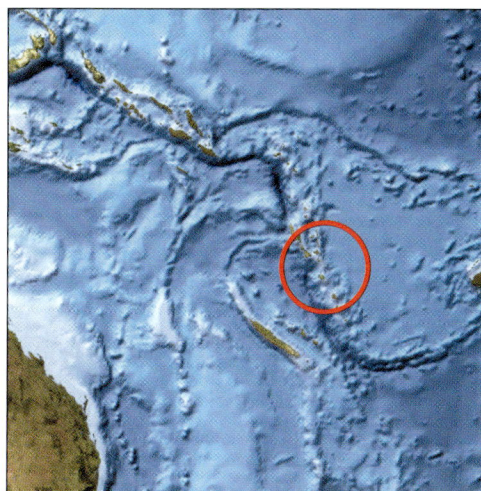

The Timeless Islands

Straddling the Pacific "rim of fire" and boasting many powerful and active volcanoes, the 80 islands that make up Vanuatu are scattered over an area slightly larger than Germany. Some of the islands have been occupied for thousands of years and pottery has been unearthed on Malo Island that is at least 4,000 years old. Separated by sea and impassable mountains, the various islands have produced a myriad of cultures with more than 100 indigenous languages. The "ni-Vanuatu", as the Vanuatuns call themselves, are made up of Melanesians who are related to the Papuans and Australian Aborigines and the lighter skinned Polynesians. Known as the "Timeless Islands" it is one of the world's most culturally diverse places. The island of Pentacost can claim to have invented Bungee jumping – between April and June, local men jump off platforms with flexible vines attached to their ankles as part of the fertility rite known as Naghol. On the island of Ambrym, villagers illustrate legends, songs and ceremonies in elaborate sand paintings.

By the end of the 18th Century, both French and English subjects had settled here and, in 1902, each nation appointed a Resident Commissioner. This arrangement continued until October 1906 when Britain and France signed the Condominium Agreement, resolving their claims to the country and placing it under the joint management of both nations. At the end of 1978, this arrangement ended and, following elections in November 1979, the nation became independent from France and the United Kingdom (on 30 July 1980). On 15 September 1981, Vanuatu joined the United Nations. In 1999, Vanuatu hosted the South Pacific Games where it won a total of 22 medals, including two gold medals in Athletics. Mary Estelle-Kapalu is Vanuatu's greatest sports woman, competing at the 1996 Olympics in the 400m flat and hurdles.

Bronze Seal

Turin Sofa Bed

Timor Sofa Bed

...and the prize for comfort goes to Slumberland

Don't lose sleep about the daunting task of selecting the right bed. Simply choose Slumberland and be confident you have chosen a manufacturer with an impeccable 80-year pedigree.

Our commitment to providing exceptional quality and value is unrivalled. That's why we have been crowned with two Royal Warrants and awarded the prestigious Guild Mark. So enjoy the games and then return home to a good nights sleep.

For a brochure contact Slumberland...

Salmon Fields, Royton, Oldham OL2 6SB
Tel: 0161 628 4886 Fax: 0161 628 4820
Email: enquiries@slumberland.co.uk

Slumberland products are available around the world, including the following Commonwealth countries: Australia/Cyprus/Kenya/Malaysia/South Africa.

Silver Seal

Gold Seal

www.slumberland.co.uk

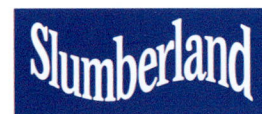
Slumberland

Too comfortable by far

WALES

CAPITAL: **CARDIFF**
AREA: 20,760 sq km
POPULATION: 2,921,000
CURRENCY: BRITISH POUND
LANGUAGE: BOTH WELSH AND ENGLISH ARE OFFICIAL LANGUAGES
THE PEOPLE/CULTURE: CAUCASIAN/EUROPEAN, INDIAN, PAKISTANI, WEST INDIAN AND AFRICAN

Wild Wales

Wales is one of the oldest countries in the world, with evidence to show that it was inhabited as early as 250,000 BC. It wasn't until the retreat of the glaciers during the Ice Age around 10,000 BC, however, that real settlement began, and by the Neolithic period (around 5,000 years ago) people were building the mysterious "Megaliths" that still dot the landscape. The Celts arrived around 1000 BC, bringing with them iron and a new language. After the departure of the Romans in the 5th Century, Wales was besieged by Irish pirates, the Scots from the North and Anglo Saxons from the East. It is thought that the legendary King Arthur led the Cymry or "fellow Countrymen" against the Anglo-Saxons (who called them Weallas, meaning "foreigner"). Viking raids in the 9th and 10th Centuries unified the various Welsh Kingdoms, although in 927 AD, the kings recognised the Anglo-Saxon, King Athelstan, as their overlord. After the Norman invasion, King William took over this mantel and so began a punitive era. The Welsh were first hemmed in by the powerful "Marcher" lords who controlled the Welsh borders and finally conquered by the bellicose Edward I who crowned himself Prince of Wales in 1302, constructing a series of massive castles. The crushing of the last armed rebellion led by Owain Glyndwr in 1400 would cause bitter enmity for centuries to come.

Coal, copper, slate and tin production – plus the arrival of the Methodism – during the Industrial Revolution gave a Wales a new identity. The growth of the new cities and colliery towns, plus trade unionism, liberalism and non-conformity, brought with it a resurgent nationalism. In 1925, Plaid Cymru (the Welsh National Party) was formed and the Welsh language was made legally acceptable in 1942, while Cardiff became the official capital in 1955. By the end of the last century, Wales had a new National Assembly.

FABULOUS FACTS

Legend says that Welsh prince Madog ab Owain Gwynedd, landed eight ships in America in 1169 – before Columbus

Many scholars believe that St Patrick was born in the still Welsh-speaking Northern Kingdom of Strathclyde c 385 AD

In 1805, Oliver Evans (a Welsh descendent) drove the first self-propelled vehicle in the US (in Philadelphia)

Llanfairpwllgwyngyll gogerychwyrndrobwyll-llantisiliogogogoch is the longest town name in England

Cambrian, a geological division in the Paleozoic era, is derived from the Latin name for Wales (Cambria)

COLIN JACKSON, 110M-HURDLE WORLD RECORD HOLDER, OLYMPIC SILVER MEDALLIST AND THREE-TIME EUROPEAN CHAMPION, IS AN OBVIOUS NAME TO LOOK OUT FOR.
WITH THE POSSIBILITY OF RETIREMENT AFTER 2002, HE SUMMED UP HIS INTENTIONS IN A RECENT INTERVIEW WITH THE BBC: "I WOULD LIKE TO ADD MORE TITLES TO MY COLLECTION." OTHER STRONG CONTENDERS ARE IWAN THOMAS, 400M GOLD MEDALLIST AT THE LAST COMMONWEALTH GAMES, AND JAMIE BAULCH, 4X400M OLYMPIC GOLD MEDALLIST AND WORLD INDOOR 400M EUROPEAN INDOOR CHAMPION.

Darren England, Alex Livesey (Getty Images)

The Association of Greater Manchester Authorities (AGMA) welcomes all visitors to the XVII Commonwealth Games

AGMA represents the ten districts in Greater Manchester and is delighted to have the opportunity to support the Commonwealth games in Manchester. Co-operation of all public services in Greater Manchester will be one of the keys to providing a smooth and successful Commonwealth Games.

Whilst you are in Greater Manchester and enjoying the games you will also be in what is now a thriving sports and cultural centre of regional, national and international renown. We hope you will take the chance to –

- Experience the wide range of museums, art galleries and visitor centres across the County
- Take advantage of our excellent shopping facilities, clubs, restaurants and cafes
- Join in the many festivals and events taking place across the city region alongside the games

Enjoy the Greater Manchester experience and come back soon!

For further details contact: **David Fletcher, AGMA Policy Unit, Waterside Drive, Off Swan Meadow Road, Wigan, WN3 5BA; Tel: 01942/705724; Fax: 01942/705728; e-mail: d.fletcher@wiganmbc.gov.uk**

ZAMBIA

CAPITAL: LUSAKA
AREA: 752,614 sq km
POPULATION: 9,872,007
CURRENCY: ZAMBIAN KWACHA
LANGUAGE: ENGLISH, BEMBA, LUAPULA, NYANJA, TONGA, LOZI, KIKAONDE, LUNDA, AND LUVALE
THE PEOPLE: AFRICAN (REPRESENTING MORE THAN 70 ETHNIC GROUPS) AND EUROPEAN

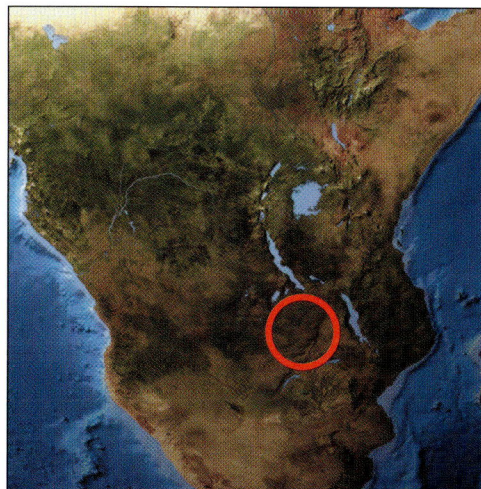

Man's birthplace

In 1921, excavations at Kabwe (Zambia) revealed the almost complete skull of Homo sapiens rhodesiensis ("Broken Hill Man"), which may be well over 100,000 years old. The earliest evidence of Homo sapiens sapiens have also been found in much of central and northern Zambia, while evidence of pottery and copper industries prior to the 15th Centuries abound throughout the country.

Trade between Zambia and Europe started early in the 17th Century, when the Portuguese ousted Muslims from the gold trade of central Africa. The Portuguese founded trading posts in the early 18th Century and by 1762, they were regularly acquiring ivory and copper from Zambians in exchange for cotton cloth. During the later 18th Century, Goans and Portuguese mined gold and hunted elephants. By the mid-19th Century, Zambia was submerged with a flood of raiders and traders from neighbouring tribes hunting for slaves and ivory, although local rulers attempted to turn the trade to their advantage.

British interest in the region was first aroused by the missionary-explorer David Livingstone, who crossed Zambia during three great expeditions between 1853 and his death, near Lake Bangweulu, in 1873. In 1889, the British government granted a charter to Rhodes' British South Africa Company (BSAC), which sought to prevent expansion from other European countries.

In 1911, the area became known as Northern Rhodesia under BSAC, and soon after vast copper ore deposits were found. The colony came under direct British rule in 1924. In the1950s, Kenneth Kuanda founded the United National Independence Party (UNIP). In 1963, British Rule ended and northern Rhodesia became Zambia, named after the Zambezi River.

FABULOUS FACTS

Lusaka, the Zambian capital didn't even exist before the 20th Century and only became the capital in 1931.

The Victoria Falls (at 1.2 miles wide and dropping over 330 ft) is one of the world's most spectacular and well known waterfalls

The Busanga Plains flood between March and May, to become a vast lake attracting hippos and birds.

Zambia's Chirundu Fossil Forest includes 150 million-year-old trees, as well as Stone Age artefacts.

Zambia boasts some of the best bird watching for enthusiasts in Africa, with over 700 hundred different species.

ZAMBIA'S BEST-KNOWN ATHLETE IS SAMUEL MATETE, WHO WON A SILVER MEDAL IN THE 400M HURDLES AT THE 1996 OLYMPICS. HOWEVER, THERE ARE A NUMBER OF PROMISING MARATHON AND LONG DISTANCE RUNNERS, INCLUDING VENRY HAMALILA, MACMILLAN MWANSA, MEDSON CHIBWE, VINCENT HATULEKE AND CHANDA MWANSA. BOXING IS ALSO VERY POPULAR – LOTTIE MWALE IS THE FORMER COMMONWEALTH LIGHT HEAVYWEIGHT BOXING CHAMPION AND KEITH MWILA IS OLYMPIC BRONZE MEDALLIST IN LIGHT FLYWEIGHT BOXING. ZAMBIA ALSO HOPES TO TAKE PART IN THE CYCLING AND JUDO EVENTS.

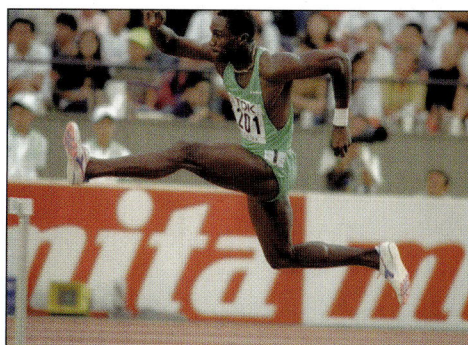

Tony Duffy (Allsport)

Make the most of your swimming with Swimfit

Introducing Swimfit - a new initiative from the Amateur Swimming Association which is designed to help you maximise your efforts in the pool. Check out our new website where you can update your own personal **LogBook**, enabling you to track your swims and analyse calories burned, as well as monitor your average speed by stroke. With password protected access to the personal **My Swimfit** area of the site you can also select appropriate **Training Programmes** and set yourself distance challenges with **Planet Swimfit**.

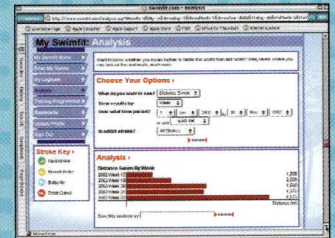

Benefits of ASA Swimfit Membership include:

- your own copy of SWIMMER magazine, worth £2.95, delivered to you each month

- Access your own personal Training LogBook on the Swimfit Website at www.swimfit.com

- £5 discount voucher and free cap & goggles with your first purchase from SwimShop

- 10% discount on both ASA Swimfit Awards and ASA merchandise including an extensive range of publications

For further details get connected to..

www.swimfit.com

call the Amateur Swimming Association's Membership Services Department on 01509 264357 or Email: enquiries@swimfit.com

swimfit

ZIMBABWE

CAPITAL: HARARE
AREA: 390,759 sq km
POPULATION: 11,272,013
CURRENCY: ZIMBABWE DOLLAR
LANGUAGE: SHONA, NDEBELE, CAUCASIAN/EUROPEAN
THE PEOPLE/CULTURE: POLYNESIAN (WITH SOME 200 EUROPEANS, SAMOANS AND TONGANS)

All Rhodes lead to home

Present-day Zimbabwe was the site of a complex African civilisation in the 13th and 14th Centuries. The first contact with Europeans was with the Portuguese at the end of the 15th Century. The Portuguese were largely concerned with ensuring communications between their colonies in Angola and Mozambique on either side of Zimbabwe. In the 1830s, Ndebele people fleeing Zulu violence and Boer migration in present-day South Africa moved north and settled in what is now known as Matabeleland. At this point, colonists arrived in the form of British mining interests led by Cecil John Rhodes' British South Africa Company (BSAC). The BSAC took control of the country, which they called Southern Rhodesia, until 1923, when it became, nominally, a British colony. From 1953-63, Southern Rhodesia formed part of the Central African Federation with neighbouring Northern Rhodesia (now Zambia) and Nyasaland (now Malawi). In 1965, the settlers, with South African support, issued a Unilateral Declaration of Independence (UDI). This triggered a civil war between the white minority government and fighters for African independence, ending in 1980 with the granting of independence and a general election held under British auspices, won by Robert Mugabe's ZANU Party. The main focus of dissent in the early years was Joshua Nkomo's ZAPU opposition party – ZANU's former ally in the "Patriotic Front", which fought the guerrilla war against Rhodesia from Zambia and Mozambique. From 1985, the two parties moved toward a merger, achieved in January 1988. Named ZANU-PF, the party won the 1990 national elections, taking 147 of 150 seats. With no broad-based opposition, Mugabe won another six-year term in 1996. He was also declared winner of the 2002 presidential elections, which observers say were suspect and Zimbabwe has since been suspended from the Commonwealth for a year as a result.

FABULOUS FACTS

English is the official language of Zimbabwe, but it is a first language for only about two per cent of the population.

The alcoholic drink of choice is chibuku, "the beer of good cheer" – it is served in buckets and shared between drinkers.

Zimbabwe's Victoria Falls measure 1.7km wide and drop between 90m and 107m into the Zambezi Gorge.

An average of 550,000 cubic metres of water plummet over the edge of the Victoria Falls every minute.

The modern nation of Zimbabwe took its name from Great Zimbabwe, the greatest medieval city in sub-Saharan Africa.

ALTHOUGH ZIMBABWE HAS BEEN SUSPENDED FROM THE COMMONWEALTH PROPER, THE COUNTRY WILL BE ALLOWED TO COMPETE IN THE 2002 COMMONWEALTH GAMES. WITH THIS IN MIND, THE ATHLETES WILL BE LOOKING TO ADD TO THEIR IMPRESSIVE TALLY OF FIVE GOLDS, SEVEN SILVERS AND EIGHT BRONZES OVER ALL. NAMES TO WATCH FOR INCLUDE RUNNERS SAMUKELISO MOYO AND LEWIS MASUNDA. IN KUALA LUMPUR IN 1998, MOYO TOOK BRONZE IN THE 5,000M WHILE HIS FEMALE COMPATRIOT JUKIA SAKARA GAINED THIRD PLACE IN THE 1,500M.

Simon Bruty (Allsport)

Born in Australia, now swimming all around the world.

Serious swimmers prefer

ZOGGS

The events

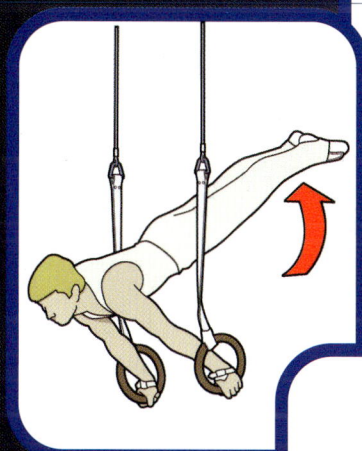

AQUATICS

VENUE: THE MANCHESTER AQUATICS CENTRE
DATES: DIVING (25–27 JULY); SWIMMING (30 JULY–4 AUG);
SYNCHRONISED SWIMMING (26–27 JULY)

Diving – History

Egyptians and Romans enjoyed diving as far back as 400BC and while
the Vikings practiced cliff diving they did so with less flair and passion than
Polynesians and the Mexicans who put Acapulco on the map. Swedish and
German divers turned the sport into an art form in the 19th Century by introducing
gymnastic movements – twists and somersaults – and using apparatus, such
as hoops, into the basic swallow dive. By the time, Germany hosted the first
recorded diving competition, the "circus" element had been dropped in favour
of skill, speed, grace and mental toughness.
Diving formed part of the inaugural British Empire Games in 1930.
Since then, the gold medal tally suggests tight competition.
Brian Phelps (1962-66), for England, was the first man to retain both
springboard and highboard Commonwealth titles, his feat later
matched by Australia's Donald Wagstaff (1970-74) and England's
Chris Snode (1978-82). The three gold medals of Peter Heatley
(now Sir Peter), for Scotland, spanned three Games (1950-58),
his first and last victories coming off the highboard. Canada's
Sylvie Bernier remains the only Commonwealth diver ever
to hold an Olympic title (in 1984), while among men only
Phelps has ever won an individual Olympic medal of
any colour and no male Commonwealth diver has
ever won a medal at the world championships.

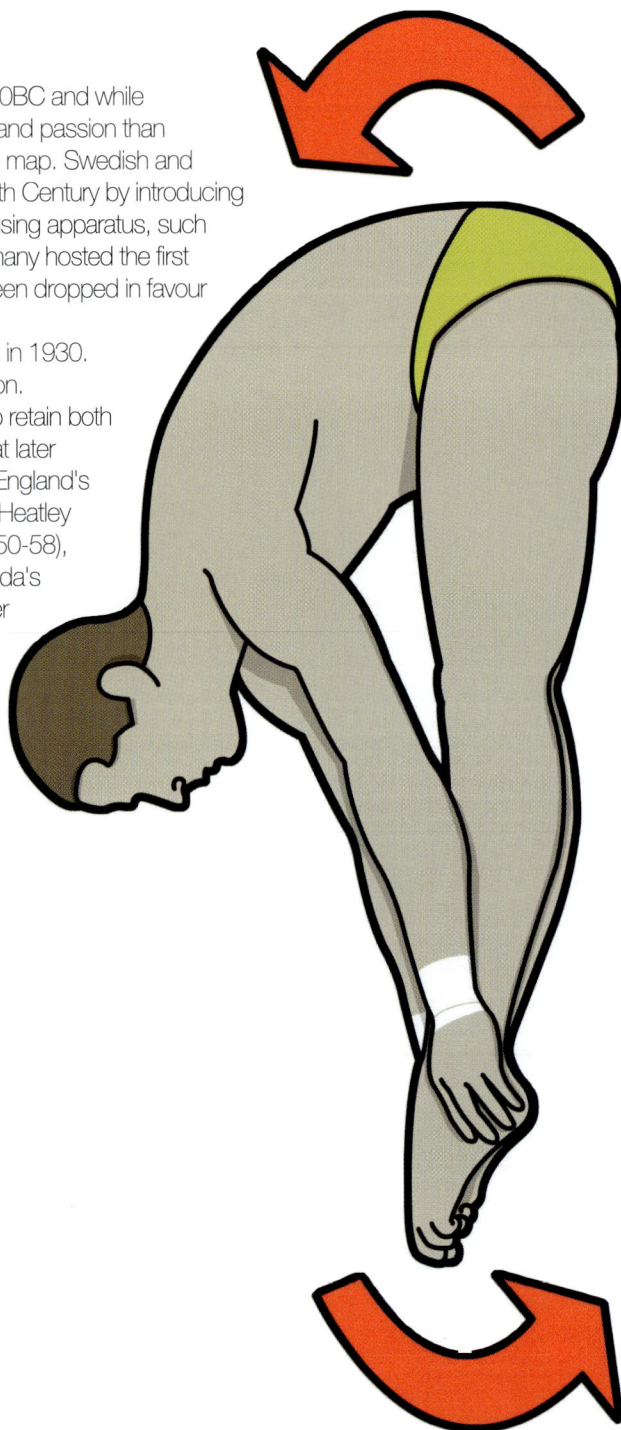

AUSTRALIA'S SWIMMING KING
IAN "THE THORPEDO" THORPE
SHOULD ADD SOME SERIOUS
FIREPOWER TO THE GAMES.
"I'M EXCITED ABOUT IT," HE SAYS.
"I CAN'T WAIT TO RACE IN THE
MANCHESTER POOL – IT'S
GOING TO BE A GREAT
COMPETITION."

Craig Lord (The Times)

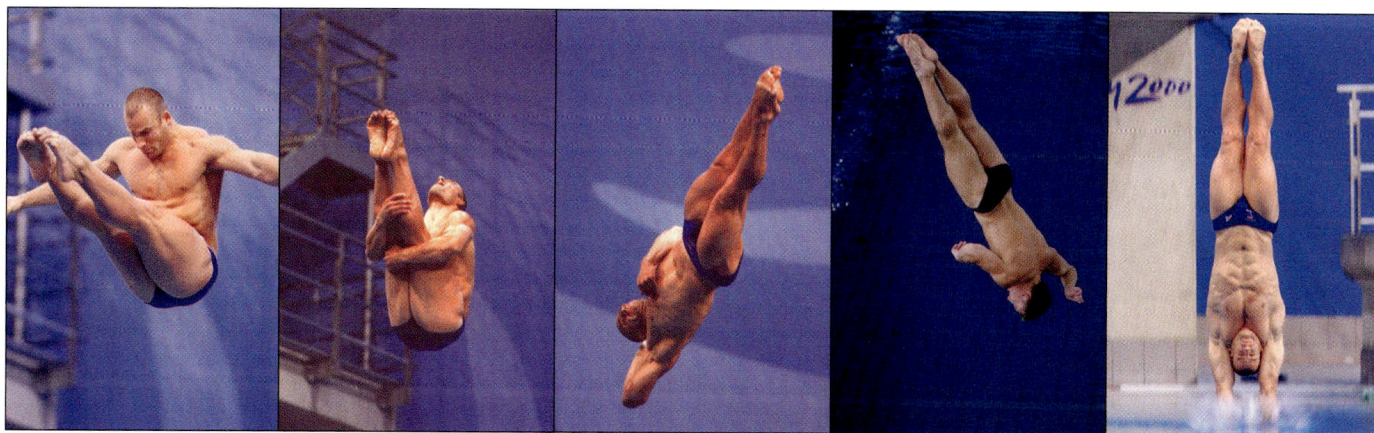

Diving – the basics

At the Commonwealth Games, divers compete off one metre and three metre springboards, and the 10-metre highboard (or platform). There are compulsory and optional dives, marked out of 10 points by each of seven judges. Divers are marked on starting position, the approach, the take-off, height, the execution of a set dive – degrees of difficulty ranging from 1.5 to 3.5 – and the entry into the water, which must be vertical, with body straight and splash minimal. Lowest and highest scores are discarded, the five remaining added up and multiplied by the degree of difficulty for a total score.

The divers

Australia overhauled Canada in diving for the first time in Kuala Lumpur, taking three titles to the two for Canada's Alexandre Despatie and Eryn Bulmer, who will be back this year to defend their crowns. Australia's Loudy Tourky, an Olympic synchronised diving medal winner, will be one to watch, while among England's men, Tony Ally, Mark Shipman and Peter Waterfield are all gold medal prospects.

EAD aquatics

The 2002 Manchester Games is the first wholly-inclusive multi-sport event. This means that, for the first time ever, medals won by Elite Athletes with a Disability (EAD) will count toward the final medal tally.

The EAD swimming programme contains four multi-disability events specifically for swimmers with a disability: women's 50m multi-disability freestyle, men's 50m multi-disability freestyle, women's 100m multi-disability freestyle and men's 100m multi-disability freestyle. In terms of eligibility, classification is the grouping of swimmers with like abilities for the purpose of fair competition. Each swimmer is classified according to functional ability and not according to their disability. The events are being run on a multi-disability format, which includes both physically disabled and visually impaired swimmers.

2002 Manchester
THE XVII COMMONWEALTH GAMES

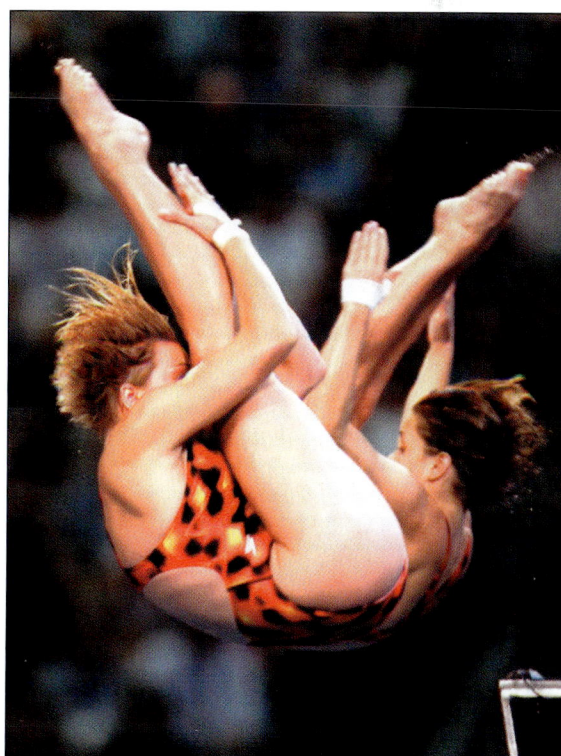

Clive Brunskill, Jed Jacobsohn, Jamie Squire, Ezra Shaw (Allsport)

Serco is a leading provider of management services.

We work in partnership with governments, local authorities and companies worldwide, designing operational solutions and then taking responsibility for delivering performance.

Our activities range from controlling satellites and managing computer networks for the European Space Agency to operating the Great Southern Railway in Australia, one of the world's great train journeys.

Serco Group plc

We work in partnership with Manchester City Council in delivering a number of services including the Metrolink tram service, ten Community Leisure Centres and the five English Institute of Sport facilities currently being used to host the Commonwealth Games.

Being part of the community where we work is an important part of the Serco approach. In Manchester, we have recently agreed with the City Council to fund a community sports initiative over the next five years which will give more young people a chance to participate in athletics.

Serco would like to wish Manchester and the Commonwealth Games every success.

SOLUTIONS FOR THE FUTURE

Serco Group plc
Dolphin House
Windmill Road
Sunbury-on-Thames
TW16 7HT
United Kingdom

T +44 (0)1932 755900
F +44 (0)1932 755854

serco

www.serco.com

Swimming – the history

Swimming has come a long way since the first known competition was held in the time of the Japanese Emperor Suigiu in 36BC. The sport was popular with ancient Greeks and Romans but fell from favour during the Dark Ages as water was linked with the spread of disease. During the 18th Century, however, George III's love of swimming in the sea helped to regenerate interest and a century later breaststroke, or variations on the same theme, was well established.

Swimming for both men and women formed part of the inaugural British Empire Games in 1930. Australia has dominated events since, winning 184 gold medals to Canada's 90 and England's 37. Legends of the Green and Gold shoal have included Dawn Fraser, Murray Rose, Jon Konrads, Kieren Perkins and Michael Wenden, the only man in history to have won the same title, 100m freestyle, three times (1966, 70 and 74).

The strokes

There are four official strokes: butterfly, backstroke, breaststroke and freestyle, and all four make up a medley. The races take place in a pool 50 metres long and divided by eight lanes 2.5 metres wide. Rules govern the arm and leg motions in each stroke as well as the way in which the start and turn must be executed. Inaugural events in Manchester are the 50m in butterfly, backstroke and breaststroke, and the women's 4x200m freestyle relay.

The swimmers

In Kuala Lumpur, Australia lost only nine out of 31 races. The Olympic tally of Sydney 2000 stacked up 18 medals, including five gold, for Australia, against three medals for the rest of the Commonwealth, none of them gold, while at the world championships in Japan last year Australia took back aquatic supremacy from the USA for the first time since 1956.

Leading the Dolphins from Down Under in Manchester will be freestylers Ian Thorpe and Grant Hackett, the two most outstanding talents of all-time, while Petria Thomas will attempt to become the first women in the pool to win the same title, 100m butterfly, three times.

Alex Livesey (Allsport)

Synchronised swimming – the history

Synchronised swimming was created when a group of Canadian women in the 1920s teamed up to demonstrate the aquatic skills they had mastered in the course of taking their life saving diplomas. The popularity of their new activity caused rules to be laid down – and a sport was born. Although it was a demonstration sport at the 1948 and 1952 Olympic Games, it was not until 1973 that World Championships were held and not until 1984 that the sport joined the Olympic movement. It has formed part of the Commonwealth Games programme since 1986.

There is no doubt who the stars of the show are – Canada, which has won all nine gold medals on offer since 1986. The most famous among those winners are Carolyn Waldo and Sylvie Frechette, Olympic duet champions of 1988.

The moves

The quirk of the Commonwealth Games programme is that the two events are solo and duet; there is no team event of eight women as exists at world level. Each entry must perform a technical routine including seven obligatory elements, all worth 35 per cent of the total score. The free routine is worth 65 per cent. There are two panels of judges, one for technical merit covering execution, synchronisation and difficulty, and the other artistic impression covering choreography, body patterns and effect of the music in relation to the routine. Points are deducted for rule infringements, such as touching the bottom of the pool. Highest and lowest scores are discarded and the other three are averaged out to give a total.

The synchronised swimmers

The Canadians are yet again tipped to dominate events, Claire Carver-Dias and Fanny Létourneau having won bronze medals in the duet and team events at the world championships in Japan last year, when no other swimmers from the Commonwealth made the final cut. Watch for Naomi Young, of Australia, however, in both the solo and duet. Born with club feet and encouraged by doctors to take up swimming to help improve their condition, Naomi took up the sport after being inspired as she watched the 1984 Los Angeles Olympics on the television.

all time aquatic gold medals

Below is a list of the all-time gold medal tally for aquatic events, including diving, synchronised swimming and swimming events:

1. Australia – 212 gold medals
2. Canada – 119 gold medals
3. England – 79 gold medals
4. New Zealand – 12 gold medals
5. Scotland – 11 gold medals
6. South Africa – 7 gold medals
7. Wales – 4 gold medals
8. Zimbabwe – 1 gold medals

Note: The leading gold medallist is swimmer Susie O'Neill of Australia who won a remarkable 10 gold medals between 1990 and 1998

Manchester 2002
THE XVII COMMONWEALTH GAMES

Allsport UK

SPEEDO fast·skin™

WE'VE USED SHARKS TO MAKE PEOPLE SWIM FASTER

The shark shouldn't be extremely fast in water. But it is. The secret's in its skin. Nature has perfected the design over 350 million years. And at SPEEDO we've mimicked it to design a swimsuit with a fabric that minimises drag and moulds to the body like a second skin.

With a level of detail that means even its seaming increases the co-ordination of your muscles. The result - a swimsuit that's faster than any other suit tested.

SPEEDO FAST.SKIN
The ultimate swimsuit. For the ultimate swim.

today, make a molehill out of a mountain.

M715GT MEN'S RUNNING SHOE

A supportive cushioned trainer

- Abzorb® cushioning in the heel and forefoot
- Medial EVA Post provides support for mild to moderate over-pronators
- Stability Web® provides midfoot support and torsional stability
- Solid Rubber Outsole for a cushioned ride with N-durance™ Heel Pad for long-lasting heel strike durability
- Available in different widths

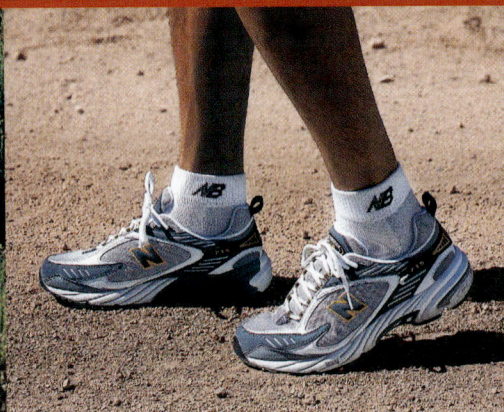

new balance ⟩B®

www.newbalance.co.uk
Freephone: 0800 389 1055
© 2002 New Balance Athletic Shoe, Inc.

VENUE: THE CITY OF MANCHESTER STADIUM
DATES: JULY 26 – JULY 31

ATHLETICS

Straight sprints – 100m, 200m, 400m, 100m Blind (EAD)

The 100m is a test of sheer speed and competitors go through several qualifying rounds before advancing to an eight runner final in the fight to be crowned "fastest human in the Commonwealth." The 200m is a sustained sprint of half a lap, requiring a sprinter with good endurance, while the 400m is a battle of sheer willpower and measured speed. In addition, the elite athletes with a disability compete in the 100m blind, which requires athletes to run with a guide. Each race comprises a maximum of four runners, each with a guide runner.

Caribbean and African athletes are expected to feature strongly in the women's 100m and 200m, with Chandra Sturrup, the defending champion from Bahamas, among the favourites. Trinidad's Olympic silver medallist Ato Boldon bids to defend his 100m men's title, but he faces fierce opposition from Namibia's Frankie Fredericks, Obadele Thompson of Barbados and a strong home nations challenge led by England's Darren Campbell, Dwain Chambers and Mark Lewis-Francis. Watch out for Boldon, Fredericks, Campbell and Wales' Christian Malcolm in the 200m. The 400m pitches reigning world champion Avard Moncur (Barbados) against Jamaica's Olympic bronze medallist Greg Haughton.

Relays – 4x100m and 4x400m

The 4x100m relay requires the passing of a baton among four teammates who are running at maximum speed. The exchange must be accomplished within a 20m passing zone, spaced at 100m intervals around the track. The 4x400m requires less baton-passing skill, but simply the speed of four great one-lap runners. England, the defending champions, will start favourites in the men's 4x100m relay, although last year's world silver medallist South Africa is an emerging force and could pose a serious threat.

A Caribbean duel between defending champions Jamaica and Barbados is likely to ensue in the men's 4x400m relay.

In the women's 4x100m, Jamaica and Nigeria are expected to fight for gold. Meanwhile, in the women's long relay the Jamaican quartet start clear favourites.

Hurdles – 100m (women), 110m (men) and 400m (both)

The essence of 100m and 110m hurdling is fast sprinting over barriers. The 400m hurdles requires athletes to run one lap of the track over ten hurdles and demands great endurance and natural speed. Arguably the finest sprint hurdler in history, Wales' Colin Jackson bids to add a third Commonwealth gold, some 16 years after he won Commonwealth silver in his debut Games in Edinburgh. In the men's 400m hurdles, South African pair Alwyn Myburgh and Llewellyn Herbert will start as marginal favourites, but they face a big threat from the Jamaicans and England's Chris Rawlinson.

Jamaica is expected to play a significant role in the women's hurdles events, with Olympic fourth-placer Delloreen Ennis-London taking on Olympic silver medallist Glory Alozie of Nigeria. In the longer hurdles, Jamaica's former Olympic champion Deon Hemmings and compatriot Debbie Anne-Parris will be the women to beat.

Words: Steve Landells

What: 'Provamel in preference to dairy milk, **Soya Fruity**... and Briannah has a bit of a passion for **Chocolate Oy** and Chocolate flavoured Desserts.'

Why:
- Low in saturated fats.
- Lactose and gluten free.
- High in polyunsaturates and soya protein.
- Helps promote healthy cholesterol levels.

www.provamel.co.uk
www.familyheart.org

Dairy free alternative to fresh milk.

Dairy free alternative to a fruit smoothie.

PROVAMEL
FROM
alpro soya
Dairy free & delicious

Dairy free chocolate flavoured dessert.

Approved by the
FAMILY HEART ASSOCIATION
as part of a healthy balanced diet.

Linford & Briannah Christie
ENJOY THE TASTE OF
DAIRY FREE

THE SOYABEANS IN PROVAMEL ARE GMO FREE, TESTED BY INDEPENDENT LABORATORIES AND FULLY TRACEABLE.

Middle distance – 800m, 1,500m

The 800m is the metric half mile, just two strides less than 880 yards. The athlete must have a sprinter's speed, and also the strong heart and lungs of a mid-distance runner. The 1,500m – also known as the metric mile – is the blue ribbon event of the track programme. The three-and-three-quarter lap race requires great speed, endurance, economy of motion, efficiency of stride and the will to endure. The men's 800m could provide a stirring battle between Kenya's Wilfred Bungei, the quickest 800m runner in the Commonwealth last year and South Africa's eternal bridesmaid Hezekiel Sepeng, a former Olympic World and Commonwealth silver medallist, who will be looking to stand on top of the medal podium in Manchester. In the 1,500m, Kenya will be looking for a clean sweep headed by Commonwealth record holder Bernard Lagat. Mozambique's Olympic 800m champion Maria Mutola will be hoping to defend her Commonwealth crown, although England's Olympic bronze medallist Kelly Holmes and Canadian Diane Cummins could threaten. In the 1,500m, Kenya might not have things all there own way, as Wales' Hayley Tullett and Holmes hope to feature. The second of the EAD events will be open to physically disabled wheelchair athletes, who will race around two laps of the track at the City of Manchester Stadium. The favourite will be world champion Louise Sauvage of Australia, but she will face fierce opposition from Canada's Paralympic champion Chantal Peticlerc. Also watch out for Wales' Tanni-Grey Thompson, who gave birth to her first child in January.

Long distance – 5,000m, 10,000m, 3,000m steeplechase (men)

The steeplechase takes place over seven and a half laps and consists of 28 barriers and seven water jumps. The wide spacing of these obstacles means the essential skill of the steeplechaser is his long distance ability. The 5000m is 12-and-a-half times around the 400m track. The 10,000m is the longest race on the track, totalling 25 laps.

The long-distance events are likely to be dominated by the all-conquering Kenyans, who took all but one of the nine medals in the long distance events in Kuala Lumpur. World champion Richard Limo (Kenya) leads the Commonwealth 5000m rankings, but Australia's emerging young talent Craig Mottram will be looking to make his mark on the event.

In the 10,000m, Abraham Chebii lead the rankings in 2001 and the red vest of Kenyan is expected to be at the head of the field.

However, in the women's 5000m, the darling of the Manchester crowd, England's London Marathon winner Paula Radcliffe will hope to add her first major track title to the glut of gold medals she has picked up on the road. In the women's 10,000m Kenyans Leah Malot and Tegla Loroupe could feature, as well as the Australian Suzie Power. Kenya will expect a clean sweep in the men's steeplechase.

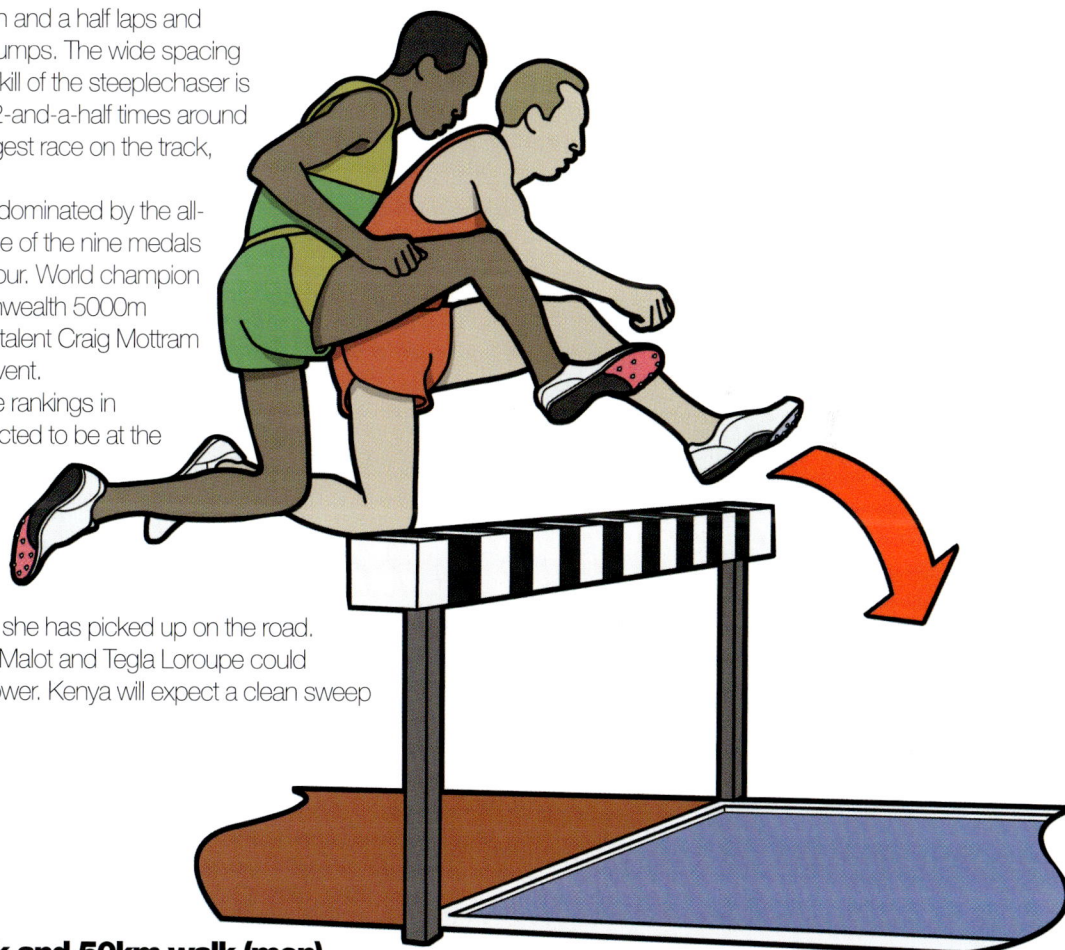

Road – marathon, 20km walk and 50km walk (men)

The Marathon is the longest running event in the Games and is run over a strength sapping 26 miles 385 yards. Race walking is defined as a succession of steps during which contact with the ground is maintained at all times. With each stride, the advancing foot must strike the road before the rear foot leaves. Disqualification occurs, if, in the opinion of three judges, a competitor's walking action breaks contact. The last men's Commonwealth Games marathon produced a major surprise, as Lesotho's Thabiso Moqhali claimed gold; this year's version is as difficult to predict. The women's marathon is equally difficult to call, with Kenyan and Australian athletes among the favourites. Watch out for Australia's Jane Saville in the 20km walk; compatriot Nathan Deakes starts favourite in the men's race. New Zealand's 50km walker Craig Barrett will be hoping 2002 is his year, after collapsing just 1km from the finish while leading in the Kuala Lumpur Games.

Throwing – shot, discus, hammer and javelin

The shot is thrown from the confines of a concrete ring, encircled by a steel rim with a wooden stop board at the front. The thrower attempts to use as much of the circle as possible in accelerating to the point of release. The discus is one of the oldest events and is thrown from a circle 2.50m in diameter. The hammer is a composite steel ball, cable and handle, weighing 8.257kg. The thrower seeks to accelerate the hammer to maximum release within the confines of the circle. The javelin thrower approaches the foul line through a series of cross steps, the thrower then bringing the javelin back into a cocked position. The feet are planted and the javelin is pulled powerfully through the axis of the javelin.

The men's shot could be a two-way battle between South African Janus Robberts, who led the Commonwealth rankings last year, and England's Carl Myerscough, who started competing again earlier this year after a two-year ban. South African duo Dreinkie Van Wyk and Veronica Abrahamse are expected to fight for gold in the women's shot.

Manchester-born Alison Lever (Australia) starts favourite in the women's discus and in a potential world-class men's discus, South Africa's Olympic bronze medallist Frantz Kruger takes on Jason Tunks of Canada.

The men's hammer is weakened by the withdrawal of South Africa's Commonwealth record holder Chris Harmse, whose Christian beliefs won't allow him to compete on a Sunday. In his absence, Australia's Stuart Rendall will be favourite to retain his crown. In the women's hammer, Commonwealth record holder Bronwyn Eagles will be the woman to beat.

Laverne Eve of the Bahamas will be hoping to secure victory in the women's javelin, while in the men's event Olympic silver medallist Steve Backley will be hoping to land a third Commonwealth gold. Backley explained: "I'm really looking forward to the Commonwealth Games. I've always enjoyed competing on home soil and I think there's always an element of pride about competing at home."

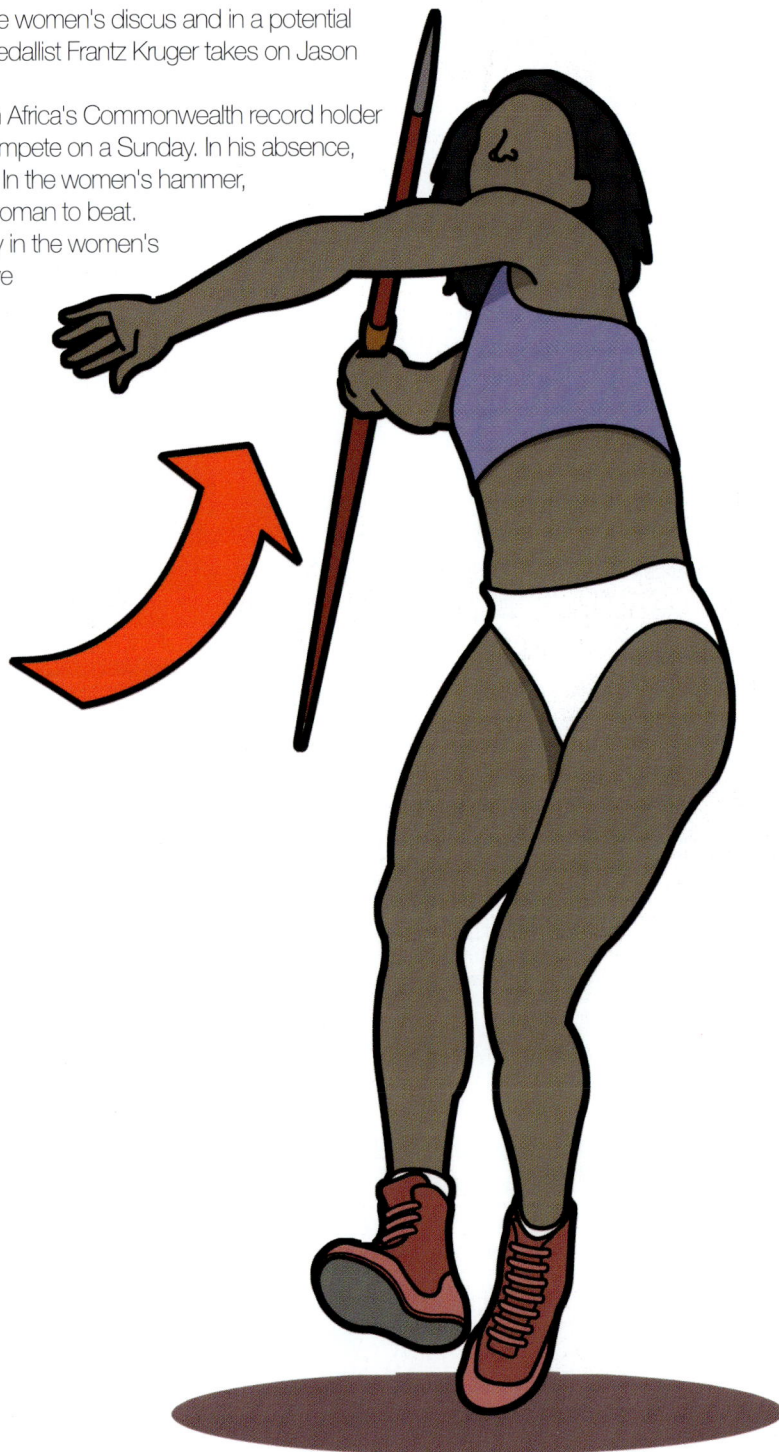

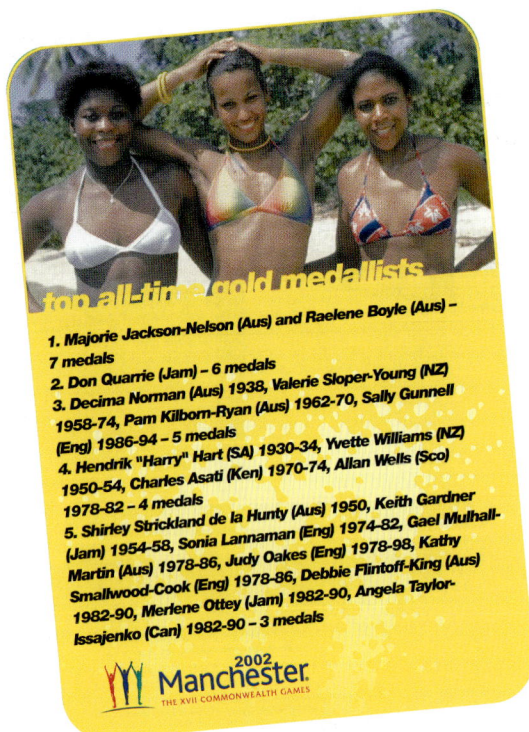

top all-time gold medallists

1. Majorie Jackson-Nelson (Aus) and Raelene Boyle (Aus) – 7 medals
2. Don Quarrie (Jam) – 6 medals
3. Decima Norman (Aus) 1938, Valerie Sloper-Young (NZ) 1958-74, Pam Kilborn-Ryan (Aus) 1962-70, Sally Gunnell (Eng) 1986-94 – 5 medals
4. Hendrik "Harry" Hart (SA) 1930-34, Yvette Williams (NZ) 1950-54, Charles Asati (Ken) 1970-74, Allan Wells (Sco) 1978-82 – 4 medals
5. Shirley Strickland de la Hunty (Aus) 1950, Keith Gardner (Jam) 1954-58, Sonia Lannaman (Eng) 1974-82, Gael Mulhall-Martin (Aus) 1978-86, Judy Oakes (Eng) 1978-98, Kathy Smallwood-Cook (Eng) 1978-86, Debbie Flintoff-King (Aus) 1982-90, Merlene Ottey (Jam) 1982-90, Angela Taylor-Issajenko (Can) 1982-90 – 3 medals

2002 Manchester
THE XVII COMMONWEALTH GAMES

Tony Duffy (Allsport)

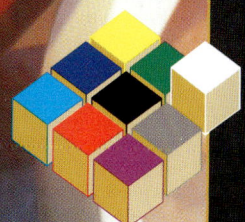

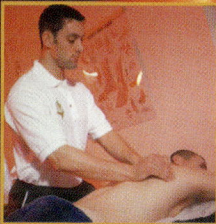

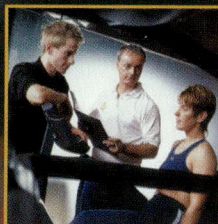

Jumping – high jump, pole vault, long jump, triple jump

The high jump rules allow athletes to have three attempts at every height. The vast majority of athletes use the "Fosbury Flop" technique as made famous by 1968 Olympic champion Dick Fosbury (illustrated below).

The pole vault is a dramatic synthesis of speed, strength and risk, requiring the skills of a circus acrobat. Long jump combines raw speed and jumping ability. The triple jump requires good running speed on the approach to take-off. During the hop phase, the triple jumper tries to cover as much distance as possible, while preserving momentum and control in order to execute the lengthy step and an effective jump.

South Africa's reigning world champion Hestrie Cloete appears to stand head and shoulders above the opposition in the women's high jump and South Africa will be hoping for a high jump double in the shape of 20-year-old Jacques Freitag.

Australia's world champion Dmitri Markov and compatriot Viktor Chistiakov, if fit, will expect to contest gold in the men's pole vault. Chistiakov's wife Tatiana Grigorieva will be the best bet in the women's pole vault. Australia's Commonwealth record holder Bronwyn Thompson has enjoyed an excellent first half of the year and starts red-hot favourite in the women's long jump. Meanwhile, Jamaica's former Olympic silver medallist James Beckford should start a marginal favourite in the men's long jump, although a special eye should be kept on England's 20-year-old sensation Chris Tomlinson.

The hosts will be hoping for gold in the women's triple jump, in the shape of defending champion Ashia Hansen. However, England's best chance of gold lies with World and Olympic champion Jonathan Edwards in the men's triple jump. The world record holder stated: "I hope the Commonwealths are well supported and we can show the world that England can stage a major championship."

Multi events – decathlon (men), heptathlon (women)

The decathlon is the ultimate test for any athlete and combines ten events spread over two days. Day one includes: 100m, long jump, shot, high jump and 400m and day two, 110m hurdles, discus, pole vault, javelin and 1,500m. The heptathlon for women is seven events, with 100m hurdles, high jump, shot and 200m on the first day and long jump, javelin and 800m on day two.

England world bronze medallist Dean Macey should have far too much class for the opposition in the decathlon. As Macey said of the Commonwealth Games: "It is my main priority this summer, because it is an event I know I can win. I'm both nervous and excited for the Commonwealth Games." Denise Lewis, England's Olympic heptathlon champion is not expected to compete after giving birth to a daughter in April. In a wide-open competition, Australia's Jane Jamieson may start slight favourite.

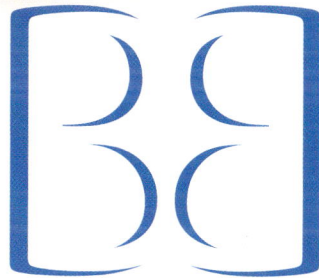

ENHANCE YOUR PERFORMANCE

BRIGHAM BRINING £ CO.

- Independent Financial Advisers -

Investment Specialists • Wealth Management
Retirement Solutions • Corporate Planning • Business Protection

If you have over £25,000 to invest *OR* your income is over £30,000 per annum you need to talk to the specialists on...

0800 328 0867
or email: mail@bb-co.net

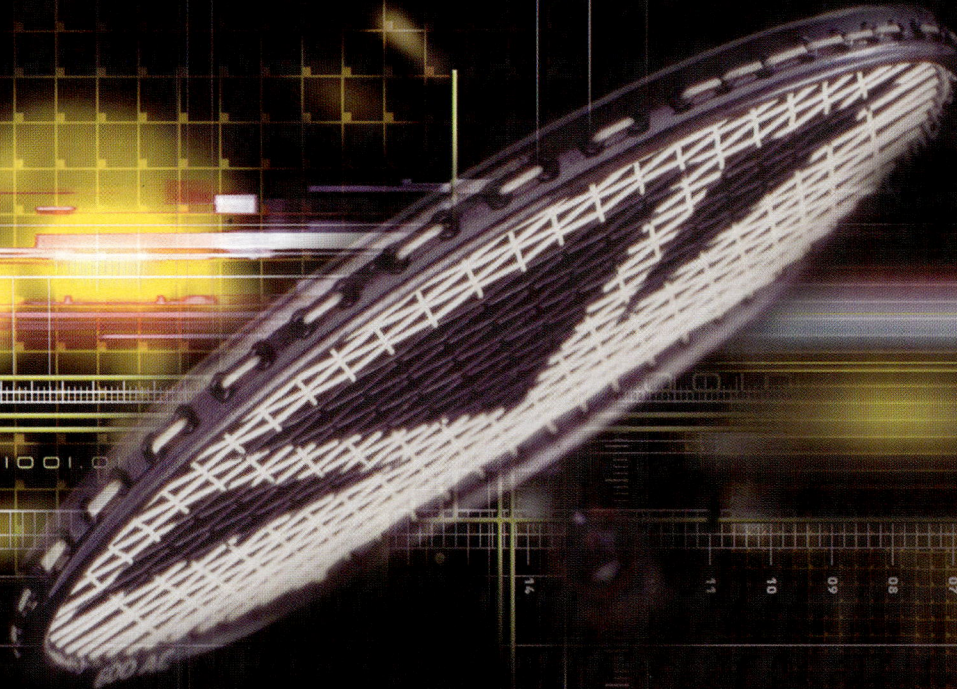

VENUE: BOLTON ARENA
DATES: 26–30 JULY (TEAM); 31–4 JULY (INDIVIDUAL)

BADMINTON

History

Badminton is a game with ancient roots – a version of the game was played as far back as 100 BC in Greece, India and China. Around 1873, the game got its name from the Duke of Beaufort's estate, Badminton, where he played the game (originally called "Poona") with friends. In 1934, the International Badminton Federation was established and, 32 years later, in 1966, the sport was introduced as a participant sport in the Commonwealth Games. The game's attempts to move with the times will be reflected the spectacular new £15m Bolton Arena. For the first time since badminton's Games debut in Jamaica, the sport will use the best of 5x7 scoring system instead of the traditional 3x15. In 5x7, the action is shorter and sharper, but every bit as skillful – and still with plenty of power.

Equipment

The shuttle consists of a rounded cork base covered in a thin layer of leather. Sixteen goose feathers are attached to this base. Each shuttle requires three birds because a wing has six feathers and manufacturers cannot mix those from left and right wings, as they have different curvatures. Rackets are now state-of-the-art – in fact, England's defending mixed doubles champion Simon Archer will still be blasting world record 162mph smashes with a graphite/titanium racket weighing just 90 gm (less than the weight of a small apple).

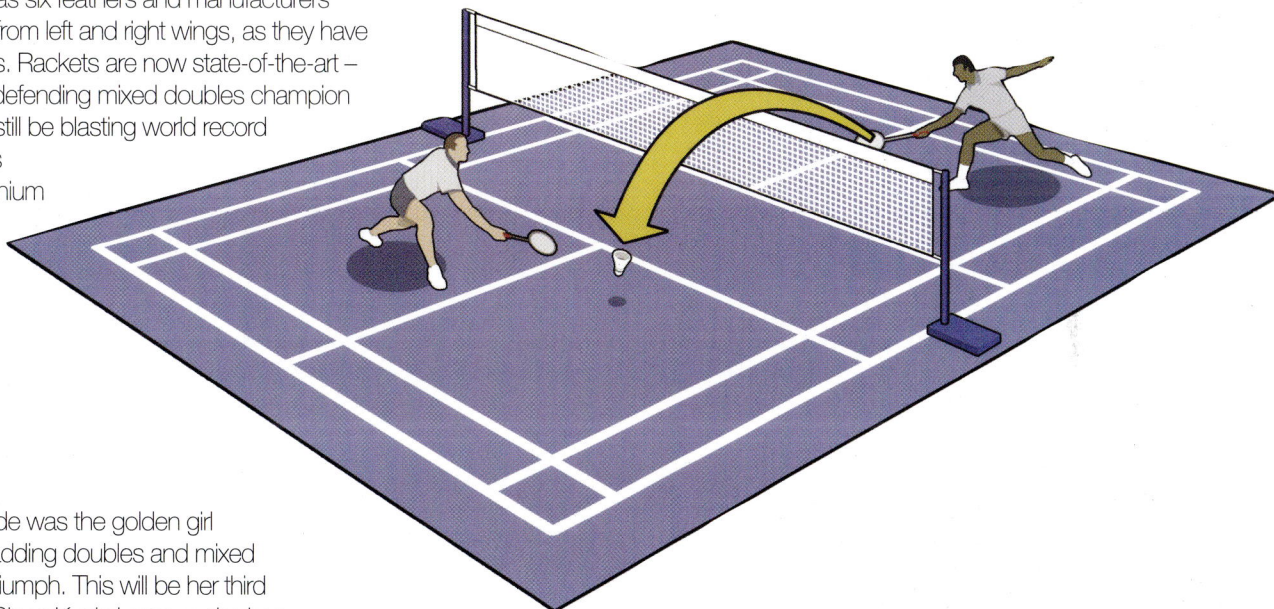

Big hitters

England's Jo Goode was the golden girl in Kuala Lumpur, adding doubles and mixed gold to her team triumph. This will be her third and final Games. Since Kuala Lumpur, she has scored Britain's first Olympic badminton medal. Pullela Gopichand of India has already tasted success in England. The 2001 All England champion is an artist just like his great predecessor, 1978 Commonwealth and 1980 All England champion Prakash Padukone. Padukone recalls: "My wins brought badminton to the forefront of Indian sport, but Gopi has revitalised our game. He became a national hero overnight." Malaysia's men are also strong, producing Kuala Lumpur finalists in both singles (Wong Choong Hann beat Yong Hock Kin) and doubles (Lee Wan Wah and Choong Tan Fook beat Cheah Soon Kit and Yap Hock Kim). Now they have the coaching skills of Korea's ex-world and Olympic champion Park Joo Bong, the former England coach who is acclaimed as the greatest ever doubles player – formidable indeed.

KELLY MORGAN OF WALES IS AIMING TO BE THE FIRST WOMAN TO RETAIN HER SINGLES TITLE SINCE HELEN TROKE IN 1986. SHE SAYS: "I'M REALLY LOOKING FORWARD TO DEFENDING MY TITLE SO CLOSE TO HOME. BADMINTON HAS RECEIVED A LOT OF ATTENTION IN WALES FOLLOWING MY SUCCESS."

Words: William Kings

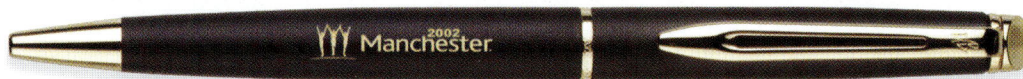

WATERMAN ◈ PARIS

The Winning Team

The Pen Shop are official merchandise suppliers for the
XVII Commonwealth Games

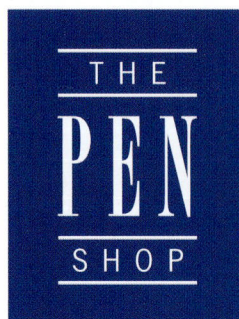

THE
PEN
SHOP

CORPORATE

3 Regent Crescent | The Trafford Centre | Manchester | 01617 477432
54 King Street | Manchester | 01618 393966
www.penshop.co.uk

BOXING

VENUE: FORUM CENTRE, WYTHENSHAWE AND MEN ARENA
DATES: 26 JULY – 3 AUGUST (REST DAY: 2 AUGUST)

History

Boxing is possibly the oldest sport in history – in fact, it's probably been in existence since the first caveman hit his friend and their buddy (in a bow-tie, of course) stepped in to referee.

Arguments over the morality and brutality of the sport rage, but to many, it is still the purest test of skill, strength and stamina. Boxing, abolished in 393 BC during the Roman gladiator period (due to excessive brutality – being thrown to the lions was presumably less brutal), has seen many changes over the years.

Headgear was made compulsory for all amateur competitions in 1984 while 10 oz gloves, that no doubt feel more like 10 lbs when worn by 1986 Commonwealth gold winner Lennox Lewis, are the order of the day. Amateur boxing was one of the founder sports at the 1930 Commonwealth Games in Hamilton. The Commonwealth Games have been the springboard for a number of professional careers including Olympic gold medallist Audley Harrison and the aforementioned Lewis. Northern Ireland's Barry McGuigan won gold in the featherweight category at Hamilton in 1978 and the "Clones Cyclone" (later a world champion) burst into tears on the winner's podium.

Words: Christopher Davies (Daily Telegraph)

Rules and equipment

The bell sounds for three, three-minute rounds and the two pugilists step toward each other ready to do battle. Each will be properly attired in 10 oz gloves; compulsory headgear and coloured singlets. Each boxer attempts to score points by landing good hits on his opponent. A point is gained by three or more of the five judges pressing the button on the computer score pad within one second of each other. At the end of the bout, the boxer with the most points is declared the winner. Other methods of victory include knockouts or if the referee decides that one contestant is taking too much punishment.

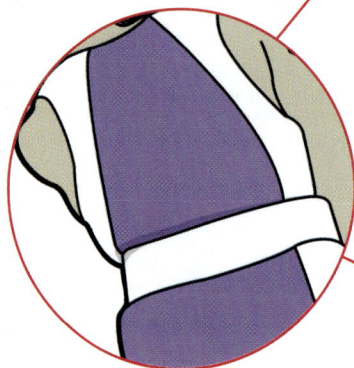

Kings of the ring

Australia, whose sporting profile has never been higher, is sending two outstanding prospects in Paul Miller and Justin Kane. "Mr Magic" Miller has already collected a trophy in the North-West of England when he won the Liverpool Cup and he hopes to become the first Australian middleweight to collect a gold medal since Philip McElwaine in Edmonton 1976. Another in whom Boxing Australia has confidence is bantamweight Justin "Sugar" Kane, who says his greatest characteristic is "never giving up." Kane places much emphasis on motivation and plans to add Commonwealth gold to his impressive haul of state, national and international medals.

There will also be strong support for Kevin Evans of Wales, who defeated British and Welsh super-heavyweight champion Scott Grammer at the WBA championships to book his place in his country's 2002 Games team.

"I am now fully focused on winning a gold medal in Manchester," says Evans, who competed at Kuala Lumpur four years ago.

"I was inexperienced then," he says. "I've had over a dozen international fights since then so I think I might be a serious contender."

England's Lightweight challenger Andy Morris will particularly relish his opportunity as he boxes for the West Wythenshawe Club, which trains at the Wythenshawe Forum – the venue for the competition's preliminary rounds.

From further afield, hopefuls will arrive with varying levels of preparation. African sport, especially at amateur level, often suffers from lack of finance, but Uganda has big expectations for light middleweight Isaac "Zedbra" Ssenyange and welterweights Hamza Wandera and Paul Sserunjogi.

the divisions

The 12 different weights in amateur boxing are as follows:

1. Light-flyweight (48 kg)
2. Flyweight (51 kg)
3. Bantamweight (54 kg)
4. Featherweight (57 kg)
5. Lightweight (60 kg)
6. Light-welterweight (63.5 kg)
7. Welterweight (67 kg)
8. Light-middleweight (71 kg)
9. Middleweight (75 kg)
10. Light-heavyweight (81 kg)
11. Heavyweight (91kg)
12. Super-heavyweight (over 91kg)

2002
Manchester
THE XVII COMMONWEALTH GAMES

High fliers, welcome aboard.

Excellent communications by road, rail and air, a high skill base which has attracted and retained world class companies and a quality of life second to none.

If you are looking for a location to match your highest aspirations, the sky's the limit in Lancashire West.

To find out more call 01772 206012 or visit our website: **www.lancashirewest.org.uk**

"driving the future"

Lancaster

Wyre

Blackpool Preston

Fylde

South Ribble

Chorley

West Lancashire

lwp
LANCASHIRE
WEST PARTNERSHIP

LWP/22

CYCLING

VENUE: NATIONAL CYCLING CENTRE (TRACK); RIVINGTON (TIME TRIAL; MOUNTAIN BIKES; ROAD)
DATES: 28 JULY – 2 AUGUST (TRACK); 27 JULY (TIME TRIAL – INDIVIDUAL);
29 JULY (MOUNTAIN BIKES); 3 AUGUST (ROAD)

Road race

The ultimate two-wheeled test of stamina and savvy, the road races on the Rivington circuit will be the grand finale to cycling events for the Games. The rules are simple: the riders start together and the first across the line wins. Slipstreaming is permitted, meaning that there is no point in merely putting your head down and pushing: the preferred tactic is to conserve energy before selecting the perfect moment to escape, so a calculating mind is as vital as strong legs.

Road racing bikes resemble everyday sports bikes, with drop handlebars and thin, light tyres, but have 18 gears, pre-set to be selected at the touch of a button, with frames made of superlight steel, aluminium or titanium. With the cyclists spending much of the race in a tightly packed group, crashes are a big risk and helmets are compulsory.

Go speed racers

The five-hour men's race will be a three-way battle between England, Scotland and Australia, with the English led by the Anglo-Italian Max Sciandri, a stage winner in the Tour de France – "I don't get many chances to race in Britain, and in a championship like this, that will something else," he says. The Scots will look to another Tour star, David Millar, nicknamed "the Dandy" for his rock-star looks, while Australia will bank on 35-year-old Scott Sunderland, back to his best after coming close to death three years ago in a racing crash. In the two-and-a-half-hour women's event, all eyes will be on Nicole Cooke, the 18-year-old triple junior world champion from Wales who won three big races in her first two months as a pro this spring.

"There will be so much home support, it will be fantastic," she says.

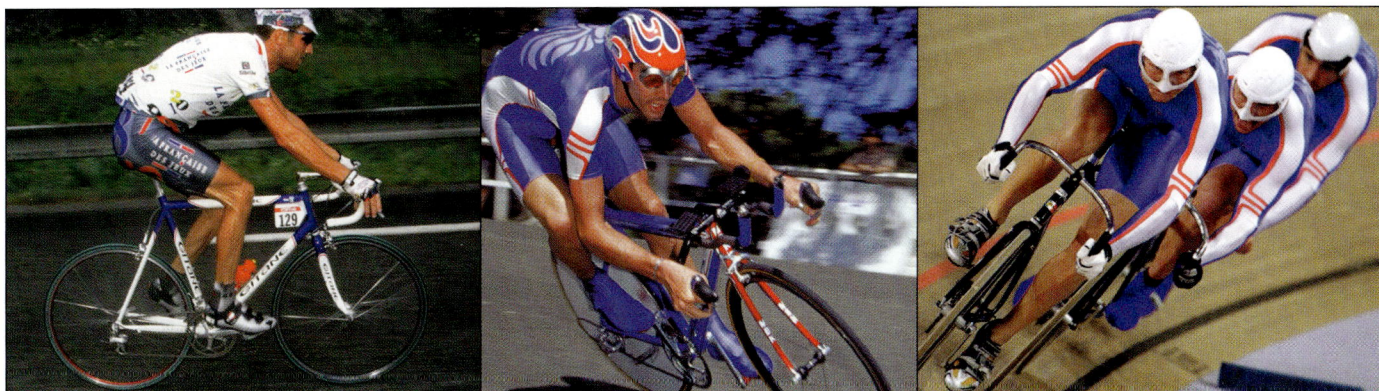

Words: William Fotheringham. Photos: Alex Livesey, Mike Powell (Allsport)

Time trials

In the road time trials, which open the Games, the cyclists start at two-minute intervals and are timed around the circuit, with slipstreaming strictly forbidden. Aerodynamic handlebars, tear-drop shaped helmets and skin-tight lycra catsuits help save vital seconds.

all-time top cycling medallists

The following are the leading Commonwealth Games gold medal winners since cycling made its debut in 1934:
1= Jocelyn Lovell (Can) 1970-78 – 4 golds
1= Brad McGee (Aus) 1990-94 – 4 golds
3= Kevin Nichols (Aus) 1978-82 – 3 golds
3= Gary Niewand (Aus) 1986-94 – 3 golds
3= Gary Anderson (NZ) 1990 – 3 golds
3= Kathy Watt (Aus) 1994 – 3 golds

The following are the top three gold medal countries of all-time:
1. Australia (54 gold medals)
2. England (21 gold medals)
3. New Zealand (12 gold medals)

Manchester 2002
THE XVII COMMONWEALTH GAMES

Time triallists

While the Olympic medallist Bradley Wiggins will lead the English challenge and Canada will look to Ryder Hesdjal, who also rides the mountain bike race, the dark horse could be Northern Ireland's Michael Hutchinson, the best time triallist in Britain's domestic scene last year – "As the next best thing to the Olympics, the Games have massive appeal for me," he says. "Being part of something of that magnitude is really something to look forward to and I'm keen to measure myself against some of the best in the world."

Track cycling

This event is a spectator's joy, with high speeds, inch-perfect bike handling and pure power on the banked curves of the Manchester velodrome, on bikes pared down to the bones – no brakes, no gears, just a single fixed cog, which the rider uses to slow down by pushing down against the pedals. The blue riband discipline is the sprint, a knock-out competition over three 250m laps of the velodrome, with a two-man final. It's tactical stuff as each rider attempts to trick the other into taking the lead to win the benefit of surprise in the last-lap's 40mph dash for the line.

tales from the track

The most intriguing story on the track is that of the Great Britain Olympic sprint team. The team members won medals at World and Olympic level for the last three years, but must split up for the Games: Englishman Jason Queally and two Scots, Chris Hoy and Craig Maclean.
The Olympic champion Queally will take on Hoy in the standing-start kilometre time trial – a minute of pure pain, at close to 38mph average speed. He will then face both Hoy and Maclean in the Olympic sprint, a timed, three lap, three rider sprint, with each man setting the pace for a lap.
"There will be lots of friendly banter with Jason, I don't doubt," laughs Maclean, "but I'm looking forward to racing for Scotland. There's a lot of expectation being put on me, and I'm sure I'll live up to it."

Manchester 2002
THE XVII COMMONWEALTH GAMES

Track cyclists

The Australians are the masters here, so expect to see riders like Jobie Dajka and Sean Eadie in the men's medals; in the women's event, Canada's 2001 world championship bronze medallist Lari Ann Muenzer will be favourite. England's Bradley Wiggins, a former world junior champion, is the man to watch in the individual 4,000 metre pursuit, a timed race in which two cyclists start on either side of the track and "pursue" each other. He could well end up facing his professional teammate Bradley McGee of Australia in the final. In the team competition, where four riders share the pace over the distance, Australia will be out to make amends for a disastrous crash in last year's World Championships.

Michael Steele, Jamie McDonald (Allsport)

Start here. Go anywhere.

The Halfords Bikehut. If we don't stock it, you don't need it.

halfords

halfords.com

Mountain biking

This event is the new kid on the cycling block, an Olympic discipline only since 1996 and included in the Games this year for the second time. Mountain biking was born in California's Marin County in the early 1980s, when a bunch of aging hippies began modifying their city bikes – "clunkers" with fat tyres and wide handlebars.

Today's mountain bike is no clunker. It's made of titanium, carbon fibre or aluminium, with 24 gears, including special low ratios to deal with steep climbs on loose stones and slippery mud. Tyres are fat and studded for grip, while oil-damped front and rear suspension systems and disc brakes owe much to cross-country motorbike technology.

The cross-country event on the Lancashire landmark of Rivington Pike is a two-hour mass-start race over terrain varying from tarmac roads to thick mud. It's a severe test of endurance for man and machine with rocks and tree roots to test bike-handling skills, high-speed descents that push the cyclists' reactions and long steep climbs where heart, lungs and legs work overtime.

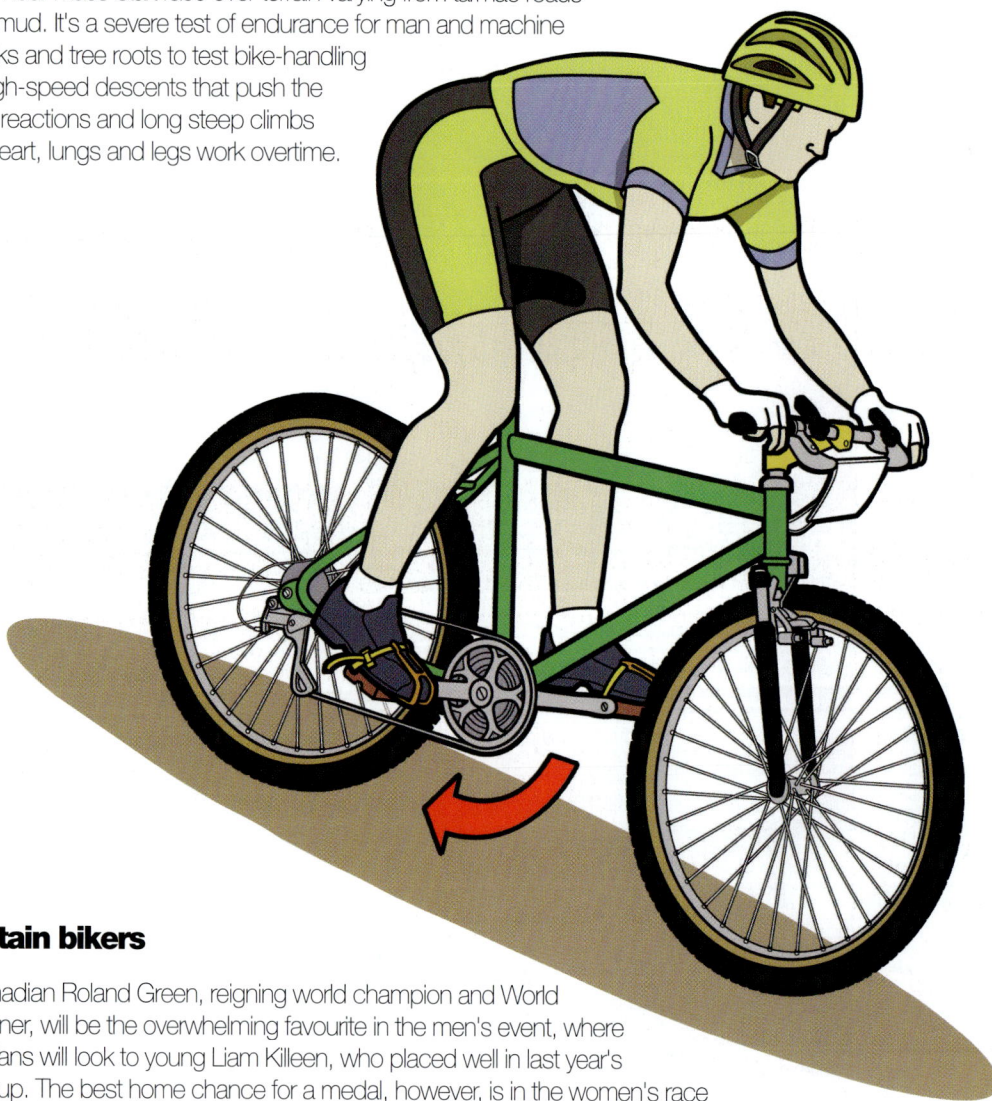

"I'M REALLY EXCITED ABOUT IT," SAYS SCOTLAND'S CAROLINE ALEXANDER. "THE GAMES MEAN A LOT TO ME, AND I WANT TO WIN... I'VE BEEN ROUND THE COURSE AND IT'S A GOOD HARD NORTHERN CIRCUIT – RIGHT UP MY STREET."

Mountain bikers

The Canadian Roland Green, reigning world champion and World Cup winner, will be the overwhelming favourite in the men's event, where English fans will look to young Liam Killeen, who placed well in last year's World Cup. The best home chance for a medal, however, is in the women's race where Scotland's Caroline Alexander, who lives just up the M6 in the Lake District, will have her best chance ever to take a major title.

"I'm really excited about it," she says. "The Games mean a lot to me and I want to win: it's rare to have a title like this in my back garden, where my friends and family can come and see me. I've been round the course and it's a good hard Northern circuit – right up my street."

Alexander, a stalwart of British women's mountain biking for the last decade, will retire at the end of the season and knows that gold would be the perfect way to sign off.

THE FAST TRACK TO VICTORY

JASON QUELLY
(WINNING)

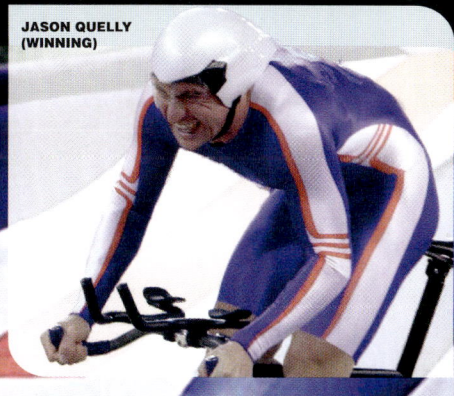

LANCE ARMSTRONG
3 X TOUR DE FRANCE WINNER

UNITED STATES
POSTAL SERVICE

LANCE ARMSTRONG
(WINNING)

NICOLE COOKE
JUNIOR WORLD CHAMPION
(MTB, ROAD & TIME TRIAL!)

NICOLE COOKE
(WINNING)

JASON QUELLY
OLYMPIC 1000M TRACK GOLD MEDALIST

SHIMANO®

components for champions

VENUE: G-MEX
DATES: 26-29 JULY

GYMNASTICS

The basics

There are three separate competitions each for men's and women's gymnastics at the Commonwealth Games. The men compete in six events: floor exercises, pommel horse, rings, vault, parallel bars and high bar. Women compete in four events: vault, asymmetric bars, beam and floor exercises.

The first competition is the Team Championships. Each team consists of five gymnasts, with the best four competing in each of the events. The best three scores on each event count toward the team total. Some gymnasts will compete in all the events; others might only compete on the one or two events at which they excel.

The scores from each of the men's and women's team competitions are also used to find the top 24 qualifiers for the finals of the Individual Championship (six events in total for men and four events for women). To find the Commonwealth champion in each of the events, the top eight qualifiers for the apparatus finals are taken out of the event rankings from the team competition. The judging of gymnastics exercises is done using a strict code that specifies how each of the events must be constructed and performed.

The teams

When gymnastics was first introduced as a Commonwealth Games sport the Canadian national anthem dominated the presentation ceremonies. At the last Games in Malaysia, the medals returned to nations throughout the Commonwealth. England is defending the men's team competition with some great all-around gymnasts and a number of remarkable event specialists, whose high scores can be used to lift the team total. For the past two years Canada has had perhaps the best all-round team. The success of the specialists in each team may tip the result. Australia has some awesome gymnasts but will have to dig deep to find the depth to win. Scotland has its best team for many decades and might just challenge for a medal position.

The women's competition could see England win the gold medal. Over the past four years, Australia has been ranked first with England, while Canada is a close third. Scores in 2002 show that England has improved and with Beth Tweddle, European bars bronze medallist heading the England team, it is certain to post a high team total.

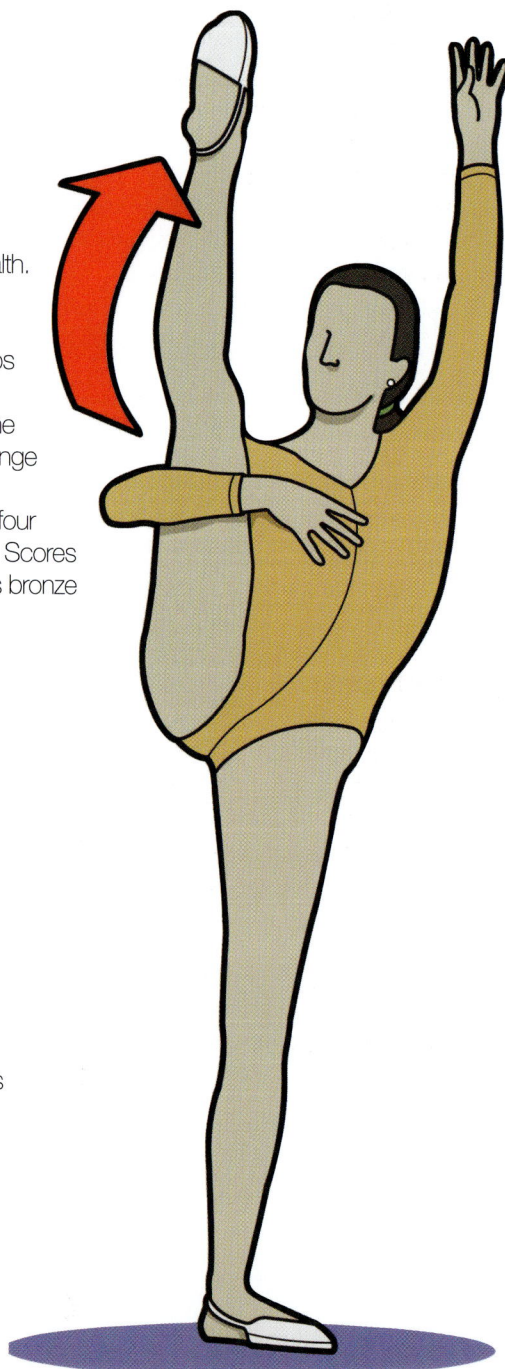

Discipline 1: floor

Floor exercises comprise acrobatics and choreographed movements designed to display dynamic skill, agility and suppleness. Backflips and handsprings are used to build up speed before spinning somersaults that can be performed with a tuck shape, piked or straight body. Double somersaults and twists add to the difficulty of the exercise, with consecutive somersaults earning bonus points. Women perform floor exercises to music, with dance movements adding drama and emotion. Alana Slater of Australia must be a predictable medal winner of the women's floor exercises. Also watch out for Canadian Grant Golding in the men's floor competition. He will be pressed by England's Darren Gerrard and this might be the closest final of them all.

Words: Trevor LOW

Discipline 2: vault

The traditional vaulting horse was abandoned a year ago to make way for a vaulting table to allow more difficult and interesting vaults to be performed. Women vault at a lower height than the men, but many of the vaults are similar. The most difficult vaults have more than one somersault or contain up to two twists. Some vaults begin by jumping backwards from the springboard and are called Yurchenko vaults after their inventor. The English men's duo of Kanukai Jackson and Darren Gerrard have the most difficult vaults; both made the European finals, with Kanukai winning the bronze medal. Malaysia has shown immense ability in men's vaulting over the past few years. Recent new rules, making potential vault finalists complete two vaults during the team competition, make this very much a specialist event. Northern Ireland's Holly Murdoch is one of the Commonwealth's greatest vaulters.

Discipline 3: parallel bars

This event is the most difficult in which to achieve a Start Value near 10.00 points. Swinging in and around a handstand is combined with giant swings under the bars to make a complex exercise with critical hand changes. As the end of one movement is the start of the next, the mechanics of every skill leave no margin for error – this is the gymnastic equivalent of jumping ten double decker buses on a pushbike. It requires strength, dynamic power, agility, endurance and a tremendous sense of swing rhythm.

Discipline 4: high bar

The most spectacular of the gymnastic events is the men's high bar. Giant swings with turns and hops are combined with somersaults over the bar to recatch. Tkachev, Geinger and Jager somersaults can all be done with or without twists. The most recent addition to the excitement of high bar is the Kovac double somersault, which passes over the top of the bar – this is an event for the seriously courageous. Scotland's Barry Collie has the ability to challenge for a medal, but the World bronze medallist (2001), Australian Phillippe Rizzo, is the odds-on favourite. Canadian Richard Ikeda and Welshman David Eaton also have World Class routines.

Discipline 5: pommel horse

This is the most difficult exercise to judge and perform. Many hand changes occur while the gymnast moves from one part of the horse to another. One small error of balance can cause a chain reaction of errors and give the judges cause to frown. England's Kanukai Jackson, David Eaton from Wales and Richard Ikeda from Canada are all capable of taking medals. The real star might be Kwang Tung Onn of Malaysia, who has perfected a routine awash with extreme difficulty.

Flags courtesy of www.theodora.com/flags used with permission.

Diversity, involvement, commitment, passion.
be in Birmingham 2008.

Birmingham is bidding to become the European Capital of Culture in 2008. It is Britain's most culturally rich and diverse city.

More than any British city, Birmingham has invested in its culture for decades: £3billion over the last 25 years and more than £850million annually.

Birmingham has a track record of staging major events brilliantly, from the Eurovision Song Contest to the G8 summit.

So, be in Birmingham in 2008.

Discipline 6: rings

Muscle, muscle and muscle. Crucifix, Maltese Cross, Azyrian – the names of the strength elements conjure up years of dedicated power training. With a few swings to handstand and a dismount, the gymnast must be above all, strong. Damian Istria of Australia and Kanukai Jackson of England are the Commonwealth "men of men", but much depends on the seconds that sort the strong from the strongest.

Discipline 7: balance beams

Light and dynamic acrobatic skills, leaps and jumps, spins and turns are choreographed into an exercise that should look easy. However, on a beam 10cm wide, nothing is easy. The best Commonwealth gymnasts on this apparatus are from Australia, but England's Tweddle, who qualified for the beam finals (top eight) at the recent European Championships may surprise everyone.

Discipline 8: asymmetric bars

For the women gymnasts, vault, floor and beam share similar "families" of skills and movements. For bars, an entirely different physical ability is required and very high scores will be rare. The gymnast must use both bars, making giant swings around the bars and "in bar" elements where the hips pass close to a bar. Different hand grips are used, with the most spectacular movements involving a swing with a release of the bar before somersaulting and recatching. There is a great expectation of a medal for Tweddle at this event. The English gymnast won the bronze medal for her bar exercise at the last European Championships, making gymnastics history as the first woman from the home nations to win a European medal. Watch out for Jacqui Dunn of Australia, who has the most classic line and form.

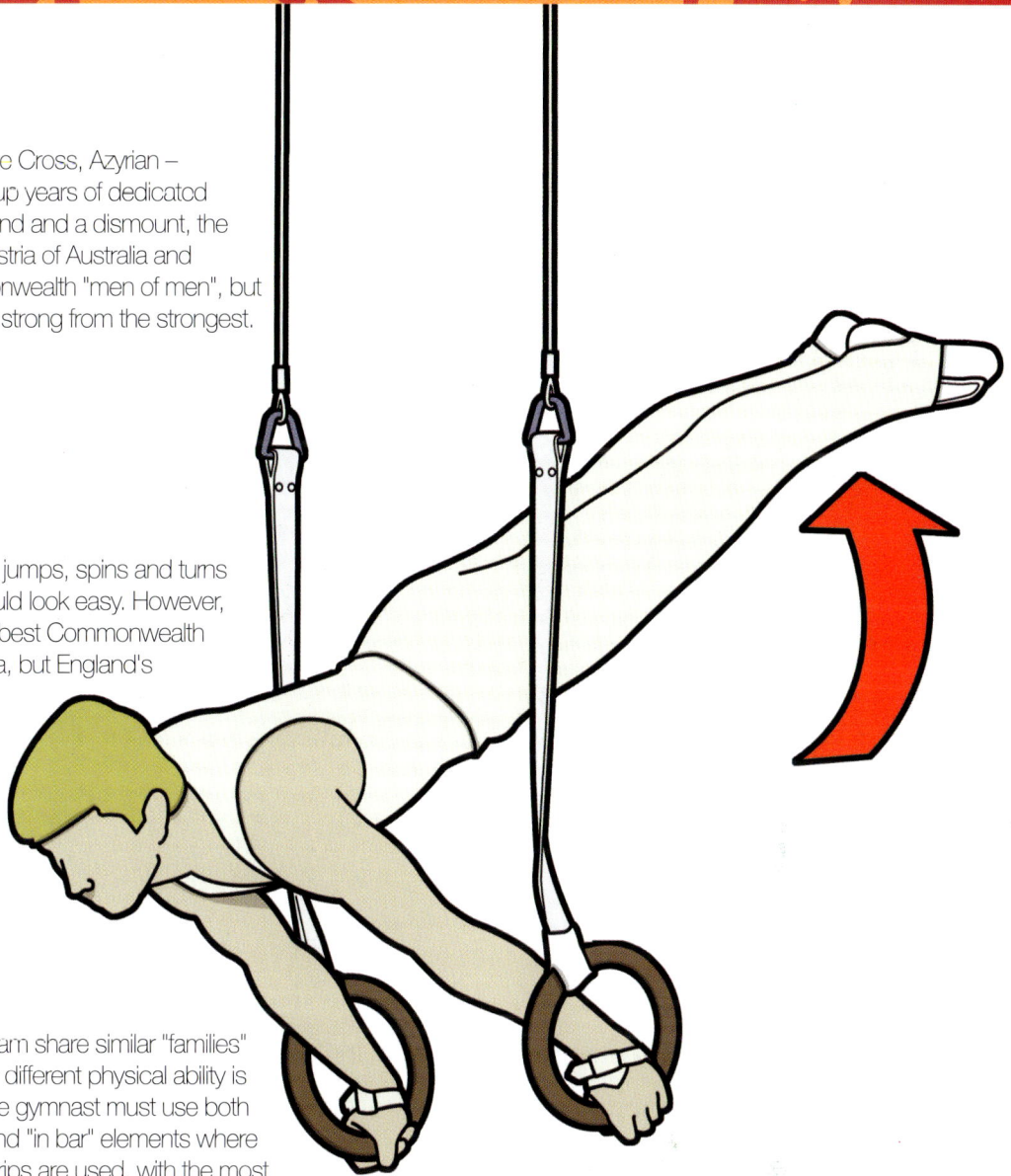

"THE COMMONWEALTH GAMES ARE A HUGE MILESTONE ON THE WAY TO ATHENS IN 2004. IT GIVES THE ENGLISH TEAM A CHANCE TO SEE WHERE THEY ARE IN THE STANDINGS... THE BIGGEST RIVALS ARE AUSTRALIA AND CANADA," SAYS BETH TWEDDLE (ENGLAND).

Official Kit Supplier to England's Hockey, Squash and Badminton Teams

Julian Robertson

Simon Parke

Ian Sullivan

Leisa King

Jimmy Wallace

Jane Smith

Slazenger®

www.slazenger.com

VENUE: BELLE VUE REGIONAL HOCKEY CENTRE
DATES: 26 JULY – 4 AUGUST

HOCKEY

History

The history of hockey cannot be told without looking back at the roots of the game, which are buried deep in antiquity. Historical records show that a crude form of hockey or hurley was played in Egypt some 4,000 years ago and in Ethiopia around 1000 BC. We also know from various museums that a form of the game was played by the Romans and Greeks and even by the Aztec Indians of South America several centuries before Columbus landed in the New World.
The modern game evolved in England in the mid-18th Century around schools, including Eton and Winchester, under local rules and was followed by the creation of The (English) Hockey Association in 1886. The (English) Ladies Hockey Association was formed in 1895, having had their request to join the Men's Association turned down.
The International Hockey Federation started much later when it was formed in Paris in January 1924.The first Olympic hockey tournament was held in London in 1908, with England, Ireland and Scotland competing. The sport was dropped from the 1912 Olympics in Stockholm, reappeared in Antwerp in 1920, missed out in Paris in 1924 to begin its continuous Olympic run in Amsterdam in 1928.
Hockey emerged from the shadows in Britain in October 1986, when over six million people switched on their television sets to watch a hockey match. Hockey had come of age as England lined up to face Australia in the World Cup Final at Willesden.
Just two years later, even more got up early to watch the Olympic Hockey Final from Seoul, with Great Britain beating the Germans to win the gold medal.

Basics

"Soccer with a stick" is the best way to explain hockey to those unfamiliar with the game. Like football, it is a game played between two teams of 11 players, including a goalkeeper, with the simple objective to put the ball in the opposing goal. Sixteen players make up a squad with rolling substitutes permitted. The hockey pitch and goals are smaller than those used for soccer. Take away the football and substitute a smaller, hard ball, then give each player a stick that can only be used to move the ball around and there you have it. Like soccer, the goalkeeper plays under different rules. Within his own circle, he can kick the ball, use his hands and stop a shot with his body. Unlike football, the ball must be hit by an attacker inside a shooting circle before a goal can be scored and there is no offside rule. Many of the tactics used in hockey are similar to those of soccer, like the use of the wings, close passing and control of the midfield, but hockey is a non-contact sport (although you might find this difficult to believe) and the body cannot be used to shield the ball from an opponent when stationery. The use of aerial balls is also more limited because of the danger element of the small hard object whacking a player in the head. There are numerous other differences. Throw-ins are replaced with hit-ins when the ball goes out of play over the side lines. There are two degrees of penalty awards: a penalty corner and – for very serious offences – a penalty stroke. A yellow card is a temporary suspension for a limited period while a red card represents a permanent suspension.

Words: Bill Collwill

Stick it to them

Undoubtedly the Australians will provide major opposition along with Pakistani men to the English teams. While several of the English women will have scores to settle with the Australians having lost the final in Malaysia 8-1. 22 year old Kate Walsh, who has made great strides since given an opportunity by England's Australian coach Tricia Heberle, will be the one to watch in the heart of English defence. For the men, hopes will centre on Reading's 25 year old Mark Pearn, a gifted player with the ability to produce a goal scoring chance out of nothing. Other teams to watch out for include the Canadian men who are currently ranked 17th in the world.

Current Malaysian captain Mirnawan Mawawi is known as the "dribble king" of Malaysia and was in the Malaysian side that picked up the silver medal in Kuala Lumpur.

The Malaysians could well be among the medals in Manchester once again.

commonwealth hockey history

The history of Commonwealth Games hockey is very short, only entering the events roster in 1998 in Kuala Lumpur. This is somewhat strange considering the majority of the world's best hockey teams, both men's and women's, come from the Commonwealth. Australia, India, England, Pakistan, India and New Zealand are particularly strong while the Malaysians (who won silver in Kuala Lumpur) have arguably the best dedicated hockey stadium in the world at Balik Jalil which has a capacity of 13,000. In fact, of the 18 men's Olympic hockey golds won between 1908-1996, India took eight, Great Britain and Pakistan took three each while New Zealand grabbed one – leaving only three for the rest of the world. In the Kuala Lumpur Games, Australia took home both men's and women's gold medals while England gained bronze in the men's and silver in the women's event.

Manchester 2002
THE XVII COMMONWEALTH GAMES

Allsport

SPORT
AT MANCAT

If sport is your passion - MANCAT is the college for you!

Are you aged between 16 and 18?

Are you interested in a career in sport?

Would you like to be a sports coach, sports manager or sports player?

Give your future a head-start with a MANCAT sports course!

Programmes available include:

- **Sports and Recreation NVQ Level 1 (Introduction to Coaching & Leading)**
- **BTEC First Award Sports Studies**
- **BTEC National Diploma in Applied Sports Science**
- **Sports Academy - Football, Basketball and Individual Sports**

For more information on any of our sports courses, or to receive an application form, call the Schools Liaison Team on 0161 953 2267, or email us at slt@mancat.ac.uk

Manchester 2002
THE XVII COMMONWEALTH GAMES

MANCHESTER
College of Arts and Technology
www.mancat.ac.uk

MANCAT is host to the Broadcasting Centre for the Commonwealth Games

JUDO

VENUE: G-MEX
DATES: 30 JULY – 1 AUGUST

History

Judo originates from the ancient Japanese martial art of jujutsu – a hand-to-hand combat system derived on the battlefields of medieval Japan.

At that time, the samurai (warrior) class held an important position in Japanese society. By the end of the 19th Century, though, the samurai had lost its prestige and status, and martial arts as a whole had lost some of their mystique and popularity.

As interest in the martial arts waned, a young university student called Jigoro Kano began to develop an interest in the ancient art of jujutsu ("the pliant art").

He began studying jujutsu at the age of 17 and within five years had developed his own art, judo ("the gentle way"). Judo was based on the principle of using an opponent's force against him. Its formal beginning is believed to be in 1882 when Kano opened the Kodokan Judo Academy in Tokyo – the spiritual home of judo.

Basics

Judo is a form of jacket wrestling where opponents attempt to throw, pin down, armlock or strangle each other to secure victory. Victory can be gained either with a perfect throw, a hold lasting 25 seconds or by forcing a submission with either an armlock or strangle. Fighters compete by weight categories. There are seven weight categories for both men and women, ranging from under 60 kg and over 100 kg to under 48 kg and over 78 kg respectively. Competitors wear thick cotton open jackets tied with a belt, and cotton pants. The competition area measures 10 sq m and competitors can be penalised for a variety of infringements such as passivity or stepping out of the contest area.

Face off for gold

The Home Nations are extremely strong in judo within the Commonwealth, with the top fighters spread across the entire British Isles. Scotland's best hope lies with 1999 world champion, Graeme Randall.

"As a Scotsman, the Commonwealth Games is one of the best opportunities to represent your home country," he says. "It is a great honour to compete for Great Britain, but it is a different sensation to be able to fight for Scotland." England will be pinning its hopes on Sydney silver medallist Kate Howey MBE – if she can recover from a serious wrist injury in time. Australian Maria Pekli, winner of a bronze medal in the 52-57 kg category at the 2000 Olympic Games, is also expected to be a favourite, as is Carley Dixon from New South Wales who is a past US Open champion.

Words: Barnaby Chesterman

asics®

STEVE BACKLEY
Javelin

JONATHAN EDWARDS
Triple Jump

JASON GARDENER
100/200m Sprint

ASHIA HANSEN
Triple Jump

HEART & SOLE.

COLIN JACKSON
110m Hurdles

DEAN MACEY
Decathlon

CHRISTIAN MALCOLM
100/200m Sprint

IWAN THOMAS
400m

FOR THE LOVE OF SPORT

"You don't win with your feet, your legs or your arms. You win with your heart". The love of sport brings with it the promise and perspective of reaching the highest levels possible. Like an athlete will sacrifice everything for a new personal best, ASICS will go to extremes to develop shoes and apparel with the best performance ever. May we take this opportunity to wish all ASICS athletes every success. There's more for the love of sport at www.asics.co.uk

FOR THE LOVE OF SPORT

LAWN BOWLS

VENUE: HEATON PARK, MANCHESTER
DATES: 26 JULY – 4 AUGUST

History

The origins of the game of bowls are obscure, although there is evidence that as early as 5200 BC, the Chinese – and later the Egyptians, around 3000 BC – found amusement and demonstrated skill-at-arms by throwing or rolling one object at another and applying a measure to determine the winner. The best known antecedent of the game in modern times stems from the 16th Century, when Sir Francis Drake completed his game of bowls on Plymouth Hoe before sailing to battle against the Spanish Armada.

In England, the game is reputed to have been played first in the 11th Century. In 1999, the Southampton (Old Green) Club celebrated its 700th anniversary, having been founded in 1299.

Royalty have played and influenced the game. In the 14th Century, laws were passed prohibiting bowls because players were distracted from practicing their archery skills by spending too much time on the bowling green. In 1903, the English Bowling Association was formed with the first President being Dr WG Grace of cricketing fame. The game is now very popular throughout the world, steeped in tradition and symbolising the skill of the clear thinking and cool headed warrior.

Basics

Flat green bowls are played on a green divided into rinks. A biased ball (known as a bowl) is rolled toward a smaller unbiased ball (known as a jack). Games can be played one against another (Singles) or in teams (Pairs, Triples or Fours). The object is to get as many bowls of one team closer to the jack than the opposition. Games are played to a specified number of shots or over a number of ends.

High rollers

Lawn bowls was one of the original sports featured at the inaugural Commonwealth Games in 1930. The sport brings together 340 players from 26 countries, some with membership of over 200,000 players to others with less than 50. There is a 50 year age gap between the youngest and oldest competitors, family members will play together, players will be from all races, colours and creeds, and include the able-bodied, disabled and blind. Spectators will be particularly amazed at the skills of the Blind Women's Singles competitors, while everyone will be keeping an eye on the EAD Men's Triples, especially if England (captained by Richard Coates) plays New Zealand (skippered by Peter Horne). Playing at home, England will have the benefit of great support. Ireland, Scotland and Wales have many Commonwealth Games and World Champions in their teams. Margaret Johnston (Ireland) and Willie Wood MBE (Scotland) seem to have been winning titles forever. A very strong challenge will come from the Southern Hemisphere countries of Australia, New Zealand, South Africa and Malaysia who prepare so thoroughly for major events. Rex Johnston and Steve Glasson (Australia), Peter Belliss MBE, Rowan Brassey and Marlene Castle (New Zealand), Neil Burkett (South Africa) are still performing very consistently after many years at the top.

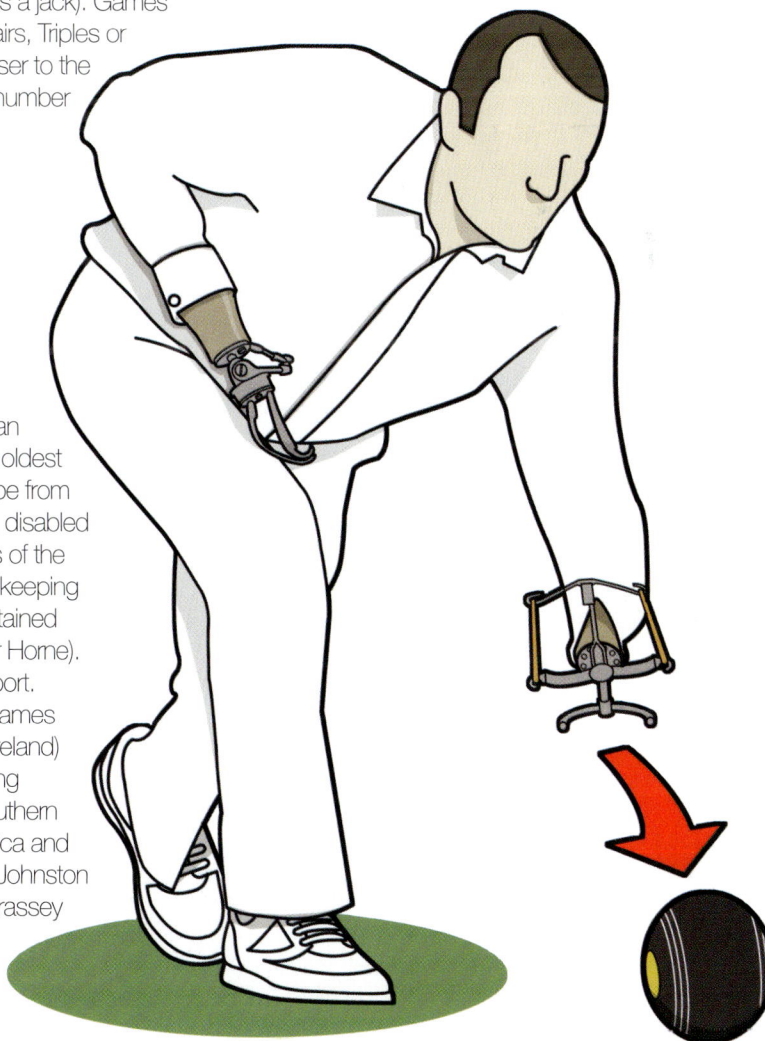

Words: George Shaw

NETBALL

VENUE: THE MEN ARENA

DATES: 26 JULY – 4 AUGUST (REST DAYS: 1 AUGUST AND 3 AUGUST)

History

Basketball was invented at the YMCA International Training School in Springfield, Massachusetts in 1891, by a young Canadian named James Naismith. In 1895, netball – a variation on the game – was introduced to England and the "nets" were two waste paper baskets hung on walls at each end of the hall. The game then moved outdoors onto grass. The students at Dartford introduced rings instead of baskets, the large ball and the division of the ground into three courts. The first official rules of netball were published in 1901, with the game and rules being introduced to USA, Canada, France, South Africa, as well as Wales, Scotland and Ireland in 1902. The International Federation of Netball Associations was formed in 1960. The World Championships have been held every four years since 1963 with Australia dominating. In 1995, the game was recognised as an Olympic sport and in 1998, it was included in the Commonwealth Games for the first time. England won the Bronze medal, beating South Africa 56-54 and Australia defeated New Zealand in the final.

The rules

Netball is played between two sides, each with seven players on the court. The netball court is a rectangular shape (30.5 by 15.25m) and divided into three equal areas. In the middle third is a small circle (0.9m in diameter) from which the game is started with a centre pass, which teams take alternatively. In each of the end thirds is an arc (4.9m in diameter). It is from this arc that goals are scored by placing the ball through a ring 3.05m high and attached to a post.
Each time a team is able to place the ball through the net, they are awarded one goal – the team with the highest score at the end of four 15-minute quarters is declared the victor. Only the positions of Goal Shooter and Goal Attack are able to score goals for their team. The seven players on court each have an allocated position, which allows them to enter only specific areas of the court and they wear a team bib with initials indicating their position to identify themselves.

Sharp shooters

There are ten teams taking part in this year's event, with the Australians and New Zealanders looking like favourites. The main Aussies to watch for are Liz Ellis (GK and vice captain) and Sharrelle McMahon (GA) who scored the final goal for Australia in the 1999 World Championships giving the title to Australia by one goal. For News Zealand, Irene Van Dyke is a standout. She is one of the tallest players in the sport (6ft 3in) and highly accurate – her shooting statistics often exceed 90 per cent. Olivia Murphy, nicknamed "The Thief" at the 1999 World Championships due to her ability to make interceptions, will be the key player in the England side.

Words: Siobhan Atkinson

POWERGEN

Powergen. Putting more energy into rugby

Powergen, sponsers of English Cup Rugby

RUGBY 7S

VENUE: CITY OF MANCHESTER STADIUM
DATES: 2–4 AUGUST

History

Scotland can claim the credit for introducing the rest of the world to the pleasures of golf and whisky, and the same applies to seven-a-side rugby. The best ideas are often the simple ones and, in 1883, a local Melrose butcher called Ned Haigh hit upon a new wheeze to raise funds for his cash-strapped local club. A shortened form of the 15-a-side game, with a mere three forwards packing down rather than the customary eight (or nine or 10 as some favoured in those days), was duly born, with the aim of giving local people some eye-catching running rugby in a competitive format. It had the added benefit of encouraging forwards to run and handle like backs and, more importantly for the Scottish Border clubs, it proved an instant financial success.

The Melrose Sevens developed into a world-renowned event, spawning illustrious competitors such as the Hong Kong Sevens and the Middlesex Sevens, where the social advantages of attending a whole day's rugby instead of a mere 80-minute game swiftly became obvious. When rugby union went professional in 1995, there were fears that sevens might be one of the casualties, with clubs reluctant to release their best players and the global calendar becoming increasingly congested.

The International Rugby Board, however, saw sevens as a perfect vehicle to encourage the game in developing rugby nations, establishing the IRB's World Sevens Series (which began in 1999/2000), with events being staged as far afield as Mar del Plata in Argentina and Singapore. Sevens has already made its Commonwealth Games debut in Kuala Lumpur in 1998 when New Zealand and Jonah Lomu enjoyed a memorable triumph. All the signs point to Manchester hosting an equally vibrant spectacle.

"NEW ZEALAND PLACE A GOOD DEAL OF PRIORITY ON SEVENS," ADMITS AUSTRALIA'S SEVENS MANAGER JULIAN GARDNER, THE FORMER DUAL WALLABY AND ITALIAN INTERNATIONAL. "THEY'RE SUPER-CONFIDENT AS A SIDE."

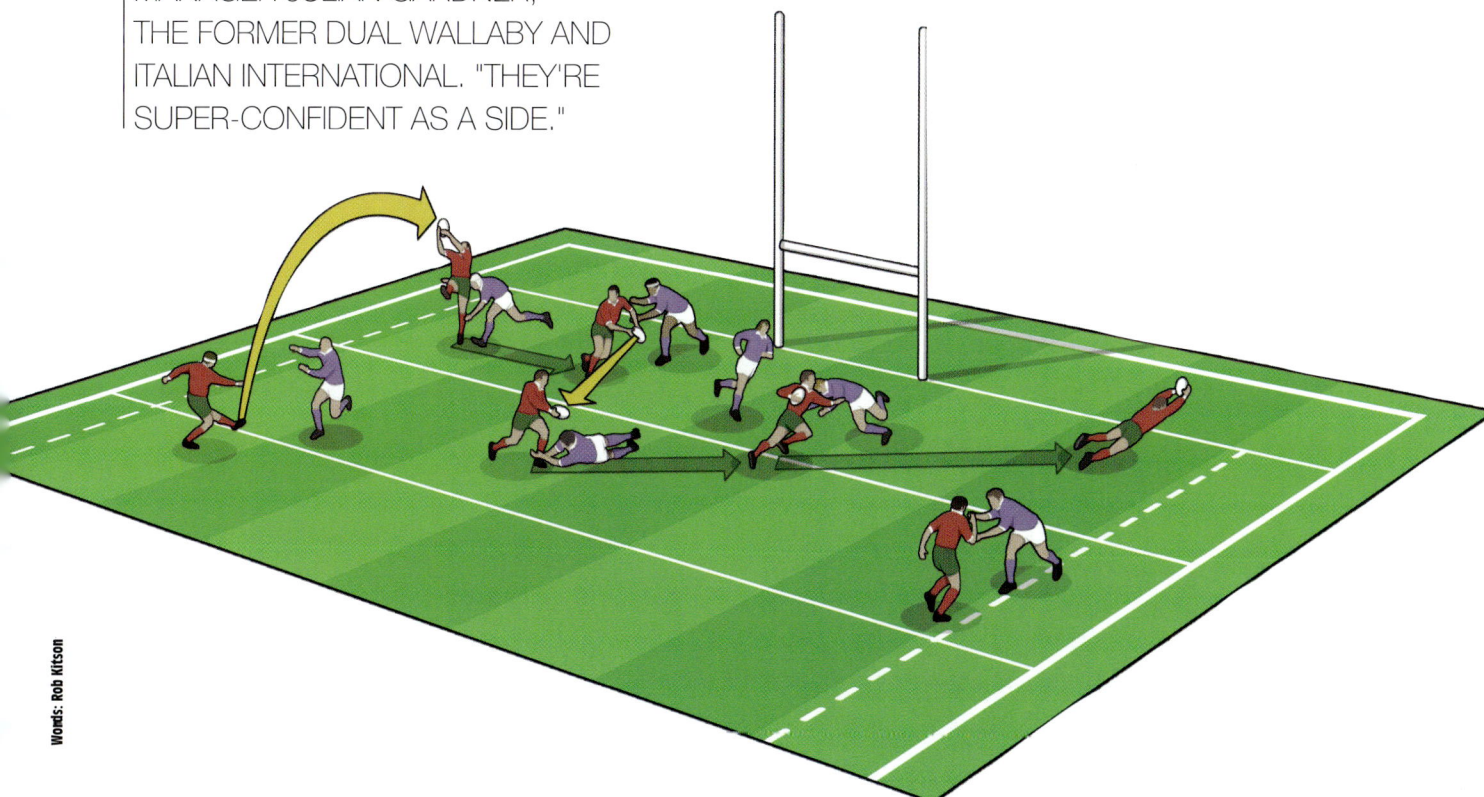

Words: Rob Kitson

Basics

The beauty of sevens is its ability to incorporate virtually all the best elements of rugby union: a good sevens player needs vision, elusiveness, pace, top-class tackling and handling skills and, above all, stamina. There are few bigger nightmares than being an unfit sevens competitor; such is the fast, non-stop nature of the game that 10 minutes each way can feel like a lifetime. The majority of rules are the same as union, the most obvious exceptions being the three-man scrums and the use of drop-kicks instead of place-kicks for conversions. Time spent on set-pieces is also considerably reduced; if a restart kick sails into touch, for example, the receiving side gets a free-kick on halfway rather than scrum possession. Three substitutes are allowed in any one match and if scores are level at full-time, the first team to score in extra-time wins. Rugby league fans may discover that sevens resembles their own game more closely than the 15-a-side version of union. The extra space available means that breaching the opposition defensive line is more likely to produce a try and, unless conditions are bad, there is much less kicking.

Lucky 7s

Those ecstatic ex-pats who roared England to victory in the Hong Kong Sevens this year will be aware that established 15-a-side international players are not necessarily an automatic passport to success. Two of England's principal heroes on a wet March night in the Far East were James Simpson-Daniel and Simon Amor, far from household names, but young men with sharp acceleration and an eye for a gap. When it comes to winning at sevens, commitment, dash and calculated risk-taking can often outweigh reputation. Having said that, New Zealand remains the team the rest have to beat. The All Blacks have won the IRB World Sevens Series in all three years of its existence and, as defending Commonwealth champions, will not easily relinquish their title.

"New Zealand places a good deal of priority on sevens," admits Australia's sevens manager Julian Gardner, the former dual Wallaby and Italian international. "They're super-confident as a side, even if they put in the players who have performed for them in this year's World Sevens Series rather than draft in players from their Super 12 teams."

The party is about to start here at the lock building!

why not join us?

Lucky 7s (cont.)

Unfortunately for those keen to see Lomu in Manchester, New Zealand's Tri-Nations test with Australia in Sydney clashes directly with the Games.

Filling the gap, though, will be talent ranging from the peerless Eric Rush to the new young sevens star from Auckland, Joe Rokocoko. England's manager Joe Lydon takes a similar view to Gardner: "I don't think it really matters to New Zealand which name is inside their jumpers. They have such strength in depth that they don't need to put any big names in."

Lydon, though, is quietly excited by his own side's potential, despite the fact his final 12-man squad will lack the unique talents of Jason Robinson.

Lydon did his best to persuade the former rugby league legend to change his plans for a summer's rest – "I became a bit of a stalker at one point" – but another cross-code export Henry Paul should feature prominently. "We're dark horses, which is what most English teams like to be. We're at home in Manchester and there'll be a lot of pressure on the players, but I'll be trying to counteract that by saying, 'This is the event of your rugby lives.'"

If he had unlimited choice, Lydon would still love to select the little Fijian genius Waisale Serevi, the only survivor of a radical Fijian squad rebuilding operation earlier this year. South Africa, under the command of Williams, are also worth watching and opponents have been particularly impressed by the talent of their young playmaker Brent Russell. Australia's challenge will depend on whether they can strengthen their youthful squad with players on the fringes of Wallaby selection and Gardner hopes league capture Wendell Sailor will be available.

"The Commonwealth Games is an event we would like to do well in. We will be arriving with the intention of winning medals – hopefully the yellow-coloured ones. We're not in the Commonwealth Games to come second, we want to win the thing." It promises to be a riveting three days.

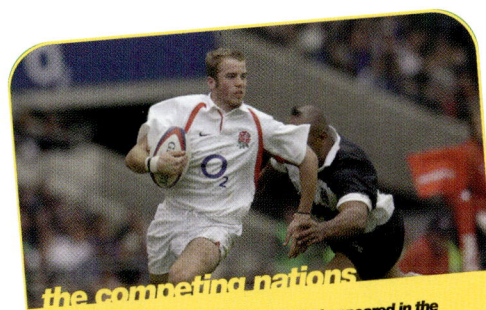

the competing nations

As with hockey, the Rugby 7s event first appeared in the Commonwealth Games in Kuala Lumpur in 1998. New Zealand took the gold with the massive wing-threequarter, Jonah Lomu proving to be one of stars of the Games. Fiji took silver while Australia beat Samoa in the third place play-off to take bronze. This year will see 16 teams in the competition with New Zealand starting as favourites again. Oceania is particularly well represented, with seven teams vying for gold.

The competing nations are as follows:
Australia, Canada, Cook Islands, England, Fiji, Kenya Malaysia, New Zealand, Papua New Guinea, Samoa, Scotland, South Africa, Tonga, Trinidad & Tobago, Wales, Zimbabwe

2002 Manchester
THE XVII COMMONWEALTH GAMES

"WE'RE DARK HORSES, WHICH IS WHAT MOST ENGLISH TEAMS LIKE TO BE. WE'RE AT HOME IN MANCHESTER AND THERE'LL BE A LOT OF PRESSURE ON THE PLAYERS, BUT I'LL BE TRYING TO COUNTERACT THAT BY SAYING, 'THIS IS THE EVENT OF YOUR RUGBY LIVES'," SAYS JOE LYDON, ENGLAND MANAGER.

Tom Shaw (Getty Images)

BISLEY

THE NATIONAL SHOOTING CENTRE

VENUE FOR THE SHOOTING EVENTS OF THE XVII COMMONWEALTH GAMES

Over 100 years ago the National Rifle Association created Bisley as the National Centre for target shooting. Now, with the help of grants from the National Lottery, its facilities have been enhanced dramatically whilst still retaining its original Victorian charm. Bisley can now be considered the World Centre for all disciplines of target shooting and is the venue for the Commonwealth Games shooting events in 2002. Whether young, old, disabled, beginner or an experienced shooter you are most welcome. Why not contact Sarah Bunch on telephone 01483 797666 to find out more and how you too can enjoy these same superb facilities.

The National Shooting Centre at Bisley provides a variety of packages for corporate hospitality, which can be tailored to suit both the pocket and the disciplines required.

Ring Sarah on 01483 797666 or e-mail info@nsc-clays.co.uk

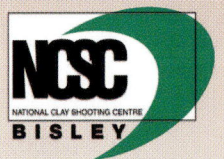

www.nra.org.uk

www.nsc-clays.co.uk

SHOOTING

VENUE: NATIONAL SHOOTING CENTRE, BISLEY
DATES: 27 JULY – 3 AUGUST

The way of the gun

Shooting, contrary to popular opinion, is an ancient sport – there is evidence that shooting clubs were around in the 13th Century and that competitions using firearms with rifled barrels has existed since the 16th Century. Shooting was included at the first modern Olympics in 1896 and, by 1920, 21 shooting events were included in the Antwerp Olympics.

Shooting was first included in the Commonwealth Games in 1966 at Kingston, Jamaica. Since then, shooting has gone from strength to strength at the Games and by 1998, the programme included 30 events for men and women.

One of the most interesting points about the sport is that men and women can compete on equal terms. In 1976, for example, Margaret Thompson Murdoch of the USA becomes the first woman in history to win an Olympic Medal in open competition against both men and women in Montreal, Canada.

Since its first inclusion in the Games, Australia leads the way with 38 gold medals in total for shooting, while smaller nations such as Jersey, Isle of Man and Cyprus have all picked up gold medals.

Clays

Clay target shooting is the art of shooting at (and hitting) flying targets with a shotgun. The target is a small clay disk, about 10 cm in diameter. Clay target events, or clay "pigeons" as they are known, have a worldwide enthusiastic following and are the most visual of shooting competitions.

Competitors in clay target events use 12 bore shotguns. The clays are made from a mixture of pitch and chalk shaped like an inverted saucer designed to break up when hit by just one or two of the pellets.

England's Richard Faulds won gold in Double Trap at Sydney while Ian Peel took silver. However, nothing can be taken for granted. Australia and New Zealand in particular will be wanting to have their say, particularly Aussies Russell Mark, Michael Diamond and Nathan Cassells. Not forgetting India's Mansher Singh, who won the 2001 Commonwealth Federation Trap event.

Expect some close competition in the women's category as well. England's Anita North is in hot form, but she will face stiff opposition – Australia's Suzanne Balogh is a particularly formidable competitor.

Words: Mike Barnes; Peter Underhill

Smallbore and air pistols

Target shooting encompasses a very broad range of disciplines: smallbore rifle; smallbore pistol; air rifle; air pistol and centre fire pistol. There are several categories in these events, each with differing ranges, shooting positions, target exposure and shot limits All the smallbore rifle events are shot at 50 metres using .22" calibre rifles and electronics targets. The smallbore pistol events using .22" calibre pistols each have their own conditions as to the course of fire and the specifications of the pistol used. All air rifle events are shot at 10 metres with .177" calibre air rifles, from the physically demanding standing position. This competition is fired with centre-fire pistols of a calibre between .30" and .38". Air pistol shooting is an increasingly popular sport that can be shot on a 10 metre indoor range. As with the other sporting events, the teams to look out for in small bore and air pistol shooting are Australia, India, Malaysia, Canada, New Zealand and England. Jaspal Rana from India will be defending the golds he won in Kuala Lumpur in the individual centre-fire pistol and in the pairs event; he'll also be trying to better the silvers he gained in 1998 in the individual air pistol and the pairs air pistol. Rana was stopped in his quest for golds in 1998 by England's Michael Gault, who'll be looking to add to the three gold medals he won in Kuala Lumpur. From the smaller nations, Dave Moore from the Isle of Man will be looking to go one better than the silver he won in 1998 in the individual free rifle prone. In the women's events, Sydney 2000 Olympic bronze medallist Annemarie Forder from Australia is a good bet in the air pistol with fellow Aussie, Christine Trefry attempting to add to her impressive medal tally from Kuala Lumpur. English interest lies with Louise Minnett and Linda Smallbone who have both had strong seasons.

Open rifle

The open rifle event is the only Commonwealth Games event contested equally by men or women. The event pits the shooters against each other and the elements over distances from 300 to 1,000 yards, using the 7.62mm calibre single shot target rifles.

Shots are fired from the prone position and rifles have to conform to rigidly enforced weight and other technical specifications. Telescopic sights are not allowed, the shooter using a "peep" sight that is adjustable to compensate for wind and elevation. A freestanding telescope is used to see the spotting disk on the target (showing where the shot has struck). The shooters rely on their experience and judgement, looking at the way the wind-flags are blowing and through their spotting telescopes at the mirage, to assess the strength and direction of the wind.

In the fullbore event, the Northern Irish are the ones to watch. In Kuala Lumpur, David Calvert and Martin Millar picked up gold and will be back to defend their title in Manchester. As in all shooting events, the Malaysians and the Indians will be strong and gunning for medals – in 1998, Malaysian Zainal Abidin Mohammed Zain grabbed silver behind Jim Paton of Canada. The Australians will be looking to get back on the podium after missing out in 1998 – they'll be staking their hopes on the pairing of Colin Cole and David Gardiner. New Zealand will certainly be hoping to improve on their performance in past Commonwealth Games as their national fullbore rifle selection panel convener Jeff Smith explains: "We've done poorly in recent Commonwealth Games, very poorly at Kuala Lumpur in 1998 in fact. For some reason or other, our Commonwealth Games performances have been less than admirable over the last four Games." They may be able to put that right in Manchester. At time of writing, Mike Collings, Mitch Maxberry and young gun John Snowden are leading the qualifying field.

At the Manchester we believe in putting our customers first

To find out about our wide range of savings and mortgage products, contact Manchesters' Number One Building Society.

Tel: 08709 900 800
Fax: 08709 900 801

www.
the**manchester**
.co.uk

Email: info@themanchester.co.uk

Manchester
BUILDING SOCIETY

Queens Court, 24 Queen Street, Manchester M2 5AH

avesco plc   DeLaRue         fredericks DAIRIES

GENERALE LOCATION   Greater Manchester Waste Limited

LAMINEX         Panasonic Broadcast   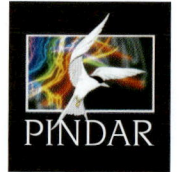

PUMA   SCHENKER Stinnes Logistics

   Gerflor Floors to match your imagination      

      mitre   Schildkröt

The usual suspects

Probationer Police Constables

With a mixture of officers from a variety of ethnic communities, of different ages and even diverse heights, there's nothing standard about Surrey Police. Join us as a Probationer (a trainee PC) and you'll soon appreciate the diversity of the force. You'll enjoy a comprehensive training programme that will enable you to develop the skills you need to become a PC. We will support you with the help of a Tutor Constable during your initial training period, who will work closely with you at your first station. On completion of your two-year probationary period, you'll be eligible to join one of our many specialist units, from Dog Handling or CID, to Financial Investigations, the Domestic Violence Unit or the Helicopter Team.

We aim to reflect the community we serve, so we're looking for people who can work with people from a variety of backgrounds. To qualify, you can be any height, or aged between 18 and 47 approximately. And, of course, we welcome men and women from all racial, cultural and religious backgrounds. Upon joining you'll need a full car driving licence and should be physically fit in all aspects – although we don't expect you to be an Olympic athlete.

So join the usual suspects. To apply contact The Recruiting Department on 01483 482600 (24 hour answerphone) or e-mail join@surrey.police.uk Please quote ref: CG/02. www.surrey.police.uk

SURREY POLICE

TRIPLE THREAT
TUNGSTEN SERIES

The pinnacle of power and precision.

To be the best you have to play with the best, and that's what PETER NICOL, the world's No.1 does. He requires only the very best racquets and footwear to keep him at the top of the sport. Prince® produce both of these in the:

TTT Sovereign racquet - an extremely strong stable frame, that Peter needs to maintain control of his game when under pressure, even though it weighs a mere 135 grams.

NFS Indoor black shoe - is very comfortable and gives the support and grip needed on all types of squash court surfaces.

PETER NICOL

prince

TRADITIONAL SWEET SPOT
TRIPLE THREAT® SWEET SPOT
TRIPLE THREAT® WITH TUNGSTEN SWEET SPOT

1. TRIPLE THREAT™ TUNGSTEN SOVEREIGN
Racquet stability and manoeuverability are maximised by fortifying the 3 Triple Threat® locations with tungsten, a strong dense metal. Tungsten provides precise weight distribution, allowing further weight reduction in noncritical areas, to deliver superior sweet spot size, power, directional control and reduced shock in a lighter racquet frame.

2. POWER RING™
Innovative and patented racquet design, where all the main strings wrap around an inverted ring. This provides longer, more uniform string lengths for a more consistent response and greater power in a more durable frame.

3. POWER SCOOP™ SHAFT
A uniquely shaped shaft which absorbs wall and floor impacts for more comfort and durability, yet provides full frame stiffness for maximum ball strike power.

INNOVATIONS
ANNOUNCING TRIPLE THREAT® WITH TUNGSTEN

VENUE: NATIONAL SQUASH CENTRE
DATES: 26–31 JULY (SINGLES); 31 JULY – 4 AUGUST (DOUBLES)

SQUASH

History

In the second half of the 19th Century, squash developed from the older game of rackets with the introduction of a rubber ball. Rackets, played within the walled yards of London taverns and prisons, found its way to Harrow School where boys improvised the new game. Squash rackets spread to public schools and gentleman's clubs, and the Forces took it overseas to the Empire. In the 1960s, squash boomed and by the mid-1970s an international circuit had started, and the British Open became the world's premier event. In the 1980s, a transparent court was innovated.

The Basics

In play, players hit alternatively and can rebound the ball off of any wall to hit the front wall above the lower line called the tin. Play continues until a mistake is made or a ball is not returned. The women use a 19-inch tin, the men and doubles play use a 17-inch tin. In standard singles scoring, only the server wins points. A game is to nine points, except that at eight-all, the receiver makes the choice to play to nine or ten. A match is a best of five games. In doubles, Point a Rally scoring to 15 points is used – at 14-all, players have the option to play to 15 or 17 points. A match is the best of three games.

Hit men

If the Commonwealth played the rest of the world at squash, the Commonwealth would win convincingly. In both the men's and women's game, eight of the top ten world ranked players are competing in these Games. World No 1 Peter Nicol, who won gold in Kuala Lumpur, called it the greatest moment of his career, while his arch-rival the Canadian Jonathon Power still regrets his slack preparation.

In fact, Power is quoted as saying, "in the 1998 Games, I was hung up on the fact that there was no prize money – then I realised what an idiot I had been. It got more attention than I have ever got for anything and I came second." Their rivalry will continue this time, but the race for gold is wide open.

Words: Ian Mackenzie; Photo: Robert Cianflone (Allsport)

queens of the court

In the women's event, Australia's Sarah Fitz-Gerald (interviewed on page 70), the world No 1, is the overwhelming favourite. She retained her British Open title in April in convincing style, but was pushed in the Grand Prix Finals in Qatar a couple of weeks later by England's Cassie Campion and the former Australian world champion Carol Owens, who is now competing for New Zealand.

Leilani Joyce, the New Zealand No 1, is another young squash player to keep your eyes on at Manchester 2002. Joyce appeared at the Kuala Lumpur Games, but failed to make much of an impression. However, since 1999, she's climbed through the rankings to reach No 3 in the world and the Maori has definitely got her sights set on Fitz-Gerald in the battle for the gold.

Manchester 2002 THE XVII COMMONWEALTH GAMES

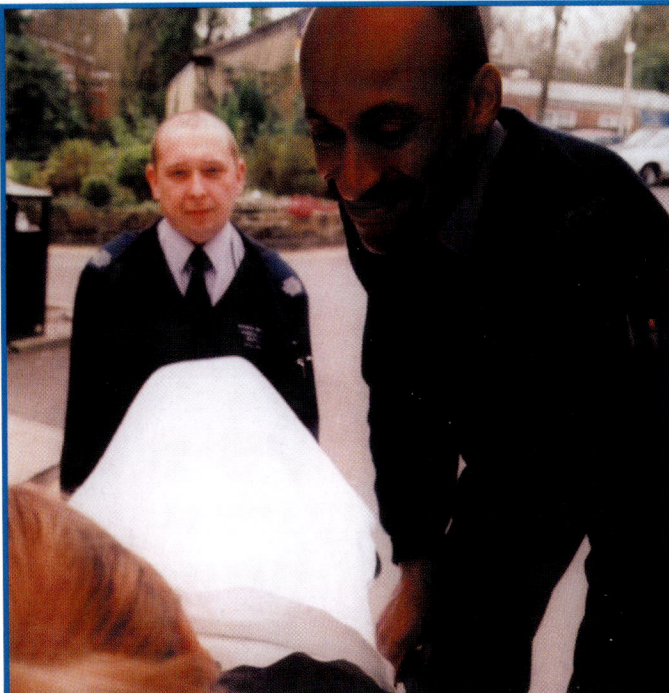

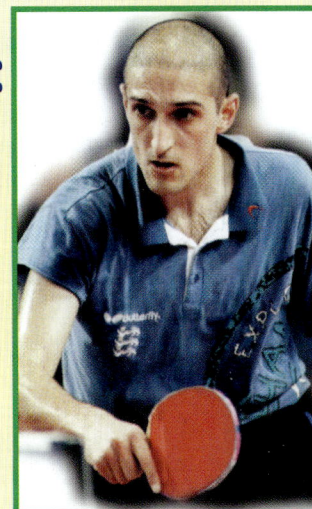

TABLE TENNIS

VENUE: TABLE TENNIS CENTRE, SPORTCITY
DATES: 26–30 JULY (TEAM); 30 JULY – 4 AUGUST (INDIVIDUAL)

History

Table tennis became extremely popular in England at the end of the 19th Century as an after-dinner pastime; the dining table was cleared, a piece of string was tied between two empty wine bottles and the lids of cigar boxes were used to hit the wine bottle cork over the makeshift net; the cork bounced irregularly and so was shaped to become the forerunner of the modern table tennis ball.

The introduction of the celluloid ball is credited to James Gibb who with John Jaques started to market "Ping Pong" in 1900 (the name being derived from the noise made by the ball striking the table and the vellum racket). The game became popular in Europe with the first ever World Championships being held in 1926, when the International Table Tennis Federation was formed; over the ensuing decades the game grew into a worldwide sport, gaining Olympic status in Seoul in 1988. Now, in 2002, in the country of its birth, table tennis celebrates another landmark, becoming part of the Commonwealth Games for the first time in its history.

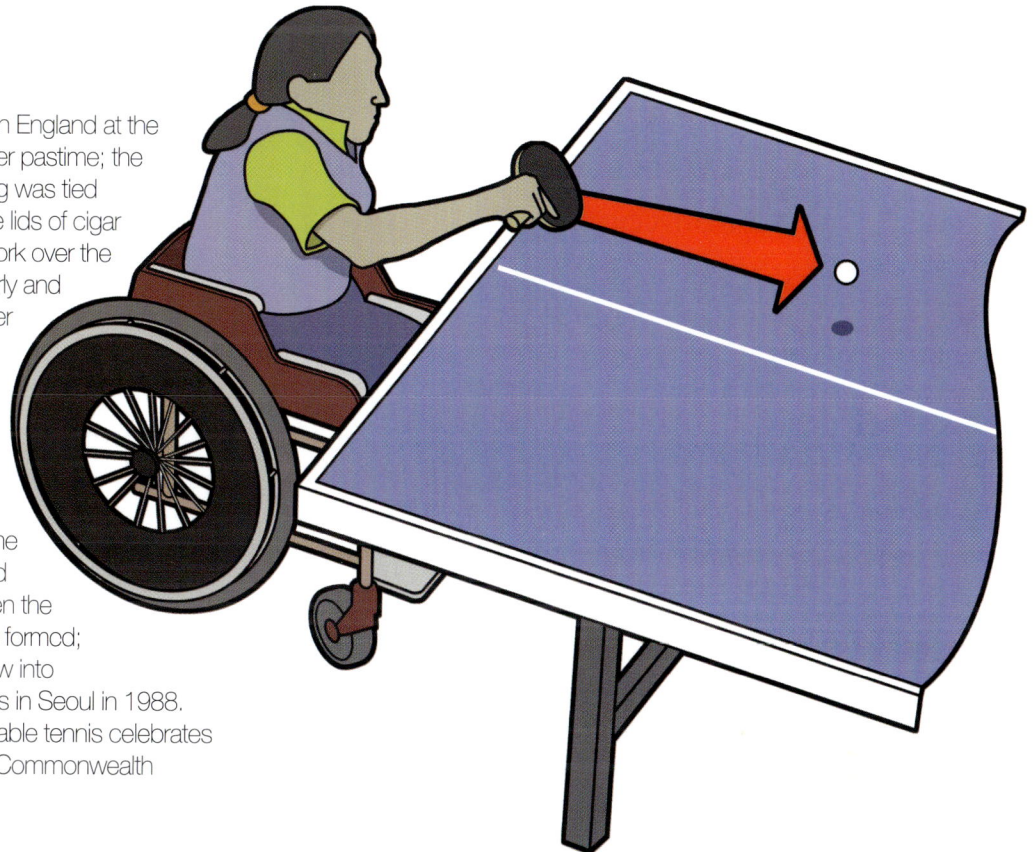

EAD table tennis

This year will see the first-ever women's wheelchair singles table tennis EAD event. This competition is set to feature many of the current stars of the EAD game.

The EAD version of the game is a much more technical and tactical affair when played from a wheelchair than the able-bodied game. Clearly, movement around the end of the table is much more restricted so the use of good angles is crucial for a successful outcome and provides a dimension rarely seen in the able-bodied version. Technically, the EAD version of the game differs only slightly. The ball, the table and the racket are all standard. The only major difference is the use of ball patrols, positioned around the court to retrieve and return the ball to the players.

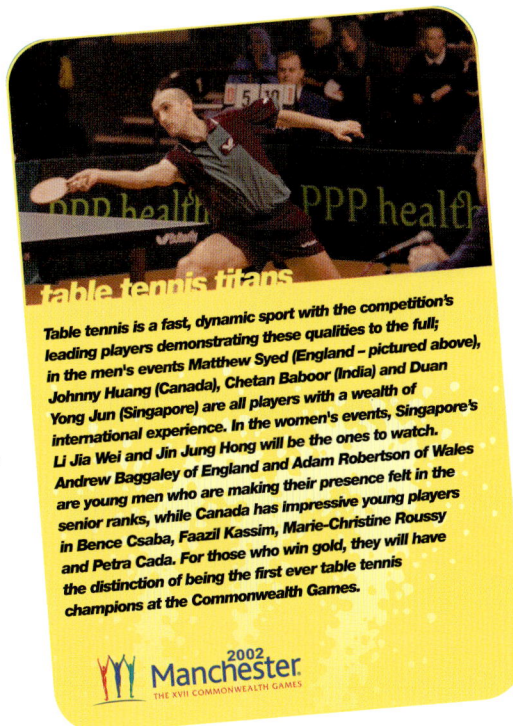

Words: Ian Marshall; Photo: Tees Sport

table tennis titans

Table tennis is a fast, dynamic sport with the competition's leading players demonstrating these qualities to the full; in the men's events Matthew Syed (England – pictured above), Johnny Huang (Canada), Chetan Baboor (India) and Duan Yong Jun (Singapore) are all players with a wealth of international experience. In the women's events, Singapore's Li Jia Wei and Jin Jung Hong will be the ones to watch. Andrew Baggaley of England and Adam Robertson of Wales are young men who are making their presence felt in the senior ranks, while Canada has impressive young players in Bence Csaba, Faazil Kassim, Marie-Christine Roussy and Petra Cada. For those who win gold, they will have the distinction of being the first ever table tennis champions at the Commonwealth Games.

2002 Manchester
THE XVII COMMONWEALTH GAMES

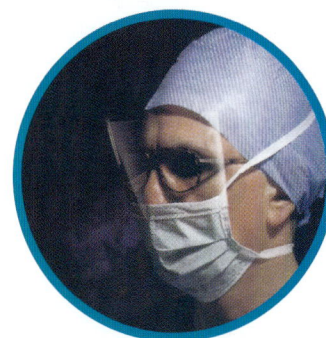

TRIATHLON

VENUE: SALFORD QUAYS

DATES: 4 AUGUST

History

Triathlon developed in the United States in the 1970s. While swimming and running races had been organised before, members of the San Diego Track Club came up with the idea for the first swim-bike-run competition in 1974. The inaugural triathlon saw 46 competitors battling it out in Mission Bay over a course comprising six miles of running, five miles cycling and 500 yards of swimming.

In 1978, the world's most famous triathlon, the Hawaii Ironman, was staged for the first time and it spawned a global series of Ironman competitions, which caught the imagination of athletes and spectators alike. Triathlons of all distances quickly became popular around the globe. The British Triathlon Association was established in 1983 in response to increased interest on this side of the Atlantic while the International Triathlon Union, the sport's world governing body, was founded in Avignon, France, in 1989. Triathlon continued to develop through the 1990s and featured in the Olympics for the first time in 2002.

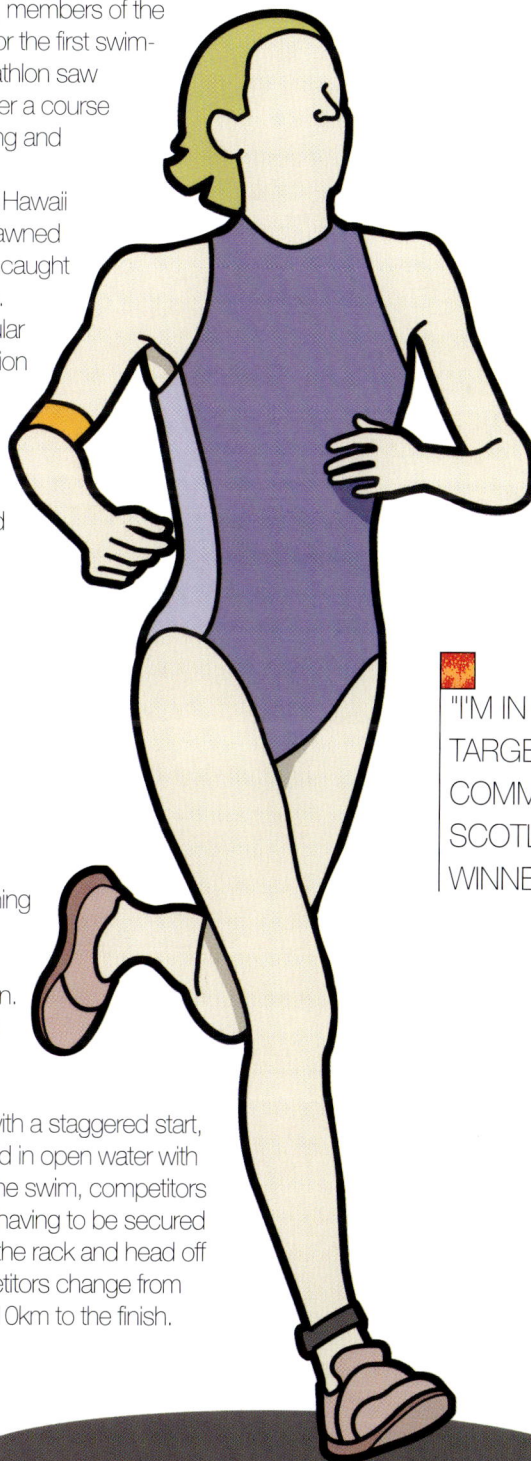

The basics

Triathlon combines swimming, cycling and running in one continuous race. Although the length of triathlons can vary enormously, the standard distance is: 1.5km swim; 40km cycle; 10km run. Transitions between the three disciplines are an integral part of the event and contribute to the overall time.

The swim can take place in a swimming pool with a staggered start, but in international competition, it's invariably held in open water with all competitors starting at the same time. After the swim, competitors swap their wetsuit for cycling gear, their helmet having to be secured before they remove their bike from its place on the rack and head off on the road. The second transition sees competitors change from bike shoes to running shoes before racing the 10km to the finish.

"I'M IN GREAT SHAPE AND ON TARGET TO PEAK FOR A GREAT COMMONWEALTH GAMES," SAYS SCOTLAND'S HALF IRONMAN UK WINNER, RICHARD ALLEN.

Words: Mat Brett

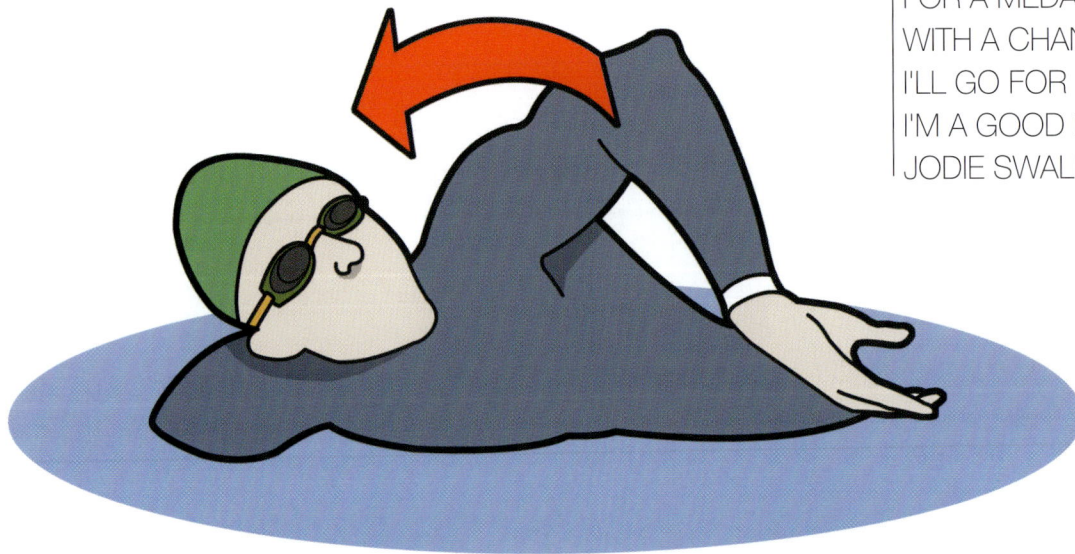

"IF YOU MAKE THE COMMONWEALTH TEAM, YOU'VE GOT TO BE AIMING FOR A MEDAL, AND IF I'M IN WITH A CHANCE ON THE RUN, I'LL GO FOR GOLD BECAUSE I'M A GOOD RUNNER," SAYS JODIE SWALLOW, ENGLAND.

The players

The Australian's boast terrific strength in depth. Their squad includes current world champion Peter Robertson as well as Chris McCormack, a former winner of the global crown, who won Ironman Australia earlier in the year. New Zealand boast athletes of a similarly high quality, including Hamish Carter, who has won several rounds of the World Cup over the years, and Craig Watson, who finished third in last year's World Championships. Of the Home Nations athletes, five-time former world champion Simon Lessing will be a serious contender for victory, as will Scotland's Half Ironman UK winner Richard Allen, who said recently, "I'm in great shape and on target to peak for a great Commonwealth Games." In the women's event, Australian's Loretta Harrop must be favourite to take gold, but the 1999 world champion is bound to be tested by compatriot Michellie Jones, two-time world champion, three-time world No 1 and Olympic silver medallist. Canada's Carol Montgomery, who broke a wrist while racing at the Sydney Olympics, will also be a major threat.

Also look out for 20-year-old Jodie Swallow. The Loughborough University student says, "If you make the Commonwealth team, you've got to be aiming for a medal – and if I'm in with a chance on the run, I'll go for gold because I'm a good runner."

triathlon facts

1. The first Olympic gold medals for triathlon were awarded to Simon Whitfield of Canada and Brigitte McMahon of Switzerland at Sydney 2000.
2. Sadly, Simon Whitfield, Canada's Olympic Champion, broke both wrists and a collar bone while racing in April, severely damaging his chances of competing.
3. Manchester 2002 sees the debut of triathlon at the Games, although it was a demonstration sport in 1990.
4. The distances for each discipline having been taken from existing events on the Olympic programme.
5. The Commonwealth countries are extraordinarily strong in triathlon. At the start of the current season, nine out of the top 10 male triathletes in the world rankings came from Australia, New Zealand, Canada and the United Kingdom.

2002 Manchester
THE XVII COMMONWEALTH GAMES

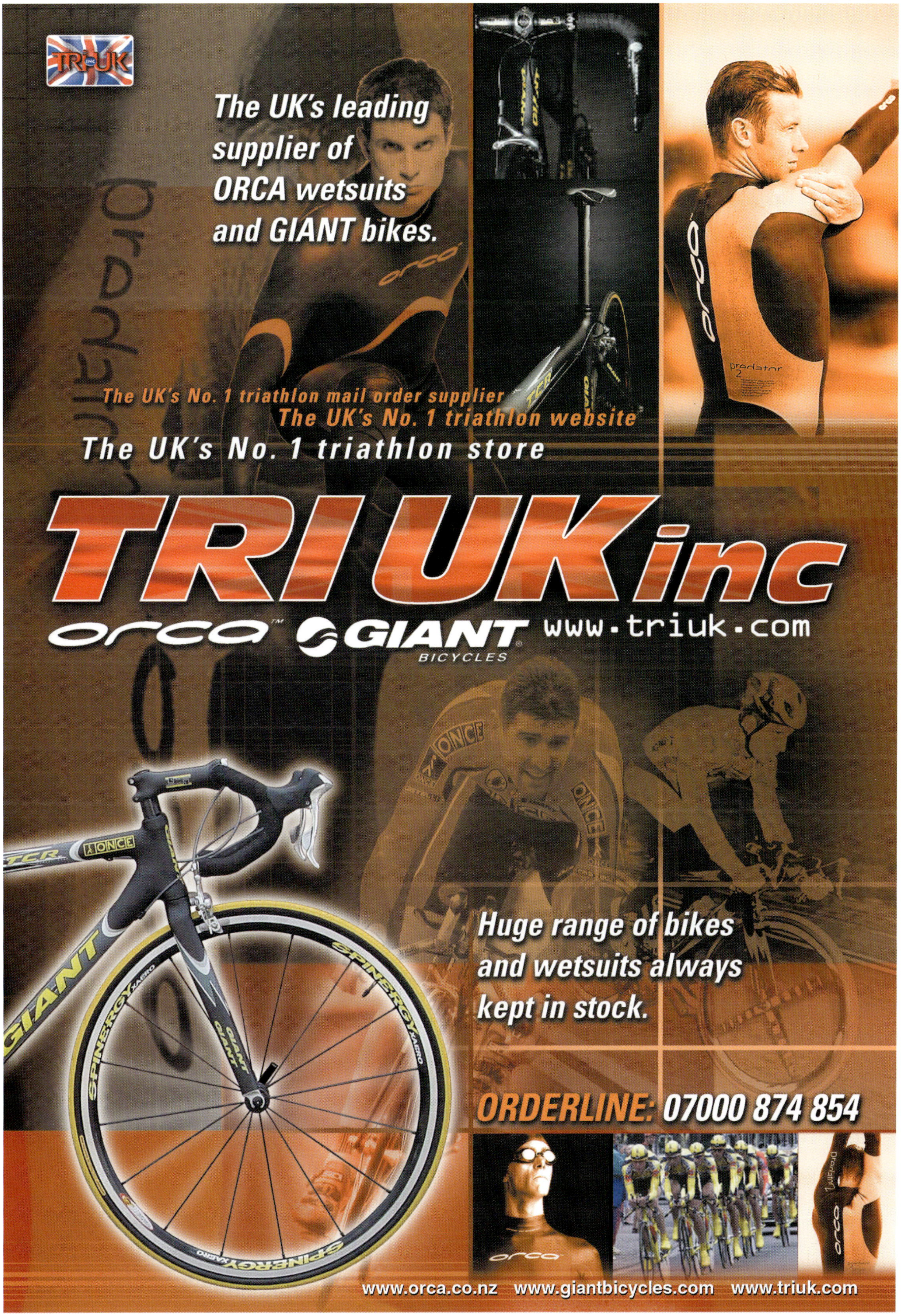

The UK's leading supplier of ORCA wetsuits and GIANT bikes.
The UK's No. 1 triathlon mail order supplier
The UK's No. 1 triathlon website
The UK's No. 1 triathlon store
TRI UK inc
orca GIANT BICYCLES www.triuk.com
Huge range of bikes and wetsuits always kept in stock.
ORDERLINE: 07000 874 854
www.orca.co.nz www.giantbicycles.com www.triuk.com

Crowns & Regalia Ltd present:
The Miniature Crown Jewel Collection
Golden Jubilee Set

This stunning collection of 1/12th scale miniatures, contains the 12 main pieces of The British Crown Jewels used during the coronation of Her Majesty Queen Elizabeth II, and is to commemorate her 50 year Golden Jubilee.

The Collection is entirely hand made by skilled artists of Crowns & Regalia Ltd, using the finest materials. Each piece is hand cast in quality pewter, then richly 22 ct. Gold or Sterling Silver plated, hand polished, set with minute Austrian Crystal stones and/or hand enamelled and finished, and presented in a luxurious jewellery presentation box.

Represented in miniature are:
The St. Edward's Crown, The Imperial State Crown, The Sovereign's Sceptre with the Cross, The Sovereign's Sceptre with the Dove, The Sovereign's Orb, The Ampulla, Anointing Spoon, George IV Diadem, The Sovereign's Ring, The Commonwealth Bracelets and The Jewelled State Sword!

The Crown Jewels of Great Britain represent not only Britain's greatest treasures; they also represent the long history of the times and the monarchs who wore them. This beautiful set of collectors miniatures will be a treasured heirloom, and a lasting reminder of the glorious 50 year reign of our Queen.

Send for this stunning collection now! and receive a gift of: 'The Crown Jewels' the superb booklet by 'Pitkin', packed full of information about the Crown Jewels, completely Free of Charge!

For more information on Crowns & Regalia Ltd, or other items in our range, please contact us as follows:
Tel: 0208 291 1233 Fax: 0208 291 4510, Online or email www.crownsandregalia.com
TO ORDER: Please complete the order form, not forgetting the postage and packing, and payment details, and send to: CROWNS & REGALIA LTD, NELSON HALL, DARTMOUTH PLACE, FOREST HILL, LONDON SE23 3HS. ENGLAND. Please allow 28 days for delivery. If you are not happy with your 'Golden Jubilee Set' please return it to us within 7 days for a full refund.
The Arrangement in the box may be subject to change.

I would like to order the following items at £92.50 per set. (Should you prefer to pay in US Dollars - $140.00 per set)

Description:	Qty.	Each:	Total
MINIATURE GOLDEN JUBILEE SET			
* Post & Packing:			
Total:			

☐ I enclose a personal cheque payable to 'Crowns & Regalia Ltd'

☐ Please debit my Credit Card: *Visa / Mastercharge / Amex / Diners Club*

Please print clearly in block capitals:

_ _ _ _ / _ _ _ _ / _ _ _ _ / _ _ _ _ / _ _

Expiry Date: _ _ _ _ _ _ _ _

Issue: _ _ _ _ _ _ _ _

Mr/Mrs _ _ _ _ _ _   First Name: _ _ _ _ _ _ _   Last Name: _ _ _ _ _ _ _

Address: _

_ _

Postcode: _ _ _ _ _ _ _   Country: _ _ _ _ _ _ _

Tel. No.: _ _ _ _ _ _ _   Signature: _ _ _ _ _ _ _

* Postage & Packing:
UK & Europe
add £3.50
(€6.00)
Other
add £7.50
(US$10.50)

WEIGHTLIFTING

VENUE: MANCHESTER INTERNATIONAL CONVENTION CENTRE
DATES: 30 JULY – 3 AUGUST

A trial of strength

Weightlifting is quite possibly one of the oldest of all sports, dating back to Ancient Greek and Roman times when trials of strength were admired. To be able to lift an object above one's head, or just off the ground, that was too heavy for anyone else often resulted in the telling of stories and building of reputations. Today, it's no different, reputations are built and stories created around a single lift by a specific person in a particular championship event.

The British Amateur Weightlifting Association (BAWLA) was started in 1910 and became the British Weight Lifters' Association (BWLA) two years ago. England, Ireland, Scotland, and Wales compete as Great Britain in Olympic Games, World Championships and European Championships, but compete as individual countries in the Commonwealth Games – and with fierce rivalry.

ACCORDING TO STEVE CANNON, TEAM MANAGER OF THE ENGLAND LIFTING SQUAD AT MANCHESTER 2002: "WE HAVE PICKED A STRONG AND EXPERIENCED ENGLAND LIFTING SQUAD FOR MANCHESTER AND I AM CONFIDENT WE WILL DO WELL AGAIN."

Words: Bill Barton

Our International Phonecards always win gold

Just like the Commonwealth Games, IDT is expert at bringing people together from all over the world. After all, we are the world's biggest phonecard company, selling over 2 million international phonecards a month across Europe alone - cards that offer you the opportunity to make huge savings on international phone calls. In many cases IDT phonecards can offer savings of up to 75% on the equivalent BT rate and you can dial from your own home or work phone, mobile or even a phone box. So you can talk for longer, more often, for less!

IDT Europe is part of the sixth biggest telecoms company in the USA and, unlike many of our competitors, we actually own the infrastructure that routes your calls - so you can be sure of call connection and phone line quality. You can buy IDT phonecards in either £5, £10 or £20 denominations from all good newsagents, convenience stores and Commonwealth Games concession outlets, so start saving money on your international calls with the phonecard company that's always out in front.

For more information contact 0845 080 0568.

IDT EUROPE
Communicating With Intelligence™

The World's Largest Phonecard Company

Rules and basics

Competitors lift an international barbell 2,200 mm long, on a platform that measures 4 sq ms. The weights (450 mm in diameter) are loaded on to the bar and are held tightly on the bar using locking collars. Weights range from 1.25 kgs to 25 kgs and are all colour specific to denote their weight.

Athletes compete in two disciplines: the two hands snatch and the two hands clean and jerk. They are allowed three attempts on each lift and the best attempts are added together to make the "total". Medals are given for each of the two lifts and for the total.

In the snatch, the athlete takes a wider grip and lifts the bar from the platform to the overhead position in one fast movement, and by "squatting" underneath the bar as it is received overhead. The clean and jerk is two movements. The athlete usually takes a grip slightly wider than "shoulder width" and pulls the bar to the front of the shoulders, again squatting under the bar to receive it. In the jerk, the athlete stands up, feet are "hip width" apart, the knees are dipped, the athlete drives upwards on to his toes and then splits his legs fore and aft to lower himself under the bar. To complete the lift, the athlete repositions his feet until they are in line.

Lifts are judged by three referees. The centre referee sits directly in front and centre of the weightlifting platform, and the two "side" referees sit corner on to the weightlifting platform. The referees press a switch at the completion of a lift resulting in a set of three lights showing to the athlete and the audience. Good lifts are decided by white lights and bad lifts by red lights on a majority of two to one or all three showing the same colour. The winner is the athlete who is judged to have lifted the heaviest weight.

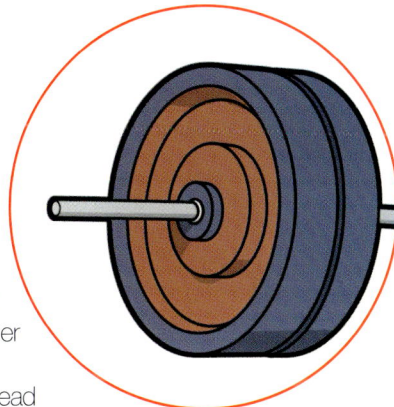

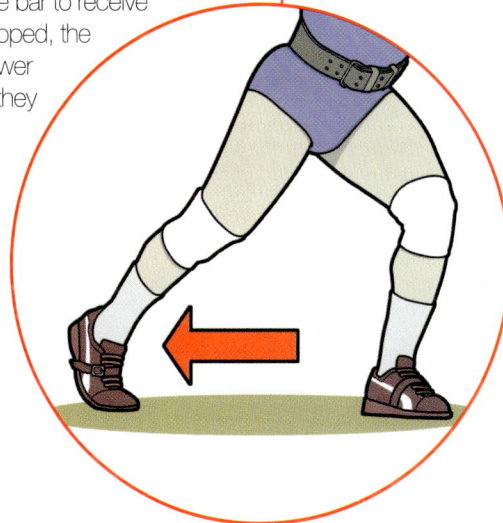

We have lift-off

Welsh weightlifter Michaela Breeze will be looking for her first Commonwealth Medals after recently finishing sixth for Great Britain in the European Senior Championships in Antalya, Turkey. Breeze was coached by Ken Price who sadly died in a car accident in 1999. In spite of this, Breeze went to Savannah, USA, to compete in the 1999 Junior World Championship and won a bronze medal. "This was Ken's medal as much as it was mine," she said at the time. "He told me never to set myself targets because they will just get in the way of progress". With this attitude, who would bet against her? England's Gurbinder Singh is a young athlete with a history. His father, Cheemah, represented England in the Commonwealth games and is now one of our National Coaches. Singh is a quiet and dedicated young athlete, but you can be sure he will be looking to go one better than Cheemah and finish this Games with a medal.

One other gentleman to watch out for is Nauru's Marcus Stephen who won three golds in Kuala Lumpur in 1998. If he's on the team, Nauru may just be on top the world again.

EAD weightlifting

The XVII Commonwealth Games in Manchester will host the men's bench press multi-disability event for the first time. On 3 August, the Manchester International Convention Centre will play host to the event in the evening. As the event is multi-disability, all classes will lift together in the same competition with all lifters competing for the same gold medal.

In order to ensure fairness between competitors with different body weights, the Wilks coefficient is used to calculate that ratio between each individual body weight against the weight they lift. In this way those who weigh less than other contestants can win the event if they lift more weight in ratio to their body weight.

2002
Manchester.
THE XVII COMMONWEALTH GAMES

Kerim Okten (European Press Association)

WRESTLING

VENUE: G-MEX
DATES: 2–4 AUG

History

Wrestling is the oldest and purest of personal combat sports. Egyptian murals on the tombs of Beni Hasan, dating back to 3000 BC, show wrestlers in combat. Wrestling was also part of the early Olympic games – it is believed to have been introduced at the 18th Olympiad about 704 BC. When the Modern Olympics resumed in Athens in 1896, wrestling became a major focus. The original Olympic Wrestling style, Greco-Roman, was derived from ancient Greek and Roman wrestling. Wrestling was not included in the 1900 Paris games, returning eight years later in St Louis, where officials added a second style called Freestyle – a less restrictive form of wrestling commonly known as "catch as catch can" or " Lancashire Wrestling". Freestyle Wrestling was a part of every Empire Games and Commonwealth Games up to the 1986 Games in Edinburgh. In Auckland four years later, it was dropped for the first time, returning in Victoria, Canada in 1994, only to be dropped again by Kuala Lumpur in 1998. The 2002 Games see wrestling return to its spiritual home in Britain – Lancashire.

Basics

Wrestling takes place on a 12m x 12m mat, with a central wrestling area (7m diameter) and a centre circle where the wrestling is started and restarted. A one-metre wide red "passivity zone" surrounds this area. The mat has a red and a blue corner, and wrestlers wear singlets of corresponding colours. Matches last for two periods of three minutes, with a 30 second break, unless concluded by a fall, technical superiority or (rarely) disqualification. A fall is when a wrestler pins both of his opponent's shoulders to the mat for one second. Technical superiority is when a wrestler leads by 10 or more points, at which point the leading wrestler is the winner. Disqualification can follow any serious misconduct, but is more likely the result of three cautions for offences such as fleeing the mat, fleeing a hold or committing a foul. A match that runs its full course is decided on points. If the match is tied (or if neither has at least three points), a three minute overtime begins (when the winner is the one who pins his opponent, reaches three points or, in a higher scoring tied match, the one who scores first).

TAKE A DOSE OF YOUR OWN MEDICINE

• Innovative 21ST century pain relief device

• Combining western science and eastern philosophy

• Non-invasive / self-healing treatment

• Stimulating the nervous system to activate the body's natural healing powers

• CE marked

GO TO WWW.LIFE–ENERGIES.COM

LIFE ENERGIES
SKENAR

EMAIL: ENQUIRIES@LIFE-ENERGIES.COM
TEL:(01722) 741 111 FAX: 741 100
THE MANOR HOUSE
27 SOUTH STREET
WILTON WILTSHIRE SP2 0JU

ENGLISH MEDAL HOPEFULS FOR WRESTLING AT THE 2002 GAMES INCLUDE ANDY HUTCHINSON, JOHN MELLING AND JOHANNES ROSSOUW. MELLING DID VERY WELL AT THE 1994 GAMES, DEFEATING IGALI BARALADEI OF NIGERIA IN THE QUARTERFINAL OF THE 62KG CLASS, AT THE 1994 COMMONWEALTH GAMES IN VICTORIA, BC, CANADA

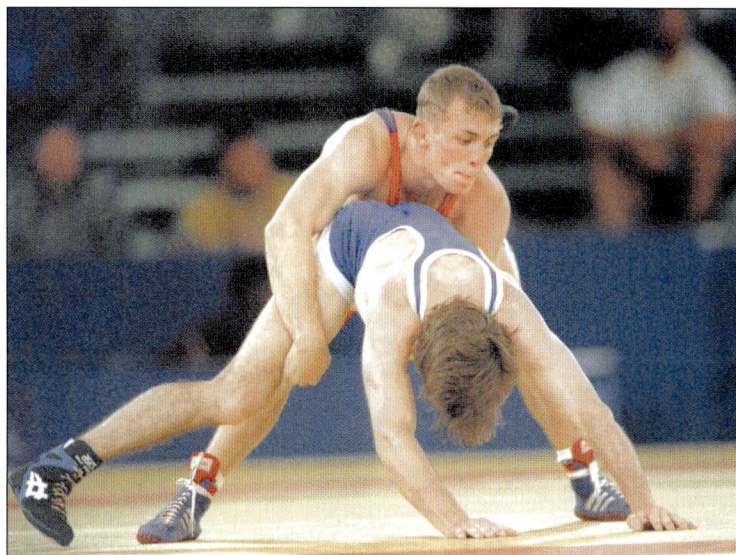

The wrestlers

Canada remains the strongest wrestling nation in the Commonwealth, having won nine out of 10 gold medals in each of the last two Games that included wrestling on the programme (1986 and 1994). FILA has reduced the number of weight categories to seven for the 2004 Olympics, which has come into force for the 2002 season and applies to the Commonwealth Games. Likely Canadian winners are 1999 world and current Olympic champion Daniel Igali (74kg), and 2001 world champion Gia Sissaouri (60kg). The other five Canadians face serious competition from a rejuvenated India team in all weight categories. Other strong nations include Nigeria and, in most weight categories, England. Hopes of any home nation gold medal success lie principally with Englishmen John Melling (66kg) and Johannes Rossouw (96kg). Other British medal possibilities include the Scots Graeme English (96kg), previous two-time Games bronze medallist and Joseph Bianco (84kg), and from England, Amarjit Singh (120kg) and Andy Hutchinson (55kg). Australian medal hopes rest principally with Rheinhold Ozoline (74kg).

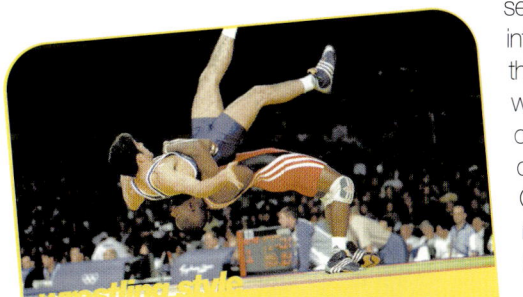

Distinctly different styles of wrestling exist today, apart from the Greco Roman Wrestling typically featured at events such as the Sydney Olympics in 2000. In Japan, for example, two types of wrestling styles are popular – sumo and jujitsu. Sumo, in which the object is to force the opponent out of the ring, is quasi-religious in nature and involves much ritual. In the traditional Turkish style of Pehlivan, wrestlers wear leather breeches and cover themselves with oil. The Schwingen style of Switzerland and the Glima of Iceland feature grips on the opponent's belt.

Manchester 2002
THE XVII COMMONWEALTH GAMES

2002 Manchester

THE XVII COMMONWEALTH GAMES

The XVII Commonwealth Games will be an incredible experience, enthralling and entertaining. You too can 'Count yourself in' by purchasing Manchester 2002 official merchandise. By doing so you are supporting Manchester 2002, The Commonwealth Games and the athletes of the Commonwealth.

Here is just a small selection of the range available. To view all the official merchandise please visit one of the retail units, details on the map opposite, or visit the e-tail store
www.commonwealthgames.com/merchandise

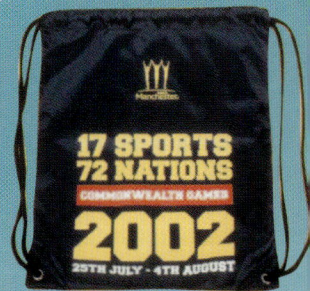

There are 100 pin designs to collect for the full range visit one of the retail outlets or visit our website

OFFICIAL MERCHANDISE

BEAN BEAR

2002 Manchester

THE XVII COMMONWEALTH GAMES

Manchester 2002 Commonwealth Games Merchandise available from the following outlets:

12 RIVINGTON

11 BOLTON

To Rivington from Bolton Arena (event days only)

To Leeds

OLDHAM

HEATON PARK

To Sportcity

MANCHESTER

TRAFFORD CENTRE

16

MEN ARENA

17

14

5

1 SPORTCITY & NATIONAL CYCLING CENTRE

LONDON

13 BISLEY

3 G-MEX & MICC

4

6

To Sheffield

M67

SALFORD QUAYS

7

CITY CENTRE

2 MANCHESTER AQUATICS CENTRE

9 BELLE VUE REGIONAL HOCKEY CENTRE

To Liverpool

Old Trafford To Sportcity & city centre

STOCKPORT

8 FORUM CENTRE, WYTHENSHAWE

To Chester

15 Manchester International Airport (10 miles from city centre)

1. Sport City Superstore & 3 Retail Units
1. National Cycling Retail Unit
2. Manchester Aquatic Centre Retail Unit
3&4. G-MEX & MICC Retail Units
5. MEN Arena Two Retail Units
7. Salford Quays Retail Unit
9. Belle Vue Regional Hockey Centre Retail Unit
10. Heaton Park Retail Unit
11. Bolton Arena Retail Unit
12. Rivington Retail Unit
14. Arndale Centre Retail Unit
15. Manchester International Airport Retail Unit
16. Trafford Centre Retail Unit
17. Piccadilly Gardens, City Centre Retail Unit

BRADFORD. CAPITAL OF CULTURE?

PREPARE TO BE AMAZED

www.bradford2008.com

BRADFORD 2008
one landscape many views